Artificial Intelligence in Telemedicine

This book explores the role of artificial intelligence in telemedicine. It explains the concepts through the detailed study and processing of biosignals, physiological parameters, and medical images. The book focuses on computational algorithms in telemedicine for the processing of biosignals, physiological parameters, and medical images. The book is presented in two sections.

The first section presents the role of computational algorithms in the processing of biosignals and medical images for disease diagnosis and treatment planning. Noise removal in ECG signal using an improved adaptive learning approach, classification of ECG signals using convolutional neural network (CNN) for cardiac arrhythmia detection, EEG signal analysis for stroke detection, and EMG signal analysis for gesture classification are discussed in this section. Application of CNN in pertussis diagnosis by temperature monitoring, physician handwriting recognition using deep learning model, melanoma detection using ABCD parameters, and transfer learning–enabled heuristic approach for pneumonia detection are also discussed in this section.

The second section focuses on the role of IoT and artificial intelligence in the healthcare sector. IoT in smart healthcare and applications of artificial intelligence in disease diagnosis and prediction are discussed in this section. The importance of 5G/6G in the pandemic scenario for telemedicine applications, wireless capsule endoscopy image compression, leukaemia detection from the microscopic cell images, and genomic signal processing using numerical mapping techniques is also discussed in this section.

This book can be used by a wide range of users including students, research scholars, faculty, and practitioners in the field of engineering for applications in biomedical signal, image analysis, and diagnosis.

Innovations in Multimedia, Virtual Reality and Augmentation

Series Editor:

Lalit Mohan Goyal,

J. C. Bose University of Science & Technology YMCA

Rashmi Agrawal,

J. C. Bose University of Science & Technology YMCA

Advanced Sensing in Image Processing and IoT

Rashmi Gupta, Korhen Cengiz, Arun Rana, Sachin Dhawan

Artificial Intelligence in Telemedicine: Processing of Biosignals and Medical images

S. N. Kumar, Sherin Zafar, Eduard Babulak, M. Afshar Alam, and Farheen Siddiqui

Artificial Intelligence in Telemedicine

Processing of Biosignals and Medical Images

Edited by
S. N. Kumar, Sherin Zafar, Eduard Babulak,
M. Afshar Alam, and Farheen Siddiqui

CRC Press
Taylor & Francis Group
Boca Raton London New York

CRC Press is an imprint of the
Taylor & Francis Group, an **informa** business

First edition published 2024
by CRC Press
6000 Broken Sound Parkway NW, Suite 300, Boca Raton, FL 33487-2742

and by CRC Press
4 Park Square, Milton Park, Abingdon, Oxon, OX14 4RN

CRC Press is an imprint of Taylor & Francis Group, LLC

ISBN: 978-1-032-30931-6 (hbk)
ISBN: 978-1-032-31046-6 (pbk)
ISBN: 978-1-003-30777-8 (ebk)

DOI: 10.1201/9781003307778

Typeset in Times
by codeMantra

Contents

PART 1 Biosignal and Medical Image Processing for Disease Diagnosis

PART 2   *Role of Artificial Intelligence and IoT in Health Care*

Editors

Dr. S. N. Kumar is Associate Professor in the Department of Electrical and Electronics Engineering, Amal Jyothi College of Engineering, Kanjirappally, Kerala. He was awarded B.E. degree in Electrical and Electronics Engineering in 2007 from Anna University, Chennai and M.E. degree in Applied Electronics in 2011 from Anna University of Technology, Tirunelveli. He was awarded his Ph.D. from Sathyabama Institute of Science and Technology, Chennai in the Department of Electronics and Communication Engineering as a part of a DST-sanctioned funded project under IDP scheme. With 13 years of teaching experience, his areas of interest include Medical Image Processing and Embedded System Applications in Telemedicine. He is an active life member of BMESI, ISTE, ISRD, Bernoulli Society, and IAENG. He was the Co-Principal Investigator of the DST IDP-funded project and research fellow of the RCA scheme, NTU Singapore. He has authored 20 peer-reviewed journal publications and eight textbooks in engineering disciplines. He also has four patent publications, 30 book chapters from prominent publications, and 36 conference publications to his credit.

Dr. Sherin Zafar is Assistant Professor of Computer Science and Engineering in the School of Engineering Sciences and Technology, Jamia Hamdard with a decade of successful experience in teaching and research management. She specializes in Wireless Networks, Soft Computing, and Network Security and has great profile in Scopus, Mendeley, Google Scholar, Research Gate, and Publons. She has about half century of papers published in Scopus, SCI, and peer-reviewed journals, as well as double century of papers reviewed. She is also Editorial Board member and Editor in Chief of many reputed and Scopus indexed journals. She has published five books and has three patents on Block Chain technology, Co-PI for FIST project of DST, and PI for two completed Unnat Bharat project. A strong believer in the power of positive thinking in the workplace, Dr. Sherin regularly develops internship and career campaigns for students through Internshala and Epoch (Literary and Cultural Society) Groups and guided huge number of graduate, postgraduate and Ph.D. students. Dr. Sherin has been session chairs for 10+ international conferences, keynote speaker, resource person for 100+ webinars and FDPs for renowned institutions, AICTE STTP, and AICTE ATAL FDP. Sherin enjoys a good Netflix and Cricket binge but can also be found on long drive rides on country roads.

Dr. Eduard Babulak is a global scholar, educator, consultant, and professional engineer with 30 years of experience. He served as Chair of the IEEE Vancouver Ethics, Professional and Conference Committee. His academic and engineering work was recognized internationally by the Engineering Council in UK, the European Federation of Engineers, and credited by the Ontario Society of Professional Engineers and APEG in British Columbia in Canada. He was awarded higher postdoctoral degree DOCENT – Doctor of Science (D.Sc.) in the Czech Republic, Ph.D., M.Sc., and High National Certificate (HNC) diplomas in the United Kingdom, as well as the M.Sc.

and B.Sc. diplomas in Electrical Engineering in Slovakia. He served as the Editor-in-Chief, Associate Editor-in-Chief, Co-Editor, and Guest-Editor. He communicates in 16 foreign languages and his biography was cited in the Cambridge Blue Book, Cambridge Index of Biographies, Stanford Who's Who, and number of issues of Who's Who in the World and America.

Dr. Mohammad Afshar Alam completed his postgraduation in MCA (Master of Computer Application) from the Aligarh Muslim University and Ph.D. from Jamia Millia Islamia. Presently, he is working as Vice-Chancellor and Professor and Dean of School of Engineering Sciences and Technology at Jamia Hamdard, New Delhi. His research areas include Software Re-Engineering, Data Mining, Bio-Informatics, Fuzzy Databases, and Sustainable Development. In his 25 years of experience in teaching and research, he was invited to many countries across the globe including UAE, Nepal, Syria, Yemen, and many more for delivering Special Lectures and as Keynote speakers in Conferences. He has authored ten books, supervised more than 30 doctoral students and more than 200 postgraduate research projects, and has more than 160 research papers in reputed journals to his credit. He is conferred with many prestigious awards like Bharat Samaj Ratna Award, AMP Award for Excellence in Education, Cooperative Citizen Award, World Environment Day Award, and Spardha Shree Award. He is also the member of various government bodies at both national and international levels including University Grants Commission (UGC), All India Council of Technical Education (AICTE), National Assessment and Accreditation Council (NAAC), Department of Science and Technology (DST).

Dr. Farheen Siddiqui is HOD of CSE and Associate Professor in Jamia Hamdard. She is actively involved in teaching, research and project supervision of undergraduate postgraduate students. She served as Ph.D. Examination Coordinator and Deputy Superintendent of Examinations. She also served as Centre Coordinator for IIT spoken tutorial, member of the Board of Studies of the Department of Computer Science, FMIT, Designed CBCS-based course structure and M.Tech. (CS) course, Programme Coordinator of M.Tech. (CS), External Member for Moderation Committee, Department of Computer Science, Jamia Millia Islamia.

Contributors

Abhirami B.
Department of ECE
Amal Jyothi College of Engineering
Kanjirappally, Kerala, India

Abubeker K. M.
Faculty of Engineering, Department
of Electronics and Communication
Engineering
Karpagam Academy of Higher
Education
Coimbatore, India

K. Aiswarya
Department of Electronics and
Communication Engineering
SRM TRP Engineering College
Tiruchirappalli, India

Quazi Mohmmad Alfred
Department of ECE
Aliah University
Kolkata, India

Arifa Begum S. K.
Department of Pharmacy
Bharat Institute of Technology
Mangalpally, Ranga Reddy, Telangana,
India

J. Asokan
Department of Electronics and
Communication Engineering
SRM TRP Engineering College
Tiruchirappalli, India

S. Baskar
Faculty of Engineering, Department
of Electronics and Communication
Engineering
Karpagam Academy of Higher
Education
Coimbatore, India

Shaheen Begum
Department of Pharmacy
Institute of Pharmaceutical Technology
Sri Padmavati Mahila Visvavidyalayam
(SPMVV)
Tirupati, Andhra Pradesh, India

Anchana P. Belmon
Department of ECE
Rajadhani Institute of Engineering and
Technology
Karavaram, Kerala, India

Rabindranath Bera
Department of ECE
Sikkim Manipal Institute of Technology
Sikkim Manipal University
Gangtok, Sikkim, India

Cindhya Charly
Department of ECE
Amal Jyothi College of Engineering
Kanjirappally, Kerala, India

C. Chellaswamy
Department of Electronics and
Communication Engineering
SRM TRP Engineering College
Tiruchirappalli, India

M. Chengathir Selvi
Department of Computer Science and
Engineering
Mepco Schlenk Engineering College
Sivakasi, India

Bihter Das
Department of Software Engineering,
Technology Faculty
University of Firat
Elazığ, Türkiye

R. Dhanagopal
Center for System Design
Chennai Institute of Technology
Chennai, India

Shiju George
Department of IT
Amal Jyothi College of Engineering
Kanjirappally, Kerala, India

Ramsundar Ghorai
Department of ECE
Sikkim Manipal Institute of Technology
Sikkim Manipal University
Sikkim, India

Seda Nur Gulocak
Department of Software Engineering,
Technology Faculty
University of Firat
Elazığ, Türkiye

P. Haritha
Department of Pharmacy
Bharat School of Pharmacy
Mangalpally, Ranga Reddy, Hyderabad,
India

S. G. Hymlin Rose
Department of ECE
R.M.D Engineering College
Kavaraipettai, Tamil Nadu, India

S. Janani
Department of ECE
Periyar Maniammai Institute of Science
and Technology
Thanjavur, India

Devika Jayakumar
Department of ECE
Amal Jyothi College of Engineering
Kanjirappally, Kerala, India

Kanimozhi T
Department of Electronics and
Communication Engineering
VelTech Ranagarajan Dr. Sagunthala,
R& D Institute of Science and
Technology
Chennai, India

Asha Joseph
Department of IT
Amal Jyothi College of Engineering
Kanjirappally, Kerala, India

K. Joseph Abraham Sundar
School of Computing
SASTRA Deemed to be University
Thanjavur, India

P. Linu Babu
Department of Electronics and
Communication Engineering
IES College of Engineering
Thrissur, Kerala, India

Therese Yamuna Mahesh
Department of ECE
Amal Jyothi College of Engineering
Kanjirappally, Kerala, India

T. Manonmani
Department of Computer Science and
Engineering
Mepco Schlenk Engineering College
Sivakasi, India

Neenu R.
Department of CSE
APJ Abdul Kalam Technological
    University
Thiruvananthapuram, Kerala, India

Nirmala V.
School of Computing
SASTRA Deemed to be University
Thanjavur, India

S. Prabu
School of Computing
SASTRA Deemed to be University
Thanjavur, India

K. Pradeep
Department of Biomedical Engineering
Chennai Institute of Technology
Chennai, India

C. Prajitha
Faculty of Engineering, Department
    of Electronics and Communication
    Engineering
Karpagam Academy of Higher
    Education
Coimbatore, India

Premaladha J.
School of Computing
SASTRA deemed to be university
Thanjavur, India

Jayanta Kumar Ray
Department of ECE
Sikkim Manipal Institute of Technology
Sikkim Manipal University
Gangtok, Sikkim, India

Della ReasaValiaveetil
Department of Electronics and
    Communication Engineering
Christ College of Engineering
Kerala, India

C. Sadak Vali
Department of Pharmacy
Browns college of Pharmacy
Khammam, Telangana, India

Arpita Sarkar
Department of ECE
Jorhat Engineering College
Assam Science and Technology
    University
Jorhat, Assam, India

Sanjib Sil
Department of ECE
Calcutta Institute of Engineering and
    Management
Kolkata, India

K. V. L. D. Spandana
Department of Pharmacy
Avanthi Institute of Pharmaceutical
    Sciences
Hayathnagar_Khalsa, Telangana, India

S. Sridevi
Department of Electronics and
    Communication Engineering
Veltech Rangarajan Dr. Sagunthala
    R&D Institute of Science and
    Technology
Chennai, India

K. P. Sridhar
Faculty of Engineering, Department
    of Electronics and Communication
    Engineering
Karpagam Academy of Higher
    Education
Coimbatore, India

Rogina Sultana
Department of ECE
Aliah University
Kolkata, India

R. Suresh Kumar
Center for System Design
Chennai Institute of Technology
Chennai, India

S. Swathi Goud
Department of Pharmacy
Vishnu Institute of Pharmaceutical
    Education & Research (VIPER)
Narsapur, Telangana, India

K. Thirumoorthy
Department of Computer Science and
    Engineering
Mepco Schlenk Engineering College
Sivakasi, India

Elsa Shaju Thomas
Department of ECE
Amal Jyothi College of Engineering
Kanjirappally, Kerala, India

Geevarghese Titus
Department of ECE
Amal Jyothi College of Engineering
Kanjirappally, Kerala, India

P. T. Vasanth Raj
Center for System Design
Chennai Institute of Technology
Chennai, India

B. Vijayakumari
Department of Electronics and
    Communication Engineering
Mepco Schlenk Engineering College
Sivakasi, India

Part 1

Biosignal and Medical Image Processing for Disease Diagnosis

Part I

1 Lightweight One-Dimensional CNN for Cardiac Arrhythmia Classification

T. Manonmani, B. Vijayakumari,
K. Thirumoorthy, and M. Chengathir Selvi
Mepco Schlenk Engineering College

CONTENTS

1.1   INTRODUCTION

Cardiovascular diseases (CVDs) [22] are ailment of the heart and blood vessels, which are particularly dangerous for the middle-aged and elderly people. When we grow old, our cardiovascular system weakens and becomes more susceptible to cardiac diseases. Arrhythmias are electrical disorders within the heart. The lack of oxygen causes the cardiac cells to depolarise, which leads to altered impulse formation or conduction. It may occur on its own or in conjunction with other cardiac diseases. Electrocardiogram (ECG) signal is a biological signal, which helps to analyse the cyclical contraction and relaxation of heart muscles. ECG signals are captured with the help of certain electrodes (ECG leads) and are used to examine the heart rhythm, i.e. the action impulse generated by the cardiac tissues. By manually interpreting the ECG signal image, medical practitioners diagnose the patient's cardiac condition.

Visual diagnosis of ECG for classifying it into normal and abnormal ones and further classification of it into different classes of arrhythmia can be a tedious process and might lead to false detection. In addition, random, noisy, low-frequency ECG recordings might result in unstable diagnosis results. As shown in Figure 1.1, the five

DOI: 10.1201/9781003307778-2

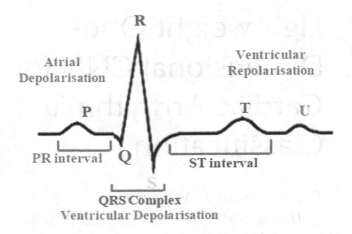

FIGURE 1.1   ECG signal wave.

distinctive points of ECG signals are P, Q, R, S, and T. Arrhythmia occurs if this path does not repeat continuously over time. Atrial depolarisation is represented by P wave. The depolarisations of right and left ventricles as well as contraction of ventricular muscles are plotted by QRS complex, while the T wave represents the repolarisation of ventricles. Unusual pattern of R-R interval, ECG baseline oscillations and abnormal heartbeats are characterised by diagnosing the ECG. Conventionally, signal features are derived from the area of QRS wave, T wave and possibly P wave. Changes in these parameters indicate a condition affecting the heart, which may be caused by a variety of factors. By utilising the peculiarities of the ECG signal, classification techniques identify the abnormalities to discriminate the signals into defined classes.

ECG signals are one-dimensional (1D) signals representing the time series. General machine learning algorithms [6,8,12,19] with the maturity of Artificial Intelligence (AI) efficiently handle vast amount of feature data from ECG signals. Traditional machine learning techniques such as Hermite function [31], principal component analysis [18], wavelet transform [6] and independent component analysis [36] help to extract and select features efficiently. Classification techniques such as Random Forest [15], support vector machine (SVM) ([19] and K-nearest neighbour (KNN) [21] are employed to classify cardiac arrhythmias based on the handcrafted features. Performance of these techniques depends upon the quality of the handcrafted features, inadequate or improperly chosen features lead to loss of information.

Having many layers to iteratively train and learn the feature, hierarchy deep learning–based frameworks [5,23,24] have gained popularity to automate the process of feature extraction and classification. Features extracted from these frameworks are more beneficial than conventional handcrafted features. Deep learning techniques play a vital role in successful detection of cardiac diseases such as myocardial infarction [32], premature ventricular contraction [20], atrial fibrillation [4], and ventricular tachycardia [3]. In recent years, health care industry recognised the knowledge gathering capabilities of neural network–based systems [21,31] in extracting high-level features for early detection and classification of diseases. With deep learning algorithms like deep convolutional neural network (CNN) [1,2,14,17,25,33,35,37,39], and deep belief network [34], it is possible to automatically extract high-level features from ECG signals. Innovative approaches like optimisation [5,9], error propagation [30], depth-wise convolution [17] and the implementation of graphical processing units lead to efficient use of multi-layer networks. Furthermore, the main drawback of employing deep learning is it requires a huge data set for training and consumes a lot of resources.

For processing multi-dimensional inputs, CNN acts as a feed-forward network in deep learning. Designed to replicate the human brain cortex, CNN utilises multiple processing units, connected by a group of neurons to handle multiple sets of data at same time. Being capable of inferring the hidden intrinsic patterns; CNN avoids the need of feature engineering process. Main layers of CNN include convolution, normalisation, pooling, and fully connected layers. The first three layers of the CNN are responsible for extracting features, while fully connected layers are responsible for classification. A 34-layer CNN layer architecture was proposed [28] for detecting arrhythmia from single-lead ECG signals. By adopting the residual connection strategy their model outperformed the analysis of cardiologist in arrhythmia classification. An optimisation-based deep CNN was proposed by [5] to classify the ECG signal into five classes with a maximal accuracy of 93.19%. In most cases, lacking in dynamic feature handling affects the overall performance of the system. A multi-channel CNN [27,29,32,38] was employed to classify the multi-lead ECG recordings and achieved 94.67% of accuracy. Removal of noise from the ECG signal has no impact on the accuracy of the system [21]. Results from the experiments show that the accuracy of the system remains same for both noisy and noiseless signals. In most current deep learning models, the focus is on improving accuracy and this often leads to models that are too large for embedding into the mobile devices.

In 1D-CNN, the input data are a single stream ECG signal and a kernel slide over it to discover patterns. To design a CNN, one must consider a number of factors, such as optimisation method, performance metrics, loss function, and hyperparameter settings. Optimisation of deep learning algorithms in different contexts is the most difficult of all neural networks. Verification and validation of the model are primarily evaluated by loss function and accuracy [11]. The hyperparameter setting includes the learning rate, batch size, hidden layers, neurons, channels for every layer, pooling, etc.

In this chapter, lightweight 1D CNN architecture with eight layers is proposed to classify the various class of cardiac arrhythmia present in the ECG signals. The objective of the study is to interpret the classification results as well as to understand the behaviour of the neural network. Confusion matrix analysis can be carried out to classify the arrhythmia classes.

In summary, this chapter made the following contributions. Section 1.2 introduces the ECG data set used and the various classes of cardiac arrhythmia present in the data set. Normalising and distributing the data for training, testing, and validation are discussed and the data imbalance is corrected using synthetic data generation technique. Section 1.3 presents the proposed lightweight 1D CNN model, it analyses the function of various layers, highlights its performance in classifying the arrhythmia in terms of confusion matrix and discusses the research trends and future challenges. In Section 1.4, we compare the performance of the proposed architecture, and a conclusion is drawn in Section 1.5.

1.2 MATERIALS AND METHODS

1.2.1 ECG DATA SET

PhysioBank MIT-BIH arrhythmia is a well-documented public data set [10] used to study the performance of the arrhythmia classifiers. It consists of ECG recordings of 30 minutes obtained with Lead II signal (received from electrodes on the chest) from 48 subjects. Performance of the Lead II signal is proved with 96.13% in research [29], where the performance accuracy of all 12-lead input is tested. 48-half-an-hour-long signals are sampled at various frequencies, and the beat tags are interpreted by multiple cardiologists.

As a first step of data set preparation, signals are divided into smaller segments to feed into the system. ECG signals' size is chosen to be between 1 and 2 seconds to ensure the presence of at least one beat in each segment. The sample rate of 360 Hz and size of 187 are taken for classification. Signal segments are normalised from 0 to 1 and corresponding labels are assigned. Typically, each ECG signal is classified into one of five classes: N (sinus-mode beats), S (supraventricular ectopic beats), V (ventricular ectopic beats), F (fusion beats), and Q (unclassifiable beats).

The presence of diverse types of ECG signals should be balanced and consistency throughout the experimental process should be ensured. For this purpose, the signal data are divided as 70% for training, 30% for testing, and for validation 20% of training data is used. Figure 1.2 shows the distribution of ECG signals employed to balance the training, testing, and validation procedures.

Table 1.1 summarises the different types of heart disease classes present in the arrhythmia data set. N, S, V, F, and Q are the macro classes of arrhythmia, with each class having several sub-classes.

TABLE 1.1

Signal Samples of Various CVD Classes from MIT-BIH Database

Class	Sample ECG Signal
Normal(N)	
Supra-ventricular premature (S)	
Premature ventricular contraction (V)	
Fusion of ventricular and normal (F)	
Unclassifiable (Q)	

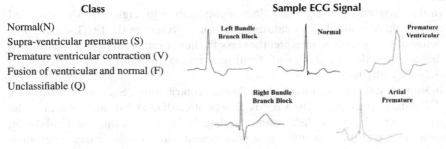

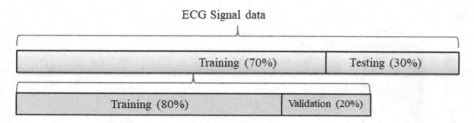

FIGURE 1.2   Data distribution for training, testing, and validation.

TABLE 1.2
Summary of ECG Class Using AAMI EC57 Standard

Classes	CVD Type	Beat Count	Total
N	Normal(N)	75,017	90,588
	Left bundle Branch block (L)	8071	
	Right bundle Branch block (R)	7255	
	Atrial escape (e)	16	
	Nodal escape (j)	229	
S	Atrial premature (A)	2546	2781
	Aberrant atrial premature (a)	150	
	Nodal premature (J)	83	
	Supra-ventricular premature (S)	2	
V	Premature ventricular contraction (V)	7129	7235
	Ventricular escape (E)	106	
F	Fusion of ventricular and normal (F)	802	802
Q	Paced(/)	7023	8038
	Fusion of paced and normal (f)	982	
	Unclassifiable (Q)	33	
	Total		101,404

Table 1.2 represents the beat counts present in various classes of arrhythmia and a total of 101,404 beats are extracted from the data set. Approximately 101,400 beats are distributed over five different classes and labelled by multiple cardiologists. To even out the number of samples synthetic data generation is introduced.

1.2.2 SYNTHETIC DATA GENERATION

Heartbeat distributions by class are highly non-uniform in MIT-BIH ECG arrhythmia database. A majority of signals belong to a single class, with the remaining 20% belonging to the other four classes.

As shown in Figure 1.3, a class imbalance problem exists in this data set, since samples taken from the majority class are 100 times greater than those taken from the minority class. Synthetic data were generated to address this problem. The minority classes were fitted with synthetic data to avoid overfitting. Using synthetic data, the five classes of ECG heartbeats (N, S, V, F, Q) are balanced.

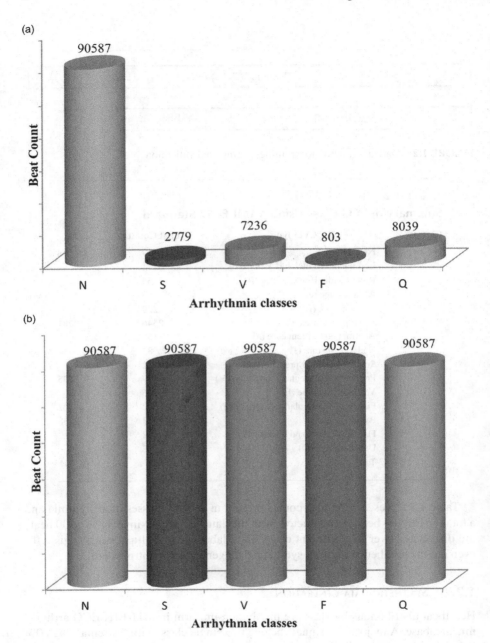

FIGURE 1.3 Distributions of signal samples: (a) Before SMOTE. (b) After SMOTE.

Synthetic minority oversampling technique (SMOTE) is a widely used oversampling technique [7], which employs KNN graphs to generate simulated data. A new synthetic minority sample can be generated by using this method without having to duplicate existing samples. Synthetic data generation is done as follows

$$S^{SD} = S^i + \left(S^j - S^i\right) * \gamma \qquad (1.1)$$

where S^i represents the minority class instance, S^j is the randomly selected minority class from KNNs. γ is a vector with random number (0 to 1) taken from the primary reference instance S^i and secondary reference instance S^j.

Synthetic data S^{SD} is generated along the line between S^i and S^j and the direction of the line joining toward S^i. Synthetically created balanced data set with equal number of instances in each class using SMOTE is shown in Figure 1.3b. Being most abundant, the segments in N class remain unchanged. Segments of the remaining types are augmented to match the number of segments in the N class. In total, 452,935 beats have been added to the N, S, V, F, and Q segments after augmentation. SMOTE method prevents over-fitting as well.

1.3 PROPOSED 1D CONVOLUTIONAL NEURAL NETWORK

The CNN is a well-known deep learning architecture inspired by human visual perception. CNN architecture draws attention in extracting the most appropriate features from input ECG signals by applying convolution operations. In a classic CNN, convolutional layers are cascaded and pooled together. Convolutional layers calculate the inner product of the linear filter and the underlying vectors of an input segment by applying a nonlinear activation function to generate feature maps. The complete structure of the proposed lightweight 1D CNN with three convolutional layers and one output layer for ECG signal classification is shown in Figure 1.4.

The proposed 1D CNN consists of three fully connected layers (L1–L3), a Max pool layer (L4), a flattening layer (L5), a dropout layer (L6), and finally a fully connected layer (L7) with softmax layer (L8). 1D convolution produces a tensor of output by convolving the input layer with a 1D convolution kernel.

The first convolution layer (L1) is fed by 187×1 sequences with a kernel size of 3 and modifies the input sequence and results with a feature space of size 256. The second (L2) and (L3) convolution layers convert the respective feature space to a shape of 187×64 with a kernel size of 3. The Maxpooling layer (L4) down samples the feature vector space to 94×64 space and flatten to feed the fully connected layer with 1024 neurons. Rectified Linear Unit (ReLU) is the non-linear activation function throughout the architecture. Most of the hyperparameters were kept same throughout the network, e.g. kernel size (also called filter size) was kept "3" for all the convolution layers, polling size was kept "2" for the pooling layer, and convolution and polling operation in all the layer was "same," i.e. with zero padding. In flatten layer (L5), the matrices are reshaped to vectors to support the subsequent non-spatial layers. In L6, the dropout rate is set as 0.5 and finally the softmax layer (L8) classifies the data into five different arrhythmia classes. The proposed 1D-CNN structure comprises a total of 6,191,493 trainable parameters.

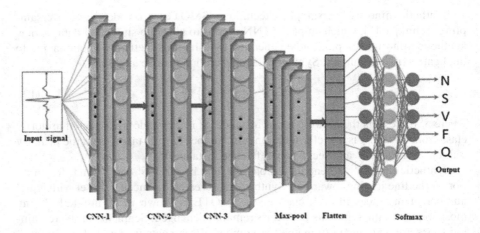

FIGURE 1.4   Proposed lightweight 1D CNN architecture.

TABLE 1.3
Trainable Parameters Contributed by Each Layer of the Network

Layer #	Layer (Type)	Output Shape	Parameters
L1	Conv1D	(None, 187, 1)	256
L2	Conv1D	(None, 187, 64)	12,352
L3	Conv1D	(None, 187, 64)	12,352
L4	MaxPool1D	(None, 94, 64)	0
L5	Flatten	(None, 6016)	0
L6	Dropout (0.5)	(None, 6016)	0
L7	FC(Dense)	(None, 1024)	6,161,408
L8	Softmax	(None, 5)	5125
Total Trainable Parameters			6,191,493

Table 1.3 presents the trainable parameters contributed by each layer of the network. Based on the categorical cross-entropy loss function [11], the neural network parameters were optimised. Using the Adam optimisation algorithm [13] categorical cross-entropy loss was minimised CNN parameters were updated. To lessen the risk of overfitting, an early stopping technique [26,27] is used to reduce the number of epochs required for training. In this technique, training is terminated when there is no improvement in the loss on the validation set for at least 20 consecutive epochs.

In the first step, we trained the proposed model using both training and validation sets. Then the CNN was evaluated on test sets that were unseen by the model during training phase. The training history of accuracy and loss function on full feature set is executed for 100 epochs based on the training and validation values. Each training epoch is followed by a validation set that is used to determine the learning efficiency. The model encounters a problem of overfitting after running the training process.

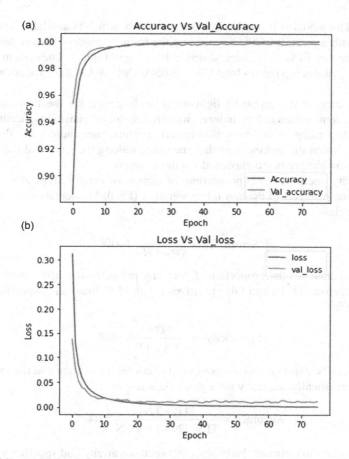

FIGURE 1.5   (a) Validation accuracy curve. (b) Validation loss curve.

The results, indeed, showed that both training loss and validation loss converge around 75 epochs. The cumulative accuracy was 99.97% in the training set with a loss of 9.7820e-04, while the cumulative accuracy in validation set was 99.8% with a loss of 0.0121.

The progression of accuracy during validation is shown in Figure 1.5a, and loss during accuracy training process is shown in Figure 1.5b. From the graphs, it is evident that the 1D CNN model performed well during the training phase and that both the training loss and validation loss converge around 75 epochs. Validation loss is closer to training loss since validation data set was never used for training and only used to prevent overfitting.

1.4   RESULTS AND DISCUSSION

Though the classification of arrhythmia didn't need to elaborate voluminous data, the CNN needs a significant volume of time for training accomplished on a low-end machine. The model is trained using Google Colab, which is available as a virtual machine with a powerful GPU to speed up the training process. Before being standardised the raw ECG signals are scaled in the range of 0 to 1. The system used for the experimental setup has an Intel Core i5-6500 CPU @3.2 GHz processor with 16 GB RAM.

Performance of the proposed lightweight architecture for the classification of arrhythmia is measured in four indexes, namely specificity, sensitivity, accuracy, and F1-score. According to the confusion matrix, performance indices are defined by the ratio between the instances of the true classes along the rows and the instance frequencies of the predicted classes along the columns.

Sensitivity measures the proportion of correctly predicted positive samples between true positives (TPs) and false negatives (FNs). Mathematically, sensitivity for a given class is

$$\text{Sensitivity} = \frac{TP}{TP + FN} * 100\% \tag{1.2}$$

Specificity calculates the proportion of correctly predicted negative samples within the true negatives (TNs) and false positives (FPs). Mathematically, specificity for a given class is

$$\text{Specificity} = \frac{TN}{TN + FP} * 100\% \tag{1.3}$$

Accuracy can be expressed in terms of ratio of correct prediction and the input samples. Mathematically, accuracy for a given class is

$$\text{Accuracy} = \frac{TP + TN}{TP + TN + FP + FN} * 100\% \tag{1.4}$$

F1-score is used to estimate the balance between sensitivity and specificity and also to evaluate the classification model performance. Mathematically, F1-score for a given class is

$$\text{F1-score} = \frac{2 * \text{Sensitivity} * \text{Specificity}}{\text{Sensitivity} + \text{Specificity}} * 100\% \tag{1.5}$$

Classification accuracy, sensitivity, specificity and F1-score for each of the five arrhythmias are presented in Table 1.4.

Researchers have developed many algorithms for detecting arrhythmias using deep learning models with different data sets. A comparison of our results to state-of-the-art techniques is undertaken in terms of number of arrhythmia classes, methodology, size of signal samples, and performance metrics.

Performance comparison of various types of classifier models tested in MIT-BIH data set is given in Table 1.5. With respect to other models, the differences between the proposed work and the state-of-the-art are rather promising both in terms of accuracy and computational cost. Considering the potential and prospects of the proposed methodology, utilising it for diagnosing different critical diseases would be an interesting endeavour.

TABLE 1.4

Confusion Matrix of the Proposed System

Class	C1	C2	C3	C4	C5	Actual	Predicted	Specificity	Sensitivity	F1 Score
C1	26,876	147	37	29	28	27,117	26,876	99.11	99.98	100
C2	0	27,080	0	0	0	27,080	27,080	100	99.45	100
C3	3	2	27,250	3	3	27,261	27,250	99.96	99.86	100
C4	0	0	0	27,119	0	27,119	27,119	100	99.88	100
C5	1	0	0	0	27,303	27,304	27,303	99.99	99.88	100

Overall classification accuracy: 99.81%

TABLE 1.5

Performance Comparison with State-of-Art Techniques

Reference	Classes	Approach	Signal Length	Performance		
				Sensitivity	Specificity	Accuracy
Kiranyaz et al. [14]	5	CNN + BPN	128	60.3	99.2	97.6
Acharya, Oh, et al. [2]	5	CNN	260	96.71	91.54	94.03
Garcia et al. [9]	3	SVM + PSO	200	94.0	98.0	92.4
Zhai & Tin [37]	5	CNN	245	97.5	76.8	98.7
Yang et al. [35]	6	Auto encoder	89 (L) 160 (R)	98.43	98.18	96.49
Z. Zheng et al. [39]	5	CNN-LSTM	300	97.87	98.57	98
Atal & Singh [5]	2	CNN-LSTM	360	93.8	95	93.19
Ullah et al. [33]	5	CNN	200	99.28%	99.63	99.12
Rashed-Al-Mahfuz et al. [28]	5	VCG16 CNN	180	97.50	98.70	**99.90**
Oh et al. [20]	5	U-net	160	94.44	98.26	97.32
Y. Li et al. [16]	5	ResNet	300	93.21	96.76	99.06
Faust & Acharya [8]	5	CNN-LSTM	300	97.87	98.57	98
Y. Li et al. [16]	5	DCNN	360	92.05	97.54	88.34
Siouda et al. [30]	3	Hybrid RBF – RVFL NN	260	55.66	80.55	93.11
Proposed model	**5**	**1D CNN**	**187**	**99.81**	**99.81**	**99.8**

1.5 CONCLUSION

Technology for automatic diagnosis of arrhythmias has important research value and can reduce the danger of CVDs. This chapter examines and assesses deep learning methods used to classify heartbeats and proposed a lightweight 1D CNN to automatically classify five different cardiac signals. There are several techniques already described in the literature for this purpose. The enlarged data from MIT-BIHECG arrhythmia database naturally complicates the task of classifying the data during testing because of the human factor. The data sets were scrutinised in order to improve the model's accuracy. The analysis of its confusion matrix revealed some misinterpretations both due to data nature and class imbalances. In comparison to other deep learning algorithms and traditional machine learning algorithms, this algorithm is more accurate at classifying cardiac arrhythmias. CNN's proposed network performs remarkably well in terms of overall performance with 99.8% classification accuracy. Thus, the proposed model offers very lightweight architecture with great generalisation which can be easily integrated with low-power consumption technologies. In future, the proposed architecture is also expected to best fit for other applications involving 1D bio signals.

REFERENCES

1. Acharya, U. R., Fujita, H., Oh, S. L., Hagiwara, Y., Tan, J. H., & Adam, M. (2017). Application of deep convolutional neural network for automated detection of myocardial infarction using ECG signals. *Information Sciences, 415–416*, 190–198. https://doi.org/10.1016/j.ins.2017.06.027.
2. Acharya, U. R., Oh, S. L., Hagiwara, Y., Tan, J. H., Adam, M., Gertych, A., & Tan, R. S. (2017). A deep convolutional neural network model to classify heartbeats. *Computers in Biology and Medicine, 89*, 389–396. https://doi.org/10.1016/j.compbiomed.2017.08.022.
3. Alwan, Y., Cvetkovic, Z., & Curtis, M. J. (2018). Methods for improved discrimination between ventricular fibrillation and tachycardia. *IEEE Transactions on Biomedical Engineering, 65*(10), 2143–2151. https://doi.org/10.1109/TBME.2017.2785442.
4. Andersen, R. S., Peimankar, A., & Puthusserypady, S. (2019). A deep learning approach for real-time detection of atrial fibrillation. *Expert Systems with Applications, 115*, 465–473. https://doi.org/10.1016/j.eswa.2018.08.011.
5. Atal, D. K., & Singh, M. (2020). Arrhythmia classification with ECG signals based on the optimization-enabled deep convolutional neural network. *Computer Methods and Programs in Biomedicine, 196*, 105607. https://doi.org/10.1016/j.cmpb.2020.105607.
6. Banerjee, S., & Mitra, M. (2014). Application of cross wavelet transform for ECG pattern analysis and classification. *IEEE Transactions on Instrumentation and Measurement, 63*(2), 326–333. https://doi.org/10.1109/TIM.2013.2279001.
7. Chawla, N. V., Bowyer, K. W., Hall, L. O., & Kegelmeyer, W. P. (2002). SMOTE: Synthetic minority over-sampling technique. *Journal of Artificial Intelligence Research, 16*, 321–357. https://doi.org/10.1613/jair.953.
8. Faust, O., & Acharya, U. R. (2021). Automated classification of five arrhythmias and normal sinus rhythm based on RR interval signals. *Expert Systems with Applications, 181*, 115031. https://doi.org/10.1016/j.eswa.2021.115031.
9. Garcia, G., Moreira, G., Menotti, D., & Luz, E. (2017). Inter-patient ECG heartbeat classification with temporal VCG optimized by PSO. *Scientific Reports, 7*(1), 10543. https://doi.org/10.1038/s41598-017-09837-3.
10. Goldberger, A. L., Amaral, L. A. N., Glass, L., Hausdorff, J. M., Ivanov, P. C., Mark, R. G., Mietus, J. E., Moody, G. B., Peng, C.-K., & Stanley, H. E. (2000). PhysioBank, physiotoolkit, and physionet. *Circulation, 101*(23). https://doi.org/10.1161/01.CIR.101.23.e215.
11. Heaton, J. (2018). Ian Goodfellow, Yoshua Bengio, and Aaron Courville: Deep learning. *Genetic Programming and Evolvable Machines, 19*(1–2), 305–307. https://doi.org/10.1007/s10710-017-9314-z.
12. Kandala, R. N. V. P. S., Dhuli, R., Pławiak, P., Naik, G. R., Moeinzadeh, H., Gargiulo, G. D., & Gunnam, S. (2019). Towards real-time heartbeat classification: Evaluation of

nonlinear morphological features and voting method. *Sensors, 19*(23), 5079. https://doi. org/10.3390/s19235079.

13. Kingma, D. P., & Ba, J. L. (2015). Adam: A method for stochastic optimization. *3rd International Conference on Learning Representations, ICLR 2015- Conference Track Proceedings*, San Diego, CA, pp. 1–15.

14. Kiranyaz, S., Ince, T., & Gabbouj, M. (2016). Real-time patient-specific ECG classification by 1-D convolutional neural networks. *IEEE Transactions on Biomedical Engineering, 63*(3), 664–675. https://doi.org/10.1109/TBME.2015.2468589.

15. Li, T., & Zhou, M. (2016). ECG classification using wavelet packet entropy and random forests. *Entropy, 18*(8), 285. Special Issue Entropy on Biosignals and Intelligent Systems, 1–16. https://doi.org/10.3390/e18080285.

16. Li, Y., Qian, R., & Li, K. (2022). Inter-patient arrhythmia classification with improved deep residual convolutional neural network. *Computer Methods and Programs in Biomedicine*, 214,106582.

17. Mahmud, T., Fattah, S. A., & Saquib, M. (2020). DeepArrNet: An efficient deep CNN architecture for automatic arrhythmia detection and classification from denoised ECG beats. *IEEE Access, 8*, 104788–104800. https://doi.org/10.1109/ACCESS.2020.2998788.

18. Martis, R. J., Acharya, U. R., Lim, C. M., & Suri, J. S. (2013). Characterization of ECG beats from cardiac arrhythmia using discrete cosine transform in PCA framework. *Knowledge-Based Systems, 45*, 76–82. https://doi.org/10.1016/j.knosys.2013.02.007.

19. Melgani, F., & Bazi, Y. (2008). Classification of electrocardiogram signals with support vector machines and particle swarm optimization. *IEEE Transactions on Information Technology in Biomedicine, 12*(5), 667–677. https://doi.org/10.1109/TITB.2008.923147.

20. Oh, S. L., Ng, E. Y. K., Tan, R. S., & Acharya, U. R. (2018). Automated diagnosis of arrhythmia using combination of CNN and LSTM techniques with variable length heart beats. *Computers in Biology and Medicine, 102*, 278–287. https://doi.org/10.1016/j. compbiomed.2018.06.002.

21. Park, J., Lee, K., & Kang, K. (2013). Arrhythmia detection from heartbeat using k-nearest neighbour classifier. *2013 IEEE International Conference on Bioinformatics and Biomedicine*, pp. 15–22. Dec. 18 2013 to Dec. 21 2013, Shanghai, China https://doi. org/10.1109/BIBM.2013.6732594.

22. Piot, O., Boveda, S., Defaye, P., Klug, D., Lacotte, J., & Marijon, E. (2022). Prospective evolution of cardiac arrhythmia care: 2030 vision. *Archives of Cardiovascular Diseases*. https://doi.org/10.1016/j.acvd.2022.02.008.

23. Pławiak, P., Abdar, M., & Rajendra Acharya, U. (2019). Application of new deep genetic cascade ensemble of SVM classifiers to predict the Australian credit scoring. *Applied Soft Computing, 84*, 105740. https://doi.org/10.1016/j.asoc.2019.105740.

24. Pławiak, P., & Acharya, U. R. (2020). Novel deep genetic ensemble of classifiers for arrhythmia detection using ECG signals. *Neural Computing and Applications, 32*(15), 11137–11161. https://doi.org/10.1007/s00521-018-03980-2.

25. Pourbabaee, B., Roshtkhari, M. J., & Khorasani, K. (2018). Deep convolutional neural networks and learning ECG features for screening paroxysmal atrial fibrillation patients. *IEEE Transactions on Systems, Man, and Cybernetics: Systems, 48*(12), 2095–2104. https://doi.org/10.1109/TSMC.2017.2705582.

26. Prechelt, L. (1998). *Early Stopping - But When?* (pp. 55–69). https://doi.org/10.1007 /3-540-49430-8_3.

27. Rajpurkar, P., Hannun, A. Y., Haghpanahi, M., Bourn, C., & Ng, A. Y. (2017). *Cardiologist-Level Arrhythmia Detection with Convolutional Neural Networks*. http:// arxiv.org/abs/1707.01836.

28. Rashed-Al-Mahfuz, M., Moni, M. A., Lio', P., Islam, S. M. S., Berkovsky, S., Khushi, M., & Quinn, J. M. W. (2021). Deep convolutional neural networks based ECG beats

classification to diagnose cardiovascular conditions. *Biomedical Engineering Letters*, *11*(2), 147–162. https://doi.org/10.1007/s13534-021-00185-w.

29. Ribeiro, A. H., Ribeiro, M. H., Paixão, G. M. M., Oliveira, D. M., Gomes, P. R., Canazart, J. A., Ferreira, M. P. S., Andersson, C. R., Macfarlane, P. W., Meira, W., Schön, T. B., & Ribeiro, A. L. P. (2020). Automatic diagnosis of the 12-lead ECG using a deep neural network. *Nature Communications*, *11*(1), 1760. https://doi.org/10.1038/s41467-020-15432-4.

30. Siouda, R., Nemissi, M., & Seridi, H. (2022). A random deep neural system for heartbeat classification. *Evolving Systems*. https://doi.org/10.1007/s12530-022-09429-1

31. Tran Hoai, L., Osowski, S., & Stodolski, M. (2003). On-line heart beat recognition using hermite polynomials and neuro-fuzzy network. *IEEE Transactions on Instrumentation and Measurement*, *52*(4), 1224–1231. https://doi.org/10.1109/TIM.2003.816841.

32. Tripathy, R. K., Bhattacharyya, A., & Pachori, R. B. (2019). A novel approach for detection of myocardial infarction from ECG signals of multiple electrodes. *IEEE Sensors Journal*, *19*(12), 4509–4517. https://doi.org/10.1109/JSEN.2019.2896308.

33. Ullah, W., Siddique, I., Zulqarnain, R. M., Alam, M. M., Ahmad, I., & Raza, U. A. (2021). Classification of arrhythmia in heartbeat detection using deep learning. *Computational Intelligence and Neuroscience*, *2021*, 1–13. https://doi.org/10.1155/2021/2195922.

34. Wu, Z., Ding, X., & Zhang, G. (2016). A novel method for classification of ECG arrhythmias using deep belief networks. *International Journal of Computational Intelligence and Applications*, *15*(04), 1650021. https://doi.org/10.1142/S1469026816500218.

35. Yang, J., Bai, Y., Lin, F., Liu, M., Hou, Z., & Liu, X. (2018). A novel electrocardiogram arrhythmia classification method based on stacked sparse auto-encoders and softmax regression. *International Journal of Machine Learning and Cybernetics*, *9*(10), 1733–1740. https://doi.org/10.1007/s13042-017-0677-5.

36. Yu, S., & Chou, K. (2008). Integration of independent component analysis and neural networks for ECG beat classification. *Expert Systems with Applications*, *34*(4), 2841–2846. https://doi.org/10.1016/j.eswa.2007.05.006.

37. Zhai, X., & Tin, C. (2018). Automated ECG classification using dual heartbeat coupling based on convolutional neural network. *IEEE Access*, *6*, 27465–27472. https://doi.org/10.1109/ACCESS.2018.2833841.

38. Zheng, Y., Liu, Q., Chen, E., Ge, Y., & Zhao, J. L. (2014). *Time Series Classification Using Multi-Channels Deep Convolutional Neural Networks* (pp. 298–310). https://doi.org/10.1007/978-3-319-08010-9_33.

39. Zheng, Z., Chen, Z., Hu, F., Zhu, J., Tang, Q., & Liang, Y. (2020). An automatic diagnosis of arrhythmias using a combination of CNN and LSTM technology. *Electronics*, *9*(1), 121. https://doi.org/10.3390/electronics9010121.

2 An Automatic System for Pertussis Diagnosis with Temperature Monitoring Using CNN

Therese Yamuna Mahesh, Abhirami B, Cindhya Charly, Devika Jayakumar, and Elsa Shaju Thomas
Amal Jyothi College of Engineering

CONTENTS

2.1 INTRODUCTION

The project aims to develop a pertussis diagnosis system that is fully automatic, user-friendly and highly accurate. The system should be able to analyze audio signals and provide quick diagnostic results. This helps in suggesting efficient treatment methods to people with limited access to resources. Also, along with this, a temperature sensor is used so that a comprehensible result is obtained, which when uploaded to a cloud platform can be accessed by anyone from anywhere, thus providing an easy way for continuous monitoring purposes.

Pertussis is a contagious respiratory disease that is caused by the bacteria *Bordetella pertussis*. It causes infection in the lungs and airways. The symptoms of pertussis range from running nose to serious conditions of apnea, where there is a pause in breathing of babies. Cough of a patient with pertussis is characterized by a whooping sound, which immediately follows the cough, and, hence, pertussis is commonly known as whooping cough [1]. Pertussis, if left untreated can cause serious health risks and can even be dangerous to life. Hence, there is a need for immediate attention if pertussis is detected. But, for providing immediate medical care for diseases like

DOI: 10.1201/9781003307778-3

pertussis, there is a need for faster detection systems, which can diagnose the disease immediately by looking at earlier symptoms and identifying the underlying characteristics, which may prove to be a gold standard when it comes to the detection of that particular disease. Like most respiratory diseases, cough is a symptom of pertussis. But, unlike any other disease, cough in pertussis is characterized by whooping sound, which may or may not be present in patients suffering from pertussis. Still, doctors usually look for the presence of whooping sound, when it comes to the preliminary examination of pertussis.

2.2 RELATED WORKS

Even if whooping sound is not present, it was found by researchers that coughs of different diseases may have different spectral characteristics [2–4] depending on various features like the gender of the patient, part of infection and whether there is expectoration following cough or not. Therefore, it is possible that different diseases can be detected from cough by properly identifying their underlying properties [1,5]. This discovery can be proved to be a major breakthrough when it comes to the diagnosis of respiratory diseases [6–8]. For diseases like pertussis, there is an urgent need for systems that are able to detect pertussis quickly. But it is equally important that such systems need to be highly accurate and provide results in the shortest time possible [9,10]. Therefore, it is highly preferable that the system is fully automatic in order to reduce the time lost by manual labor [9,11]. As per the report of the World Health Organization, 16 million cases of pertussis occur worldwide, resulting in approximately 200,000 deaths [12]. Most of these cases are reported mainly in rural areas and are extremely dangerous for children below one year of age. The graph in Figure 2.1 shows the incidence of pertussis across different age groups.

It is clearly evident from the figure that pertussis mainly affects infants. Also, pertussis is an airborne disease, which is highly contagious and requires faster

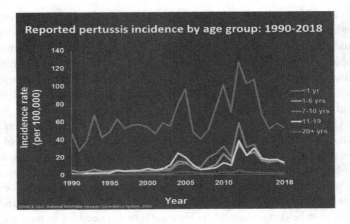

FIGURE 2.1   Pertussis incidence across different age groups (pertussis surveillance trend reporting and case definition 2022) [13].

treatment. Doctors rely on whooping sound and other symptoms when it comes to diagnosis of pertussis. However, the gold standard for pertussis diagnosis is by taking nasopharyngeal specimens. Also, there are other diagnosis tests like blood analysis with serology and polymerase chain reaction (PCR). But a downside to all these tests are they are time consuming and expensive and may not be easily available especially in rural areas of developing countries. Thus, there are chances of delay in the effective treatment of patients. This worsens their condition and further spreads the infection to others. Therefore, there is a need for a quick diagnosis system, which provides accurate results for the tests carried out. It had been found out earlier that cough signals can act as a guideline when it comes to diagnosis of respiratory diseases. Attempts have been made by early researchers toward this end for developing systems capable of detecting diseases by the analysis of cough sounds of the patients. But the current systems available for cough detection are semi-automatic as they require help from experts to manually count the cough sounds before further classification. The sound recording systems used are microphones, which had to be attached to a person for collecting sounds, which may cause some difficulty for the person wearing it [14]. This may also cause violation of privacy as the microphones record not only cough sounds but also other sounds in the background. Also, the use of complex classifiers leads to cases of overfitting which reduces accuracy and causes false alarms. Our aim is to develop a cough classifier which overcomes the above difficulties and provides accurate results for pertussis diagnosis. We collected the cough samples, took the spectrogram and classified the image using convolutional neural network (CNN) [15]. Alerts were sent to the concerned medical personnel when the number of coughs and the temperature of the patient exceeded a set threshold value.

2.3   DATABASE DESCRIPTION FOR PERTUSSIS DETECTION

Our database consists of cough sounds in two classes. They are classified into pertussis cough samples and non-pertussis cough samples. The sources of our database are the cough sound samples extracted from YouTube and also from some websites dedicated for whooping cough or pertussis.

The total dataset is split into a testing set, validation set and training set in the ratio 15:15:70. Training set is the dataset that we use for training the model (weights and biases in the case of a neural network). The model learns from these data. A validation dataset is a sample of data, set aside from training the model and used to give an estimate of model skill as we tune the model's hyperparameters. Testing set is the sample of data used to provide an evaluation on the extent to which the final model fits on the training dataset.

The classification of cough samples into two classes is based on the fact that pertussis cough samples contain a whooping sound along with the cough sound, where the patient gasps for air. This is what makes the whooping cough samples different from the normal non-pertussis coughs. Since whooping sound is a unique feature specific to pertussis cough samples, this turns out to be the most important characteristic, which helps us to perform further classification and for the final diagnosis of pertussis disease.

2.4 DETECTION OF PERTUSSIS USING CONVOLUTION NEURAL NETWORK

The block diagram of the proposed model is shown in Figure 2.2. The first part of the work deals with pertussis diagnosis from the input cough sounds, and the next part deals with temperature monitoring of the diagnosed patients using DS18B20.

The first stage in the development of our model is data collection. Here, the required number of audio samples is collected, which are fed as the input for the first stage. The main sources of data are the sound samples extracted from YouTube and from some of the websites particularly dedicated for whooping cough [16].

Then, the input audio samples are given to the pre-processing stage. Pre-processing is an important step for building an accurate and better-performing model [17]. Pre-processing is defined as all the transformation processes performed on the raw input data before feeding them to the deep neural network. This is because training a CNN on raw input data can lead to poor classification performance. The pre-processing stage also helps to speed up the training process. Here, all the input audio samples are resampled to 16,000 Hz with a bit resolution of 16 bits, and all the sound samples are made mono in nature.

Since the input to CNN are images, the pre-processed audio signals are then converted to spectrograms [11]. A spectrogram gives a representation of the signal strength of the signal over time at various frequencies that are present in a particular waveform. In a spectrogram, the y-axis represents frequency, and the x-axis represents time. The different colors in the spectrogram represent the intensity at that particular frequency.

The input to CNN is the spectrograms generated from the previous stage. This is where training of the model is performed. CNN is a class of deep neural networks

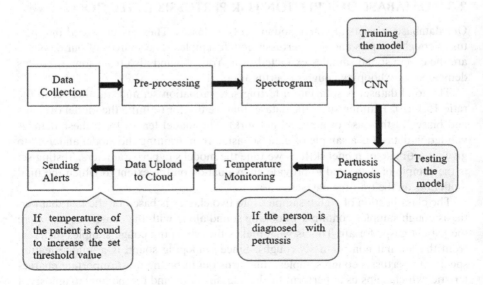

FIGURE 2.2 Block diagram of the proposed system.

[18], which is most commonly applied to analyze visual imagery. The CNN consists of an input layer, hidden layers and an output layer. The convolution kernel generates a feature map, which is the input of the next layer. The other layers include fully connected layers, pooling layers and normalization layers. The final output layer of the CNN model performs the classification of sound signals.

The pertussis diagnosis stage uses the trained CNN model to predict whether the person has pertussis disease or not. Here, the input cough samples are provided, which will be tested on the trained CNN model. And this cough sample will then be classified into one of the two classes, i.e. pertussis cough or non-pertussis cough. Hence, an accurate diagnosis can be provided if a person is suffering from pertussis, just by using the patient's cough sound, without using any laboratory tests [12]. We are also providing an account of temperature for pertussis-diagnosed patients. Here, we are using a DS18B20 temperature sensor for the continuous monitoring of temperature of the patients, which is connected to Raspberry Pi 3B+. DS18B20 temperature sensor [19] is an electronic device, which measures the patient's temperature and converts it into digital data to record, monitor, or signal temperature changes. Raspberry Pi is a single-board computer that allows connecting a temperature sensor and streams the data to a data visualization software. The digital output of the DS18B20 temperature sensor works well with the Raspberry Pi. Hence, the temperature of the patient is measured using the DS18B20 temperature sensor and the Raspberry Pi 3B+, which can be used for the further stages.

The temperature of the patients which is monitored continuously with a DS18B20 [19] temperature sensor is fed to a cloud platform called Thing Speak using Raspberry Pi. Thing Speak is an IOT Cloud platform where we can send the temperature sensor data to the cloud server, which allows us to analyze, visualize, and aggregate live data streams in the cloud. Since these data are stored in a cloud platform, the temperature of the patient can be monitored from anywhere in the world at any time by anyone having access to this cloud platform.

We can also use the temperature stored in the Thing Speak cloud server to send alerts. This is done using the facilities offered by the IFTTT [20] platform. Here, we can set a threshold temperature such that, when the patient's temperature exceeds the set threshold limit, alert messages can be sent to anybody including the doctors or patient's relatives via emails, messages, or calls. In this manner, we can ensure continuous monitoring of the patients, and it can also help in quicker diagnosis and providing early treatments.

This research work uses CNN [18] for distinguishing whooping cough sounds from other sounds. CNNs have been traditionally used for image recognition and classification purposes. But the project involves the application of audio signal processing. Audio signals cannot be directly fed as input to CNN. Therefore, the one-dimensional audio signals have to be converted to two-dimensional images before inputting them to the network. This conversion is carried out by performing short-term Fourier transform (STFT) on the signal. The entire audio is divided into frames of fixed duration and Fourier transform is performed on each frame. These frames are put together to form the spectrogram of an audio signal. Spectrogram is also known as the waterfall model. Figure 2.3 shows the waveform and spectrogram of a sample audio.

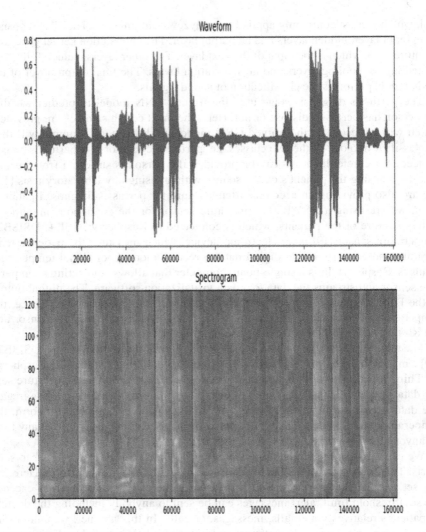

FIGURE 2.3   Waveform and spectrogram of sample audio.

Similarly, the spectrogram of the entire dataset is taken and is fed to a CNN. The system uses a CNN with two convolutional layers, a fully connected layer and a max-pooling layer [18].

The input spectrogram of size (1405 × 129) is rescaled to a size of (32 × 32) before inputting it to the convolutional layer. This is done in order to reduce the computational complexity. The rescaled image is normalized and is fed into the convolutional layer. The first convolutional layer contains 32 (3 × 3) filters which pass over the spectrogram to extract the relevant features. The first convolutional layer outputs a feature map of size (30 × 30). The total number of parameters learnt from this layer is 320. The feature map outputted by the first convolutional layer is fed to the second convolutional layer. This layer also has 64 filters and they are of (3×3) dimension. This layer again learns the relevant features and thus produces a feature map containing all this information. The size of this feature map is (28×28) and the number of learnable parameters from this layer is 18,496.

Both the convolutional layers employ Rectified Linear Unit (ReLU) [18] as their activation function. Neural networks employ a wide class of activation functions. Some of them are step functions, sigmoid functions and hyperbolic tangents and so on. Step functions can only be used for linear classification scenarios. Since the project involves complex and non-linear classification problems, step functions cannot be employed as the activation function. Sigmoid as well as hyperbolic tangents have proven to be useful in case of non-linear problems. But the problem with these activation functions is that they tend to saturate. Saturation problem arises because sigmoid activation function tends to compress the output of neurons to a value between 0 and 1. That is, negative values are compressed to a value of 0 and high positive values are compressed to a value of 1. Similarly, hyperbolic tangent (tanh) tends to compress high negative values to -1 and high positive values to 1. This is not good as the model will find it difficult to understand between relevant features and unnecessary ones. But ReLU [18] on the other hand, compresses only negative values to 0 and passes every positive value. Thus, the model will be able to distinguish between relevant and not-so-relevant features.

The final feature map from the second convolutional layer is fed to the pooling layer which scales down the size of the image to 14×14. This helps not only in reducing complexity but also in filtering out the most relevant and important features from the rest. Dropout regularization of 25% is involved in this layer. Dropout refers to dropping out certain neurons in a neural network so as to avoid the problems of overfitting. Dropout reduces the co-dependency that sometimes arises between neurons while training so that the training set always encounters a different architecture while training takes place. The output of the pooling layer is fed to a flattening layer so as to convert the feature map to a column vector, which is compatible with the fully connected layer.

The fully connected neural network has 128 neurons in each layer. It is in this part of the architecture that the neural network learns the different dependencies that exist between various features extracted by the collective effort of convolutional layer and pooling layer. Here also, a dropout of 50% is employed so as to reduce the chances of overfitting. ReLU is employed as the activation function. The output of this fully connected layer is fed to a small dense layer having only two neurons so as to predict the final output. The model summary of the deep learning architecture is shown in Figure 2.4.

The whole training takes place by using Adaptive Momentum (Adam) optimizer. This optimizer is a variant of stochastic gradient descent (SGD), which is one of the popularly used optimizers. Adam estimates the learning rate for all the parameters involved in the training of gradients. Adam helps in reducing the computational cost and requires only less memory for implementation and is best suitable for complex learning problems in CNN. The training samples are divided into batch size of 10. That is, after 10 training samples are fed to the network, parameter updation takes place [17,21].

For finding the difference between the expected prediction and actual prediction, we are using sparse categorical cross entropy loss. This is the usual cross entropy

```
Input shape: (1405, 129, 1)
Model: "sequential_1"
```

Layer (type)	Output Shape	Param #
===	===	===
resizing_1 (Resizing)	(None, 32, 32, 1)	0
normalization_1 (Normalizati	(None, 32, 32, 1)	3
conv2d_2 (Conv2D)	(None, 30, 30, 32)	320
conv2d_3 (Conv2D)	(None, 28, 28, 64)	18496
max_pooling2d_1 (MaxPooling2	(None, 14, 14, 64)	0
dropout_2 (Dropout)	(None, 14, 14, 64)	0
flatten_1 (Flatten)	(None, 12544)	0
dense_2 (Dense)	(None, 128)	1605760
dropout_3 (Dropout)	(None, 128)	0
dense_3 (Dense)	(None, 2)	258

```
Total params: 1,624,837
Trainable params: 1,624,834
Non-trainable params: 3
```

FIGURE 2.4 Model summary of the deep learning architecture.

loss, but better since computation can be performed on simple integers rather than encoding them as in the case of calculating cross entropy using TensorFlow in Python. Memory requirement is also less. This loss is mainly used when the classes are mutually exclusive. Sparse categorical cross entropy together with Adam optimizer is one of the standard models used in very generic scenarios. Additionally, here accuracy is also used as a metric in order to evaluate the model performance. The number of epochs used here is 500. Number of epochs refers to the total number of times the model is introduced to the whole dataset. A part of the whole dataset is dedicated for validation purposes termed as the validation data. Validation data help in evaluating the overall performance of the model. It is a common notion that the training loss decreases as the training progresses. But the validation loss first decreases, then increases as the training proceeds. This increase in validation loss serves as an indicator of overfitting. Hence, early stopping is introduced so that the training halts when validation loss begins to climb up. Finally, after the model is properly trained, it is evaluated on the test data, which are completely independent of the training dataset and is unknown to the model.

2.5 TEMPERATURE MONITORING

Since pertussis is a contagious disease, it is very difficult to monitor those who are under treatment. Temperature devices are often used to measure body temperature.

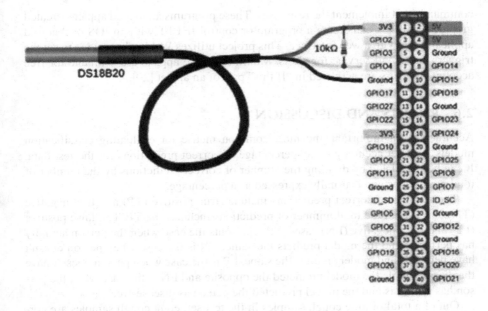

FIGURE 2.5 DS18B20 with Raspberry Pi.

Temperature sensor will keep in touch with the patient, and measure body temperature automatically. Sensor data will be sent to Thing Speak cloud and give alerts to medical practitioners to take appropriate medical attention when the temperature exceeds a particular limit. In this project, DS18B20 [18] temperature sensor is interfaced with Raspberry Pi, stores data in Thing Speak cloud and sends the email alerts along with the patient details, when the temperature of the patient exceeds the threshold value.

DS18B20 [19] temperature sensor has three terminals, Data line (yellow), VCC (red) and Ground (black). VCC is connected to 3.3 V (pin 1) of Raspberry Pi, Data line is connected to GPI04 (pin 7) and ground is connected to ground (pin 9). Figure 2.5 shows the interfacing of DS18B20 with Raspberry Pi.

Thing Speak is an Internet of Things (IOT) analytics platform, a service that allows users to analyze, visualize and collect live data streams in the cloud. Sensor data can be sent to Thing Speak from devices like Raspberry Pi and other hardware platforms. These data are stored in the cloud. Users can send and receive data from the stored place through the communicating Thing Speak channel. A maximum of eight fields is supported by each channel. In addition, each channel consists of different data types, three location fields and one channel field for status value. The data can be issued into the channel after creating the channel. The data are analyzed and evaluated by Thing Speak, and the results can be viewed according to our convenience.

A service that allows users to give a response to certain events can be done by using IFTTT (If This Then That). This service has collaborations with different service providers. They supply event notifications to IFTTT and then execute the commands that implement the responses. These programs are called applets, created graphically. Users can create a program or control IFTTT with an IOS or Android application or with a web interface. This project utilizes Webhooks service to set the triggers and email service for alerts. Maximum three applets are available for free account. Triggers are activated in "If this" part of an applet [20].

2.6   RESULTS AND DISCUSSION

Accuracy is an important and most common metric for evaluating classification models. Test set accuracy is the percentage of correct predictions for the test data. It can be calculated by dividing the number of correct predictions by the number of total predictions and is usually expressed as a percentage.

The number of correct predictions includes true positive (TP) and true negative (TN) cases. And the total number of predictions includes the TP, TN, false positive (FP) and false negative (FN) cases. TP represents the case when the person actually has pertussis and the model predicts the same. TN is the case when person doesn't have pertussis and model predicts the same. FP is the case when person doesn't have the disease while the model predicted the opposite and FN is the case when the person has pertussis and the model predicted the person as disease-free.

Out of a total of nine cough samples in the test set, eight cough samples are correctly predicted (TP and TN). Hence, we have obtained a testing accuracy of 89%.

Figure 2.6 represents a 2×2 confusion matrix we have obtained for the two classes, pertussis, and non-pertussis coughs.

We have taken a total of nine cough samples for testing purpose, which consists of five non-pertussis cough samples and four pertussis cough samples. From this, four non-pertussis cough samples out of a total of five, and the whole four whooping cough samples are correctly classified into their respective classes. And one of the non-pertussis cough samples got incorrectly classified as pertussis. The model was tested using unknown cough samples that the model has not encountered during the whole training process. It has made more correct predictions for the unknown samples as belonging to their respective classes, in comparison with a few misclassifications. This helped us to reach a conclusion that the model can be used to predict pertussis disease with a high degree of confidence.

Out of a number of predictions made, two of them belonging to the two classes are shown in Figure 2.7.

Figure 2.7 represents the output of an unknown pertussis cough sample, which is fed to the trained CNN model. First, the unknown sound sample is pre-processed. As the next step, spectrogram of the unknown cough sample is generated, which is fed to the trained CNN model, which then predicts the class of the unknown whooping cough sample based on the training provided for the model. And as seen in Figure 2.8, the sample got correctly classified into pertussis class with a high probability of above 95%.

The DS18B20 temperature sensor connected to the Raspberry Pi measures the temperature of the patients. Figure 2.9 displays the measured temperature values which have been obtained on Raspberry Pi Python shell.

The patient's temperature, monitored continuously using the DS18B20 temperature sensor, is uploaded to the Thing Speak cloud platform. The chart shown in

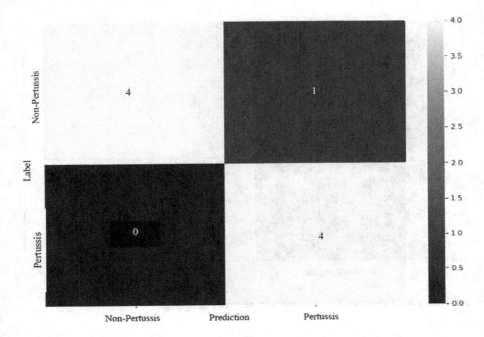

FIGURE 2.6 Confusion matrix.

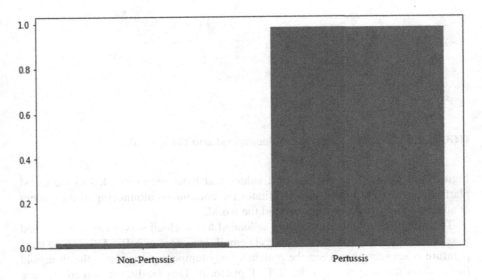

FIGURE 2.7 Prediction for unknown pertussis sample.

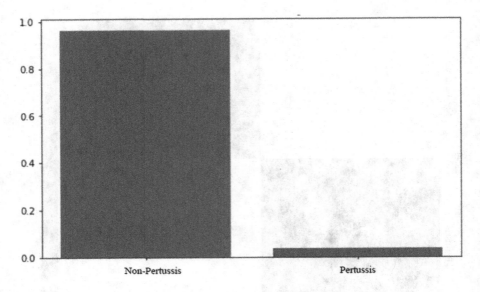

FIGURE 2.8   Prediction for unknown non-pertussis sample.

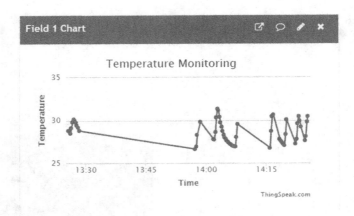

FIGURE 2.9   Measured temperature values uploaded to Thing Speak.

Figure 2.10 displays the temperature values that have been uploaded to the cloud platform at different times. This facilitates the continuous monitoring of the patient at any time and from anywhere around the world.

The measured temperature values uploaded to the cloud server can also be used to send alerts to the concerned people via email, messages or calls. A threshold temperature is set such that when the patient's body temperature exceeds the threshold limit, alerts are sent through the IFTTT platform. This facilitates immediate care and faster treatment for patients suffering from pertussis.

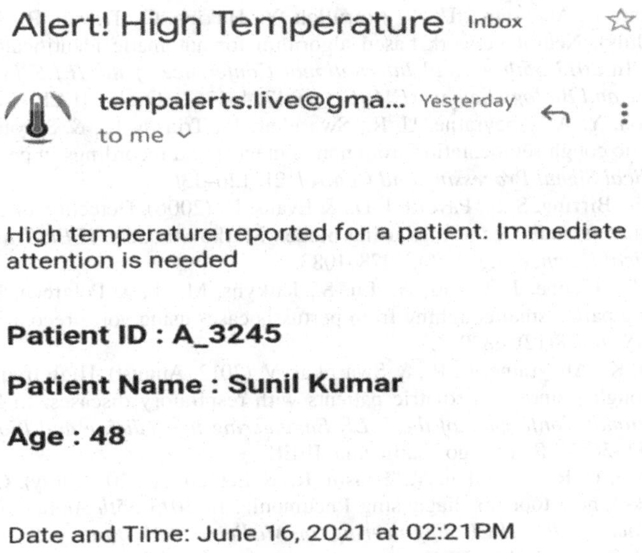

Alert! High Temperature Inbox ☆

tempalerts.live@gma... Yesterday ↩ ⋮
to me ⌄

High temperature reported for a patient. Immediate attention is needed

Patient ID : A_3245

Patient Name : Sunil Kumar

Age : 48

Date and Time: June 16, 2021 at 02:21PM

FIGURE 2.10 Email alert generated in the proposed system.

2.7 CONCLUSION

Through our research work, we have developed a model that can be used for automatic diagnosis of pertussis disease along with temperature monitoring. The algorithm serves as a fully automated, end-to-end solution with the incorporation of spectrogram generation, classification of cough sounds and pertussis detection along with temperature monitoring. As a result, no laboratory tests need to be performed allowing the algorithm to be used as a stand-alone solution in real time. Additionally, it will not require any person-specific tuning of thresholds and the usage of CNN helps the model to achieve less complexity and quick output. And, since all the details including the temperature along with pertussis diagnosis are uploaded to the cloud platform, it can be easily accessed by doctors along with the common people, anytime from anywhere in the world. Overall, we have developed a quick, user friendly and easily available system with a high pertussis identification performance using classification methods. We have proved that a pertussis cough can be automatically identified using its sound characteristics with a high degree of confidence. Besides its application in pertussis detection, it is useful for preventing the spread of the disease as the patient can be monitored with minimal contact.

REFERENCES

1. Tracey, B. H., Comina, G., Larson, S., Bravard, M., López, J. W., & Gilman, R. H. (2011, August). Cough detection algorithm for monitoring patient recovery from pulmonary tuberculosis. In *2011 Annual International Conference of the IEEE Engineering in Medicine and Biology Society* (pp. 6017–6020). Boston, MA, IEEE.

2. Swarnkar, V., Abeyratne, U. R., Amrulloh, Y., Hukins, C., Triasih, R., & Setyati, A. (2013, July). Neural network based algorithm for automatic identification of cough sounds. In *2013 35th Annual International Conference of the IEEE Engineering in Medicine and Biology Society (EMBC)* (pp. 1764–1767). Osaka, IEEE.

3. Amrulloh, Y. A., Abeyratne, U. R., Swarnkar, V., Triasih, R., & Setyati, A. (2015). Automatic cough segmentation from non-contact sound recordings in pediatric wards. *Biomedical Signal Processing and Control*, 21, 126–136.

4. Matos, S., Birring, S. S., Pavord, I. D., & Evans, H. (2006). Detection of cough signals in continuous audio recordings using hidden Markov models. *IEEE Transactions on Biomedical Engineering*, 53(6), 1078–1083.

5. Parker, D., Picone, J., Harati, A., Lu, S., Jenkyns, M. H., & Polgreen, P. M. (2013). Detecting paroxysmal coughing from pertussis cases using voice recognition technology. *PloS One*, 8(12), e82971.

6. Kosasih, K., Abeyratne, U. R., & Swarnkar, V. (2012, August). High frequency analysis of cough sounds in pediatric patients with respiratory diseases. In *2012 Annual International Conference of the IEEE Engineering in Medicine and Biology Society* (pp. 5654–5657). San Diego, California, IEEE.

7. Abeyratne, U. R., Swarnkar, V., Triasih, R., & Setyati, A. (2013, July). Cough Sound Analysis-A new tool for diagnosing Pneumonia. In *2013 35th Annual International Conference of the IEEE Engineering in Medicine and Biology Society (EMBC)* (pp. 5216–5219). Osaka, IEEE.

8. Al-Khassaweneh, M., & Bani Abdelrahman, R. E. (2013). A signal processing approach for the diagnosis of asthma from cough sounds. *Journal of Medical Engineering & Technology*, 37(3), 165–171.

9. Liu, J. M., You, M., Li, G. Z., Wang, Z., Xu, X., Qiu, Z., ... & Chen, S. (2013, July). Cough signal recognition with gammatone cepstral coefficients. In *2013 IEEE China Summit and International Conference on Signal and Information Processing* (pp. 160–164). Beijing, IEEE.

10. Lúcio, C., Teixeira, C., Henriques, J., de Carvalho, P., & Paiva, R. P. (2014, October). Voluntary cough detection by internal sound analysis. In *2014 7th International Conference on Biomedical Engineering and Informatics* (pp. 405–409). Dalian, IEEE.

11. Swarnkar, V., Abeyratne, U. R., Amrulloh, Y. A., & Chang, A. (2012, November). Automated algorithm for Wet/Dry cough sounds classification. In *2012 Annual International Conference of the IEEE Engineering in Medicine and Biology Society* (pp. 3147–3150). San Diego, CA, IEEE.

12. Pramono, R. X. A., Imtiaz, S. A., & Rodriguez-Villegas, E. (2016). A cough-based algorithm for automatic diagnosis of pertussis. *PloS One*, 11(9), e0162128.

13. Centers for Disease Control and Prevention. https://microbewiki.kenyon.edu/index.php/Bordetella_pertussis_and_the_Importance_of_Vaccination This graph shows the reported B. pertussis incidences for 1990-2018 by age group (per 100,00 persons). Source of information:[https://www.cdc.gov/pertussis/surv-reporting.html]

14. Larson, E. C., Lee, T., Liu, S., Rosenfeld, M., & Patel, S. N. (2011, September). Accurate and privacy preserving cough sensing using a low-cost microphone. In *Proceedings of the 13th International Conference on Ubiquitous Computing* University of Florida, SIGSPATIAL (pp. 375–384).

15. Liu, J. M., You, M., Wang, Z., Li, G. Z., Xu, X., & Qiu, Z. (2014, November). Cough detection using deep neural networks. In *2014 IEEE International Conference on Bioinformatics and Biomedicine (BIBM)* (pp. 560–563). Belfast, IEEE.

16. *Doug Jenkinson.* https://www.msdmanuals.com/professional/multimedia/audio/whooping_cough_classic_whoop//whoopingcough.net.Audio file courtesy of Doug Jenkinson, MD. Brought to you by Merck & Co, Inc., Rahway, NJ, (known as MSD outside the US and Canada)

17. Swarnkar, V., Abeyratne, U. R., Chang, A. B., Amrulloh, Y. A., Setyati, A., & Triasih, R. (2013). Automatic identification of wet and dry cough in pediatric patients with respiratory diseases. *Annals of Biomedical Engineering*, 41(5), 1016–1028.
18. Chen, L., Li, S., Bai, Q., Yang, J., Jiang, S., & Miao, Y. (2021). Review of image classification algorithms based on convolutional neural networks. *Remote Sensing*, 13(22), 4712.
19. Les Pounder https://bigl.es/ds18b20-temperature-sensor-with-python-raspberry-pi DS18B20 Temperature Sensor With Python (Raspberry Pi). Updated on June 2017.
20. Freeman. https://github.com/DrGFreeman/IFTTT-Webhook, A Python module to trigger IFTTT events using webhooks, updated 2022.
21. Chatrzarrin, H., Arcelus, A., Goubran, R., & Knoefel, F. (2011, May). Feature extraction for the differentiation of dry and wet cough sounds. In *2011 IEEE International Symposium on Medical Measurements and Applications* (pp. 162–166). Bari, IEEE.

3 DocPresRec
Doctor's Handwritten Prescription Recognition Using Deep Learning Algorithm

S. Prabu and K. Joseph Abraham Sundar
SASTRA Deemed to be University

CONTENTS

3.1 INTRODUCTION

A medical prescription is a document written by the doctor that provides medicines for people suffering from time illness, injuries, or other disabilities. Medical prescription is a crucial component in the healthcare system. Usually, the doctor knows what is written in the prescription, but patients find it challenging to read and interpret the text written in the prescription. Patients may be interested in knowing their recommended drugs before purchasing them. Doctors use complicated medical names, medical terminologies, and Latin abbreviations to write prescriptions; most patients and some pharmacists find it challenging to decipher doctor's handwritten prescriptions. Due to illegible handwriting, the pharmacist may deliver false medicines to patients by misinterpreting medicine names in medical prescriptions, which may cause severe and lethal effects. A doctor's illegible handwriting is one of the most significant contributors to medical errors. The first possible reason for sloppy/illegible handwriting is that they spend an hour or more a day in the hospital and write medical prescriptions for patients waiting outside for their turn. The second reason is pharmacists, and doctors could have an unholy alliance. The doctors encrypt the prescription so that no one else can decipher it. A doctor's illegible handwriting is the third-highest contributing factor to medical error. Some study claims that male doctors have considerably worse handwriting than female doctors. In the later stages, many doctors find it difficult to decipher their handwriting.

According to the Institute of Medicine of the National Academies of Science (IOM) report, medical errors kill 44,000–98,000 people in the United States every year. Approximately 7000 of them died because of illegible handwriting. The survey predicted that avoidable adverse events in healthcare cost the country 17–29 billion dollars. Another study states that medical errors claim the lives of over 30,000 people annually in the United Kingdom, and illegible prescriptions account for a significant portion. A few years back, a staff nurse could testify that a doctor in Delhi had given her the medicine "Duodil," which was used to treat muscular spasms and the pain and discomfort that accompanied them. Because of the doctor's sluggish handwriting, the pharmacist at a drugstore gave her the medicine "Daonil," a diabetic drug. She took it for a few days. That resulted in a sharp drop in her blood sugar levels, resulting in convulsions. The incomprehensible handwriting of the doctor who treated her in Delhi was primarily to blame for such a severe outcome. To make pharmacist's work easier and reduce the risk of misinterpreted medicine names and dosages, it is sometimes advisable to convert handwritten text into digital characters. The major contribution of this chapter is proposing a solution for both patients and pharmacists by providing a model that detects and recognizes doctor's handwritten text from the medical prescription and returns a legible digital text of the drug and its dosage.

A deep learning model, DocPresRec, is proposed to recognize handwritten English medical prescriptions. DocPresRec converts handwritten drug names into readable digital text. This chapter employs an end-to-end trained text-spotting approach named "MaskTextSpotterv3" [1] to detect and recognize handwritten drug names from the prescription. The text spotting algorithm comprises six main modules: Network Backbone, Proposal Segmentation, Refining Proposals module, Text instance segmentation module, CSM (Character Segmentation Module) and SAM (Spatial Attention Module). MaskTextSpotter v3 is additionally trained with handwritten datasets such as MNIST [2] and IAM-OnDB [3] to detect and recognize densely oriented/curved text [4]. The proposed model also assists the pharmacist and patient in dispensing and verifying correct medicines.

3.2   RELATED WORKS

The research communities have extensively researched STR (Scene Text Recognition) and OCR (Optical Character Recognition). But in particular, doctor's handwritten prescription recognition is less explored. Some of the previous works are summarized in the literature.

Alday and Pagayon [5] developed a mobile application, "MediPic," which uses the OCR library "Tesseract" to convert illegible handwritten text into digital text. The inner algorithm matches the recognized text with the database text. Kumar et al. [6] used traditional OCR techniques and CNN (Convolutional Neural Network) to identify the handwritten text from the prescription. OCR algorithm works well in documents. In the medical scenario, it promptly failed to recognize complex shape text from the medical images. Najafiragheb et al. [7] followed a three-stage process to segregate the text from the images, including noise removal and line and word extraction. Finally, a KNN (K-Nearest Neighbor) classification algorithm is used to classify the handwritten and printed text. This method achieves a recognition accuracy of 83%, which is low compared to the state-of-the-art algorithm. Dhande and Kharat [8] introduced a system to recognize cursive characters. The modules used to perform text-line segmentation, word segmentation, feature extraction, and classification are the horizontal projection, vertical projection, convex hull algorithm, and SVM (Support Vector Machine). The author's taken different doctor's prescription samples to assess their system's performance. Text-line and word segmentation modules achieve 95% and 92% accuracy. However, the system obtains an overall recognition accuracy of 85%.

Wu et al. [9] integrated three individual classifiers CNN, PCA and KNN, combined and made a multi-classifier system to recognize Chinese medicine prescriptions. The individual characters are cropped and trained to perform the recognition. Kamalanaban et al. [10] developed a mobile application called "Medicine Box." It employs CNN and LSTM (Long Short-Term Memory) to extract text features and predict characters. Recognized text can be compared with the database to verify the drug name using the string-matching approach. Since the application reaches the recognized text with the database, it is unaware that the application can retrieve the correct drug name because the recognized text can be empty or invalid. To overcome this problem, Hassan et al. [11] developed an android application for both pharmacists and patients to understand the drug details by converting the handwritten text into more readable digital text. The image processing techniques are incorporated to perform pre-processing tasks, including noise removal and resizing. Then, a CNN is used to obtain the text. The OCR technique is incorporated to correct the drug name if the predicted text accuracy is less than 50%. The main disadvantage of this technique is that it uses the OCR technique to refine the text in the later stages, and the usage of CNN remains void.

Ou et al. [12] use Google text detection API (Application Programming Interface) to identify text in the doctor's prescription. The pre-processing step scans the medication and removes the irrelevant information [13], providing only essential information such as drug name, quantity, NRI code, and usage. The framework is evaluated using 20 different prescriptions, yielding a recognition accuracy of 92.42%. Achkar et al. [14] employed convolutional recurrent neural network (CRNN) to recognize handwritten text from the prescription. Here, the text lines are cropped and used for the training. However, the problem with this technique is that it does not follow character-level training because the network may find it hard to read the individual character's in the handwritten prescription. Fajardo et al. [15] assessed the performance of standalone CRNN and model-based CRNN using the doctor's handwritten prescription images. However, the model-based CRNN (76%) performs marginally better than the standalone CRNN (73%). Kulathunga et al. [16] developed a mobile application called "PatientCare" using Otsu's binarization method and OCR technique. Butala et al. [17] proposed an online handwriting recognition system. It uses the character segmentation step to segment individual characters from the word image and the character classification step to recognize the segmented characters with the help of a neural network classifier. The post-processing step incorporates a spell checker to improve the accuracy of the word.

Jain et al. [18] proposed a deep learning framework (CNN-Bi-LSTM) comprising three models; a CNN is used to extract features from the input image. Bi-LSTM (Bi-directional Long-Short Term Memory) generates the text sequences from the feature map. Finally, CTC (Connectionist Temporal Classification) loss function sums up the alignment scores between the predicted text and ground truth. Kumar et al. [19] proposed a Medical Prescription and Report Analyzer application to assist the patient in understanding their prescribed medicine and health report. Image processing and segmentation techniques enhance image quality and segment text regions. Character level and handwritten recognition capture the RoI (Region of Interest). Finally, sloppy handwriting corrections remove spelling mistakes and retrieve exact medicine names. However, this method is not efficient for severely curved texts.

Tabassum et al. [20] proposed novel data augmentation techniques such as stroke rotation, parallel shift, and regenerating sequence data to generate more training samples and improve recognition accuracy. The medicine name predicted by Bi-LSTM can be verified using a newly established "Handwritten Medical Term Corpus" database, which contains 17,431 handwritten, 480 English words. Shaw et al. [21] used ANN (Artificial Neural Network) to recognize handwritten medical prescriptions. This model uses the EMNIST dataset to identify the doctor's illegible handwriting. Dhar et al. [22] created a new dataset named "HP DocPres" and proposed an algorithm to localize and classify the texts in the medical prescription. This dataset contains printed, handwritten, blank spaces, and mixed text. A series of steps, including grayscale conversion, morphological operations (erosion followed by dilation), image subtraction, Otsu's binarization, and localization shape-based feature extraction, are carried out before giving it to the Random Forest Classifier. The performance of the HP DocPres is assessed using four regularly used classifiers [23]: Decision table, Random tree, REPT tree and J48, and the Random Forest classifier.

3.3 PROPOSED FRAMEWORK

Figure 3.1 shows the overall architecture of the DocPresRec. This framework employs MaskTextSpotterv3 to detect and recognize handwritten text from the prescription. The text spotting algorithm performs three important tasks: feature extraction,

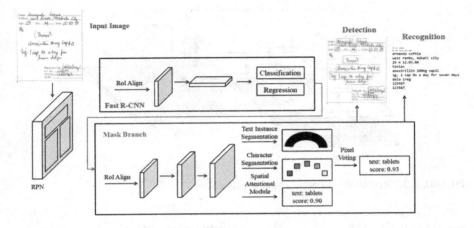

FIGURE 3.1 Illustration of the DocPresRec architecture.

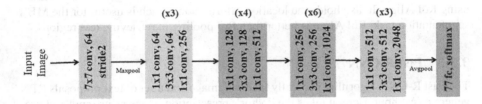

FIGURE 3.2 ResNet50 backbone architecture.

handwritten text detection, and text recognition using ResNet (Residual Network), Fast R-CNN and Mask branch (MB), respectively.

3.3.1 BACKBONE NETWORK

The text in medical prescriptions comes in a variety of forms. Here, a feature extractor Feature Pyramid Network (FPN), is combined with a backbone ResNet [24] of depth 50 (see Figure 3.2) to generate the most critical semantically rich feature maps at different scales, as shown in Figure 3.3. FPN uses a top-down architecture to combine low-level features of different resolutions with high-level semantic feature maps, enhancing recognition accuracy at a minimal cost.

3.3.2 REGION PROPOSAL NETWORK

Region proposal network (RPN) is originally designed for object detection. Here, RPN is used to generate the text proposals given to the subsequent blocks, such as object detection (Fast R-CNN) and object recognition (MB). Depending on the size of the anchor, it is allocated to various stages [25]. Five important stages $\{S_2, S_3, S_4, S_5, S_6\}$ are the anchors for the different regions, whose set pixels values, respectively,

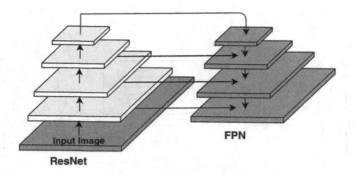

FIGURE 3.3   ResNet50 – FPN backbone architecture.

are $\{32^2\}$, $\{64^2\}$, $\{128^2\}$, $\{256^2\}$, $\{512^2\}$. As in Ref. [26], different aspect ratios and scales are used at each step in the detection process. Likewise, the RPN can handle words of different sizes and aspect ratios. The features of text regions are extracted using RoI Align. It also holds the location information, which is useful for the MB's segmentation task. RoI Align is better than RoI pooling in retrieving text regions.

3.3.3 Fast R-CNN

The Fast R-CNN algorithm generally takes an image and a set of text proposals RPN generates as input. Here, it takes the doctor's prescription image as its input and processes it with multiple convolution and max-pooling layers to produce a feature map. The RoI pooling layer derives a fixed-length feature vector from the feature map for each text proposal. Each feature vector is given as input to a series of fully connected (fc) layers, which branch out into two output layers: regression and classification [27]. Regression, which generates four real-valued integers, encodes bounding-box positions over the text regions and classification, which provides softmax probability for the text region.

3.3.4 Mask Branch

The MB plays a vital function in the proposed framework by detecting and recognizing the arbitrary shape text from the medical prescription. It comprises three important tasks: segmentation (character and text instance) and text recognition.

3.3.5 Character and Text Instance Segmentation

This section passes a 16×64 RoI feature through four convolutional layers and a de-convolutional layer with 3×3 and 2×2 filters. The generated features are given as input to the Character and Text Instance Segmentation (CTIS) module. The text instance module generates the text instance map, which gives the accurate location of the text regions, irrespective of the shape of text instances. The character segmentation maps are created directly from the combined feature maps in the character

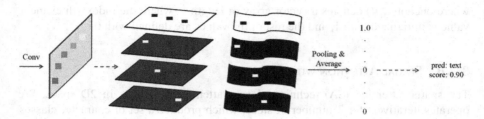

FIGURE 3.4   Illustration of character segmentation module.

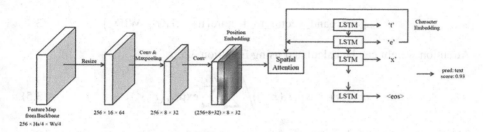

FIGURE 3.5   Illustration of Spatial Attentional Module (SAM).

segmentation module, as shown in Figure 3.4. The generated character segmentation maps are of the form $N_C \times 32 \times 128$, where N_C is set to 37, indicating the number of classes, including 1 for the background class and 36 for alphanumeric characters.

3.3.6 SPATIAL ATTENTIONAL MODULE

The Spatial Attentional Module (SAM) is trained end-to-end to decipher the character set from the shared feature maps. Unlike existing methods, which initially encode the high-level feature map into a 1D array and interpret the character set. SAM decodes the 2D feature maps directly to represent different shapes accurately.

3.3.7 POSITION EMBEDDING

Figure 3.5 shows the pipeline of the SAM. The normalization operators in SAM are not positioning variants, and hence position embedding is adopted in the final convolutional block. FM_{pe} represents the positional embedding feature map of shape $(WID_p + HIG_p, WID_p, HIG_p)$, where WID_p and HIG_p are set to 8 and 32, respectively. Equations 3.1–3.3 calculate the position embedding feature map:

$$FM_{pe}^x(r,s,:) = \text{onehot}(r, WID_p) \tag{3.1}$$

$$FM_{pe}^y(r,s,:) = \text{onehot}(s, HIG_p) \tag{3.2}$$

$$F_{pe} = \text{concat}(FM_{pe}^x, FM_{pe}^y) \tag{3.3}$$

where onehot(x, V) denotes a vector array of length V, where the index xth element value is initialized with 1, and the rest of the values are defined with 0.

3.3.8 SPATIAL ATTENTION WITH RNNS

The spatial attention (SA) technique learns attentional weights in 2D space. SA operates iteratively for T number of steps, which produce a set of character classes $cc = (cc_1, cc_2, \ldots, cc_T)$. There are three inputs at step t: input feature map FM, final hidden state hs_{t-1} and generated character class cc_{t-1}. The last hidden state hs_{t-1} can be expanded from a feature vector to a feature map (FS_{t-1}) using Equation 3.4.

$$FS_{t-1} = \text{expand\_vector\_to\_feature}\left(hs_{t-1}, HIG_p, WID_p\right) \tag{3.4}$$

Attention weight can be calculated using Equation 3.5.

$$\alpha_t(r,s) = \exp\left(t_e(r,s)\right) \bigg/ \sum_{r'=1}^{HIG_p} \sum_{s'=1}^{WID_p} \exp\left(t_e(r',s')\right) \tag{3.5}$$

The final anticipated character class y_{t-1} is computed using Equations 3.6 and 3.7.

$$f(cc_{t-1}) = \text{Weight}_y \times \text{onehot}(cc_{t-1}, NO_c) + \text{bias}_y \tag{3.6}$$

$$M_t = \text{contact}\ (gl_t, f(cc_{t-1})) \tag{3.7}$$

where gl_t is a glimpse at step t, Weight_y and bias_y are trainable parameters. NO_c denotes the number of character classes. NO_c is initialized to 37, 36 for alphanumeric characters and one for an end-of-sequence character (EOS). Finally, a softmax function and a linear transformation determine the conditional probability at step t (see Equations 3.8 and 3.9).

$$p(cc_t) = \text{softmax}\left(\text{Weight}_o \times x_t + \text{bias}_o\right) \tag{3.8}$$

$$cc_t \sim p(cc_t) \tag{3.9}$$

3.3.9 DECODING

Two recognition modules are used in the standalone recognition paradigm: character segmentation and SAM. The character segmentation segment anticipates the character sequence on a pixel-by-pixel basis, and the SAM module anticipates the character sequence in a 2D perspective in an end-to-end manner. The pixel voting approach in the character segmentation module arranges and clusters pixels to generate the last character sequence. The pseudocode and workflow for the pixel voting approach are shown in Table 3.1 and Figure 3.6.

The pixel voting technique decodes the predicted text maps into text sequences. The background map is binarized first, with a threshold value of 0.75, ranging from 0

TABLE 3.1
Pseudocode of the Pixel Voting Approach

Procedure: Pixel voting
Input: Character map (CM), background map (BM)
Connected regions (CRs) are generated using BM and CM on a binarized background map

```
D = Ø
for i in CR do
    Count = Ø
  for j in CM do
    M = Mean (j[i])
    Count = Count + M
  end for
  D = D+ Argmax(Count)
end for
return S
```

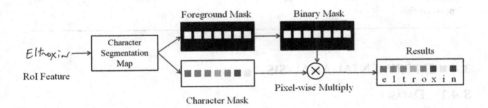

FIGURE 3.6 Workflow of the pixel voting approach.

to 1. Then, all the character regions are obtained from the binarized map's connected regions. The mean values are calculated for all the character and binary masks connected regions. The obtained result can be considered the region's character class likelihood, which can also be interpreted as a character confidence score. The region will be given to the character class with the highest mean value. All the characters are grouped and sorted from left to right under English writing conventions.

SAM uses two decoding techniques to generate the final character sequence. The first method uses a beam search algorithm to preserve the topmost probabilities at each stage. The beam search methodology is adopted in this work and set k to 6. The second method is to select a character class with a maximum likelihood value at each stage using the greedy decoding approach. The two recognition results are combined for better accuracy. The character segmentation module's confidence score is the average of all character confidence scores in Table 3.1. In contrast, SAM's confidence score is the average of character probabilities in Equation 3.8. The recognition result with the highest confidence score is selected.

TABLE 3.2

Datasets Used to Train and Test the DocPresRec Framework

Task	Dataset	Image			Text Instance		
		Total	Train	Test	Total	Train	Test
Text detection	ICDAR2013	462	229	233	1944	849	1095
	ICDAR2015	1500	1000	500	17548	122318	5230
	COCO-Text	63686	43686	20000	145859	118309	27550
	Total-Text	1525	1225	300	9330	–	¬
	MLT2017	18000	7200	10800	–	–	–
Text	IIIT5K	1120	380	740	5000	2000	3000
recognition	SVT	350	100	250	725	211	514
	ICDAR2003	509	258	251	2268	1157	1111
	ICDAR2013	561	420	141	5003	3564	1439
	ICDAR2015	500	1000	500	6545	4468	2077
	SVT - P	238	–	238	639	–	639
	CUTE80	80	–	80	288	–	288
	IAM-OnDB	13017	10413	2604	104136	83309	20827
	MNIST	70000	60000	10000	–	–	–
Medical prescription	HP Labs	82	66	16	11340	9072	2268

3.4 EXPERIMENTAL ANALYSIS

3.4.1 DATASET

The DocPresRec framework is trained and tested with benchmark datasets such as ICDAR2013 [28], ICDAR2015 [29], COCO-Text [30], Total-Text [31], MLT [32], IIIT5k-Words [33], Street View Text (SVT) [34], ICDAR2003 [35], SVT-Perspective [36], and CUTE80 [37]. Table 3.2 describes the datasets used to carry out the experiments. Figure 3.7 shows the dataset images of the sample HP Labs [22].

3.4.2 IMPLEMENTATION DETAILS

The proposed framework was implemented using PyTorch, and all our experiments are carried out on a standard workstation (DELL Precision Tower 7810) with NVIDIA Quadro K2200 GPUs. A single GPU is used to train and evaluate the model. For all our experiments, the mini-batch size is set to 8. SGD (Stochastic Gradient Descent) optimizer is used to improve the performance of our model, which has a weight decay of 0.001 and a momentum of 0.9, where the initial learning rate is set to 0.01. Due to the inadequacy of handwritten word images, data augmentation operations are performed to generate additional samples at the fine-tuning step. The input images are rotated at specific angles [−30°; 30°]. Other augmentation techniques include randomly changing the color, brightness, and contrast, which are also used.

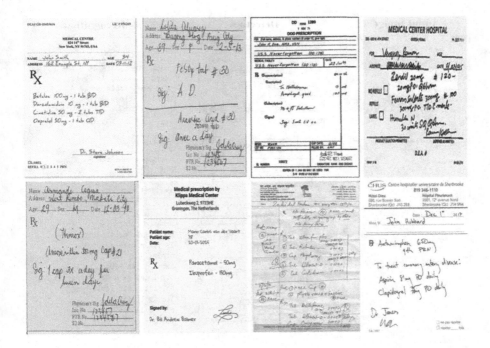

FIGURE 3.7   Sample dataset images.

3.5   RESULTS AND DISCUSSION

In the HP Labs dataset [22], there are 11340 text instances, including 3114 handwritten texts, 5220 non-texts, and 126 texts in mixed formats and 2880 texts printed as words or phrases. Table 3.3 shows the performance of the proposed framework with existing approaches. Figure 3.8 shows sample results obtained by the proposed framework on the HP Labs dataset. It recognized 11,271 texts and missed 69, achieving a recognition accuracy of 99.4%.

Figures 3.9 and 3.10 show the framework's accuracy and loss, respectively. The performance of the DocPresRec framework is shown in Table 3.3. The proposed framework outperforms most of the existing methods by a large margin. The current state-of-the-art algorithms [9,18] and [19] are not trained with any text benchmark datasets. Additional layers in the CNN make the network structure more complicated. Still, [6,10] and [18] use CNN as their backbone network. CNN faces difficulties in solving complex problems. To cover the pitfalls of CNN, DocPresRec uses ResNet as its backbone network, which has a skip connection to avoid vanishing gradient problems and improve recognition performance. DocPresRec trained using IAM-OnDB and MNIST handwritten dataset, whereas [21] uses only the EMNIST dataset, which is insufficient to solve complex problems.

Input Image   **Detection**   **Recognition**

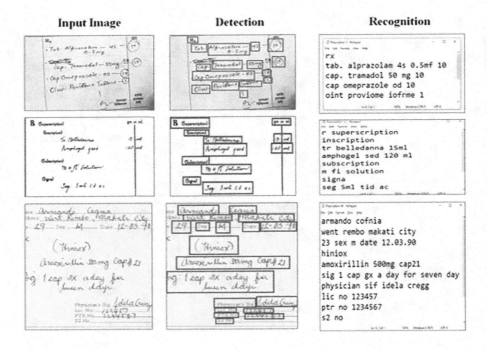

FIGURE 3.8   Sample result of the DocPresRec: First: the input image is the doctor's hand-written prescription. Next: text detection result. Last: the text recognition result contains the drug name, quantity and other information.

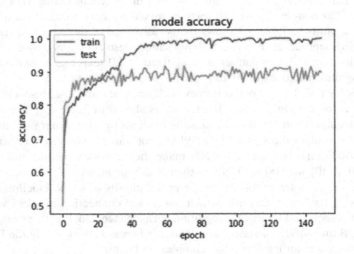

FIGURE 3.9   Illustration of training and testing accuracy of the DocPresRec.

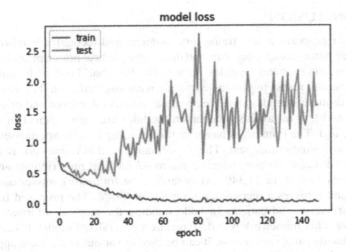

FIGURE 3.10   Illustration of training and testing loss of the DocPresRec.

TABLE 3.3
Comparison of the DocPresRec Framework's Performance with Existing Approaches

Authors	Methods Used	HP Labs Recognition Accuracy
Alday and Pagayon [5]	OCR + string matching algorithm	72.0%
Kumar et al. [6]	OCR + CNN	70.1%
Najafiragheb et al. [7]	KNN	83.0%
Dhande and Kharat [8]	Horizontal projection and vertical projection + convex hull algorithm + SVM	85.0%
Wu et al. [9]	CNN + PCA + KNN	96.1%
Kamalanaban et al. [10]	CNN + LSTM	95.0%
Hassan et al. [11]	Image processing techniques + CNN + OCR	61.5%
Ou et al. [12]	Google text detection API	92.4%
Fajardo et al. [15]	CRNN	73.0%
	CRNN + model-based normalization	76.0%
Kulathunga et al. [16]	Otsu binarization + OCR	70.0%
Butala et al. [17]	OCR + neural network classifier	87.5%
Jain et al. [18]	CNN + Bi-LSTM + CTC	88.4%
Kumar et al. [19]	OCR + image processing techniques	90.7%
Tabassum et al. [20]	Bi-LSTM	89.5%
Shaw et al. [21]	ANN	87.6%
Proposed method (DocPresRec)	**ResNet + Fast R-CNN + Mask Branch**	**99.4%**

3.6 CONCLUSION

This chapter proposes a new framework to detect and recognize handwritten text such as drug name, dosage, quantity, and date in the medical prescription. It improves accuracy by using several modules, such as the FPN backbone with ResNet50, to fuse the features maps, improving accuracy with minimal cost. The Fast R-CNN algorithm captures complex shape text such as horizontal, curved and oriented text. Character and text instance segmentation modules are very efficient in recognizing cursive text. The framework has been trained using benchmark datasets, including scene and handwritten text. The performance of this framework is evaluated using the "HP Labs" dataset, which contains 82 medical prescriptions and 11,340 text instances. Out of the 11,340 text instances, the framework misses only 69 text instances and achieves a recognition accuracy of 99.4%. The proposed framework assists pharmacists and patients in understanding the medical information in the prescription. This framework was designed as a generalized model; hence, it is not limited to handwritten recognition. It can be used in various text-related applications such as number plate recognition and scene text recognition. It can also assist the visually impaired in reading the text on the signboards.

REFERENCES

1. Liao, M., Pang, G., Huang, J., Hassner, T., & Bai, X. (2020, August). Mask textspotter v3: Segmentation proposal network for robust scene text spotting. In *European Conference on Computer Vision*. Glasgow, (pp. 706–722). Springer, Cham.
2. Cireşan, D. C., Meier, U., Masci, J., Gambardella, L. M., & Schmidhuber, J. (2011). High-performance neural networks for visual object classification. arXiv preprint arXiv:1102.0183 (pp. 1–11).
3. Liwicki, M., & Bunke, H. (2005, August). IAM-OnDB-an on-line English sentence database acquired from handwritten text on a whiteboard. In *Eighth International Conference on Document Analysis and Recognition (ICDAR'05)* (pp. 956–961). IEEE.
4. Selvam, P., Koilraj, J. A. S., Romero, C. A. T., Alharbi, M., Mehbodniya, A., Webber, J. L., & Sengan, S. (2022). A transformer-based framework for scene text recognition. *IEEE Access*, 10, pp. 100895–100910.
5. Alday, R. B., & Pagayon, R. M. (2013, July). MediPic: A mobile application for medical prescriptions. In *IISA 2013* (pp. 1–4). IEEE.
6. Kumar, S., Sahu, N., Deep, A., Gavel, K., & Ghos, R. (2016). Offline handwriting character recognition (for use of medical purpose) using neural network. *International Journal of Engineering and Computer Science*, 5(10), pp. 18612–18615.
7. Najafiragheb, N., Hatam, A., & Harifi, A. (2017). An approach for handwritten prescribed medications detection using KNN. In *6th International Conference on Electrical, Computer, Mechanical and Mechatronics Engineering (ICE2017)*. Dubai, pp. 1–5.
8. Dhande, P., & Kharat, R. (2017, May). Recognition of cursive English handwritten characters. In *2017 International Conference on Trends in Electronics and Informatics (ICEI)*. Tirunelveli (pp. 199–203). IEEE.
9. Wu, P., Wang, F., & Liu, J. (2018, November). An integrated multi-classifier method for handwritten Chinese medicine prescription recognition. In *2018 IEEE 9th International Conference on Software Engineering and Service Science (ICSESS)*. Beijing (pp. 1–4). IEEE.

10. Kamalanaban, E., Gopinath, M., & Premkumar, S. (2018). Medicine box: Doctor's prescription recognition using deep machine learning. *International Journal of Engineering and Technology (UAE)*, 7, 114–117.
11. Hassan, E., Tarek, H., Hazem, M., Bahnacy, S., Shaheen, L., & Elashmwai, W. H. (2021, January). Medical prescription recognition using machine learning. In *2021 IEEE 11th Annual Computing and Communication Workshop and Conference (CCWC)*. Las Vegas, NV (pp. 0973–0979). IEEE.
12. Ou, Y. Y., Tseng, S. P., Lin, J., Zhou, X. P., Wang, J. F., & Kuan, T. W. (2018, October). Automatic prescription recognition system. In *2018 International Conference on Orange Technologies (ICOT)*. Nusa Dua, Bali (pp. 1–4). IEEE.
13. Selvam, P., & Koilraj, J. A. S. (2022). A deep learning framework for grocery product detection and recognition. *Food Analytical Methods*. 15. 3498–3522.
14. Achkar, R., Ghayad, K., Haidar, R., Saleh, S., & Al Hajj, R. (2019, August). Medical handwritten prescription recognition using CRNN. In *2019 International Conference on Computer, Information and Telecommunication Systems* (CITS). Beijing (pp. 1–5). IEEE.
15. Fajardo, L. J., Sorillo, N. J., Garlit, J., Tomines, C. D., Abisado, M. B., Imperial, J. M. R.,... & Fabito, B. S. (2019, November). Doctor's cursive handwriting recognition system using deep learning. In *2019 IEEE 11th International Conference on Humanoid, Nanotechnology, Information Technology, Communication and Control, Environment, and Management (HNICEM)*. Piscataway (pp. 1–6). IEEE.
16. Kulathunga, D., Muthukumarana, C., Pasan, U., Hemachandra, C., Tissera, M., & De Silva, H. (2020, December). PatientCare: Patient assistive tool with automatic handwritten prescription reader. In *2020 2nd International Conference on Advancements in Computing (ICAC)*. Colombo (Vol. 1, pp. 275–280). IEEE.
17. Butala, S., Lad, A., Chheda, H., Bhat, M., & Nimkar, A. (2020, February). Natural language parser for physician's handwritten prescription. In *2020 International Conference on Emerging Trends in Information Technology and Engineering (ic-ETITE)*. VIT Vellore (pp. 1–7). IEEE.
18. Jain, T., Sharma, R., & Malhotra, R. (2021, April). Handwriting recognition for medical prescriptions using a CNN-Bi-LSTM model. In *2021 6th International Conference for Convergence in Technology (I2CT)*. Pune (pp. 1–4). IEEE.
19. Kumar, A., Goyal, A., Rai, B. K., & Sharma, S. (2022, March). OCR based medical prescription and report analyzer. In *AIP Conference Proceedings*. 2424(1). (pp. 070006). AIP Publishing LLC.
20. Tabassum, S., Takahashi, R., Rahman, M. M., Imamura, Y., Sixian, L., Rahman, M. M., & Ahmed, A. (2021, May). Recognition of doctors' cursive handwritten medical words by using bidirectional LSTM and SRP data augmentation. In *2021 IEEE Technology & Engineering Management Conference-Europe (TEMSCON-EUR)*. Judge Business School, Cambridge (pp. 1–6). IEEE.
21. Shaw, U., Mamgai, R., & Malhotra, I. (2021, October). Medical Handwritten Prescription Recognition and Information Retrieval using Neural Network. In *2021 6th International Conference on Signal Processing, Computing and Control (ISPCC)*. Waknaghat (pp. 46–50). IEEE.
22. Dhar, D., Garain, A., Singh, P. K., & Sarkar, R. (2021). HP_DocPres: A method for classifying printed and handwritten texts in doctor's prescription. *Multimedia Tools and Applications*, 80(7), pp. 9779–9812.
23. Prabu, S. (2022). Real-time pill detection and recognition framework based on a deep learning algorithm. In *Advancement, Opportunities, and Practices in Telehealth Technology*, S.N Kumar,Sherin Zafar, S Suresh, Padmanabhan Vivekananth (eds.) (pp. 117–137). IGI Global, ,United States.

24. He, K., Zhang, X., Ren, S., & Sun, J. (2016). Deep residual learning for image recognition. In *Proceedings of the IEEE Conference on Computer Vision and Pattern Recognition*. Las Vegas, NV, USA. (pp. 770–778).

25. Prabu, S., & Abraham Sundar, K. J. (2023). Enhanced attention-based encoder-decoder framework for text recognition. *Intelligent Automation & Soft Computing*, 35(2). pp. 2071–2086.

26. Ren, S., He, K., Girshick, R., & Sun, J. (2015). Faster R-CNN: Towards real-time object detection with region proposal networks. *Advances in Neural Information Processing Systems*, 28. pp. 1–14.

27. Prabu, S. (2022, March). Object segmentation based on the integration of adaptive K-means and GrabCut algorithm. In *2022 International Conference on Wireless Communications Signal Processing and Networking (WiSPNET)*. Chennai (pp. 213–216). IEEE.

28. Karatzas, D., Shafait, F., Uchida, S., Iwamura, M., i Bigorda, L. G., Mestre, S. R., ... & De Las Heras, L. P. (2013, August). ICDAR 2013 robust reading competition. In *2013 12th International Conference on Document Analysis and Recognition*. Washington, DC (pp. 1484–1493). IEEE.

29. Karatzas, D., Gomez-Bigorda, L., Nicolaou, A., Ghosh, S., Bagdanov, A., Iwamura, M.,... & Valveny, E. (2015, August). ICDAR 2015 competition on robust reading. In *2015 13th International Conference on Document Analysis and Recognition (ICDAR)*. NW Washington, DC (pp. 1156–1160). IEEE.

30. Bazazian, D., Gomez, R., Nicolaou, A., Gomez, L., Karatzas, D., & Bagdanov, A. D. (2017). Improving text proposals for scene images with fully convolutional networks. arXiv preprint arXiv:1702.05089. Las Vegas, NV (pp. 1–6).

31. Ch'ng, C. K., Chan, C. S., & Liu, C. L. (2020). Total-text: Toward orientation robustness in scene text detection. *International Journal on Document Analysis and Recognition (IJDAR)*, 23(1), pp. 31–52.

32. Nayef, N., Patel, Y., Busta, M., Chowdhury, P. N., Karatzas, D., Khlif, W., ... & Ogier, J. M. (2019, September). ICDAR2019 robust reading challenge on multi-lingual scene text detection and recognition—RRC-MLT-2019. In *2019 International Conference on Document Analysis and Recognition (ICDAR)*. Sydney (pp. 1582–1587). IEEE.

33. Shi, B., Bai, X., & Yao, C. (2016). An end-to-end trainable neural network for image-based sequence recognition and its application to scene text recognition. *IEEE Transactions on Pattern Analysis and Machine Intelligence*, 39(11), 2298–2304.

34. Wang, K., Babenko, B., & Belongie, S. (2011, November). End-to-end scene text recognition. In *2011 International Conference on Computer Vision*. Barcelona (pp. 1457–1464). IEEE.

35. Lucas, S. M., Panaretos, A., Sosa, L., Tang, A., Wong, S., Young, R., ... & Lin, X. (2005). ICDAR 2003 robust reading competitions: Entries, results, and future directions. *International Journal of Document Analysis and Recognition (IJDAR)*, 7(2), 105–122.

36. Phan, T. Q., Shivakumara, P., Tian, S., & Tan, C. L. (2013). Recognizing text with perspective distortion in natural scenes. In *Proceedings of the IEEE International Conference on Computer Vision*. Sydney (pp. 569–576).

37. Risnumawan, A., Shivakumara, P., Chan, C. S., & Tan, C. L. (2014). A robust arbitrary text detection system for natural scene images. *Expert Systems with Applications*, 41(-18), 8027–8048.

4 An Efficient Deep Learning Approach for Brain Stroke Detection
Application of Telemedicine

C. Chellaswamy, K. Aiswarya, and J. Asokan
SRM TRP Engineering College

CONTENTS

4.1 INTRODUCTION

The foremost deadly ailment that demands the lives of myriad personnel is brain stroke. Pathologists find it more perplexing to classify its types under telemedicine. A novel method of detecting its importance was found in order to lessen the mortality owing to the deferment in identifying and classifying it at an earlier stage. Stroke is the leading cause of adult mortality worldwide, claiming the lives of 6.2 million people each year [1]. Stroke accounts for 26% of all deaths worldwide. Across the globe, stroke is the most prominent cause of death. As a result, more research into developing an accurate and better methodology for detecting stroke with ease is required in practice [2]. The advent of stroke in the brain befalls due to obstruction in the flow of either blood to the brain or when sarcasm of blood to the brain is witnessed. Accordingly, a condition of blood scarcity in a peculiar part of the brain makes it non-responsive [3], which creates a syndrome for its connected organelles, suggested an intelligent data analysis method for ischemic patients with and without diabetes. Initially, the data have been analysed, and the mean and covariance are observed, and the correlated components are investigated. The classification is influenced by the obstruction of blood supply to the brain as in haemorrhagic stroke and ischemic stroke. The profound reason for ischemic stroke is obstruction of blood vessels that makes it 87% fatal [4]. Haemorrhagic stroke is instigated by weak blood vessel breakage due to malformations in arteriovenous and aneurysmal vessels, another of which is high blood pressure. A study has been conducted by Mohamad et al. on the interaction of the heart and the brain [5]. Saver studied the blood flow in the primary area of the brain, the outcome of the thrombolysis, and the salvage of the penumbral [6].

A multifocus image fusion method has been used to improve the quality of computed tomography (CT) images. A 13-layer convolution neural network (CNN) was proposed for the classification of brain strokes. An optimised imaging workflow has been introduced by Rowley and Vagal [7]. To make it more precise, individuals alleged to have strokes are used to categorise the types of strokes through their CT scans. A CT scan provides emergency procedures after the onset of stroke [8]. It is best suited because of its affordable cost and less noise perception, which makes its reach faster than the other methods like MRI. The first radiological examination through non-enhanced CT was done [9]. In an ischemic lesion, the CT images utilise hypodense structures, yet visibility of abnormal lesions is still in vain, such as locating minute infarcts in the cerebellum, the interiors of the cerebral hemispheres, and brain stem. Henceforth, MRI has become a suitable alternative for this [10]. Regardless of its benefits, MRI is expensive, with access only to certain healthcare centres. Another limitation of MRI scans is their length of time in comparison to others [11]. As an alternative to CT, detection is done at an earlier stage through MRI. Over decades, quite a few computer-aided systems have been developed for detecting brain abnormalities at the earliest. In particular, for attaining accurate and automated results, deep learning [12] and artificial intelligence are mainly used. This goes hand in hand as a complementary approach to give assistance to the doctors in discovering the location of the stroke [13]. There are a lot of things that can go wrong when using these methods, like getting high-resolution images, which is expensive these days, and having different types of brain tissue, which makes it harder to tell the difference between old and new stroke areas [14].

In recent years, deep learning applications using medical imaging have reached their pinnacle, with performance close to that of humans. A couple of studies have gained importance for detecting thrombus or occlusion. One is anticipated through CNN applied to non-contract CT from the afflicted side as well as the opposite side together with atlas information [15], and yet another for case prediction on computed tomography angiography (CTA) using ResNet-50 for maximum intensity projections. Certain industry methods lack methodological and evaluation details where neither conventional nor deep learning methods are used for 4D-CTA. Through multimodal and unimodal images, hybrid deep learning methods are used to tell the difference between haemorrhagic strokes and ischemic strokes.

A flower pollination optimisation was used to optimise the CNN, where the best hyperparameters were chosen to achieve the least loss function [16]. An alternative way of calculating haemorrhagic and ischemic strokes was made by Marbun and Andayani [17]. A meticulous approach has been made by Kuo et al. [18] that incorporates various deep architectures such as VGG16, MobileNet, and InceptionV3 along with customised learning approaches like SVM, logistic regressions, and artificial neural networks. The Bayesian classifier-based MobileNet architecture, which was best suited, achieved an accuracy of 91.57%. A study on multimodal MRI images for the identification of haemorrhagic and ischemic stroke was carried out by Xue et al. For post-processing, a 3D convolutional kernel is added to a modified U-network. This is done to take advantage of the fact that larger datasets can be merged [19]. Care coordination, patient education, and counselling are all responsibilities of the anaesthesiology preoperative clinic in order to make sure patients are as safe as possible and get the best possible results [20]. Patient risks for surgery may be assessed via telemedicine in preoperative anaesthesiology clinics. For paediatric patients, healthcare practitioners have to deal with not just assessing the children themselves but also soothing, connecting, and guiding their parents or guardians [21]. Patients should be included in strategies to protect and increase patient happiness across all modes of healthcare delivery as telemedicine continues to expand. After the COVID-19 epidemic has passed, provider and patient gratification must be a major factor in the long-term viability of telemedicine. During the pandemic, people all over the world who used telemedicine services were very happy with them [22].

In this chapter, the main focus is on the major types of brain stroke (haemorrhagic and ischemic) detection for telemedicine using minimal training sets of MRI images. A recent study has demonstrated that convolutional neural networks (CNNs) are better for brain stroke classification than others in terms of segmentation, detection, and classification. The classification in the method stated tends to be a bottleneck when the number of test samples is increased. In the proposed model, it is overcome through transfer learning subjected to small changes in the VGG16 network architecture model. At the output end, a Network-in-Network (NiN) architecture is put in place, which makes the images of the Spatial Pyramid Pooling (SPP) layer look like they were put together.

The segregation of anomalous tissues from healthy tissues makes brain stroke identification a daunting task. The diagnosis should be done earlier so that you can carry out healing with ease. When treated earlier, stronger therapy can also be put to use. Instantaneously recognising the brain's stem structures makes a stroke with better definition, the lesions of which tend to be a theme of this chapter. The significant impacts of the chapter are as follows:

- A deep network model from BSD-VNS for greater accuracy and faster estimation.
- The effectiveness of the proposed system is estimated using five different performance metrics.
- The deep learning model that is recommended sorts brain strokes into three groups: ischemic strokes, haemorrhagic strokes, and images that are not strokes.

- The system works as a whole with the help of a SoftMax classifier and a Stochastic Gradient optimiser.

The remaining part of this chapter is organised as follows: Section 4.2 describes the materials and methods (types of strokes, proposed stroke detection method, parameter metrics, and parameter settings). Section 4.3 explains the obtained results using the proposed method. Finally, the conclusion is given in Section 4.4.

4.2   MATERIALS AND METHODS

In the course of the last two decades, methods of deep learning have been beautifully implemented in the fields of medical image analysis, language processing, speech recognition, etc. but with a few drawbacks. They are a wonderful example of the on-hand crafting characteristics that were designed by subject matter specialists. By the way, the observed datasets differ from one person to the next, and the perception of those differences differs depending on the level of knowledge of the expert. That might result in errors both across and among observers. Moreover, it captures various hidden features of the images, analyses them efficiently, and helps the doctors with the precise result. Typically, the deep network has a greater number of layers that quickly diminish the backpropagation error, which causes a minor update of their weights in these layers for detecting various features precisely [23]. Henceforth, none of the significant features will be missed. In healthcare applications, big data analytics are handled by a Graphics Processing Unit (GPU).

4.2.1   TYPES OF STROKES

A stroke is a sign of a medical emergency that interrupts or breaks the flow of blood to the brain. In this paradigm, the following strokes have gained importance: ischemic stroke, haemorrhagic stroke, transient ischemic stroke (mini-stroke), and brain stem stroke are the four types of strokes. (i) Face drooping: a condition characterised by facial numbness or drooping and an uneven or lopsided smile. (ii) Arm weakness: numbness of the weaker arm, which keeps it down while trying to raise both arms. (iii) Difficult to speak: a condition characterised by slurred speech that makes understanding and speaking difficult. (iv) Contact the emergency services: If this sign persists, contact emergency services for immediate assistance.

Ischemic stroke: A stroke of this type is predominant and arises due to blockage in the supply of blood to the brain by a blood clot. The symptoms may vary according to the affected region of the brain. It includes the following symptoms: (i) sudden numbness of a leg, arm, or face, usually in a single location; (ii) communication and comprehension stumbling block; and (iii) Imbalanced walking, dizziness, or lack of coordination. Blindness and double vision are examples of visual impairments.

Haemorrhagic stroke: A condition of cell bleeding that damages the cells lying nearby. Every year, it accounts for 10%–20% of all strokes [24]. In countries such as the UK, USA, and Australia, haemorrhagic stroke cases have been found to be 8%–15%, but 18%–24% have been found in Japan and Korea. The number of cases per 1,000,000 people per year ranges between 12% and 15%. The incidence is high in nations with poor and moderate incomes as well as among Asians. It is more prevalent in men, with an increase in age. In African and Asian countries, a strategic increase is witnessed. Due to hypertension control, the incidence of ICH is reduced at a greater rate in Japan. Henceforth, the fatality rate is about 30%–48% in nations with low to moderate levels of income, and 25%–30% in nations with a high per capita income and that rely on the effectiveness of intensive medical treatment. The reason for haemorrhagic stroke is an aneurysm (a vulnerable spot in a blood vessel that causes it to burst open), abnormal blood vessels, consumption of cocaine, bleeding disorders, injury, and hypertension. The symptoms usually upsurge gradually over minutes to hours in haemorrhagic stroke, but the onset of subarachnoid haemorrhage occurs suddenly. Certain normal things we come across that contribute to such haemorrhagic strokes include the following: issues with one's eyesight, as well as passing out; sensitivity to light; strangeness; and intense headaches.

Brain stem stroke: It is a type of stroke that damages the brain stems. It has the bad effect of making the person "locked in" and unable to speak or move below the neck.

4.2.2 PROPOSED HYBRID METHOD FOR STROKE DETECTION

The proposed method is a blend of SPP [25], VGG16 [26], and NiN [27] architectures. The block diagram of the proposed model is portrayed in Figure 4.1.

Karen Simonyan and Andrew Zisserman have put forward their ideas using a deep CNN, where the acronym VGG stands for Visual Geometry Group, from Oxford University [28]. This exemplary innovation has secured second place in the ILSVRC 2014 competition for attaining 92.7% performance. This model starts with a small convolutional filter size (3×3) and extends up to larger-scale images. Every VGG block has a series of convolutional layers followed by a max-pooling layer with

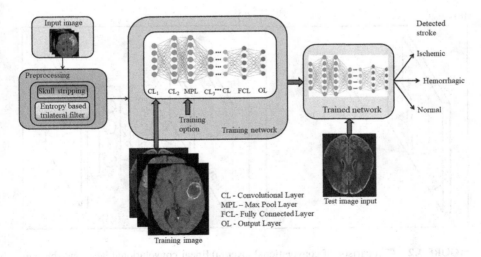

FIGURE 4.1 Block diagram of the proposed BSD-VNS.

a uniform distribution of the kernel size (3×3), over every other convolutional layer. Furthermore, the padding size of 1 is kept fixed at the output. To resolve down to half for subsequent blocks, a max-pooling of size 2×2 with strides of two is made. VGG16 is named so as it comprises 16 tunable parameters (13 convolutional layers and 3 fully connected layers) added together with 5 max-pooling layers. In each section, the number of filters doubled, starting with 64 and decreasing to 512. This model is broken off into two fully connected hidden layers with 4096 neurons each and an output layer comprising 100 neurons based on the ImageNet dataset. In the following section, the implementation of this using Keras is depicted. The NiN is the *mlpconv* layer, which would be a collection of micro-networks. It is based on the multilayer perceptron paradigm. A comparison between the linear convolutional layer and *mlpconv* is pictured in Figure 4.2.

A NiN layer can be constructed by arranging multiple layers of *mlpconv* layers. The non-linear properties are encoded via a stack of multilayer perceptrons, which results in the maximum level of abstraction. To enumerate the activations of *"mlpconv"* sub-layers, the Parametric Relu (PRelu) function is utilized.

$$f_{i,j,1} = \max\left(w_{1x_{i,j}}^T + b_1, \alpha\left(w_{1x_{i,j}}^T + b_1 \right) \right) \tag{4.1}$$

$$f_{i,j,n} = \max\left(w_n^T f_{i,j,n-1} + b_n, \alpha\left(w_n^T f_{i,j,n-1} + b_n \right) \right) \tag{4.2}$$

where n denotes the layer count in micro net *"mlpconv"*. The term $x_{i,j}$ indicates the feature patch centred at (i, j). w's and b's indicate the weights and biases of different sub-layers respectively. The PRelu adaptively learns the parameters, thereby reducing the possibility of model overfitting. The softmax classifier is used for classification activation in the final layer. A loss function is utilised, and it is categorical cross-entropy. The Stochastic Gradient Decent optimiser is used to carry out the training.

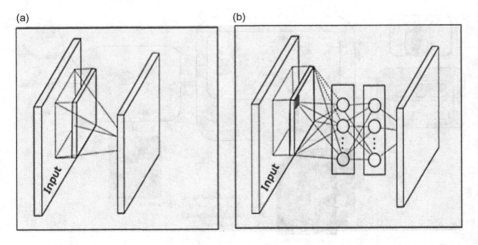

FIGURE 4.2 Comparison of convolutional layer (a) linear convolutional layer and (b) multilayer perception convolutional layer.

Yet another deep CNN called NiN, the structure of which is in contrast with the classic CNN models. In general, classical models incorporate a linear convolution layer followed by an activation function for scanning the input, whereas NiN assimilates multilayer perceptron convolution layers that include micro-networks at each layer. Another variance is that in classic models for object classification, fully connected layers are used at the end of the model, but in contrast, NiN has a global average pooling layer before the output is fed to the softmax layer. The global average pooling layer has certain advantages over the traditional fully connected layers. The foremost thing with regard to the global average pooling layer is its nativity towards the convolution structure by imposing correspondence between feature maps and categories. The overfitting phenomenon is no more as there is no parameter of optimisation in these pooling layers, which makes it more robust towards the spatial translations as the input itself is the sum of these spatial parameters.

The assortment of micro-networks is the *mlpconv* layer of NiN, developed in the multilayer perceptron paradigm. The difference between the linear convolutional layer and *mlpconv* is depicted in Figure 4.2. The fabrication of the NiN layer is achieved by the arrangement of multiple *mlpconv* layers whose non-linear properties are encoded through a multilayer perceptron stack with a higher level of abstraction. For the successful computation of "*mlpconv*" sub-layers, the Parametric Relu (PRelu) function is utilised. The PRelu lessens the possibility of model overfitting through rectifier parameters. The classification activation is done by the softmax classifier usage. Other than this, a loss function, which is a cross-entropy by its category, is manipulated. For successful training, a Stochastic Gradient Descent optimiser goes hand in hand.

4.2.3 INITIALISATION AND HYPER-PARAMETER SETTING

A new architecture combined with the VGG network, SPP layer, and NiN model has been utilised in the proposed model. The VGG network model received a score of 92.75%. Transfer learning froze the convolution layers of the trained VGG network, yet the fully connected layers are fine-tuned. Table 4.1 shows various hyperparameters and their values. The learning rate is primarily set to make the learning adaptive and to make it devoid of overfitting. If the validation loss doesn't fit with five consecutive iterations, then the value is diminished by a factor of 0.1.

4.2.4 IMAGE PROCESSING AND TELEMEDICINE

It is possible to provide long-distance clinical treatment, as well as training and education for both patients and professionals, via the use of telecommunications and electronic information technology in the field of healthcare. Most telemedicine applications nowadays are based on two basic types of technologies: (i) "Store and forward" refers to the process of transferring digital photographs from one location to another. (ii) With the use of a digital camera, a picture may be captured and then "stored" on a computer before being "transmitted" somewhere. If the diagnostic or consultation can be done and returned within 24–48 hours, this is often employed for non-emergency circumstances. Some examples include teleradiology, teledermatology,

TABLE 4.1
Hyper Parameters Used in the Proposed BSD-VNS

Hyper Parameters	Values
Size of the batch	8
Learning rate at the beginning	0.01
Momentum	0.9
Minimal rate of learning	0.0001
Epoch size	50

and telepathology. Imaging procedures such as X-rays, CT, and MRI are useful in the diagnosis of many different disorders. The internet has made rapid progress in facilitating the movement of huge volumes of data. Telemedicine services, such as teleconsultation and telesurgery, and the urgent necessity of transferring medical pictures between patients, physicians, and scan centres are particularly important. To safeguard the privacy of patients' personal medical data, these photos must be sent through a secure communication channel [29]. Using computer-aided diagnosis (CAD), digital image processing has become a strong standard for recognising common disorders from medical pictures, such as cancer. An automated technique for diagnosing acute lymphoblastic leukaemia has been presented by Bhupendra et al. [30]. The researchers used two important processes for the medical picture segmentation: feature extraction and classification.

4.2.5 DATASET DESCRIPTION

In this chapter, the Kaggle dataset is used for training our network. For the experiment, 5720 MRI images have been taken, of which 1745 are ischemic, 1950 as haemorrhagic, and the remaining 2025 as no stroke. The different classifications of brain stroke are done using supervised learning where only labelled images are considered. The extension to the unlabelled datasets via unsupervised learning techniques will be developed in the near future. The distribution of the data between these stroke types is interpreted in Table 4.2. In this study, 75% of the data was taken for training and 25% was taken for testing, respectively.

4.2.6 PERFORMANCE PARAMETERS

Performance metrics like accuracy, area under the curve (AUC) [31], and receiver-operating curve (ROC) [32] are used to judge the quality of our proposed model.

Accuracy: The negative and positive classes define the accuracy of the prediction. It can be expressed as:

$$\text{Acc} = \frac{T_{\text{POS}} + T_{\text{NEG}}}{T_{\text{POS}} + T_{\text{NEG}} + F_{\text{POS}} + F_{\text{NEG}}} \tag{4.3}$$

where $T_{\text{POS}}, T_{\text{NEG}}, F_{\text{POS}}, F_{\text{NEG}}$ denote, respectively, the true-positive, true-negative, false-positive, and false-negative values.

TABLE 4.2
Dataset Used for Training and Testing of Brain Tumour Classification

Category	Name of the Dataset	Number of Images	Training	Testing
Ischemic	Dataset-1	1745	1309	436
Haemorrhagic	Dataset-2	1950	1463	487
No stroke	Dataset-3	2025	1519	506
Total		5720	4291	1429

True positive (T_{POS}) indicates correctly identified DR images, and true negatives (T_{NEG}) are negative classes ahead of given T_{POS} instance that are identified as negative. False positives (T_{NEG}) are positive prediction of negative classes, and false negatives are negative prediction of positive classes.

Specificity: Specificity is termed as a true negative rate. It can be calculated as follows:

$$Spe = \frac{TN}{TN + FP} \qquad (4.4)$$

Recall/sensitivity: Sensitivity, otherwise called true-positive rate (TPR), is calculated as:

$$Sen = \frac{T_{POS}}{T_{POS} + F_{NEG}} \qquad (4.5)$$

Precision: A proportion of truly classified results is made up of true-positive and false-positive sample results. It can be calculated as follows:

$$Pre = \frac{TP}{TP + FP} \qquad (4.6)$$

F1-score: It is a blend of specificity and precision in harmonic form and is been calculated as:

$$F1 = 2 \times \frac{Pre \times Spe}{Pre + Spe} \qquad (4.7)$$

It ranges from 0 to 1. When the score is 1, the best and worst case scenario is 0. The ROC is plotted between TPR and false-positive rate (FPR). FPR is generated as:

$$FPR = 1 - Specificity \qquad (4.8)$$

The degree of class separation is proliferated as AUC that directs how well the model has earned and been evaluated to the core.

4.3   RESULTS AND DISCUSSION

4.3.1   EXPERIMENTAL SETUP

To analyse the working competence of the incorporated method, gliomas, meningiomas, and pituitary adenoma brain strokes are taken into consideration. It is instigated by using the Kaggle dataset of brain stroke images for its classification. The experimentation is carried out using MATLAB 2021a, with a configuration of Window 10, AMD Radeon RX 6900 XT with NVIDIA Tesla k40 Graphics with 64 GB RAM. The results are examined using healthy and ailment images from the Kaggle dataset.

4.3.2   TRAINING AND VALIDATION

Brain stroke diseases are identified using MRI images with 16 convolutional layers (Table 4.3) and a customised BSD-VNS architecture. To make it noteworthy, 80% of the dataset is subjective as a training set and 20% as a validation set. In the architecture proposed, the diagnosis of three types of strokes is witnessed. By incorporating data augmentation, each image is reduced to a standard size of 224×224. For training purposes, customisation of the training set is done through Stochastic Gradient Descent Optimisation and BSD-VNS architecture for brain stroke image classification. By implicating these optimisation strategies, various layers of the proposed BSD-VNS are enlisted in Table 4.3 with typical brain stroke images as depicted in Figure 4.3.

4.3.3   TESTING PHASE

To instigate, scaling of brain stroke images with 224×224 pixels pertaining to data augmentation and trained datasets. For training rationale, the test images were

TABLE 4.3
Different Layers of VGG-NiN Architecture

Layer	Filter Dimensions	Layer	Filter
Con-1	$3 \times 3 \times 64$	Conv-12	$3 \times 3 \times 512$
Con-2	$3 \times 3 \times 64$	Conv-13	$3 \times 3 \times 512$
MaxPool	$2 \times 2 \times 64$	MaxPool	$2 \times 2 \times 512$
Con-3	$3 \times 3 \times 128$	SPP	(1,2,4)
Con-4	$3 \times 3 \times 128$	FC – 1	512
MaxPool	$2 \times 2 \times 128$	FC – 2	4096
Conv-5	$3 \times 3 \times 256$	Conv – 1	$1 \times 1 \times 11$
Conv-6	$3 \times 3 \times 256$	FC – 1	400
Conv-7	$3 \times 3 \times 256$	FC – 2	400
MaxPool	$2 \times 2 \times 256$	Conv – 2	$1 \times 1 \times 11$
Conv-8	$3 \times 3 \times 512$	FC – 3	100
Conv-9	$3 \times 3 \times 512$	FC – 4	100
Conv-10	$3 \times 3 \times 512$	Conv – 3	$1 \times 1 \times 11$
MaxPool	$2 \times 2 \times 512$	FC – 5	4096
Conv-11	$3 \times 3 \times 512$	Output	5

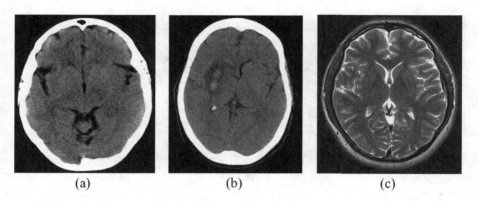

(a) (b) (c)

FIGURE 4.3 Types of strokes (a) ischemic, (b) haemorrhagic, and (c) normal.

TABLE 4.4
Comparison of SPP-VGG-NiN with Other Methods

Methods	ACC (%)	SPE (%)	SEN (%)	PRE (%)	F1-score (%)
Data-1					
Inception V3	86.42	84.61	81.52	77.27	81.56
Densnet201	88.95	85.24	83.68	80.63	86.34
Nasnet	89.32	89.41	90.32	84.58	90.52
BSD-VNS	94.01	95.06	94.90	93.12	93.96
Data-2					
Inception V3	90.34	87.32	89.30	82.67	86.59
Densnet201	92.34	90.32	90.15	87.54	90.36
Nasnet	94.51	92.90	93.42	90.20	91.80
BSD-VNS	96.20	95.85	96.80	94.79	96.21
Data-3					
Inception V3	82.36	76.56	83.16	80.06	82.37
Densnet201	84.68	80.27	86.87	85.38	86.50
Nasnet	89.22	83.17	91.40	87.27	90.24
BSD-VNS	93.80	91.42	95.24	91.29	94.15

portrayed as inputs with multiple CL and FCL refined parameters. Well ahead of time, the Softmax classifier was built into the VGG-NiN features to classify different brain stroke diseases. Surveying of the suggested BSD-VNS efficacy is done by indulging various performance metrics like ACC, SPE, SEN, PRE, and F1-score. Various input samples were fed to SPP-VGG-NiN input, and the quantitative results are enlisted in Table 4.4. The results are equated by means of Inception V3, Densnet201, and Nasnet. Greater effects are proliferated by the proposed SPP-VGG-NiN model's overall performance metrics owing to the towering score of 90.57% for ACC, 94.21% for SPE, 100% for SEN, 92.76% for PRE, and 95.34% for F1-score.

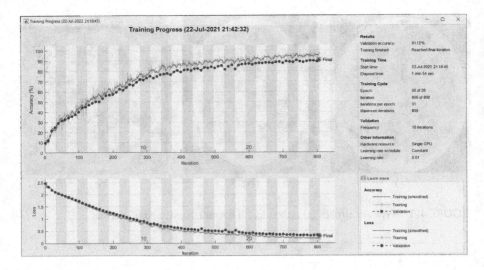

FIGURE 4.4   Training progress plots of CNN without using VNS.

The last row of Table 4.4 compares the performance of the suggested methods to the other three strategies. It is proven that the suggested method reaches its pinnacle over the other novel methodologies with the following performance metrics: ACC = 91.53%, SPE = 88.36%, SEN = 94.18%, PRE = 90.50%, and F1-score = 93.25%.

4.3.4   Performance of SPP-VGG-NiN

The performance is rated with and without the use of the *SPP-VGG-NiN* model. Better performance is seen by assimilating the learning rate of 0.01 with 26 epochs. Every epoch contains 31 iterations and a maximum of 806 iterations. The comparison plot between the usage of the proposed BSD-VNS model and without the same is shown in Figure 4.4. However, the *x*-axis and *y*-axis are embraced with the number of iterations and training accuracy, respectively. A validation accuracy of 91.10% was attained through the training process that lasts for 52 seconds (Figure 4.4). Hence, the figure beholding the accuracy and loss pertaining to BSD-VNS was shown in Figure 4.5. The comparison reveals an improvement of 7% when the proposed BSD-VNS is assimilated rather than with the inclusion of a normal CNN model.

4.3.5   Performance Comparison

The evaluation of performance exploited to analyse and measure the developed VGG16-NiN model with prior methods is pronounced herewith. In addition to this performance metric comparison, the profound description of hyper-parameter settings is depicted in Table 4.2. Further ahead, the layer-by-layer description of our method proposed is predicted in Table 4.3. The training dataset is quite unbalanced, whose analysis of each class is exposed in Table 4.5. Certain other classes tend to have an influence on several performance measures like precision, accuracy, specificity,

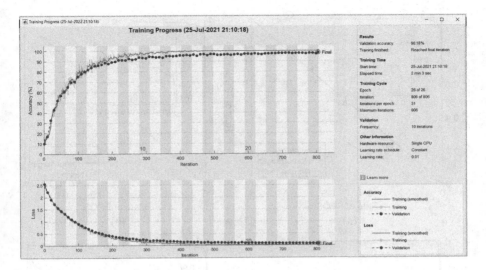

FIGURE 4.5 Training progress plots of CNN with VNS.

TABLE 4.5

Comparison of Performance Metrics with Guangming et al. [25]

	ACC (%)		SPE (%)		SEN (%)		PRE (%)		F1-score (%)	
Types	**PBV**	**CMG**	**PBV**	**CMG**	**PBV**	**CMG**	**PBV**	**CMG**	**PBV**	**CMG**
Meningioma	98.2	89.4	93.6	76.9	98.2	88.6	93.3	88.9	98.2	91.3
Pituitary tumour	96.3	88.3	94.2	81.4	99.3	83.7	95.5	91.4	96.1	90.5
No tumour	99.5	91.7	94.3	83.1	91.5	89.5	97.1	90.6	96.5	91.1
Average	97.75	88.4	94.275	80.875	96.325	85.8	95.3	90.3	96.9	90.9

PBV, Proposed BSD-VNS; CMG, Comparison method of Guangming et al. [25]

and F1-Score. The variance in the VGG work in prior work with the proposed VGG-NiN is 6% higher. In Table 4.5, this comparison is made between Guangming et al. [25] and VGG-NiN.

In addition, among the various evaluation strategies, the ROC curve is one among those that serves as the most effective assessment of performance for categorisation. The ROC curve serves as a primary parameter for the evaluation of the proposed method for class differentiation. The performance of the proposed method is compared with three different benchmark networks, namely, Inception V3, Densnet201, and Nasnet. Details of the results of the ROC curve obtained for Inception V3, Densnet201, Nasnet, and the proposed BSD-VNS are shown in Figure 4.6. The proposed BSD-VNS provided an improvement of 3.59%, 5.59%, and 9.62% for the detection of AMD compared to Inception V3, Densnet201, and Nasnet, respectively. Similarly, in other cases such as cataract, normal, DR, and glaucoma, the

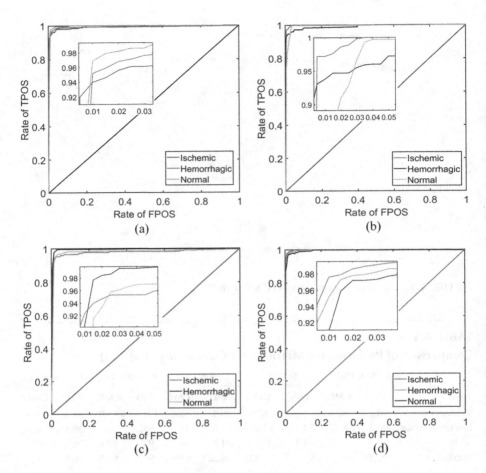

FIGURE 4.6 ROC curve for various algorithms (a) Inception V3, (b) Densnet201, (c) Nasnet, and (d) BSD-VNS.

proposed BSD-VNS provided better results compared to Inception V3, Densnet201, and Nasnet. Figure 4.6 indicates that the proposed BSD-VNS provides the best performance compared to other methods. So, the BSD-VNS can be used to reliably find brain strokes in real-time applications.

4.4 CONCLUSION

This chapter is proposed with variations on the existing CNN architecture that combine linear convolutional layers with SPP with fully connected layers and NiN. Fewer learning parameters are required to achieve efficacy and accuracy in the classification of brain MRI images into different strokes. The datasets are obtained from Kaggle, which are imbalanced for validating the performance metrics. The proposed

BSD-VNS model training processes provide an improvement of 7.06% over the existing CNN model. The SPP-VGG-NiN results witnessed an accuracy of 89.2%, 90.9%, 94.3%, and 96.2% for ischemic, haemorrhagic, and instances with no stroke, respectively. For the training and implementation processes, a lesser number of resources are put to good use.

The findings disclose that the proposed model out performs the existing state-of-art methodology. The proposed BSD-VNS provided an improvement of 4.69%, 5.06%, and 7.59% for the detection of dataset-1 compared to Nasnet, Densnet201, and Inception V3, respectively. It can be deliberated with changes in the present model, and enhancement in pre-processing techniques can be made shortly to address how these changes get an impact with brain stroke classification of MRI images in specific when it is in the earlier stage of diagnosis.

REFERENCES

1. Natsumi, M., Kaori, T., Ami, O., Hideaki, A., Aika, H., Zhiheng, L., Ching-Ting, W., Satoko, A., Toru, M. (2021). AIM/CD5L attenuates DAMPs in the injured brain and thereby ameliorates ischemic stroke. *Cell Reports*, 36(11), 109693, https://doi.org/ 10.1016/j.celrep.2021.109693.
2. Apoorva, M., Shankaranarayana, S.G., Manikandan, N., Chitralakshmi, K.B., & John, M.S. (2021). Gait training interventions for patients with stroke in India: A systematic review. *Gait & Posture*, 83, 132–140, https://doi.org/10.1016/j.gaitpost.2020.10.012.
3. Vlisides, P., & Mashour, G.A. (2016). Perioperative stroke. *Canadian Journal of Anesthesia*, 63(2), 193–204, https://doi.org/10.1007/s12630-015-0494-9.
4. Semyachkina-Glushkovskaya, O., et al. (2016). Stress plays provoking role in hypertension-related stroke: Injuries of blood-brain barrier function. *Asia Communications and Photonics Conference (ACP)*, Wuhan, pp. 1–3.
5. Mohamad, A., Issam, M., Abhishek, D., Nasser, M.A., James, P.K., & David, R.H. (2022). The heart brain team and patient-centered management of ischemic stroke. *JACC: Advances*, 1(1), 100014, https://doi.org/10.1016/j.jacadv.2022.100014.
6. Saver, J.L. (2017). Penumbral salvage and thrombolysis outcome: A drop of brain, a week of life. *Brain*, 140, 519–522, https://doi.org/10.1093/brain/awx0.
7. Rowley, H., & Vagal, A. (2020). Stroke and stroke mimics: Diagnosis and treatment. In: Hodler J, Kubik-Huch RA, von Schulthess GK, editors. *Diseases of the Brain, Head and Neck, Spine 2020–2023: Diagnostic Imaging*. Cham: Springer; 2020, https://doi.org/10.1007/978-3-030-38490-6_3.
8. Kambali, I., & H. Suryanto. (2020). Cancer imaging using positron emission tomography/computed tomography. *2020 International Seminar on Intelligent Technology and Its Applications (ISITIA)*, Surabaya, pp. 170–174, https://doi.org/10.1109/ISITIA49792.2020.9163740.
9. Van Helvoort, M., & Harberts, D.W. (2018). Frequency-dependent shielding of electronics inside an MRI system. *International Symposium on Electromagnetic Compatibility (EMC EUROPE)*, 763–766, https://doi.org/10.1109/EMCEurope.2018.8485078.
10. Bhattacharjee, S., Ghatak, S., Dutta, S., Chatterjee, B., & Gupta, M. (2018). A survey on comparison analysis between EEG signal and MRI for brain stroke detection. *Emerging Technologies in Data Mining and Information Security: Proceedings of IEMIS 2018*, pp. 377–382, https://doi.org/10.1007/978-981-13-1501-5_32.
11. Lisowska, A., Beveridge, E., Muir, K., & Poole, I. (2017). Thrombus detection in CT brain scans using a convolutional neural network. In: Peixoto N, Silveira M, Ali HH, Maciel C, van den Broek EL, editors. *Bioimaging*, pp. 24–33. Science and Technology Publications, Lda, Portugal.

12. Ganesh, B.R., Chellaswamy, C., Surya, B.R.M., Saravanan, M., Kanchana, E., & Shalini, J. (2020). Deep learning based pothole detection and reporting system. *IEEE International Conference on Smart Structures and Systems (ICSSS)*, Chennai, pp. 1–6, https://doi.org/10.1109/ICSSS49621.2020.9202061.

13. Stib, M.T., Dong, M.P., Kim, Y.H., Subzwari, S.S., Triedman, H.J., Wang, A., Yao, A.D., Zhu, L.L., Boxerman, J.L., Baird, G., Cetintemel, U., Eickhoff, C., & McTaggart, R.A., (2018). Deep learning in emergent large vessel occlusion detection using maximum intensity projections via CT angiography. *SIIM Conference on Machine Intelligence in Medical Imaging*, San Francisco, CA, pp. 1–3.

14. Litjens, G., Kooi, T., Ehteshami Bejnordi, B., Setio, A.A.A., Ciompi, F., Ghafoorian, M., van der Laak, J., van Ginneken, B., & Sánchez, C. (2017). A survey on deep learning in medical image analysis. 42, 60–88, https://doi.org/10.1016/j.media.2017.07.005.

15. Chatterjee, A., Somayaji, N.R., & Kabakis, I.M. (2019). Abstract wmp16: Artificial intelligence detection of cerebrovascular large vessel occlusion-nine month, 650 patient evaluation of the diagnostic accuracy and performance of the viz. ai lvo algorithm. *Stroke*, 50(Suppl_1), AWMP16–AWMP16.

16. Subba Rao, C., Geetha, T.S., Chellaswamy, C., & Arul, S. (2021). Optimized convolutional neural network-based multigas detection using fiber optic sensor. *Optical Engineering*, 60(12), 127108, https://doi.org/10.1117/1.OE.60.12.127108

17. Marbun, J.T., & Andayani, S. U. (2018). Classification of stroke disease using convolutional neural network. *Journal of Physics: Conference Series*, 978, 012092, https://doi.org/10.1088/1742-6596/978/1/012092.

18. Kuo, W., Häne, C., Mukherjee, P., Malik, J., & Yuh, E.L. (2019). Expert-level detection of acute intracranial hemorrhage on head computed tomography using deep learning. *Proceedings of the National Academy of Sciences of the United States of America*, 116, 22737–22745, https://doi.org/10.1073/pnas.1908021116.

19. Xue, Y., Farhat, F.G., Boukrina, O., Barrett, A., Binder, J.R., Roshan, U.W., et al. (2020). A multi-path 2.5-dimensional convolutional neural network system for segmenting stroke lesions in brain MRI images. *NeuroImage: Clinical*, 25, 102118, https://doi.org/10.1016/j.nicl.2019.102118.

20. Azizad, O., & Joshi, G.P. (2021). Telemedicine for preanesthesia evaluation: Review of current literature and recommendations for future implementation. *Current Opinion in Anesthesiology*, 34(6), 672–677.

21. Andrews, E., Berghofer, K., Long, J., Prescott, A., & Caboral-Stevens, M. (2020). Satisfaction with the use of telehealth during COVID-19: An integrative review. *International Journal of Nursing Studies Advances*, 2, Article 100008, https://doi.org/10.1016/j.ijnsa.2020.100008.

22. Prasad, A., Brewster, R., Newman, J.G., & Rajasekaran, K. (2020). Optimizing your telemedicine visit during the COVID-19 pandemic: Practice guidelines for patients with head and neck cancer. *Head Neck*, 42(6), 1317–1321, https://doi.org/10.1002/hed.26197.

23. Ganesh babu, R., & Chellaswamy, C. (2022). Different stages of disease detection in squash plant based on machine learning. *Journal of Bioscience*, 47(9), 1–14, https://doi.org/10.1007/s12038-021-00241-8.

24. An, S.J., Kim, T.J., & Yoon, B.W. (2017). Epidemiology, risk factors, and clinical features of intracerebral hemorrhage: An update. *Journal of Stroke*, 19(1), 3–10.

25. Guangming, Z., Hui, C., Bin, J., Fei, C., Yuan, X., & Max, W. (2022). Application of deep learning to ischemic and hemorrhagic stroke CT and MR imaging. *Seminars in Ultrasound, CT and MRI*, https://doi.org/10.1053/j.sult.2022.02.004.

26. Khaled, A., Adel, K., & Zidane, F. (2018). Fully Automated brain tumor segmentation system in 3D MRI using symmetry analysis of brain and level sets. *IET Image Processing*, 12(11), 1964–1971.

27. He, K., Zhang, X. Ren, S., & Sun, J. (2015). Spatial pyramid pooling in deep convolutional networks for visual recognition. *IEEE Transactions on Pattern Analysis and Machine Intelligence*, 37(9), 1904–1916.

28. Karen, S., & Andrew, Z. (2015). Very deep convolutional networks for large-scale image recognition, ICLR 2015. arXiv preprint arXiv:1409.1556.

29. Karthik, J.V., & Reddy, B.V. (2014). Authentication of secret information in image stenography. *International Journal of Computer Science and Information Security*, 14(6), 58–63.

30. Bhupendra, F., Joshi, M., Modi, U., & Zaveri, T. (2015). Automatic identification of licorice and rhubarb by microscopic image processing. *Procedia Computer Science*, 58, 723–730, https://doi.org/10.1016/j.procs.2015.08.093.

31. Cho, S., Kim, Y.J., Lee, M. et al. (2021). Cut-off points between pain intensities of the postoperative pain using receiver operating characteristic (ROC) curves. *BMC Anesthesiology*, 21, 29, https://doi.org/10.1186/s12871021-01245-5.

32. Kumar, R., & Indrayan, A. (2011). Receiver operating characteristic (ROC) curve for medical researchers. *Indian Pediatrics*, 48, 277–287, https://doi.org/10.1007/s13312-011-0055-4.

5 An Automated Detection of Notable ABCD Diagnostics of Melanoma in Dermoscopic Images

Nirmala V. and Premaladha J.
SASTRA Deemed to be University

CONTENTS

5.1 INTRODUCTION

Melanoma is the most dangerous of all the other types of skin malignancies [1]. Doctors and physicians do not readily identify melanoma at an early stage. Over the years, the treatment for skin melanoma has improved significantly. Early identification of skin cancers increases the chance of survival by around 5 years. The 5-year survival rate [2] observed in patients for stage I and stage IV skin melanoma are 98.4% and 22.5%, respectively. The "ABCD" rule is a set of guidelines that a scientist group discovered at New York University for dermatologists, physicians and doctors for accessing pigmented lesions at an early stage. Each letter in the rule stands for a property [3]. A stands for asymmetry, B for border irregularities, C for color variegation and D for diameter, which is the skin lesions' properties. Skin melanoma is identified by three strong indicators: asymmetry, color variegation and diameter. The American Cancer Society promoted this rule for identifying any irregularities in skin lesions. However, this type of cancer can be rectified if diagnosed at an initial stage [4].

Asymmetry is one of the three strong indicators of malignant skin melanoma. Benign skin pigmentation tends to be symmetric [5] in fashion. However, malignant melanoma tends to grow irregularly and asymmetrically. For accessing asymmetry, the skin lesion is bisected in a 90-degree axis positioned such that it is bisected on a symmetric plane and thereby producing the lowest asymmetry score. Scale Invariant Feature Transform (SIFT) similarity is a feature detector algorithm [6] used in machine vision to find critical points in an image. SIFT was utilized to compare the picture similarity between the two portions using 128-dimensional key point vectors after the retrieved lesions were divided lengthwise across the center into two halves. The higher the value, the closer the two portions of the skin lesion are to each other, and vice versa. The idea that the two sides are not identical is called asymmetry. A projection profile utilizes data highly related to storing the number of pixels in the foreground when the input image is intended to be projected over the X and Y axes. Correlation is processed for the image pixels, and the asymmetry of the lesion is measured. This asymmetric information on the human skin lesion reveals the distinguishing feature for classifying malignant lesions from benign ones. Also, intermediate skin lesions such as actinic keratosis can be identified with the same feature; but later, it becomes malignant. Figure 5.1 depicts the ABCD parameters of human skin lesions for quantifying the melanoma.

Border irregularity defines the nature of melanoma [7]. Suppose the border has randomness and peaks in the distribution of the neighboring pixels. In that case, it is then said to have the maximum chance of being malignant. On the other hand, the irregularity has no significant variations while overlapping the coordinate axes of the edges; it can then be considered the nature of benignness. This feature also gives us clear information on its evenness, texture and sometimes the evolution of the skin lesion.

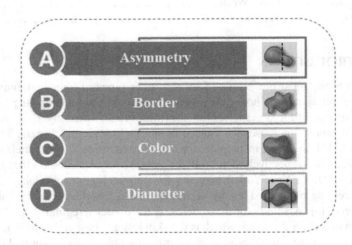

FIGURE 5.1   The ABCD of human skin lesions for quantifying the melanoma.

Color variegation is another crucial parameter in identifying skin melanoma. Skin melanoma or tumors has a wide range of color distribution [8], where specific colors describe the intensity of the disease. Variegated coloring is one of the earliest signs of this disease. Benign skin melanoma tends to have a singular color distribution, whereas malignant melanomas have a varied distribution of colors. Lighter and darker shades of brown, white, red, black and bluish-gray are the six most suspicious colors that correspond to malignant skin melanoma. Therefore, segmenting the digital skin melanoma images into various color objects would be helpful for dermatologists and physicians to provide easy aid in diagnosing the disease. The procedure entails using K-means [9] with a specific set of clusters equivalent to the total colors that will make up the color palette. The color of each pixel is then changed by the Euclidean distance [10] to the closest cluster centroid. 3D scatter plot [11] sophisticates the identification of the various spread of colors, which exhibits the distribution of pixel colors.

Diameter is one of the other indicators of skin melanoma. Doctors and physicians must distinguish a specific skin disease from skin melanoma [12]. An ordinary nevus has a diameter of less than 6 mm. However, a skin melanoma lesion is considered to have a diameter of 6 mm and more. Feret's diameters are the method to find the distance between the farthest points on the edges of the skin lesion that are outlined to determine the diameter measurement to know the size of the lesion spread in the human skin images. The distance between an object's two farthest points is its maximum Feret's diameter [13]. The distance between the two closest points is the minimum Feret's diameter. The maximum diameter measure is identified as the diameter measure in this work.

5.2 LITERATURE SURVEY

5.2.1 Limitations of Existing Methods

Various methods have been developed to automatically detect asymmetry, border irregularities, evenness, color variegation and the diameter of skin melanocytic patches. This [14] work, "Measuring asymmetry of skin lesions", investigated the use of symmetric distance (SD) to measure the dissymmetry of skin lesions. He mentioned circularity in previous works, which was used to reflect the asymmetrical property of skin lesions. Here, color images are digitized, and the primary SD, fuzzy SD and simple circularity were calculated. He concluded his work by stating that fuzzy SD gave the best results in gray-level images. Computer vision system for extracting features from skin lesions [15] based on their spectral information. When the front-end visual system was finalized, it automatically recognized the most predictive aspects, allowing the skilled system software to identify a tumor based on recorded data with limited human interaction. This classification will be a differential diagnosis, providing a list of probable diagnoses and their associated probability. The research aimed to create an algorithm that would identify the essential features in the image and can be used as an application in a microprocessor-based computer system. This work [16] developed a prototype that–processes, segments, extracts features and classifies to yield the Total Dermoscopy Score (TDS). Pre-processing includes contrast-enhancing and filtering. Localizing the lesions using thresholding techniques was used in the segmentation process. Entropy and bifold techniques were used to calculate the asymmetry of the lesions and averaged. The diameter was measured and converted into millimeters. TDS was calculated, and the lesions were classified as benign, suspicious and malignant. In this work, the classification of the melanocytic lesion [13] with the help of the framed rules implemented ABCD scores for skin lesions.

TDS was calculated [1] to classify the lesion as benign or malignant. The research mainly revolves around the preprocessing techniques, which made use of the Gabor filter [17] with different frequencies, and the lesions were segmented by Geodesic Active Contours (GAC) [18]. The extracted features from the preprocessing stage could be applied to a good classifier that best classifies the images as malignant or benign.

5.2.2 MOTIVATION AND CONTRIBUTION

Our work contributes by presenting a segmentation approach that performs better than the standard segmentation approaches by making use of Otsu thresholding techniques to separate the foreground and background, a dissymmetry measurement technique in our proposed work comprising a SIFT similarity, skewness measure and projection profiles, color variegation that uses K-means clustering techniques to identify suspicious colors, and then plotted in 3D for visualization purposes. A skin lesion's diameter is identified by using Feret's diameter. It is a crucial indicator for specifying the human skin lesion's class type, either benign or malignant. Maximum Feret's diameter measure is considered for measuring the diameter of a lesion.

5.3 PROPOSED METHODOLOGY

5.3.1 ABCD FEATURES OF MELANOMA

The ABCD features of melanoma refer to the Asymmetry, Border, Color and Diameter of the human melanocytic skin lesion characteristics, which are more susceptible to skin cancer diagnosis, especially melanoma. These factors influence discriminant feature analyses to distinguish between benign and malignant classes. Thus, the feature analysis of melanoma diagnosis should be given the most care for early-stage skin cancer detection. The workflow overview is given in Figure 5.2, which exhibits the list of feature indicators used in the segmentation. These features also help in the intra-class classification, where the nevus skin lesions are transformed into malignant lesions in later stages. Hence, evaluating skin lesions at their early stage concerning these ABCD features serves a more significant impact.

5.3.2 ASYMMETRY

The asymmetry of the skin lesion is to be measured. Here, we constructed a vector consisting of three measurement values that will be utilized to train and test a decision tree classifier. The decision tree is adopted to design a structured segmentation method on the input image, which highly cooperates with the pattern recognition of the skin lesions to emphasize the features. It also serves in an ordered fashion

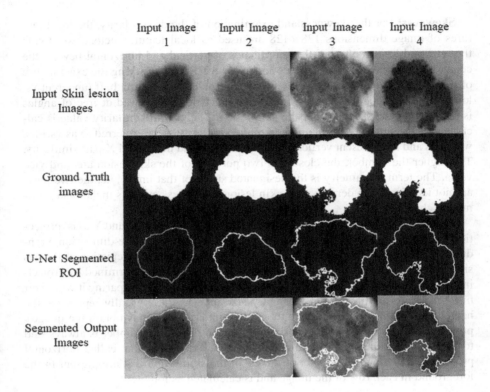

FIGURE 5.2   The workflow architecture of extraction of ABCD features for segmentation.

which has the set nodes. Here, each of its nodes internally present is associated with a decision-making variable concerning one or many within the features [19]. The utilization of two classes is represented as the two branches of the adopted decision tree algorithm called the binary tree. Here, the tree depths are expanded to the extent where all the leaf nodes are considered pure so that it does not have any possibilities of splitting, which is achieved in later steps.

SIFT measures of similarity: To describe the invariant features of the skin lesion, such as unwavering to the dominant changes of image scaling, image translation and rotation [20] in a local path, a shape descriptor is employed. These shape descriptors provide the features in a 128-dimensional vector representing the local features, such as the region of the image. The main aim of the shape descriptor is to validate the collation of two-dimensional (2D) object delineation by uniquely characterizing the object's shape. SIFT's feature vector group would thus constitute the form of the image. SIFT detects reliable feature points and then provides a collection of features that distinguish a tiny region encompassing the pixel for each point. This implies we finally grab the necessary local information from the input skin dermoscopic images. These retrieved characteristics are subsequently utilized to match entities across contexts.

Skewness: For the skewness and examination of the dissimilarity, the local features of image dimensions 128×128 are used as local feature vectors; we divide the retrieved lesions on both the coordinates of vertical and horizontal beyond the center into four non-different halves and apply SIFT to quantifying the exact nature of the images (showing correspondences) between each opposing half (uppercut vs. lower cut and proper cut vs. left cut) counterparts for the skewed degree of angles is recorded as the skewness for the skin lesion. The overall similarity value is calculated as the sum of vertical and horizontal similarity scores referred to as vs + hs, where vs and hs represent vertical Y-part similarity and horizontal X-part similarity. The higher the number, the closer the two portions of the skin lesion are, and vice versa. The term asymmetry is the designated status of that image, i.e. the two parts are not identical. The dermoscopic skin lesion's skewness exhibits melanoma information characteristics.

Projection profile: When an image is extrapolated over the X and Y axis, projection profiles hold the number of foreground pixels. They are a one-dimensional rendition of 2D image [21] material. They are considered the firm depiction of images since they preserve much relevant information. Symmetry is determined by projecting in the x and y directions of the segmented skin lesion and comparing it with their histograms. Assuming we have a binary size image, $M \times N$ usually represents the height and width. By breaking the thread line into bins, we may obtain the image's projection onto a line. While counting one valued pixel, that number is always said to be lies perpendicular to the bin. The straight axis projection, called horizontal projection, is defined as the No. of. Pixels of the skin lesion that are present in the foreground in each row of the image and is calculated as follows:

$$H_p[i] = \sum_{j=0}^{m-1} P[i,j] \quad \text{where } 0 < i < N \tag{5.1}$$

where $P[i, j]$ represents the values of the corresponding pixels at an image, $I\,(i, j)$ and $H_p[i]$ is the count of foreground pixels in the ith horizontal row. Thus, the No. of. Foreground pixels are determined for each X-plane line of pixels. The vertical projection, on the other hand, indicates the No. of. foreground pixels in each column and is defined as:

$$V_p[j] = \sum_{i=0}^{n-1} P[i,j] \quad \text{where } 0 < j < M \tag{5.2}$$

$V_p[j]$ is the no. of pixels in the foreground in the jth vertical column. Each column's upright projection is therefore determined. A histogram can be used to show the horizontal and vertical projection profiles. Each histogram's values indicate the density distribution of the pixels in the region of the lesion.

$$\text{den}(H_1, H_2) = \frac{\sum_I (H_1(\text{Int}) - H_1')(H_2(\text{Int}) - H_2')}{\sqrt{\sum_I (H_1(\text{Int}) - H_1')(H_2(\text{Int}) - H_2')}} \tag{5.3}$$

5.3.3 BORDERS

The border of the skin lesion images says a lot about the diameter [22] and spread of the lesion in the human skin. Let us consider that border B is the boundary line of the lesion. Suppose the value of B is spread apart from its overlapping. In that case, it can be inferred that the diameter intended to be greater in size. Moreover, the diameter is said to have a smaller value when they are huddled together. This quantifying skin lesion helps distinguish the complex features for the disease diagnosis and classification framework.

5.3.4 COLOR VARIEGATION

Even experienced dermatologists regard color identification in skin lesions as a subjective activity, making it important to create an automated objective technique for skin lesions. To assess the apprehensive colors prevalent in each skin lesion, we adopt the same logic as in Ref. [23]. On the other hand, employ the CIELab color system, which is more representative of sensory consciousness than the Red, Green and Blue color space.

Furthermore, we generate the lesion colors CIELab values from our dataset's color distribution, leading to better detection of the suspicious colors. Furthermore, it is still a perplexing query on how keen and precise the lesions' colors are determined (excluding the usual red, black, and white colors in Ref. [24], which utilize typical RGB values). Because it has been observed that the white color in RGB [25] does not reflect the wholesome color, on the other hand, another color was produced as a substitute in the dye of correspondence. Because we might have numerous levels (tints) of the same hue, the authors utilized only the single suspicious color value, which fails to enough representation of distinct features for their research work, in contrast here we employed the representation of six colors, which the top dominant three colors are validated in our future work of those two studies utilized just one typical value for each suspicious color, which may not be a representative enough (i.e. light brown). In opposition to such two studies, we employ Minkowski distance rather than Euclidean distance.

When working on color variegation, portraying the image in its prevalent colors is a reasonable approach. However, it is exceptionally chaotic to obtain the range of lesion dyes representing the six suspicious color values of melanoma in Table 5.1. It is adapted from the article [26] in our research work. It facilitates a range of maximum and minimum possibilities.

Color values ranging from black, deep brown color or pastel brown are regarded to have hues on skin lesions with those random pixels in CIELab. Skin lesion images can have any tone of the colors white, red or blue-gray, which are neglected as our dataset does not include those colors in the images. If an image, I used the Minkowski method for calculating the distance between any of the two-pixel colors to look up the values represented in Table 5.1. Eventually, if it has less than a cutoff point T, assessed as half the Minkowski distance between any two extremes of color referred white and deep black, which quantifies to 0.50. The pixel value related to the suspicious color represents >0.5 of the skin lesion pixels. The Minkowski distance is defined as a generalization of Euclidean and Manhattan distances [27].

TABLE 5.1

Suspicious Values of Color in Melanoma with CIELab Color

Color	Minimum Value	Maximum Value
Black	[0.0600, 0.2700, 0.10]	[39.91, 30.23, 22.10]
Dark brown	[14.32, 6.85, 6.96]	[47.57, 27.14, 46.81]
Light brown	[47.94, 11.89, 19.86]	[71.65, 44.81, 64.78]
White	[100, 0, 0]	–
Red	[54.29, 80.81, 69.89]	–
Blue-gray	[50.28, −30.14, −11.96]	–

5.3.5 DIAMETER

In the mathematical computations, the diameter of a skin lesion impression in clinical reports is in millimeters (mm). Our diameter results are delivered in pixels after the conversion metric for the clinical assessment. This can be accomplished through geometric correction (spatial calibration), which involves the image calibration technique against a known conversion value and afterward applying those calibrations to the imprecise image (i.e. in pixels). A spatial calibrated image is created in units. However, to do such calibration, one must first determine the original measurement in real time and then map it to pixels. We utilized the images from our dataset (the ISIC 2020 dataset) [28] with a ruler shown to estimate the skin lesion in millimeters and determine how many pixels would be in 1 mm. In addition, the image was magnified to match the skin lesions' magnitude better for our test sample images. After performing such calibration, we discovered that our 256×256 images had 27.80 pixels/mm of dermoscopy images, segmentation and Feret's diameter values.

5.4 RESULTS AND DISCUSSION

Applying the unique ABCD feature analysis technique of melanoma is carried out in our proposed work with the integrated U-Net segmentation [29] for the benchmark ISIC 2020 dataset images. Our approaches for the analytical symmetry of the skin lesion, with the help of projection profiles and SIFT key points, ascertained the ground truth values. Each iterative step for justifying the vital features is depicted and discussed in detail. The comparison chart confirms that our approach outperforms the other state-of-the-art method.

The input skin lesion acquired from the dataset is shown in Figure 5.3a, which has the different regions of interest, textures and sizes. The conversion of the RGB to CIELab color space is done, shown in Figure 5.3b. The process of removing the artifact's occlusions and color corrections is adjusted in the preprocessing. The thresholding with the pixels' histogram distribution is analyzed in our approach's early phases. Here, the samples from each class have been experimented with. The comparable results are shared to infer the effect of our proposed feature extraction process and the relative segmentation results.

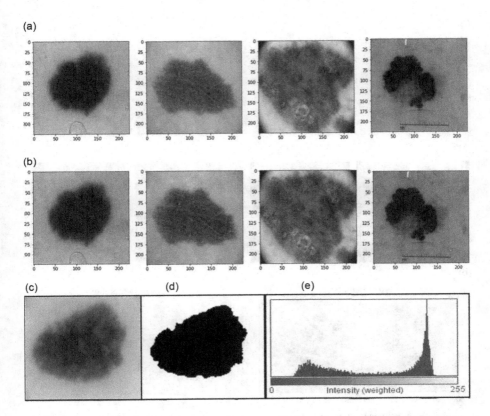

FIGURE 5.3 (a) Input image from the ISIC dataset. (b) Conversion of RGB to CIE Lab color space image. (c) Skin lesion image before thresholding. (d) Lesion image after thresholding. The optimal threshold for this image is 134. (e) Histogram showing the distribution of pixels in the image.

The asymmetricity of the input skin lesions was analyzed with the confirmation of the values of SIFT similarity and lesion projection profiles and also considering the skewness of the image region of interest. Notably, on either skew, that is referred to as horizontal and vertical skewness. In Figure 5.4a, the sliced images of the coordinate of X and Y for each image are depicted. The values are then maintained in a separate log file for the clinical statistical analysis.

The projection profile is shown in Figure 5.5. The values accelerate the probability of the skin lesion belonging to the particular class between the life-threatening cancerous and non-cancerous lesions.

The decision tree algorithm decides the status of the skin lesion by pulling out the symmetric images precisely from the group of test sample images. Also, the skin lesion's suspicious border irregularity and the color ranges are identified and analyzed with the scatter plot by the K-means clustering method, which has more reliable information that exhibits the class relevance information and the texture information, as shown in Figure 5.6. Each human skin lesion sample from the acquired dataset is

(a)

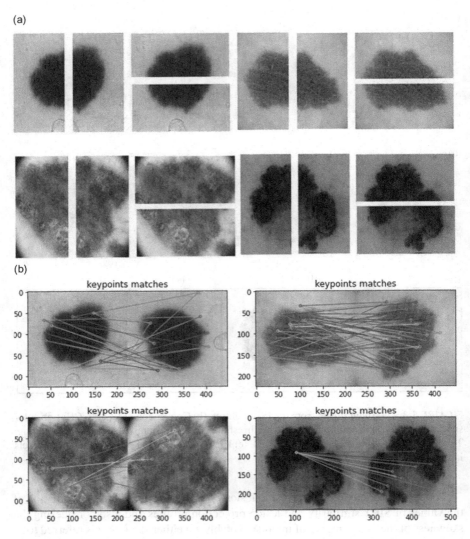

(b)

FIGURE 5.4 (a). The lesion image was split into two halves to check for the similarity between the halves using SIFT similarity. (b) The SIFT generated key points for the symmetry check the skewness to the horizontal and vertical axes.

passed into the model for the feature extraction process. The results are stored in a separate local path in the workstation. Later, these resulting images are used in the Segmentation module for the precisely segmented lesion from the wholesome input dermoscopic images that helps in classification.

The most beneficial factor of utilizing this Minkowski parameter p is to set the color code value of seven numbers in our research work. Out of these, the most suspicious skin lesion are depicted with their corresponding values for all three channels,

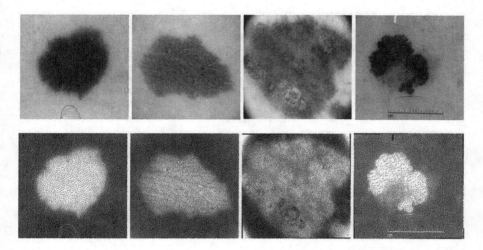

FIGURE 5.5 Skin lesion image after projection profiling to find the asymmetry measure.

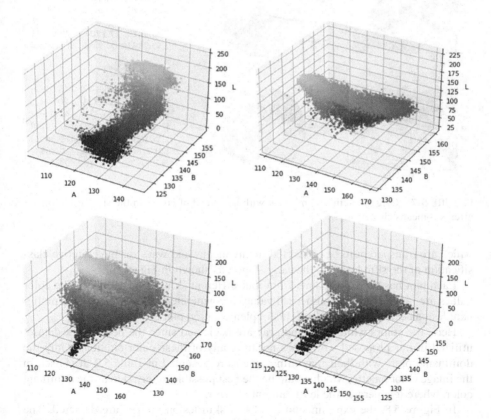

FIGURE 5.6 Skin lesion images 3D scatter plot of various colors.

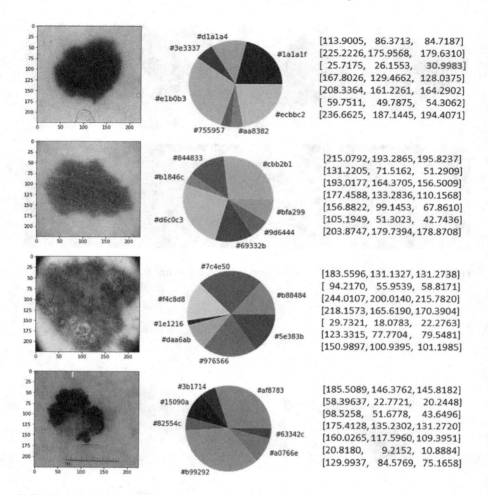

FIGURE 5.7   Original skin lesion image with its spread of colors in the skin lesion image after K – means clustering.

which are transparent to be converted in any means and ways for the effective classification of the skin lesion at the early stages, as shown in Figure 5.7.

Each plot has the color points from four different skin lesion samples. The color values are plotted, and the numerical values are generated as a.csv file for the malignant lesions extraction module at this implementation phase.

Here, the colors white, blue and gray are neglected since the benchmark dataset utilized in our proposed work does not have any of these color citations. Only the dominant colors with their max-min range as represented in Table 5.2. It is used in the image color palette, which would be the best possible, referred to as the dominant color, where it generates the least amount of error.

In Figure 5.8, the experimental results of skin lesion images are depicted. The Feret's diameter resulted in Table 5.2 is the technical representation of the furthest

TABLE.5.2
Minimum and Maximum Feret's Diameter Calculated for a Skin Lesion Image

Parameters/Inputs	Input Image 1	Input Image 2	Input Image 3	Input Image 4
Area	50,176	50,176	49,952	62,194
StdDev	30.575	47.862	64.254	52.231
MaxFeret	316.784	316.784	316.078	353.006
MinFeret	224.000	224.000	223.021	242.325
Skew	8.097	4.88	3.379	4.454

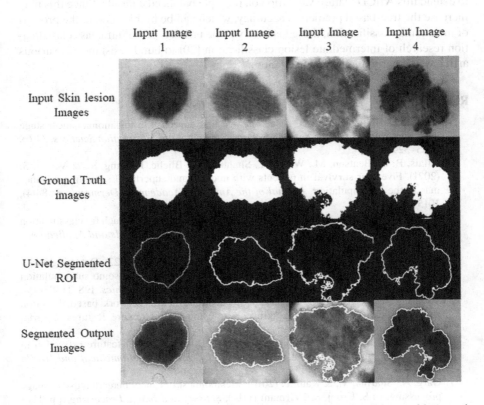

FIGURE 5.8 Proposed work results on input dermoscopy skin lesion images with ground truth.

point distance measurements in which it is calibrated in the calculated conversion from the number of pixels into millimeters. In general, the rule framed was said to have a diameter value of fewer than 6 mm with isolated corner pixels of the 2D lesion images. Hence, the values of the maximum and the minimum Feret are determined to state the shape analysis of the lesion accurately.

5.5 CONCLUSION AND FUTURE WORK

An empirical approach has been presented to remove variability in quantifying asymmetry and color variegation and to potentially prevent losing melanoma identification in the initial stage due to a diameter being less than 6 mm. In summary, this research proposes a UNet segmentation approach with notable ABCD features that resulted in an accuracy of 92.8% with 80% and 87% precision and recall, respectively. The model efficiency is evaluated using the F1 score and the Jaccard Indexing results in 80.29% and 71%, respectively, which ascertains that it performs better than conventional segmentation. An unbiased approach that utilizes the features analyzed and segments potentially malicious skin melanocytic lesions. In the future, we plan to extend this ABCD feature validation on multiple balanced datasets. Since this may increase the tree-based prediction accuracy, which can be highlighted in the process of melanoma classification, these features will be utilized in the intraclass classification research of intermediate lesion classification [20] to build resistance to various artifacts and early diagnosis of melanoma.

REFERENCES

1. Patil, R., & Bellary, S. (2020). Machine learning approach in melanoma cancer stage detection. *Journal of King Saud University-Computer and Information Sciences*, 34(6), 3285–3293.
2. Allais, B. S., Beatson, M., Wang, H., Shahbazi, S., Bijelic, L., Jang, S., & Venna, S. (2021). Five-year survival in patients with nodular and superficial spreading melanomas in the US population. *Journal of the American Academy of Dermatology*, 84(4), 1015–1022.
3. Salma, W., & Eltrass, A. S. (2022). Automated deep learning approach for classification of malignant melanoma and benign skin lesions. *Multimedia Tools and Applications*, 81(22), 1–18.
4. Choi, D. Y., Park, J. N., Paek, S. H., Choi, S. C., & Paek, S. H. (2022). Detecting early-stage malignant melanoma using a calcium switch-enriched exosome subpopulation containing tumor markers as a sample. *Biosensors and Bioelectronics*, 198, 113828.
5. Tumpa, P. P., & Kabir, M. A. (2021). An artificial neural network based detection and classification of melanoma skin cancer using hybrid texture features. *Sensors International*, 2, 100128.
6. Barata, C., Celebi, M. E., & Marques, J. S. (2018). A survey of feature extraction in dermoscopy image analysis of skin cancer. *IEEE Journal of Biomedical and Health Informatics*, 23(3), 1096–1109.
7. Garg, N., Sharma, V., & Kaur, P. (2018). Melanoma skin cancer detection using image processing. In S. Urooj, & J.Virmani (Eds.), *Sensors and Image Processing* (pp. 111–119). Springer, Singapore.
8. Lingala, M., Stanley, R. J., Rader, R. K., Hagerty, J., Rabinovitz, H. S., Oliviero, M., ... & Stoecker, W. V. (2014). Fuzzy logic color detection: Blue areas in melanoma dermoscopy images. *Computerized Medical Imaging and Graphics*, 38(5), 403–410.
9. Celebi, M. E., Mendonca, T., & Marques, J. S. (Eds.). (2015). *Dermoscopy Image Analysis* (Vol. 10). CRC Press, Boca Raton, FL.
10. Khatami, A., Mirghasemi, S., Khosravi, A., & Nahavandi, S. (2015, October). A new color space based on k-medoids clustering for fire detection. In *2015 IEEE International Conference on Systems, Man, and Cybernetic* (pp. 2755–2760). Hong Kong.

11. Hirano, G., Nemoto, M., Kimura, Y., Kiyohara, Y., Koga, H., Yamazaki, N., ... & Nagaoka, T. (2020). Automatic diagnosis of melanoma using hyperspectral data and GoogLeNet. *Skin Research and Technology*, 26(6), 891–897.

12. Birkenfeld, J. S., Tucker-Schwartz, J. M., Soenksen, L. R., Avilés-Izquierdo, J. A., & Marti-Fuster, B. (2020). Computer-aided classification of suspicious pigmented lesions using wide-field images. *Computer Methods and Programs in Biomedicine*, 195, 105631.

13. Kasmi, R., & Mokrani, K. (2016). Classification of malignant melanoma and benign skin lesions: Implementation of automatic ABCD rule. *IET Image Processing*, 10(6), 448–455.

14. Ng, V., & Cheung, D. (1997, October). Measuring asymmetries of skin lesions. In *1997 IEEE International Conference on Systems, Man, and Cybernetics. Computational Cybernetics and Simulation* (Vol. 5, pp. 4211–4216). IEEE, Orlando, FL.

15. Umbaugh, S. E., Moss, R. H., & Stoecker, W. V. (1989). Automatic color segmentation of images with application to detection of variegated coloring in skin tumors. *IEEE Engineering in Medicine and Biology Magazine*, 8(4), 43–50.

16. Zaqout, I. (2019). Diagnosis of skin lesions based on dermoscopic images using image processing techniques. *Pattern Recognition-Selected Methods and Applications*, Andrzej Zak (Ed.) (pp. 77–94). DOI: 10.5772/intechopen.88065

17. Yoshida, T., Celebi, M. E., Schaefer, G., & Iyatomi, H. (2016, December). Simple and effective pre-processing for automated melanoma discrimination based on cytological findings. In *2016 IEEE International Conference on Big Data (Big Data)* (pp. 3439–3442). IEEE, Washington, DC.

18. Jayaraman, P., Veeramani, N., Krishankumar, R., Ravichandran, K. S., Cavallaro, F., Rani, P., & Mardani, A. (2022). Wavelet-based classification of enhanced melanoma skin lesions through deep neural architectures. *Information*, 13(12), 583.

19. Pathan, S., Aggarwal, V., Prabhu, K. G., & Siddalingaswamy, P. C. (2019). Melanoma detection in dermoscopic images using color features. *Biomedical and Pharmacology Journal*, 12(1), 107–115.

20. Yang, S., Xiao, W., Zhang, M., Guo, S., Zhao, J., & Shen, F. (2022). Image Data Augmentation for Deep Learning: A Survey. arXiv preprint arXiv:2204.08610.

21. Aarthi, S., Geetha, K., Premaladha, J., & Nirmala, V. (2022, March). Medical color image encryption using chaotic framework and AES through Poisson regression model. In *2022 International Conference on Wireless Communications Signal Processing and Networking (WiSPNET)* (pp. 316–321). IEEE, Chennai.

22. Monisha, M, Suresh, A, Bapu, B. R., & Rashmi, M. R. (2019). Classification of malignant melanoma and benign skin lesion by using back propagation neural network and ABCD rule. *Cluster Computing*, 22(5), 12897–12907. https://doi.org/10.1007/s10586-018-1798-7.

23. Glorindal, G., Mozhiselvi, S. A., Kumar, T. A., Kumaran, K., Katema, P. C., & Kandimba, T. (2021, July). A simplified approach for melanoma skin disease identification. In *2021 International Conference on System, Computation, Automation and Networking (ICSCAN)* (pp. 1–5). IEEE, Puducherry.

24. Li, H., Pan, Y., Zhao, J., & Zhang, L. (2021). Skin disease diagnosis with deep learning: A review. *Neurocomputing*, 464, 364–393.

25. Tschandl, P., Codella, N., Akay, B. N., Argenziano, G., Braun, R. P., Cabo, H., ... & Kittler, H. (2019). Comparison of the accuracy of human readers versus machine-learning algorithms for pigmented skin lesion classification: An open, web-based, international, diagnostic study. *The Lancet Oncology*, 20(7), 938–947.

26. Ali, A. R., Li, J., & O'Shea, S. J. (2020). Towards the automatic detection of skin lesion shape asymmetry, color variegation and diameter in dermoscopic images. *Plos One*, 15(6), e0234352.

27. Khatami, A., Mirghasemi, S., Khosravi, A., Lim, C. P., Asadi, H., & Nahavandi, S. (2017, November). A swarm optimization-based kmedoids clustering technique for extracting melanoma cancer features. In *International Conference on Neural Information Processing* (pp. 307–316). Springer, Cham.

28. Cassidy, B., Kendrick, C., Brodzicki, A., Jaworek-Korjakowska, J., & Yap, M. H. (2022). Analysis of the ISIC image datasets: Usage, benchmarks and recommendations. *Medical Image Analysis*, 75, 102305.

29. Jojoa Acosta, M. F., Caballero Tovar, L. Y., Garcia-Zapirain, M. B., & Percybrooks, W. S. (2021). Melanoma diagnosis using deep learning techniques on dermatoscopic images. *BMC Medical Imaging*, 21(1), 1–11.

6 Comparative Study of CNN and LSTM-Based Hand Gesture Classification Using EMG Signals

Neenu R.
APJ Abdul Kalam Technological University

Geevarghese Titus
Amal Jyothi College of Engineering

CONTENTS

6.1 INTRODUCTION: BACKGROUND AND DRIVING FORCES

Gesture means a form of non-verbal communication in which a message is conveyed using movements of body parts like arms, hands, head, and face. Human gestures are a natural mode of communication that is more efficient than any other mode of interaction. Even though the origin of gestures can be of any body part, most of them are produced by the movements of the hand or face. In this literature, the main focus is

DOI: 10.1201/9781003307778-7

given to hand gesture recognition (HGR). Gesture recognition means identifying the meaning of the gesture performed by a person. A gesture recognition system should be able to identify what gesture is performed and when a gesture is performed. HGR systems have applications in various areas like human–computer interaction, sign language recognition, medical diagnosis, robotics, and virtual reality.

Over the years, different technologies have been developed for HGR. Among them, one of the earliest technologies is the data glove that can be worn on the hand. It contains various sensors like motion trackers to track the position or rotation of the data glove. Vision-based systems, which use algorithms based on computer vision methods to detect gestures from images captured using different types of cameras, are one of the most prominent HGR methods nowadays. Various other methods have also been developed, which use sensors like electromyographic sensors, acoustic sensors, accelerometers, and gyroscopes to identify gestures. The primary focus of this work is on HGR using electromyographic sensors.

Electromyography (EMG) is a diagnostic tool to evaluate and record the electrical signals emitted by skeletal muscles. The EMG signals are the electrical currents generated by the contractions of muscles, representing their neuromuscular activities. Like any other biomedical signal, an EMG signal is a function of time and can be represented in terms of its amplitude, frequency, and phase. EMG signals have proved to be a very effective method for HGR and can be used efficiently for human–computer interaction. They can also be used for controlling prosthetic devices like prosthetic hands, arms, and lower limbs. The major advantage of EMG-based HGR systems is that even upper-arm amputees can interact with computer systems, which is not possible in all other approaches.

Earlier HGR systems used machine learning (ML) models like K-nearest neighbor (KNN), support vector machine (SVM), random forests, and artificial neural network (ANN) for feature extraction and classification of gestures. But with the advancement of deep learning (DL) techniques, ML models are replaced with models like convolutional neural network (CNN), long short-term memory (LSTM), and Bi-LSTM. This work explores two basic DL models for the classification of gestures. The subsequent sections aim to throw light on the different processes involved in EMG-based HGR recognition followed by a detailed study of two prominent DL techniques CNN and LSTM for the classification of electromyographic signals.

6.2 EMG-BASED HGR SYSTEMS

6.2.1 DATASETS

There are many publicly available benchmark datasets that can be used for testing and training EMG-based HGR systems. Ninapro, UCI ML repository, and Kaggle are some of the most widely used repositories. This study uses the Ninapro datasets for training and testing the models. The repository provides different datasets, and we have used DB1 for the proposed work. The dataset which includes 10 repetitions of 52 different hand gestures performed by 27 subjects is detailed in Ref. [1]. The 52 movements include movements of fingers (12) and wrist (9), hand postures (8), and grasping and functional movements (23).

6.2.2 Generic System

An EMG-based HGR system mainly consists of modules for preprocessing, segmentation, feature extraction, and classification. Figure 6.1 shows a block diagram of an EMG-based system.

6.2.3 Preprocessing

The preprocessing module is responsible for noise removal from the signal. EMG measurements measure the performance of a group of muscles. The output of an sEMG sensor is a sum of the motor action potentials from the muscles being analyzed and may be affected by interference from nearby muscles.

The different sources of noise in an EMG signal include electrical noise from power lines and external sources, motion artifacts caused by the relative movement of the sensors, cross-talk contamination caused by the superimposition of signals from neighboring muscles, and physiological noises originating from tissues and other than muscles that generate electrical signals such as ECG and EOG signals [2,3].

Some of the techniques used in EMG noise reduction include digital filters, canonical correlation analysis (CCA), higher-order statistics (HOS), adaptive filters, principal component analysis (PCA), independent component analysis (ICA), and signal decomposition techniques.

CCA is a prominent method used in blind source separation (Figure 6.2). CCA is a statistical technique that is used to identify the correlation between two sets of data. In Ref. [4], CCA was used for denoising sEMG signals. In the proposed method, the canonical components (variates) derived from the raw sEMG signal by applying the CCA algorithm are ranked higher to lower delayed autocorrelation. The components having high correlation will be retained and those with correlation coefficients

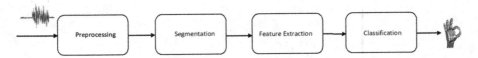

FIGURE 6.1 Block diagram of an EMG-based HGR system.

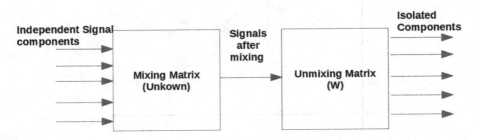

FIGURE 6.2 Blind source separation (BSS) techniques find out the optimal matrix *W*, which can separate the original components without much distortion.

less than a specific threshold (based on intensity ratio) are considered noise and are removed.

HOS methods have been proven efficient in identifying signals with non-Gaussian and non-linear behavior. Lots of information can be obtained from the higher-order moments and cumulants (third-order to Nth-order) and their spectral representation (higher-order spectra). As HOS are capable of recovering information about non-Gaussian signals, they can be used in systems involving non-Gaussian input signals as in EMG [5].

Adaptive filtering techniques can be used effectively to remove ECG components from EMG signals [6,7]. Various optimization algorithms like Ant Colony Optimization (ACO), Particle Swarm Optimization (PSO), Artificial Bee Colony, Cuckoo search, Squirrel Search, and Gray Wolf optimization are used by adaptive filters to adjust the coefficients of the filter [8,9].

PCA is a non-parametric, statistical technique that is used to reduce the dimensionality of the data (Figure 6.3). This is achieved by translating an extremely large set of correlated variables into a few variables known as 'principal components', without affecting the statistical property of the data, namely the variability. PCA can be used in various stages of signal processing like dimensionality reduction, noise removal, and feature extraction. In sEMG noise reduction techniques, the initial principal components having large variance are assumed to be related to the MUAP signals from the muscles and those components with minimum variance are considered noise [10].

ICA is a statistical method that is used to extract an original signal from a mixture of signals. It is one of the most powerful methods used in EMG signal filtering. The method assumes that the subcomponents are independent of each other and that

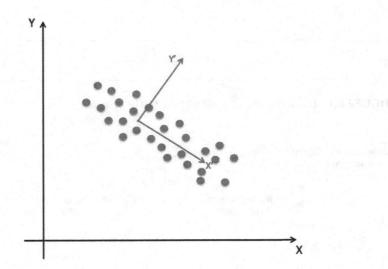

FIGURE 6.3 PCA. The principal component is the direction that has the maximum variance. Here X and Y represent the principal components.

they are non-Gaussian signals [11]. Well-known algorithms for ICA include info-max, FastICA, Joint Approximate Diagonalization of Eigen-matrices (JADE), and kernel-ICA.

The most effective and widely used technique in noise filtering of 1D signals is the signal decomposition technique. It is the process of breaking down a complex signal into simple components which are similar but independent of each other. The original signal can be reproduced by combining these components. Some of the commonly used decomposition techniques include singular value decomposition, empirical mode decomposition, discrete wavelet transform (DWT), wavelet packet decomposition (WPD), and variational mode decomposition.

In the past few decades, we have seen the influence of different types of neural networks in solving various problems. Literature has proved the effectiveness of neural in filtering noise from sEMG signals also. The filtering problem is a type of function approximation problem in which the function values are represented using time series and can be solved using neural networks. Different variations of neural networks like fully recurrent networks, Jordan networks, multilayer perceptron approach, Elman neural networks, radial basis function, and focused time lagged recurrent neural networks can be used to perform noise reduction in sEMG signals [12].

6.2.4 SEGMENTATION

After the preprocessing stage datasets are divided into segments. A time slot for extracting the required features from a signal is termed a segment. According to Ref. [13], to handle real-time scenarios, the total duration should be within 300 ms. This duration should encompass the length of the next segment along with the processing time for generating the specific control commands. As a general observation, it can be seen that the time required for processing is often less than 50 ms, and the segment duration varies between 32 and 250 ms. Segmentation is normally performed using the windowing technique. The two main techniques used in windowing are adjacent windowing and overlapped windowing. In adjacent windowing, fixed-length disjoint segments are selected whereas in overlapped windowing, the segments selected overlap.

6.2.5 FEATURE EXTRACTION

In the classification of EMG signals, the types of features extracted make a major contribution to the classification accuracy. The features can be classified as time-domain features, frequency-domain features, and time-frequency-domain features. Some of the widely used time-domain features include root mean square, mean absolute value, variance, waveform length, and zero crossing. Frequency-domain features include mean frequency, median frequency, peak frequency, mean power, and total power. DWT, continuous wavelet transform, empirical mode decomposition, and WPT are some of the techniques used to extract time-frequency-domain features [14].

6.2.6 Classification

Over the years, different researchers have used different classification models for HGR recognition using EMG signals. Various ML techniques like ANN, SVM, KNN, and decision trees have been used by different researchers for classification in earlier years. Later, with the advancement in DL techniques, ML techniques were replaced with DL techniques like CNNs, recurrent neural networks (RNNs), and LSTM networks. Section 6.3 focuses on the research done in this area over the past years.

6.3 RELATED WORKS

As discussed in the previous section, HGR-based research is progressing at a relatively fast pace. Most of these computer vision models employ various ML- and DL-based systems like SVM and CNN for the classification of HGR images [15–18]. Gesture recognition systems using impulse radio signals are another area of research [19]. Some of the research also focuses on skeleton-based gesture recognition systems that use DL models like CNN, RNN, and LSTM for classification [20,21].

Some of the pioneering work in HGR includes the classification of EMG signals using ANN [22–24]. In Ref. [25], the effects of using a genetic algorithm for feature selection (FS) and dimensionality reduction in EMG classification were analyzed. A model which uses the combination of the Hidden Markov Model, genetic algorithm, and multilayer perceptron for EMG classification is proposed in Ref. [26]. Researchers also used fuzzy-based approaches, which replaced the ANN layer with a fuzzy inference system [27,28]. ML models like SVM, KNN, and decision trees were also used to perform HGR [14,29,30]. The performance of ANNs and LDA for hand movement classification for multiple EMG datasets were analyzed in Ref. [31]. According to the work, ANN works better than LDA for the recognition of hand movements. A framework that combines logarithmic spectrogram-based graph signal (LSGS), AdaBoost k-means (AB-k-means), and an ensemble of FS techniques have been discussed in Ref. [32]. EMG signals are collected using two channels, and feature extraction was performed using the LSGS model and an ensemble FS performed FS. The selected features were classified into different hand grasps using AB-k-means.

With the advancement of technology, ML models are being replaced by DL models. A CNN model for hand movement prediction is proposed in Ref. [33]. The CNN architecture includes an input layer, four convolutional layers, four subsampling layers, and two fully connected layers along with a dropout. The model improved the accuracy of classification over conventional ML methods. A 15-layered CNN has been designed for the classification of sEMG signals in Ref. [34]. The model's performance is analyzed for different hyperparameters like learning rate and no of epochs. A CNN-based robotic arm that does not require relearning even after being reseated is discussed in Ref. [35]. In Ref. [36], a fully connected feed-forward deep neural network based classification system was proposed in which the time-domain power spectral descriptors is used as the contributing feature in the feature space.

A combined feature approach method, in which features derived from time-spectral analysis and deep features from a CNN are combined to form a feature vector for the classification of EMG signals obtained from a single-channel device [37]. The feature vector was then classified using a multilayer perceptron classifier.

A model using RNNs was developed for the real-time classification of EMG signals, and features were extracted from a hybrid time-frequency domain [38]. An HGR model using R-CNN. Feature extraction is done using the WPT proposed in Ref. [39].

An EMG classification model using LSTM networks, where four different feature sets were extracted and fed to LSTM [40]. Performance evaluation of different variants of neural networks such as feed-forward neural networks, RNN, LSTM, and a gated recurrent unit (GRU) to classify hand gesture–based features extracted from EMG of the forearm muscles is focused by Ref. [41].

A hybrid model with four CNN and two Bi-LSTM networks was developed by Ref. [42]. The model was also analyzed with different RNNs like LSTN, GRU, Bi-GRU, RNN, and Bi-RNN.

Image processing–aided DL approach for the detection and classification of hand movement from EMG signals is discussed in Ref. [43]. The model initially chose two references of either hand for a movement, which is later used to compute the 2D cross-spectrum employing the cross-wavelet transform for the subsequent data. This 2D spectrum representation is given as input to a pretrained CNN for performing the gesture classification task.

6.4 CONVOLUTIONAL NEURAL NETWORK

A CNN is a form of multilayer ANN. CNNs are designed mainly to handle grid-structured input which has strong spatial dependencies. CNN proved to be very effective in handling time series data. Each layer in the network is a three-dimensional structure, which has a height, width, and depth. Here, depth means the number of input channels.

The input EMG images in the study are obtained by windowing operation with a window length of 150 ms with 90 ms overlap. The signal is sampled at 100 Hz. Thus, the size of the input image is 15×10 where 10 is the number of channels. The CNN model used is based on the architecture proposed by Ref. [44]. The architecture mainly consists of five blocks that perform convolution 2D operations on the input as shown in Figure 6.4.

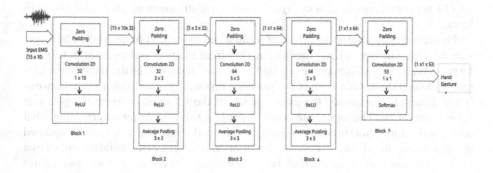

FIGURE 6.4 The CNN model for sEMG classification.

Convolution Layer: The main building block in a CNN is the convolution layer. This layer is responsible for most of the computations in the network. In the convolution process, a kernel (filter) will scan the input matrix for the presence of features. The kernel is a 2D matrix of weights that walk over the input image performing a dot product between the input matrix and the kernel. The output is called a feature map. The depth of the output is determined by the number of filters. For example, in block 1 of the model, 32 filters of size 1×10 are applied on the input image of size 15×10, which produces a feature map of size $15 \times 10 \times 32$. Zero padding is applied to maintain the original input dimension.

ReLu layer: This layer helps to increase the non-linearity in the output by applying a rectifier function on the output of the convolution layer.

Pooling layer: This layer performs dimensionality reduction and reduces the number of parameters in the input. Maximum pooling and average pooling are the two main types of pooling. This layer is responsible for complexity reduction, efficiency improvement, and limits the risk of overfitting. In the model illustrated in Figure 6.4, average pooling is used.

Softmax layer: This layer performs the classification based on the features extracted in the previous layers. It outputs a probability distribution representing the probability of each gesture class. The gesture with the highest probability will be taken as the output.

6.5   LONG SHORT-TERM MEMORY

RNNs are adaptations of ANNs with feedback connections so that the output of the present cycle depends on the output obtained in the previous cycle. RNNs are capable of storing short-term dependencies only. Also, there is no control over which part of the context should be forwarded and how much to be forgotten.

LSTM networks are advanced versions of RNNs, which are capable of handling long-term dependencies. It solves the vanishing gradient problem in RNNS. Like other RNNs, LSTM also has the form of a chain of repeating modules which are called gated cells. These gated cells consist of different layers that communicate with one another to generate the output of that cell along with the cell state. Both the output and cell state are then passed to the next hidden layer. A gated cell in the LSTM network consists of four layers – three logistic sigmoid gates and one tanh layer.

Figure 6.5 shows the architecture of a gated cell in the LSTM network. The forget gate decides whether to keep the information from the previous cycle or not. In the forget gate, a sigmoid function is applied to the weighted sum of the input in the current cycle and the hidden state of the previous timestamp. It outputs a value between 0 and 1, which determines the extent to which the information from the previous cycle is forgotten. The input gate is the one that is responsible for determining what additional information needs to be stored in the cell state. The values to be updated are decided by the sigmoid layer and the creation of a vector of candidate values that could be added is done by the tanh layer. The input gate combines these two values to update the state. The output gate decides which part of the cell state will be present in the output. The new information that is passed to the next cell state is obtained

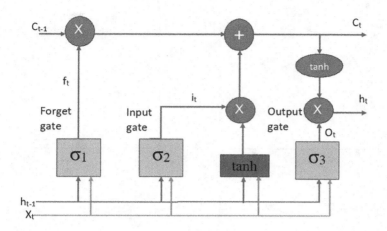

FIGURE 6.5 Architecture of a gated cell in LSTM.

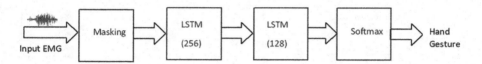

FIGURE 6.6 Architecture of two-layer LSTM model.

by applying the tanh activation function on a function of hidden state at the previous time step $t - 1$ and input at time step t.

Figure 6.6 shows the LSTM model used in this work. Two LSTM models are arranged sequentially. A masking layer is applied before LSTM layers to handle the variable length inputs. The output of the second LSTM is given to a fully connected Softmax layer for classification.

6.6 RESULTS AND DISCUSSION

Both the CNNs and LSTM networks were implemented with the Keras library using the Tensorflow background and were trained and tested. To evaluate the performance for different conditions like variation of computation cost, and accuracy, both the models were trained for different epochs.

From Figure 6.7a, it can be seen that the CNN model obtained 97% training accuracy, but the testing accuracy of the model dropped to about 67%. In the plot, the scale of the y-axis is normalized and takes values in the range of 0 and 1. To validate if there would be any variation in the accuracy for larger epochs, the performance of the model was studied by changing the number of epochs to 50, but still, the problem exists. The possible cause for the reduction in testing accuracy may be due to overfitting of the model. Adding dropout layers may help to reduce the overfitting problem.

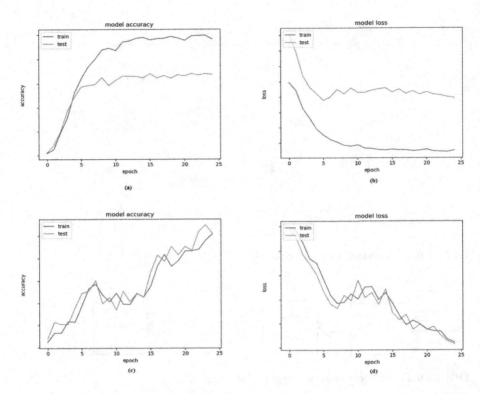

FIGURE 6.7   Variation in model accuracy and loss during training and testing of CNN model (a and b) and LSTM model (c and d) for 25 epochs.

The model may give better results by selecting different kernel sizes. Also, the model fails to classify inter-subject gestures.

The LSTM model was studied using a single LSTM layer and a double LSTM layer. And the latter one performed better. Figure 6.8 shows the accuracy of both models obtained after 10 epochs. While single-layer LSTM could obtain less than 7% accuracy, double-layer LSTM obtained more than 30% accuracy after 10 epochs.

The two-layer LSTM model illustrated in Figure 6.7 obtained training accuracy slightly lesser than the CNN model, but the model could give a stable performance during both training and testing. The graphs showing the variations in accuracy and loss of both the CNN and LSTM model are shown in Figure 6.7.

Also, the performance of the double-layer LSTM model was studied by changing the number of gated cells in the first layer from 128 to 256. The accuracy of single-layer and double-layer LSTM model for 10 epochs is depicted in Figure 6.8. Figure 6.9 shows the variation in accuracy of the two models after 25 epochs. Increasing the gated cells had a positive impact on the model performance in terms of accuracy, as seen in Figure 6.9. But the downside is the extremely high computational complexity in terms of space and time. This could greatly affect the usage of LSTM-based models for real-time applications.

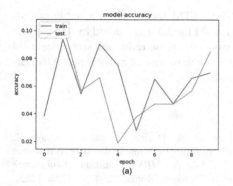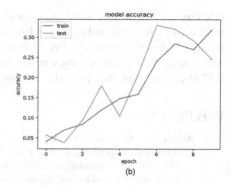

FIGURE 6.8 Accuracy of single-layer and double-layer LSTM models for ten epochs. (a) Single-layer LSTM. (b) Double-layer LSTM.

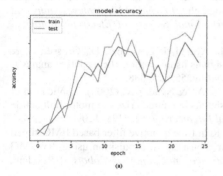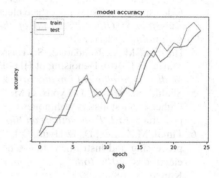

FIGURE 6.9 Accuracy of double-layer LSTM with (a) 128 gated cells in layer 1 and (b) 256 gated cells in layer 1.

The training time taken by the LSTM models is much higher than that taken by the CNN model. Also, as the number of parameters increases the system configurations needed for training the model also should be improved. Throughout this study, the models were trained and tested using subject-specific gestures. The performance of the model is not good when inter-subject gestures are used. Also, when noisy signals are given as input, the performance of both models deteriorates. Some mechanisms to improve the system performance would be to improvise the model's architecture, by adjusting and fine-tuning various hyperparameters, by incorporating more convolution layers, kernel function refinement, and checking the effectiveness of a Leaky ReLU layer.

6.7 CONCLUSION

In this work, the various stages of EMG signal classification are studied and two basic DL models are compared. Even though the CNN model gives a slightly greater accuracy than the LSTM model, the variation in training and testing accuracy of

CNN is very high and is not acceptable. The LSTM model gives a stable performance while training and testing. Also, the LSTM model was studied by varying the number of layers and gated units. In future work, the noise reduction strategies need to be focused on as the accuracy of the model is low in case of noisy input. Also, Bi-LSTM can be tried instead of the current model.

REFERENCES

1. Atzori, M., Gijsberts, A., Heynen, S., Hager, A.M., Deriaz, O., van der Smagt, P., Castellini, C., Caputo, B., & Muller, H. (2012). Building the Ninapro database: A resource for the biorobotics community. *2012 4th IEEE RAS & EMBS International Conference on Biomedical Robotics and Biomechatronics (BioRob)*, (Roma, Italy), pp. 1258–1265.
2. Chowdhury, R.H., Reaz, M.B., Ali, M.A., Bakar, A.A., Chellappan, K., & Chang, T.G. (2013). Surface electromyography signal processing and classification techniques. *Sensors (Basel, Switzerland)*, 13, 12431–12466.
3. Clancy, E.A., Morin, E.L., & Merletti, R. (2002). Sampling, noise-reduction and amplitude estimation issues in surface electromyography. *Journal of Electromyography and Kinesiology: Official Journal of the International Society of Electrophysiological Kinesiology*, 12(1), 1–16.
4. Harrach, M.A., Boudaoud, S., Hassan, M., Ayachi, F.S., Gamet, D., Grosset, J., & Marin, F. (2016). Denoising of HD-sEMG signals using canonical correlation analysis. *Medical & Biological Engineering & Computing*, 55, 375–388.
5. Shahid, S., Walker, J., Lyons, G.M., Byrne, C.A., & Nene, A.V. (2005). Application of higher order statistics techniques to EMG signals to characterize the motor unit action potential. *IEEE Transactions on Biomedical Engineering*, 52, 1195–1209.
6. Jamal, M.Z., Lee, D., & Hyun, D.J. (2019). Real time adaptive filter based EMG signal processing and instrumentation scheme for robust signal acquisition using dry EMG electrodes. *2019 16th International Conference on Ubiquitous Robots (UR)*, (Jeju, Korea), pp. 683–688.
7. Marque, C., Bisch, C., Dantas, R., Elayoubi, S., Brosse, V., & Pérot, C. (2005). Adaptive filtering for ECG rejection from surface EMG recordings. *Journal of Electromyography and Kinesiology: Official Journal of the International Society of Electrophysiological Kinesiology*, 15(3), 310–315.
8. Nagasirisha, B., & Prasad, V.V. (2020). Noise removal from EMG signal using adaptive enhanced squirrel search algorithm. *Fluctuation and Noise Letters*, 19(04), 2050039.
9. Verma, A.R., & Gupta, B. (2019). A novel approach adaptive filtering method for electromyogram signal using Gray Wolf optimization algorithm. *SN Applied Sciences*, 2(1), 16.
10. Naik, G.R., Selvan, S.E., Gobbo, M., Acharyya, A., & Nguyen, H.T. (2016). Principal component analysis applied to surface electromyography: A comprehensive review. *IEEE Access*, 4, 4025–4037.
11. Heistermann, T., Janke, M., Wand, M., Schulte, C., & Rabe, D. (2013). Decomposition of multichannel electromyographic signals for a silent speech interface. Bachelorarbeit, Karlsruhe Institute of Technology (KIT), Germany.
12. Kale, S.N., & Dudul, D.V. (2009). Intelligent noise removal from EMG signal using focused time-lagged recurrent neural network. *Applied Computational Intelligence and Soft Computing*, 2009, 129761: 1–129761: 12.
13. Oskoei, M.A., & Hu, H. (2007). Myoelectric control systems - A survey. *Biomedical Signal Processing and Control*, 2, 275–294.
14. Nazmi, N., Rahman, M.A., Yamamoto, S., Ahmad, S.A., Zamzuri, H., & Mazlan, S.A. (2016). A review of classification techniques of EMG signals during isotonic and isometric contractions. *Sensors (Basel, Switzerland)*, 16, 1304.

15. Parvathy, P., Subramaniam, K., Prasanna Venkatesan, G., Karthikaikumar, P., Varghese, J., & Jayasankar, T. (2020). Development of hand gesture recognition system using machine learning. *Journal of Ambient Intelligence and Humanized Computing*, 12(6), 6793–6800.

16. Gadekallu, T.R., Srivastava, G., Liyanage, M., Meenakshisundaram, I., Chowdhary, C.L., Koppu, S., & Maddikunta, P.K. (2022). Hand gesture recognition based on a Harris Hawks optimized convolution neural network. *Computers and Electrical Engineering*, 100, 107836.

17. Oyedotun, O.K., & Khashman, A. (2017). Deep learning in vision-based static hand gesture recognition. *Neural Computing and Applications*, 28(12), 3941–3951.

18. Sharma, S., & Singh, S. (2021). Vision-based hand gesture recognition using deep learning for the interpretation of sign language. *Expert Systems with Applications*, 182, 115657.

19. Kim, S.Y., Han, H.G., Kim, J.W., Lee, S., & Kim, T.W. (2017). A hand gesture recognition sensor using reflected impulses. *IEEE Sensors Journal*, 17(10), 2975–2976.

20. Núñez, J.C., Cabido, R., Pantrigo, J.J., Montemayor, A.S., & Vélez, J.F. (2018). Convolutional Neural Networks and Long Short-Term Memory for skeleton-based human activity and hand gesture recognition. *Pattern Recognition*, 76, 80–94.

21. Lai, K., & Yanushkevich, S.N. (2018). CNN+RNN depth and skeleton based dynamic hand gesture recognition. *2018 24th International Conference on Pattern Recognition (ICPR)*, (Beijing, China), pp. 3451–3456.

22. Hiraiwa, A., Shimohara, K., & Tokunaga, Y. (1989). EMG pattern analysis and classification by neural network. *Conference Proceedings, IEEE International Conference on Systems, Man and Cybernetics*, (Cambridge, MA), pp. 1113–1115, vol. 3.

23. Kelly, M., Parker, P.A., & Scott, R.N. (1991). Neural network classification of myoelectric signal for prosthesis control. *Journal of Electromyography and Kinesiology: Official Journal of the International Society of Electrophysiological Kinesiology*, 1(4), 229–236.

24. Lee, K.H., Min, J.Y., & Byun, S. (2022). Electromyogram-based classification of hand and finger gestures using artificial neural networks, *Sensors*, 22(1), 225.

25. Jain, R., & Garg, V.K. (2021). EMG classification using nature-inspired computing and neural architecture. *2021 9th International Conference on Reliability, Infocom Technologies and Optimization (Trends and Future Directions)* (ICRITO), (Noida, India), pp. 1–5.

26. Kwon, J., Lee, S., Shin, C., Jang, Y.G., & Hong, S. (1998). Signal hybrid HMM-GA-MLP classifier for continuous EMG classification purpose. *Proceedings of the 20th Annual International Conference of the IEEE Engineering in Medicine and Biology Society*, (Hong Kong, China), Vol. 20 Biomedical Engineering towards the Year 2000 and Beyond (Cat. No.98CH36286), 3, pp. 1404–1407, vol. 3.

27. Chan, F.H.Y., Yang, Y.-S., Lam, F.K., Zhang, Y.-T., & Parker, P.A. (2000). Fuzzy EMG classification for prosthesis control. *IEEE Transactions on Rehabilitation Engineering*, 8, 305–311.

28. Hussein, S.E., & Granat, M.H. (2002). Intention detection using a neuro-fuzzy EMG classifier. *IEEE Engineering in Medicine and Biology Magazine*, 21, 123–129.

29. Alkan, A., & Günay, M. (2012). Identification of EMG signals using discriminant analysis and SVM classifier. *Expert Systems with Applications*, 39, 44–47.

30. Rabin, N., Kahlon, M., Malayev, S., & Ratnovsky, A. (2020). Classification of human hand movements based on EMG signals using nonlinear dimensionality reduction and data fusion techniques. *Expert Systems with Applications*, 149, 113281.

31. Saeed, B., Zia-Ur-Rehman, M., Gilani, S.O., Amin, F., Waris, A., Jamil, M., & Shafique, M. (2020). Leveraging ANN and LDA classifiers for characterizing different hand movements using EMG signals. *Arabian Journal for Science and Engineering*, 46, 1761–1769.

32. Miften, F.S., Diykh, M., Abdulla, S., Siuly, S., Green, J.H., & Deo, R.C. (2021). A new framework for classification of multi-category hand grasps using EMG signals. *Artificial Intelligence in Medicine*, 112, 102005, ISSN 0933-3657.

33. Park, K.-H and Lee, S.-W. (2016). Movement intention decoding based on deep learning for multiuser myoelectric interfaces. *2016 4th International Winter Conference on Brain-Computer Interface (BCI)*, (Gangwon-do, South Korea), pp. 1–2.

34. Asif, A.R., Waris, A., Gilani, S.O., Jamil, M., Ashraf, H., Shafique, M., & Niazi, I.K. (2020). Performance evaluation of convolutional neural network for hand gesture recognition using EMG. *Sensors (Basel)*, 20(6), 1642.

35. Yamanoi, Y., Ogiri, Y., & Kato, R. (2020). EMG-based posture classification using a convolutional neural network for a myoelectric hand. *Biomedical Signal Processing and Control*, 55, 101574.

36. Mukhopadhyay, A.K., & Samui, S. (2020). An experimental study on upper limb position invariant EMG signal classification based on deep neural network. *Biomedical Signal Processing and Control*, 55, 101669.

37. Fajardo, J.M., Gomez, O., & Prieto, F. (2021). EMG hand gesture classification using handcrafted and deep features. *Biomedical Signal Processing and Control*, 63, 102210, ISSN 1746-8094.

38. Azhiri, R.B., Esmaeili, M., & Nourani, M. (2021). Real-time EMG signal classification via recurrent neural networks. *2021 IEEE International Conference on Bioinformatics and Biomedicine (BIBM)*, (Virtual Conference), 2628–2635.

39. Vimal, S., Robinson, Y.H., Khan, M.S., Khari, M., & Gandomi, A.H. (2020). R-CNN and wavelet feature extraction for hand gesture recognition with EMG signals. *Neural Computing and Applications*, 32, 16723–16736.

40. Jabbari, M., Khushaba, R.N., & Nazarpour, K. (2020). EMG-based hand gesture classification with long short-term memory deep recurrent neural networks. *2020 42nd Annual International Conference of the IEEE Engineering in Medicine & Biology Society (EMBC)*, (Virtual), pp. 3302–3305.

41. Simão, M.A., Neto, P., & Gibaru, O. (2019). EMG-based online classification of gestures with recurrent neural networks. *Pattern Recognition Letters*, 128, 45–51.

42. Karnam, N.K., Dubey, S.R., Turlapaty, A., & Gokaraju, B. (2022). EMGHandNet: A hybrid CNN and Bi-LSTM architecture for hand activity classification using surface EMG signals. *Biocybernetics and Biomedical Engineering*, 42(1), 325–340.

43. Roy, S.S., Samanta, K., Chatterjee, S., Dey, S., Nandi, A., Bhowmik, R., & Mondal, S. (2020). Hand movement recognition using cross spectrum image analysis of EMG signals-A deep learning approach. *2020 National Conference on Emerging Trends on Sustainable Technology and Engineering Applications (NCETSTEA)*, (Durgapur, India) pp. 1–5.

44. Tsinganos, P., Cornelis, B., Cornelis, J., Jansen, B., & Skodras, A. N. (2018). Deep learning in EMG-based gesture recognition. *PhyCS*, pp. 107–114

7 Improved Transfer Learning-Enabled Heuristic Technique for Pneumonia Detection on Graphical Processing Unit Platform

Abubeker K. M., S. Baskar,
C. Prajitha, and K. P. Sridhar
Karpagam Academy of Higher Education

CONTENTS

7.1 INTRODUCTION

Pneumonia may be caused by bacteria, viruses, or fungus and is an acute respiratory infection that can affect either or both lungs. Alveoli, or air sacs, become inflamed and stuffed with pus and fluid in a patient with pneumonia, making it difficult for them to breathe. According to the World Health Organization (WHO), 14% of all deaths in children less than 5% and 22% in children between the ages of 1 and 5 are caused by pneumonia. Vaccination, healthy food habits, and optimizing environmental conditions all have a role in warding off this disease. Antibiotics are effective against bacterial pneumonia. Pneumonia caused by viruses and bacteria has similar signs and symptoms. However, there may be more signs of viral pneumonia than

DOI: 10.1201/9781003307778-8

bacterial pneumonia. When inhaled, viruses and bacteria may cause pneumonia; however, fungi-induced pneumonia cannot be transmitted via the air.

Pneumonia is a potentially deadly disease that may affect anybody. Breathing problems, pleural effusion, bacteremia, and lung abscesses are all possible consequences, although they are more common in high-risk populations. Pre-existing lung disorders may make breathing more difficult, and treatment options may include oxygen therapy and healing support using a ventilator if necessary. Antibiotics may cure bacteremia, the blood infection caused by bacterial pneumonia. Lung abscess and pleural effusion are both treatable by draining the pus with a catheter or surgically removing the infected tissue. Aged individuals, young children, those with weakened immune systems, lung or heart illness, pregnant women, hospitalized patients, and others are at higher risk of acquiring pneumonia. When a patient is already sick and medications aren't working as well, hospital-acquired pneumonia might develop during their stay in the hospital, which can be quite dangerous. Patients reliant on mechanical ventilation are at a higher risk for developing a form of hospital-acquired infection known as ventilator-associated pneumonia. The illustration of transfer learning (TL) is depicted in Figure 7.1.

The first raw holds normal CXR images, and the second raw is pneumonia CXR images. The proposed TL approach has been classifying normal and pneumonia images effectively without false negatives. Jain et al. [2] evaluated different models for pneumonia detection from CXR images using TL. Convolutional neural networks (CNNs) like Inception-v3, ResNet50, VGG16 and VGG19, are trained to classify X-ray images, and VGG16 outperforming the others in terms of accuracy. Abbas et al. [3] created a consistent and efficient CNN system for medical image classification. Because of the irregularities in the image dataset, transferring learning approaches in medical images has a higher loss probability than general image recognition. The authors developed a novel DeTraC architecture based on class decomposition, enhancing precision, specificity, and sensitivity by allowing learning at the subclass level. Vermaa et al. [4] proposed a framework for distinguishing between

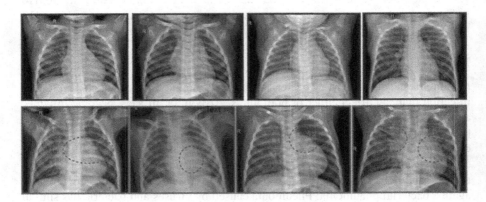

FIGURE 7.1 An illustration of transfer learning method identifies normal and pneumonia images trained and tested from the research dataset [1].

bacterial and viral pneumonia using a neural network classifier with remarkable accuracy. With pre-trained architectures such as AlexNet, ResNet18, DenseNet201, and SqueezeNet, a TL system for automated chest pneumonia detection from digital CXR is proposed. Rahman et al. [5] successfully distinguished between viral and bacterial pneumonia using DenseNet201 framework. Sai Kaushik et al. [6] developed a method for identifying COVID-19 pneumonia, bacterial, and viral pneumonia from CXR images using ResNet50-V2 CNN.

To diagnose chest X-rays, Dey et al. [7] propose a revised VGG19 architecture with superior accuracy in conjunction with a random forest classifier. An EFS scheme employs serial fusion and principal component analysis-based selection to select the primary feature set. Dina et al. [8] presented a multi-classification deep learning (DL) model for detecting lung cancer and pneumonia from CXR and CT images. The VGG19 model with CNN outperforms the other three ResNet models in their study. Wang et al. [9] model a non-invasive AI model for lung cancer diagnosis using CT images. A TL approach was used to create the model. The GPU module's role in real-time disease detection is addressed, and it can be used in the extensive application of medical image processing in several disciplines. DL developers are studied various algorithms for pneumonia detection, and the majority propose chest X-rays because of their popularity and low-cost imaging techniques [9,10]. The researchers, Bharati et al. [11] and Zhang et al. [12] have promising results and future for GPU-based implementation, and they have obtained good results with their dataset.

TL is a technique used in DL and machine learning (ML), and it involves transferring previously gained information from one model to another [13]. From a practical aspect, a reinforcement learning agent's sampling efficiency may be greatly improved by reusing or transferring knowledge from gained knowledge for the newly learned tasks. DL models need access to a huge dataset to solve a problem properly. Although it is not always the case where there are sufficient data, a pre-trained model for a related source task may be used to tackle the target job. The model is learned when the network is trained on a big dataset, which involves training all of the neural network's parameters. TL drastically reduces the time required to complete each task and expedites the process of creating multiple solutions. It also eliminates the need for a GPU and a separate Tensor Flow processing unit (TPU), which can be tedious and expensive to set up. The newly acquired dataset may be used to fine-tune the already-trained CNN. Weights from the pre-training dataset may be applied to the new dataset to extract features if the two datasets are sufficiently comparable. If the new dataset is tiny, it is recommended to train the last few layers of the network and leave the rest unaltered to prevent overfitting. The pre-trained network should, thus, have its last few levels removed. Make use of additional layers. If the new dataset is very big, it is best to retrain the whole network using the initial weights from the already trained model. The important advantage of this approach is that model consistency is increased with fewer validation data by adding weights to each layer. Furthermore, TL is a technique for accelerating neural network training and overcoming data scarcity [14]. After fine-tuning for numerous ML and CV use-cases, the pre-trained model is deployed in the interface platform. In a shorter amount of time, the GPU-based models can achieve high throughput and accuracy. The traditional ML versus TL method is depicted in Figure 7.2.

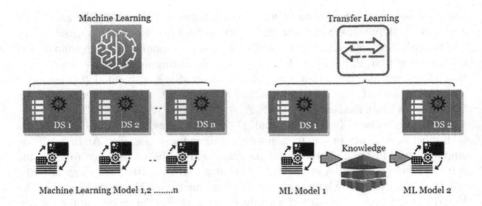

FIGURE 7.2   Traditional ML versus TL method.

Often, a DL model that has been pre-trained for a big and difficult image classification job like ImageNet is used. Available TL models for image processing include the VGG model developed at Oxford University, the Inception Model developed by Google, and the ResNet Model developed by Microsoft. Due to the enormous amount of images used in the training process, the model must effectively learn to extract features from images in order to solve the issue successfully. When it comes to saving time or improving efficiency, TL is an optimization. In most cases, it is not clear whether or not TL will be useful in the domain until after the model has been built and tested. To optimize the performance, TL models may outpace more conventional ML approaches much more quickly. This is due to the fact that models that rely upon the features, weights, etc., of other trained models already possess this information. It makes the process much quicker compared to when neural networks were trained from scratch.

The relation between traditional ML and TL approaches is seen in Figure 7.1. Both approaches use supervised learning, but the TL network is trained on various domains and source assignments and tailored to the specific area and mission. The multiple layers have frozen and fine-tuned by changing features like an optimizer and the number of epochs. Currently, supervised learning methods are replaced with TL methods and have become masters of ML and profound fields, particularly concerning medical imagery [15,16]. The philosophy of designing from scratch to using learned know-how practically to tackle other similar tasks is redeveloped. This new approach resolves the critical problems of computer vision and ML, primarily reducing the repetitive and long-lasting processing of samples. The control flow of TL method is depicted in Figure 7.3.

Obtaining a pre-trained model is the first stage in the TL method. Xception, VGG, ResNET, MobileNet, DenseNet, Inception, and EfficientNet are only a few of the resources of pre-trained models [17–19]. Layered architectures are the backbone of DL systems, allowing for understanding various features. Higher-level features are compiled in the first layers of the network and are further refined into finer characteristics as we go deeper into the network. The output of supervised learning

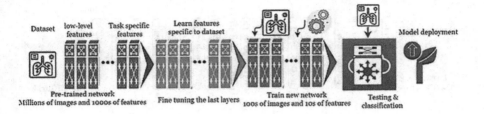

FIGURE 7.3   Control flow of transfer learning method.

consists of the connections between those layers, called a fully connected (FC) layer. This broadens the applicability of widely used pre-trained networks like the VGG model from Oxford, the Inception Model from Google, and the ResNet Model from Microsoft by removing their last layer as a fixed feature extractor. The broad nature of the pre-trained models is due to their training on a vast and diverse dataset. Feature extraction was accomplished by updating the weights of the pre-trained model during training with data pertinent to the current task. The first layers of a deep neural network are responsible for capturing high-level, abstract information. In contrast, the subsequent layers' narrow in on the particular task at hand by fine-tuning the base model's higher-order visual features. Some model layers are retrained, while others are held steady throughout training.

7.2   TRANSFER LEARNING–BASED APPROACH FOR PNEUMONIA DETECTION USING VGG16 DEEP LEARNING MODEL

VGG16 was first suggested in 2013 by Karen Simonyan and Andrew Zisserman of Oxford University. This model, built using a CNN, was presented into the ImageNet Large Scale Visual Recognition Challenge in 2014 (ILSVRC) [20]. The VGG16 model scores in the top five for accuracy by over 92.7% on the ImageNet dataset over roughly a thousand different categories. It was also among the most submitted models at ILSVRC-2014. Significant gains over AlexNet are achieved by sequentially applying a series of smaller 3 × 3 kernel-sized filters. For a considerable time (weeks), the VGG16 model was trained on Nvidia Titan Black GPUs. In addition, the 224 × 224 pixel input size is specified by the model. The VGG19 model often referred to as VGGNet-19, is similar to the VGG16 principle but includes the capability for 19 layers. VGG19 is thus three convolutional layers more advanced than VGG16, depicted in Figure 7.4.

The VGG16 has 16 layers in the network's deep neural architecture; this particular network includes a whopping 138 million parameters. However, the elegance of the VGGNet16 design lies in its apparent ease of use. Some convolution layers are used, and a pooling layer reduces the height and breadth. There are now roughly 64 usable filters, which may be increased to 128 and 256 with little work. It is possible to employ 512-bit filters in the final stages. Figure 7.4 depicts all 16 of VGG16's layers. The 16-layer design is divided into six sections. The first block consists of the following layers: a 3 × 3 convolution layer with a 64-node filter, a 3 × 3 max pooling layer; a

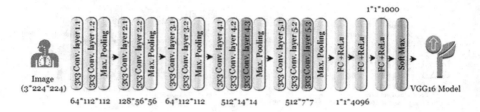

FIGURE 7.4 VGG16 architecture.

3×3 convolution layer with a 128-node filter, a 3×3 max pooling layer; a 3×3 convolution layer with a 512-node filter, a 3×3 max pooling layer; two FC layers totaling 4096 nodes. Even though VGG16 includes a total of 21 layers, only 16 of those layers are weights or layers with trainable parameters. VGG16 accepts 224×244 input tensors with three RGB channels. The design maintains a constant layout of convolution and max pooling layers with 2×2 filter of stride 2. There are 64 filters in the Conv-1.x layer, 128 in the Conv-2.x layer, 256 in the Conv-3.x layer, and 512 in the Conv-4.x and Conv-5.x layers, respectively. After a series of convolutional layers, three FC layers are used; the first two has 4096 channels each, and the third has 1000 channels to achieve a 1000-way ILSVRC classification followed by a softmax layer.

7.3 CONVOLUTIONAL NEURAL NETWORKS

Convolutional Neural Networks (ConvNets/CNN) is a type of DL used to classify the objects in the picture. In contrast to other classification techniques, ConvNet requires less pre-processing. The convolutional layer is the backbone of a CNN and relies on data input, a filter, and a feature map. Here, we'll take as input a 3D matrix of pixels representing an X-ray color image. Consequently, the input will have the same three dimensions as an image (height, width, and depth), which we refer to as the red, green, and blue channels. Also, we have a feature detector, which is also called a kernel or a filter, and it scans the image's receptive fields to see if the feature is there. The term "convolution" describes this action. This detector uses a two-dimensional array of weights as its main detectable feature. The size of the receptive field is also determined by the filter size, typically a 3×3 matrix. Next, we apply the filter to a region of the image and compute the dot product of the input pixels and the filtered version of the image. ConvNet's 3X3 filters may detect the spatial and temporal relationships present when applied to an image. As a result of using fewer parameters and making weights more broadly applicable, it achieves a more accurate fitting to the image dataset. ConvNet's job is to make the images simpler to analyze without sacrificing any important characteristics necessary to make a precise prediction. The ConvNet's 3X3 filter applied to the chest X-ray image is depicted in Figure 7.5.

An elementwise activation function, often a Rectified-Linear Unit (ReLu), receives the converted volume from the Conv. Layer as input. In a neural network, the activation function is the component that actually "activates" the node or generates an output in response to the information that was presented to it in the form of a sum

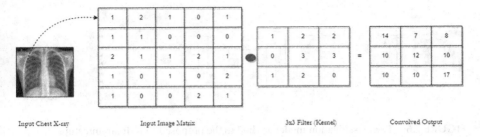

| Input Chest X-ray | Input Image Matrix | 3x3 Filter (Kernel) | Convolved Output |

FIGURE 7.5 ConvNet's 3X3 filter applied to the chest X-ray image.

of weights. If the input is positive, the ReLU t will return that value immediately; otherwise, it will return zero. A model trained using it is quicker to train and often delivers greater performance has led to it being the default activation function for various neural networks. The ReLu activation function, a non-linear one utilized in deep neural networks with several layers, is represented by Equation 7.1.

$$f(x) = \text{Max}(0, X) \tag{7.1}$$

In the first equation, the value x is used as an input, and the output of the ReLu algorithm is the greatest value that is less than or equal to the input value. According to Equation 7.2, the output value is equal to zero when the value of the input variable is negative, and the output value is equal to the value of the input variable when the value of the input variable is positive.

$$f(x) = \begin{cases} 0, & x < 0 \\ 1, & x \geq 0 \end{cases} \tag{7.2}$$

Recently, activation levels in conventional or deep neural network architectures have been computed using the ReLu function. Since ReLu requires less calculations than sigmoid and hyperbolic tangent, it has begun to replace these two functions. Since the derivative of ReLu is 1 for positive input, it may be used to speed up the training time of deep neural networks in comparison to more conventional activation functions. Deep neural networks do not waste time while training computing error terms because of the continuous nature of the data. The classification model applied to the proposed VGG16 architecture is depicted in Figure 7.6.

The activation function of ReLU is represented as,

$$R(z) = \begin{cases} z, & z > 0 \\ 0, & z \leq 0 \end{cases} \tag{7.3}$$

The basic objective of a Deep Neural Network is to extract the features in an organized manner by locating edges and gradients, followed by forming textures on top of these data. When taken as a whole, convolutional layers in Deep Neural Networks (DNN) create components of objects, and then objects themselves may summarize

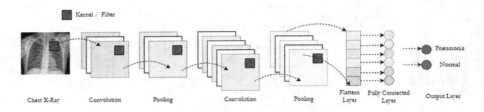

FIGURE 7.6   The classification model applied to the proposed VGG16 architecture.

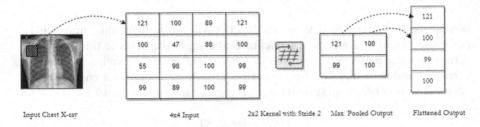

FIGURE 7.7   Illustration of max pooling and flattening applied to the chest X-ray image.

the characteristics in an input image. During this process phase, it is important to keep the image size consistent throughout the Neural Network since doing so will result in the stacking of numerous layers. Because of the vast amounts of computational resources, it requires, this cannot be maintained in the long term. Concurrently, we need a sufficient number of convolutions to extract significant features. When we look at the feature maps produced by the convolution layers, we can see that they are sensitive to the placement of the features in the input. One solution to this problem is to reduce the number of samples used in the feature maps. Therefore, downsampling or downsizing should be performed at appropriate intervals to maintain a balance between the extraction of useful characteristics and the computational resources available. We make use of a strategy known as pooling to accomplish this goal. The max pooling and flattening applied to the chest X-ray image are depicted in Figure 7.7.

Pooling is one method that may be used to downsample feature maps. This method does so by providing a summary of the features that are present in the feature maps. Max pooling and average pooling are the two types of pooling utilized most often. The maximum pooling strategy is favored in the proposed design for the system. To generate a fresh set of pooled feature maps with the same amount of features, the pooling layer processes each feature map. If the feature map is 4 by 4 pixels in size, the pooling filter will be 2 by 2 pixels in size, with a stride of 2 pixels. The pooling layer always halves the size of each feature map. Thus, a feature map with 36 pixels across by 6 pixels deep will produce a 3 by 3-pixel deep pooled feature map (9 pixels).

The pooling procedure mathematically summarizes features as a 2D filter is slid over a 3D feature map. Consider an image or feature map with height (h) dimensions and feature map (cf). Width (w) for a channel. Once the data have been pooled, the result is,

$$(h - fs + 1) / s * (w - fs + 1) * c \tag{7.4}$$

In max pooling, the layer uses the most salient feature from the feature map generated by the convolutional layer to perform its function. Fundamentally, it takes the feature map and chooses the element with the highest value inside the area caught by the filter. It is often employed after a convolutional layer. A minor degree of translation invariance is included, which means that the values of most pooled outputs are not drastically changed when the images are translated. The max pooling layer in action using a 2D feature map is seen in the following Figure 7.6. The largest value from the region of the image contained inside the kernel is what is returned by max pooling. On the other side, the average of all the values in the image region that the kernel is applied to is what average pooling will give us back. Besides its other uses, max pooling may be considered a noise suppressor. It first conducts dimensionality reduction to eliminate the noise before discarding the noisy activations. However, average pooling relies only on dimensionality reduction to dampen unwanted noise. Consequently, max pooling is superior to average pooling.

Each layer in an FC neural network is linked to every other layer in the network, and the output dimensions are dependent on the input dimensions. Let $I \in \mathbb{R}_m$ represent the input to a FC layer, $O_i \in \mathbb{R}$ be the ith output from the FC layer. Then $O_i \in \mathbb{R}$ is computed as,

$$O_i = \sigma(w_1 x_1 + \cdots + w_m x_m) \tag{7.5}$$

With enough time, FC networks may effectively remember their training data. It is not unusual for training loss to converge to zero for sufficiently big networks. An important empirical illustration of the universal approximation capabilities of FC networks is shown by this observation. High-dimensional statistics will provide many bogus correlations and patterns if we have a big enough dataset. It is not difficult for FC networks to detect and exploit such misleading connections. Mathematically, regularization is the process that puts constraints on rote learning and encourages transferable knowledge. Dropout is a sort of regularization that randomly removes some fraction of the nodes contributing to a fully linked layer. At each stage of gradient descent, the eliminated nodes are picked randomly. Due to the inability to rely on the existence of single strong neurons, dropout inhibits co-adaptation. There are two observed consequences of dropping out of the CNN layer. Dropout does two things. First, it stops the network from learning the training data. Dropouts usually improve the model's ability to forecast future data as a second point. Since it is more than simply a statistical gimmick, dropout is widely acknowledged as a significant innovation. Overfitting of the network may be avoided with the use of regularization techniques like dropout. Overlearning was prevented by adding a single dropout layer to the FC layer. All weight adjustments made during training are performed by the Adam optimizer.

When it comes to ML, the Adaptive Moment Estimation (Adam) method is a first-order, gradient-based optimization approach of stochastic objective functions.

Direction of the update may be calculated by taking the first instant and normalizing it by the second moment. Equation 7.6 provides the Adam update rule.

$$\theta_{n+1} = \left(\theta_n - \left(\alpha / \sqrt{Vn + \varepsilon} \right) \right) M_n \qquad (7.6)$$

7.4 RESULTS AND DISCUSSION

When it comes to creating accurate and optimal CNN models, TL is a cutting-edge way of training specialized neural network models. TL begins with a set of weights that have already been learned, in this case using VGG16, depicted in Figure 7.8. These models are optimized for inference on a GPU after being pre-trained with minimum further work.

This research introduces an automated portable device that is quicker and more accurate thanks to TL's inclusion, and it also demonstrates how to successfully deploy models using a GPU-based architecture. Models are trained, tested, and evaluated in Python IDLE using the Keras and Tensor Flow libraries. Using the Keras and Tensor Flow libraries in python IDLE, we train, test, and evaluate both methods. High-level APIs for the CNN library are the focus of Keras, whereas Tensor Flow serves as a general-purpose open-source framework for ML applications. For this, we used a GPU board equipped with an NVIDIA Maxwell 128 CUDA core GPU. When compared to Windows 10 machine with NVIDIA GeForce MX250 GPU, 16 GB Memory, we achieve faster testing and training times. Even though VGG and ResNet both contain variants, VGG16 fared better than human doctors and X-ray machines when it came to making diagnoses.

Figure 7.8 depicts the suggested TL model in VGG16. Each of the 64 FC layer batches has dropout rates of 0.3 and 0.2, respectively. The softmax activation function is used in the last FC layers for hyperparameter categorization. The proposed model undergoes 50 training epochs, after which the foundational models are permanently frozen. The whole process of pre-processing and training the model is included in the Tensor Flow framework's design, depicted in Figure 7.9.

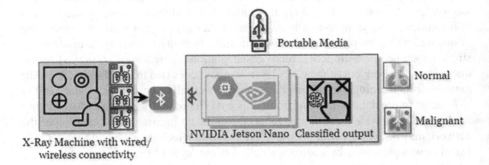

FIGURE 7.8 Deployment of improved transfer learning-enabled heuristic technique for pneumonia detection on NVIDIA 128-core Jetson Nano GPU board.

With twofold increases between the first and second max pooling layers, the 64-bit channel capacity may eventually reach 512. Each convolutional layer's output layer is computed by an FC layer that learns a function between the high-level features from the output convolutional layers by connecting all the inputs from one layer to the ReLU of the following layer. Finally, the softmax activation function from Equation 7.7 is used in the final layer to make class membership predictions about the incoming data.

$$\sigma(\theta)i = e^{\theta i}\bigg/ \sum_{j=1}^{K} e^{\theta j} \tag{7.7}$$

Furthermore, the NVIDIA Jetson Nano GPU with 128 cores is used to deploy the constructed CNN model. The whole dataset utilized in this study is seen in Figure 7.10a. A pneumonia dataset was used for the study, including 2786 instances of pneumonia and 1171 normal chest X-ray images for training. However, 715 pneumonia images and 240 normal images were used for evaluating the created VGG16 models. The comparison of VGG16 and ResNET model is represented in Table 7.1.

The research used the processing capacity of a GPU and the adaptability of ML models to implement automated pneumonia identification from chest photographs, achieving improved performance via the incorporation of previously acquired information. Figure 7.10a and b presents the training parameters of the proposed TL models.

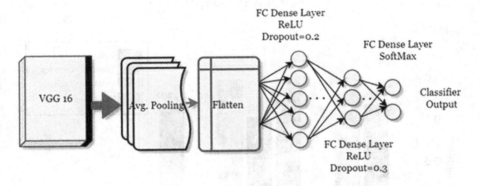

FIGURE 7.9   Proposed improved transfer learning model using VGG16.

TABLE 7.1

Comparison of VGG16 and ResNET Model

Development Platform	Convolutional Neural Network Model	Image Size	T. Loss	T. Accuracy	Val. Loss	Val. Accuracy
Python IDLE with	VGG16	224×224	0.879	0.965	0.4019	0.9054
Keras and Tensor	ResNet50	224×224	0.824	0.954	0.410	0.8902
Flow framework						

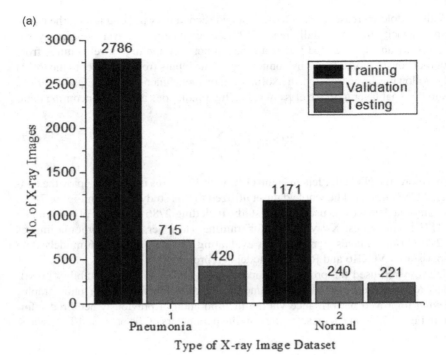

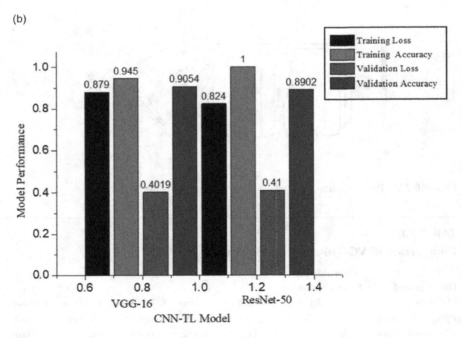

FIGURE 7.10 (a) Details of Image dataset used in training and validation process. (b) Model performance comparison chart.

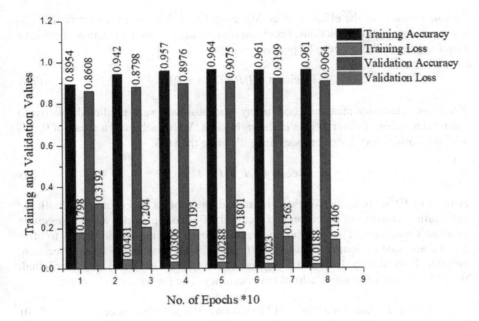

FIGURE 7.11 Number of epochs versus the training model's performance.

Overfitting is an important problem to keep in mind while training a CNN using sample data. When more epochs are utilized for training a neural network model than are strictly required, the training model picks up on artifacts unique to the sample data. The model's ability to adapt to a new dataset is severely impaired. However, although this model performs well on the training data, it struggles to replicate that success on the test data. The model is trained for as many as 150 epochs to prevent overfitting and maximize the neural network's generalization ability. To check the model's performance after each training period, a portion of the training data is set aside specifically for validation. We keep an eye on the loss and accuracy of both the training and validation sets to detect the epoch at which the model begins to overfit. The model performance in terms of the number of epochs is plotted in Figure 7.11.

7.5 EVALUATION RESULTS FOR CLASSIFICATION MODEL

Various measures are used in ML and DL to quantify the predicted accuracy of a trained model. For binary classification, accuracy may also be determined by counting the number of correct (true positives T_rP) and incorrect (true negatives T_rN) predictions. An accurate positive prediction is one in which the model accurately identifies the target class. A real negative is another result when the model successfully predicts the negative class. Incorrectly predicting the affirmative class is an example of a false positive. The model makes an inaccurate prediction of the negative class, known as a false negative.

One measure of the efficacy of an ML model is its level of precision or the reliability of its correct predictions. Precision may be defined as the fraction of positive observations that turn out to be positive.

$$\text{Precision} = T_r P / (T_r P + F_l P) \tag{7.8}$$

Recall or sensitivity measures how many true positives were predicted relative to the total number of observations in the right class. We've achieved a recall of 0.631, which is satisfactory for our model since it's more than 0.5.

$$\text{Recall} = T_r P / T_r P + F_l N \tag{7.9}$$

A model's F1 score is the weighted harmonic mean of its precision and recall. By combining measures of precision and recall, the F1 score provides a fair assessment of a test's reliability. The F1 score incorporates both accuracies and recalls to offer a more accurate evaluation of a test's efficacy. To calculate an F1 score, Precision, and Recall are averaged and then weighted. If your classes are not evenly distributed, then F1 is likely to be more helpful than accuracy. The formula for F1 score:

$$\text{F1 Score} = 2 * (\text{Recall} * \text{Precision}) / (\text{Recall} + \text{Precision}) \tag{7.10}$$

Regarding evaluation metrics, the area under the curve (AUC) is extremely popular and commonly used in binary classification. The AUC for any given classifier equals the probability that a randomly selected positive example will be ranked higher than a randomly chosen negative example. The area under the receiver operating characteristic (AUC-ROC) curve is measured from (0,0) to (1,1). Sensitivity and false-positive rates are shown on a graph to create an ROC curve. The closer the area under the curve (AUC) is to 1, the more developed the model is. The relationship and trade-off between sensitivity and specificity for each feasible cut-off for a test are graphically shown using AUC-ROC curves. Another performance metric for classification issues with varying thresholds is the AUC-ROC curve, depicted in Figure 7.12.

When the threshold is set to 1.0, at the lowest position (0, 0), the model labels all patients as free of lung illness or pneumonia. When the threshold is set to 0.0 at the maximum value (1, 1), the model labels all patients as having pneumonia. The remaining portions of the curve represent FPR and TPR values for thresholds between 0 and 1. At a certain cut-off, we see that an FPR of 0 yields a TPR of about 1. Now is when the model's predictions of which patients will get pneumonia are at their highest accuracy.

7.6 CONCLUSION

Chest X-rays are the gold standard for diagnosing pneumonia, but they are laborious and should only be performed by a trained professional. Due to recent advancements in DL and neural networks, automated pneumonia identification via analysis of chest X-rays has seen significant improvements. In this research, we employ a CNN that has been pre-trained on chest X-ray pictures as feature extractors. Then we categorize

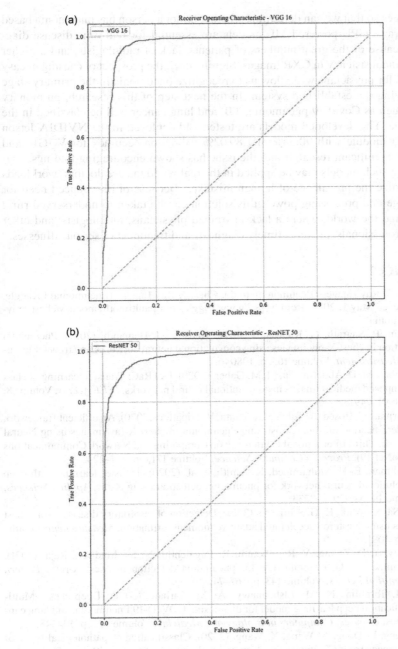

FIGURE 7.12 (a and b) ROC curve of the developed VGG16 and ResNET 50 models for pneumonia detection from chest X-ray images.

those images so that we can determine whether or not a person has pneumonia based on the X-rays. GPU-powered ML models are essential for real-time disease diagnosing because of the great numbers of patients, lack of radiologists, and a higher degree of inconsistency in CXR images. Significantly, the prospect of causing uneasy conditions for physicians will allow us to recognize pneumonia in the primary stage by employing the established system. In the next step of this research, pulmonary diseases such as Covid-19 pneumonia, TB, and lung cancer will be classified in the initial stage. The developed models are tested and deployed in the NVIDIA Jetson Nano GPU module with 90.54% and 89.02% validation accuracy for VGG16 and ResNet50. Significant research into the issue has shown encouraging findings, suggesting that such models may be applied in the real world to ease doctors' workloads and minimize the prevalence of human mistakes. Because of the reduced need for data storage and processing power, this solution can be taken to underserved rural areas around the world, where a lack of trained physicians, radiologists, and other medical professionals, prevents timely diagnosis and treatment of serious illnesses.

REFERENCES

1. Chest X-Ray Images (Pneumonia). (n.d.). Chest X-Ray Images (Pneumonia) | Kaggle. Retrieved May 1, 2022, from https://www.kaggle.com/paultimothymooney/chest-xray-pneumonia.
2. R. Jain, P. Nagrath, G. Kataria, V. Sirish Kaushik, J. Hemanth. (2021). Pneumonia detection in chest X-ray images using convolutional neural networks and transfer learning, *Measurement*, Volume 165, p. 108046.
3. A. Abbas, M. D. Abdelsamea, M. M. Gaber. (2020). DeTRaC: Transfer learning of class decomposed medical images in convolutional neural networks, *IEEE Access*, Volume 8, pp. 74901–74913.
4. D. Vermaa, C. Bosec, N. Tufchia, K. Panta, V. Tripathic. (2020). An efficient framework for identification of Tuberculosis and Pneumonia in chest X-ray images using Neural Network, Third International Conference on Computing and Network Communications (CoCoNet'19), *Procedia Computer Science*, Volume 171, pp. 217–224.
5. T. Rahman, E. H. Muhammed, K. Amith, et al. (2020). Transfer learning with deep convolutional neural network for pneumonia detection using X-ray, *Applied Sciences*, Volume 10, issue 9, p. 3233.
6. S. S. Sai Koushik, K. G. Srinivasa. (2021). Detection of respiratory diseases from chest X rays using Nesterov accelerated adaptive moment estimation, *Measurement*, Volume 176, p. 109153.
7. N. Dey, Y.-D. Zhang, V. Rajinikanth, R. Pugalenthi, N. Sri Madhava Raja. (2021). Customized VGG19 architecture for pneumonia detection in chest X-rays, *Pattern Recognition Letters*, Volume 143, pp. 67–74.
8. D. M. Ibrahim, N. M. Elshennawy, A. M. Sarhan. (2021). Deep-chest: Multi-classification deep learning model for diagnosing COVID-19 Pneumonia, and lung cancer chest diseases, *Computers in Biology and Medicine*, Volume 132, p. 104348.
9. S. Wang, L. Dong, X. Wang, X. Wang. (2020). Classification of pathological types of lung cancer from CT images by deep residual neural networks with transfer learning strategy, *Open Medicine- PMC Journals*, Volume 15, pp. 190–197.
10. C. Li, Y. Yang, H. Liang, B. Wu. (2021). Transfer learning for establishment of recognition of COVID-19 on CT imaging using small-sized training datasets, *Knowledge-Based Systems*, Volume 218, p. 106849.

11. S. Bharati, P. Podder, M. Rubaiyat Hossain Mondal. (2020). Hybrid deep learning for detecting lung diseases from X-ray images, *Informatics in Medicine Unlocked*, Volume 20, p. 100391.
12. Q. Zhang, C. Ba, Z. Liu, L. T. Yang, H. Yu, J. Zhao, H. Yuan. (2020). A GPU-based residual network for medical image classification in smart medicine, *Information Sciences*, Volume 536, pp. 91–100.
13. V. Chouhan, S. K. Singh, A. Khamparia, D. Gupta, P. Tiwari, C. Moreira, R. Damaševičius, and V. H. C. de Albuquerque. (2020). A novel transfer learning based approach for pneumonia detection in chest X-ray images, *Applied Sciences*, Volume 10, issue 2, p. 559.
14. J. Lin, L. Zhao, Q. Wang, R. Ward, & Z. J. Wang. (2020). DT-LET: Deep transfer learning by exploring where to transfer, *Neurocomputing*, Volume 390, pp. 12–17. https://doi.org/10.1016/j.neucom.2020.01.042.
15. Y. Li, Z. Zhang, C. Dai, Q. Dong, S. Badrigilan. (2020). Accuracy of deep learning for automated detection of pneumonia using chest X-Ray images: A systematic review and meta-analysis, *Computers in Biology and Medicine*, Volume 123, p. 103898.
16. G. Liang, & L. Zheng. (2020). A transfer learning method with deep residual network for pediatric pneumonia diagnosis, *Computer Methods and Programs in Biomedicine*, Volume 187, p. 104964.
17. S. S. J. Gangesh Bharadwaj. (2020). Pneumonia detection using Transfer Learning, *International Journal of Advanced Science and Technology*, Volume 29, issue 3, pp. 986–994.
18. M. Rahimzadeh, A. Attar. (2020). A modified deep convolutional neural network for detecting COVID-19 and Pneumonia from chest X-ray images based on the concatenation of Xception and ResNet50V2, *Informatics in Medicine Unlocked*, Volume 19, p. 100360.
19. R. Baskaran, B. AjayRajasekaran, V. Rajinikanth. (2020). A Deep-Learning system to classify Lung X-ray images into Normal/Pneumonia class, *International Journal of Infectious Diseases*, Volume 101, Supplement 1, pp. 202–203.
20. K. Simonyan, A. Zisserman, "Very Deep Convolutional Networks for Large-Scale Image Recognition", Published as a conference paper at ICLR 2015 University of Oxford and Google DeepMind. https://arxiv.org/pdf/1409.1556.pdf.

8 Improved Adaptive Learning Framework for an Effective Removal of Noise in ECG Signal for Telemedicine System

C. Prajitha, K. P. Sridhar, S. Baskar, and Abubeker K. M.

Karpagam Academy of Higher Education

CONTENTS

8.1   INTRODUCTION

Wearable sensors open up many opportunities for health-related queries [1]. Especially in smart wearable telehealth systems, wearable sensing technologies keep an eye on patients without help from a doctor [2]. It moreover gives distant diagnostic evaluations. Physiological parameters like electrocardiogram (ECG), electromyography (EMG), blood pressure, and body temperature can be recorded and measured with the help of wearable telehealth systems [3,4]. Heart disease is the most common illness that affects people [5]. Heart disease affects people from newborns to elderly people [6]. Arrhythmia is the medical term for an irregular heartbeat. An abnormal heartbeat is referred to as an arrhythmia [7]. Normal to deadly arrhythmias can occur in various ways [8]. When the natural rhythm of a patient's heart is out of tune with the electric signals in their heart, it results in an irregular heartbeat [9].

DOI: 10.1201/9781003307778-9

Arrhythmia, in which the heartbeat sequence is out of rhythm, is one of the most prevalent cardiovascular diseases [10]. Classification of these irregular shapes into subcategories is necessary, so patients can be given exact treatment suggestions [11]. The abnormal pattern of the human heart can be seen and predicted using an ECG [12]. The ECG is frequently utilized for effective assessment and diagnosis [13,14]. Biomedicine's healthiness and a person's qualifications or biometrics are linked to ECG signals, which carry more useful information [15,16]. However, other types of noise, such as baseline wander (BW), muscle artifact (MA), and electrode motion, can affect ECG readings [17]. Breathing electrodes that have been charged or the movement of the person all contribute to BW [18,19]. Numerous methods for ECG classification have been developed, including manual methods and machine learning approaches [20,21]. The manual procedure is time-consuming and error-prone, and noise reduction is tedious [22,23]. These disturbances may cause ECG waveforms to be deformed and obscure essential diagnostic features. As a result, noise reduction from ECG signals is required. The contribution of improved adaptive learning approach (IALM) is as follows

- The first stage in IALM is finding the symmetrical aspects of wavelet functions and the significant fluctuations in small-amplitude signals. Wavelet Thresholding (WT) and Wavelet Decomposition (WD) approaches reduce noise in the power line, and BWs reduce noise in ECG signals.
- Yule-Walker modeling is used during noise reduction to extract aspects of the ECG signal that can be used to identify different types of arrhythmias. The hidden Markov model (HMM) has been used to classify arrhythmias effectively after noise reduction.
- In terms of root mean square error (RMSE), enhancement in signal-to-noise ratio (SNR), maximum classification accuracy, sensitivity, and positive projected value, the suggested method surpasses traditional techniques like support vector machine (SVM), artificial neural network (ANN), and convolutional neural network (CNN).

8.1.1 BACKGROUND STUDY

Several kinds of literature have been carried out by different researchers Joseph Michael Jerard et al. [24] employed pipelining and look-ahead conversion methods to minimize high-frequency noise. Other designs (685.48 MHz) were not as good as the recursive pipelined 8-tap MA filter using the look-ahead technique.

Xie et al. [25] developed a multi-stage denoising framework. Noise-adaptive thresholding is used to find motion artifact candidates in the framework. After that, various measurements and decision rules are used to identify and eliminate motion artifacts using local scaling and morphological filtering techniques. An enhancement in SNR of 7%–25% is technically meaningful by the results.

Algarni et al. [26] studied three cryptosystems for ECG signal encryption. Instead of encoding and decoding the ECG signal, these cryptosystems operate on the sample values of the ECG signal, which saves a lot of time and is more resistant to noise and hacker situations. Spectral distortion, histogram, SNR, and correlation coefficient are metrics used to assess the proposed cryptosystems' effectiveness. From the experiments, it is apparent that the use of higher encryption levels improves protection. Gao et al. [27] presented a long short-term memory recurrence network (LSTM-RN) model for ECG beat data because they are in an extremely unbalanced group. The data from the arrhythmia database support the benefits of the proposed network. The LSTM network with focal loss delivered an accurate response to the problem of imbalanced datasets. Using the new technology, cardiologists may more accurately and objectively diagnose ECG signals via telemedicine.

Chowdhury et al. [28] demonstrate a programmable signal processing unit with ZedBoard, a Xilinx Zynq 7000 SoC development board. Compression rates of up to 90% can be achieved in real time with no noticeable signal distortion. An additional advantage of this method is its intrinsic capacity to reduce high-frequency noise. The suggested approach is compared and validated using six datasets from the PhysioNet databank in an implementation plan. Abdulbaqi et al. [29] enhanced the ECG signal and removed the noise from the signal by discrete wavelet transform (DWT) and extracting the critical features, followed by the construction of the peak detection algorithm. The SNR is improved as a result of the method. The heart rate has been accurately estimated following the standard benchmark databases.

Lin et al. [30] developed a stethoscope that can listen to a patient's heartbeat and display the electrical activity of the subject's heart in real time. The proposed stethoscope is possible in clinics and telemedicine because of an advanced system and a cloud database.

The pipelining methods minimize the high-frequency noise, but identifying arrhythmia is tedious. DWT extracts the critical features, which are then followed by the construction of the peak detection algorithm. IALM is used to identify and classify arrhythmia to overcome all the issues. The presence of noise in ECG signals is one of the major issues for the accurate identification of arrhythmia in telemedicine systems. The IALM is used for better identification and classification of arrhythmia. The experimental analysis is compared with the results of the theoretical analysis

8.2 AN IMPROVED ADAPTIVE LEARNING APPROACH FOR ECG SIGNAL NOISE REMOVAL

The first stage in IALM is to discover the symmetrical properties of wavelet functions and the significant fluctuations in small-amplitude signals. In addition, noise reduction is made using the Wavelet Thresholding and Wavelet Decomposition (WTWD) approach. WT reduces power line noise, while WD reduces BW noise in ECG signals. Yule-Walker modeling is used during noise reduction to extract aspects of the ECG signal that can be used to identify different types of arrhythmias. Following noise reduction, a HMM is used to classify arrhythmias accurately. The architecture of IALM is shown in Figure 8.1.

8.3 WAVELET THRESHOLDING AND WAVELET DECOMPOSITION

The symmetrical features of wavelet functions are used to identify the most significant changes in tiny amplitude data in telemedicine systems. In an ECG, the

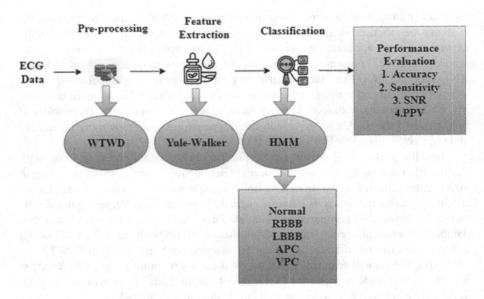

FIGURE 8.1   The architecture of IALM.

amplitude ranges from $110\,\mu V$ to $4\,mV$, and the frequency ranges from 0.05 to $100\,Hz$, making it an extremely tiny signal. The WT symmetrical qualities aid in extracting all relevant data from ECG signals. To handle ECG signals, the filtration system uses a mixture of down-sampling and a pool of filters. The transfer functions $A(s)$ and $B(s)$ for the high- and low-pass filters are used to process the ECG signal. The LPF's result is two times down-sampled. The transfer function of filters is represented as follows:

$$A(s) = a_0 + a_1 s^{-1} + a_2 s^{-2} + \cdots\cdots + a_m s^{-m}$$

$$B(s) = b_0 + b_1 s^{-1} + b_2 s^{-2} + \cdots\cdots + b_m s^{-m}$$

(8.1)

The transfer function of filters is obtained from Equation 8.1, a_0, a_1, a_2, a_m denote the low-pass filters parameters, b_0, b_1, b_2, b_m represent the high-pass filter parameters, and the filtering level is represented as m. The transfer function s^{-1}, s^{-2}, s^{-m} of the filter is shown in Figure 8.2.

When the wavelet basis is diagonal, the filter parameters in expression 8.2 must be normalized.

$$\sum_{u=0}^{m} \begin{array}{l} a_u^2 = 1 \\ b_u^2 = 1 \end{array}$$

(8.2)

The normalization u for the filter parameters a_u^2, b_u^2 is obtained from Equation 8.2, and the filtering level is represented as m. Scalability and wavelet parameters must be calculated before the wavelet can be constructed. These values convince the state, as shown in Equations 8.3 and 8.4.

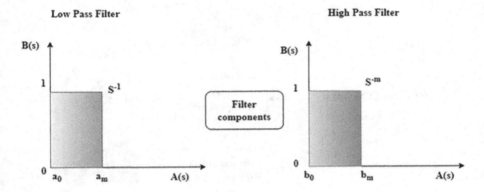

FIGURE 8.2   The transfer function of filters.

$$\varphi(s) = \sum_{m=0}^{n-1} a_1(m)\varphi(2s - m) \qquad (8.3)$$

$$v(s) = \sum_{m=0}^{n-1} b_1(m)\varphi(2s - m) \qquad (8.4)$$

The filter parameters a_1, b_1 and the duration of the signal n from Equations 8.3 and 8.4, where s represent the time under concern and the m-shifted wavelet is centered at s. The filtering level is represented as m. The wavelet-convoluted ECG signal is degraded repeatedly via a filter bank consisting of filters φ in a combined cycle to retrieve the relevant characteristics in the determined ECG signal. A down-sampler is included in the package. The down-sampler represents a twofold reduction in sampling. The filters decompose the ECG signal, resulting in sub-band values at each stage. An exponential scale is used to disperse the signal's sub-bands uniformly. In each sub-band, the sampling rate is proportional to the frequency. The symmetrical features of wavelet functions are used to discover the most significant fluctuations in small-amplitude ECG signals.

The wavelet's symmetrical features help to retrieve the essential and entire data from an ECG signal with a particular intensity range and a frequency range. Decomposition of the input signal is implemented for general signals and detail signals. The signal's position and magnitude are used to calculate the wavelet coefficients. As a result, it is possible to isolate the signal from the noise in an ECG readily.

ECG's highest values can be quickly retrieved by using WT coefficients that automatically take values over a predetermined threshold, thus reducing the amount of time it takes to acquire important information from an ECG. The variables have been quantified. The WD of the ECG signal is obtained from Equations 8.5 and 8.6

$$C_{aj}(s) = y(m) \cdot a(2s - m) \qquad (8.5)$$

$$C_{io}(s) = y(m) \cdot b(2s - m) \qquad (8.6)$$

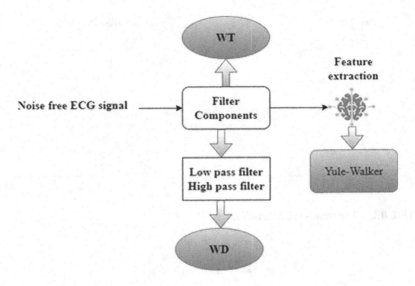

FIGURE 8.3   Pre-processing and feature extraction of ECG signal.

The wavelet is used as the mother wavelet to decompose the selected ECG signal $y(m)$. The filter input and output are obtained from Equations 8.5 and 8.6. Input signal $y(m)$ is the ECG signal that is being analyzed. a and b denote the frequency components of high- and low-pass filters, respectively. The m-shifted wavelet is centered at s. The noise-free ECG signal is obtained after pre-processing with the WTWD method. The obtained data are given for feature extraction with the Yule-Walker for accurate classification of arrhythmia. Pre-processing and the feature extraction stage is shown in Figure 8.3.

ECG signals are divided into eight levels and eight multi-resolution non-overlapping sub-bands. Initially, noise is reduced from the data before further analysis begins. Various sorts of sounds can interfere with ECG signal reliability. The signal is so tiny in amplitude that it is susceptible to interference from the surrounding environment. The original signal is distorted as a result of this. Noisy signals are difficult to detect and result in an incorrect diagnosis.

Biological and technological disturbances influence the ECG signal in clinical settings. Power lines, communication line interferences, and electrode movement are the main causes of technological noises. MAs, EMG, and motion artifacts are all examples of biological component noises. Baseline drift, power line interference, and EMG are the main sources of noise. A wavelet transform is used in the proposed model to reduce noise in an ECG signal. The signal obtained from the dataset helps to find the existence of baseline noise. BWs have a frequency range of 0–0.5 Hz. Signal restoration discards this frequency range because it appears in a particular level of decomposition. The power line and BW noise from the ECG signal are reduced by the WTWD method. The noise-reduced ECG signal is further processed by the Yule-Walker model, described below, for better detection and classification of arrhythmia.

8.4   YULE-WALKER MODELING

The type of arrhythmia is a major factor in feature extraction approaches. Many researchers have attempted to develop an automated arrhythmia diagnostic system in the literature. A different sort of arrhythmia could not be detected with the procedures that are used at present. The time sequence is defined as follows:

$$V_{m+1} = \varnothing_1 V_m + \varnothing_2 V_{m-1} + \ldots + \varnothing_j V_{m-j+1} + y_{m+1} \tag{8.7}$$

The time sequence is obtained from Equation 8.7, here $\varnothing_1, \varnothing_2, \varnothing_j$ represent the variables of the modeling process. y_{m+1} denote the white noise; the discrete time series is denoted as, $\{V_m, V_{m-1}, V_{m-j+1}\}$. The extracted feature from the ECG signal is further given to the classification stage for better identification of arrhythmia.

8.5   HIDDEN MARKOV MODEL

Machine learning approaches produce superior classification results when applied to biomedical signals to those obtained using more traditional methods. It is possible to use the system once it has been trained to recognize unknown signals. Good results can only be achieved if the dataset is trained and tested adequately. HMM, the model is implemented for better identification and classification of arrhythmia. HMM describes the development of observed occurrences that are influenced by internal factors. The MIT-BIH arrhythmia database's ECG records were classified into five categories using an HMM: normal (N), right bundle branch block (RBBB), left bundle branch block (LBBB), ventricular premature contraction (VPC), and atrial premature contraction (APC). The APC category was the most severe of the five, as shown in Figure 8.4.

Exactly a few studies in the field of ECG classification using an HMM have been implemented. There are five different forms of arrhythmia, and the suggested effort would create an enhanced HMM to categorize them. Models that use hidden Markov chains are unpredictable and can be used to forecast unknown outcomes based on prior information on state transitions. Hidden states refer to those states that are undisclosed. A Markov chain governs the hidden layer, and the basic state determines the observed' probability distribution.

An unnoticed Markov chain guides the ECG assessment. In the HMM concept, the next state's conditions depend on the initial state's conditions; therefore, this is clear. A new HMM is used to study the five various forms of cardiac arrhythmia in the IALM method. First, the parametric specification must be addressed as part of the HMM concept. (i) The description of the method, (ii) the assessment of the possibilities for each HMM, and (iii) the optimal method parameter modification for the received signal are the final steps in the process. The parameter specification in the form of $R_s, R_{s+1}, R_{s+2} \ldots R_{s-1}$, and the parameter transition likelihood matrix like m, n, K, L, A for classification of arrhythmia is shown in Figure 8.5

The characteristics of the HMM are as follows:

$$\delta = (K + L - m, \vartheta) \tag{8.8}$$

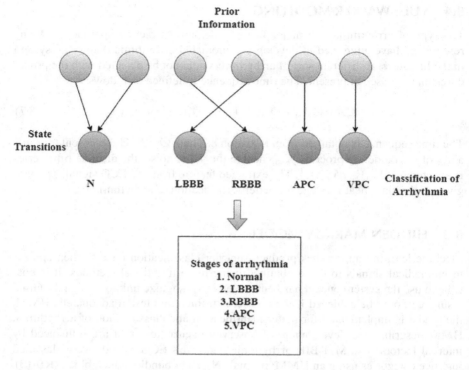

FIGURE 8.4   Classification by HMM.

The characteristics of HMM are obtained from Equation 8.8; there are three variables k, l, m that need to be assessed while designing an HMM for ECG data processing, according to Equation 8.8. Phase transitions likelihood matrix ϑ is the first variable, while model δ is the second. The transition likelihood with the parameter A is denoted as follows:

$$K = \{k_{m,n}\}; m,n = 1,2,\ldots\ldots A \qquad (8.9)$$

The possibility of a change in direction K at time $s-1$ is shown in Equation 8.9, the possibility of the system changing from one state $R_{s-1} = m$ at time $s-1$ to $R_s = n$. Different stages are denoted as m, n. The next stage representation is given as follows:

$$k_{m,n} = A(R_s = n; R_{s-1} = m) \qquad (8.10)$$

The representation of the next stage $k_{m,n}$ is shown in Equation 8.10, A denotes the parameter of transition likelihood, and one state is represented as $R_{s-1} = m$, and the other state is represented as $R_s = n$. From Equation 8.10 if $k_{m,n} > 0$; and $\sum_{n=0}^{m} k_{m,n} = 1, m,n = 0,1,\ldots A$. The different form of categorization of arrhythmia is obtained from HMM. The reduction of noise by the WTWD method achieves

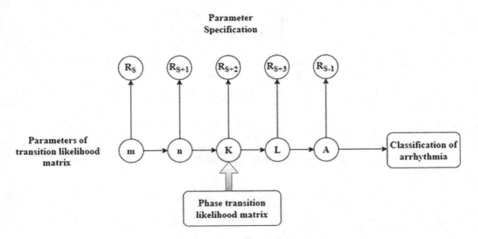

FIGURE 8.5 Phase transition likelihood for classification of arrhythmia.

arrhythmia detection. The features of the ECG signal were retrieved using Yule-Walker modeling for the effective identification of different types of arrhythmia. The performance measurement of the proposed IALM is discussed in the below section. The architecture of IALM in the form of the flow chart is shown in Figure 8.6.

8.6 EXPERIMENTAL ANALYSIS

In IALM, the initial stage is to find the symmetrical aspects of wavelet functions and the significant fluctuations in small-amplitude signals. The WTWD approach performs noise reduction. During the noise reduction procedure, elements of the ECG signal are obtained using Yule-Walker modeling, which helps optimize the retrieved characteristics to identify different arrhythmias effectively. Further, in this manuscript, HMM has been effectively used to categorize arrhythmia after the noise reduction method. The proposed method surpasses traditional techniques such as RMSE and SNR with the best classification accuracy, sensitivity, and positive projected value. IALM has been validated based on the data obtained from the MIT-BIH arrhythmia database [31]. All 4000 ambulatory ECG recordings are picked randomly from a group that includes both inpatients and outpatients.

Normal, VPC, LBBB, APC, and RBBB are all diagnosed and classified using the proposed framework. The classification accuracy is obtained by Equation 8.11.

$$\text{Accuracy} = \frac{tp + tn}{tp + tn + fp + fn} \tag{8.11}$$

In the above equation, tp is a true positive, which indicates the number of instances that were correctly classified as required, fp is a false positive, which indicates the number of instances that were incorrectly classified as required, tn is a true negative, which indicates the number of instances that were correctly classified as not required, and fn is false negative, which represents the number of instances that were

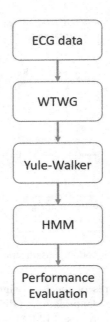

FIGURE 8.6 Flow chart of IALM.

TABLE 8.1
The Performance Measurement in the Form of Accuracy

Number of Records	Beats Detected	tp	Accuracy
20	234	234	98.92
40	267	269	90.23
60	289	287	91.45
80	292	296	97.55
100	309	307	98.11
120	321	327	92.56
140	343	347	93.56
160	367	369	94.56
180	386	388	95.22
200	390	392	95.67

incorrectly classified as not necessary. The performance measurement in the form of the accuracy of IALM is shown in Table 8.1.

Table 8.2 shows the SNR as a function of noise level and filtering in dB. ECG signals are analyzed using an altered periodogram of the same duration as the input ECG signal. The formula S yields the SNR as shown in Equation 8.12. The original signal references the raw ECG R obtained from the arrhythmia database. The SNR parameter is determined according to Equation 8.12.

TABLE 8.2

Noise Analysis for the Recorded ECG Signal

Number of Records	Q (Noisy Signal)	SNR (dB)	R (Filtered Signal)
20	−8.22	−0.98	−1.22
40	−4.56	−0.12	−2.3
60	−2.21	0.23	−3.45
80	−3.56	1.24	−1.67
100	−7.55	1.67	4.56
120	−0.21	0.98	0.98
140	−4.54	0.67	0.34
160	−5.66	1.45	1.34
180	−3.12	0.56	−1.56
200	−2.67	0.11	−2.34

$$S = R(\text{Original signal})$$

$$SNR(dB) = Q(Q_x * D * SD) \tag{8.12}$$

The one-sided spectral density SD estimate is referred to as Q_x. D is a vector of the frequency at which Q_x forecasts are made. The comparison of SNR values for both the noisy R and the filtered signal S is obtained from Equation 8.12. Q represents the noisy signal. For the recorded ECG signal, the noise analysis is shown in Table 8.2.

The error rate measures expected output and real output. In the context of the error rate, a lower error rate number indicates a lower variation and improved performance. Using the root mean square difference (RMSD), the strength of the reduced signal can be measured by comparing the original data with its reconstructed version. The recovered signal is higher if the RMSD is lower. The mean absolute error (MAE) and the RMSE are obtained from Equations 8.13 and 8.14

$$MAE = \sqrt{\frac{1}{M} \times \sum_{m}^{M=1} (y - \tilde{y})^2} \tag{8.13}$$

$$RMSE = \sqrt{\frac{\sum_{m}^{M=1} (y - \tilde{y})^2}{\sum_{m}^{M=1} y^2}} \times 100 \tag{8.14}$$

From Equations 8.13 and 8.14, m represents the number of recorded samples, M represents the ECG signal after the extraction stage, y represents the original input signal, and $\tilde{y}$ denotes the noisy signal. The MAE and the RMSD of IALM are shown in Table 8.3. The performance comparison of IALM with the existing methods like LSTM and CNN is shown in Table 8.3.

TABLE 8.3
The MAE and the RMSD of IALM

Number of Records	LSTM		CNN		IALM	
	MAE (%)	RMSE (%)	MAE (%)	RMSE (%)	MAE (%)	RMSE (%)
20	2.34	2.45	4.56	3.32	1.09	0.64
40	2.67	2.98	4.89	2.89	0.89	0.67
60	3.89	2.21	4.21	2.01	0.67	0.22
80	4.66	3.56	4.67	3.89	0.34	0.78
100	5.77	3.89	3.89	3.22	0.45	0.56
120	1.22	3.12	3.33	3.56	0.67	0.45
140	2.89	3.90	3.67	2.78	0.21	0.77
160	1.34	3.67	3.21	2.90	0.99	0.97
180	1.89	3.45	4.78	2.67	0.89	1.22
200	1.67	3.89	4.67	3.67	0.98	1.09

The sensitivity and the positive predicted values (PPVs) of the proposed IALM are obtained by Equations 8.15 and 8.16.

$$\text{Sensitivity} = \frac{tp}{(tp + fn)} \tag{8.15}$$

$$\text{Positive Predicted Value (PPV)} = \frac{tp}{(tp + fp)} \tag{8.16}$$

The sensitivity and the PPV are obtained from Equations 8.15 and 8.16; the number of successfully identified samples is represented by the true metric positive (tp). True negative (tn) is the proposed algorithm's way of identifying true samples, but it is not included in the dataset. False positive (fp) is used to measure the number of samples wrongly identified by the algorithm; false negative (fn) denotes the leftover detection of the sample. The sensitivity and the PPV of IALM are shown in Table 8.4.

According to the IALM, the sensitivity, the PPV, and the detection error rate are used to evaluate the model's effectiveness. Following the processing of the selected ECG data using the suggested model, the performance metrics (tp), (tn), (fp), (fn) are determined. The classification of HMM depends on all the performance metrics, as shown in Table 8.5.

The classification of arrhythmia by HMM with all tp, tn, fp, fn evaluates the overall performance of the proposed IALM. The proposed IALM achieves the highest accuracy, lower error rate, sensitivity, PPV, and enhancement in SNR.

The performance of IALM, in the form of the accuracy of 98.92%, SNR of 36 dB, MAE of 0.21, RMSE of 0.22, sensitivity of 98%, PPV of 98.91%, is shown in Figure 8.7. The reduction of noise from ECG signal is implemented for effective arrhythmia detection and classification. The noise-removed signal is given with Yule-Walker modeling for extraction of specific characteristics. HMM, the model achieves final arrhythmia classification. IALM for noise cancellation in ECG signals has been

TABLE 8.4

The Sensitivity and the PPV of IALM

Records	tp	Fn	fp	Sensitivity	PPV
20	2212	4	8	92	98.76
40	2234	2	12	98	96.44
60	2289	0	16	97	94.32
80	2290	8	9	96.45	95.78
100	1478	5	5	95.56	97.99
120	2678	3	8	90.11	98.91
140	1568	2	18	94.67	92.56
160	2980	8	19	97.34	91.87
180	1324	9	6	98.90	90.99
200	1786	10	7	92.11	91.45

TABLE 8.5

The Classification of HMM

Types of Classification of Arrhythmia	tp	fp	tn	fn
Normal	198	2	5	1
VPC	197	0	0	0
LBB	200	0	2	0
APC	205	3	0	2
RBB	190	5	0	0

devised for more accurate arrhythmia detection and classification. The first stage in IALM is to single out the significant oscillations on low-amplitude signals and the symmetrical properties of wavelet functions. The WT and WD techniques can be used to lessen the impact of power line noise and BW noise in an ECG. Features of the ECG signal are obtained using Yule-Walker modeling during noise reduction; this helps to improve the retrieved characteristics for efficient diagnosis of various arrhythmias. Moreover, an HMM has been established to categorize arrhythmia following noise reduction efficiently. The performance measurement in accuracy, SNR, MAE, RMSE, sensitivity, and PPV is compared with the standard models like CNN, ANN, and SVM.

8.7 CONCLUSION

ECG helps to diagnose and monitor patients with cardiovascular disease. The non-invasive nature of the ECG signal makes it easier to detect and treat arrhythmia. Consequently, an IALM reduces ECG signals' noise so arrhythmias can be more accurately identified and classified. Initial steps in implementing IALM include

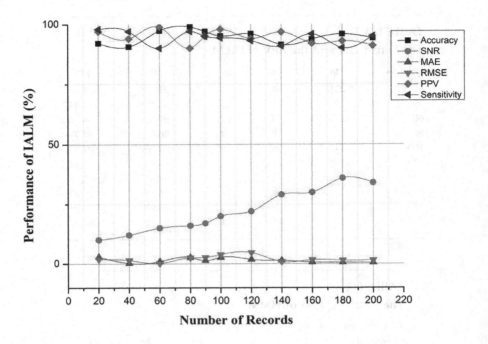

FIGURE 8.7   Performance of IALM.

spotting wavelet function symmetry and spotting large-amplitude signal fluctuations. WTWD achieve further reduction of noise. Yule-Walker modeling is used during noise reduction to extract aspects of the ECG signal that can effectively identify different arrhythmias. The HMM has been used in this study to classify arrhythmias effectively after noise reduction. In the future, other types of noise can be considered for removing noise in ECG signals. RMSE, SNR, classification accuracy, sensitivity, and PPV are all improved by the proposed strategy.

REFERENCES

1. Ali, F., El-Sappagh, S., Islam, S. R., Ali, A., Attique, M., Imran, M., & Kwak, K. S. (2021). An intelligent healthcare monitoring framework using wearable sensors and social networking data. *Future Generation Computer Systems, 114*, 23–43.
2. Awotunde, J. B., Jimoh, R. G., AbdulRaheem, M., Oladipo, I. D., Folorunso, S. O., & Ajamu, G. J. (2022). IoT-based wearable body sensor network for COVID-19 pandemic. *Advances in Data Science and Intelligent Data Communication Technologies for COVID-19, 378*, 253–275.
3. Adeniyi, E. A., Ogundokun, R. O., & Awotunde, J. B. (2021). IoMT-based wearable body sensors network healthcare monitoring system. In Gonçalo Marques, Akash Kumar Bhoi, Victor Hugo C. de Albuquerque, & K.S. Hareesha (Eds.), *IoT in Healthcare and Ambient Assisted Living* (pp. 103–121). Springer, Singapore.
4. Pradhan, B., Bhattacharyya, S., & Pal, K. (2021). IoT-based applications in healthcare devices. *Journal of Healthcare Engineering, 2021*, 1–18.

5. Nielsen, R. E., Banner, J., & Jensen, S. E. (2021). Cardiovascular disease in patients with severe mental illness. *Nature Reviews Cardiology, 18*(2), 136–145.

6. Miao, Q., Dunn, S., Wen, S. W., Lougheed, J., Reszel, J., Lavin Venegas, C., & Walker, M. (2021). Neighbourhood maternal socioeconomic status indicators and risk of congenital heart disease. *BMC Pregnancy and Childbirth, 21*(1), 1–21.

7. Faust, O., Kareem, M., Ali, A., Ciaccio, E. J., & Acharya, U. R. (2021). Automated arrhythmia detection based on RR intervals. *Diagnostics, 11*(8), 1446.

8. Rai, H. M., & Chatterjee, K. (2022). Hybrid CNN-LSTM deep learning model and ensemble technique for automatic detection of myocardial infarction using big ECG data. *Applied Intelligence, 52*(5), 5366–5384.

9. Wang, A., Nguyen, D., Sridhar, A. R., & Gollakota, S. (2021). Using smart speakers to contactlessly monitor heart rhythms. *Communications Biology, 4*(1), 1–12.

10. Luo, X., Yang, L., Cai, H., Tang, R., Chen, Y., & Li, W. (2021). Multi-classification of arrhythmias using a HCRNet on imbalanced ECG datasets. *Computer Methods and Programs in Biomedicine, 208*, 106258.

11. Iqbal, S., Mahgoub, I., Du, E., Leavitt, M. A., & Asghar, W. (2021). Advances in healthcare wearable devices. *NPJ Flexible Electronics, 5*(1), 1–14.

12. Darmawahyuni, A., Nurmaini, S., Rachmatullah, M. N., Tutuko, B., Sapitri, A. I., Firdaus, F., ... & Predyansyah, A. (2022). Deep learning-based electrocardiogram rhythm and beat features for heart abnormality classification. *PeerJ Computer Science, 8*, e825.

13. Gupta, V., Mittal, M., Mittal, V., Sharma, A. K., & Saxena, N. K. (2021). A novel feature extraction-based ECG signal analysis. *Journal of The Institution of Engineers (India): Series B, 102*(5), 903–913.

14. Faruk, N., Abdulkarim, A., Emmanuel, I., Folawiyo, Y. Y., Adewole, K. S., Mojeed, H. A., ... & Katibi, I. A. (2021). A comprehensive survey on low-cost ECG acquisition systems: Advances on design specifications, challenges and future direction. *Biocybernetics and Biomedical Engineering, 41*(2), 474–502.

15. Keskes, N., Fakhfakh, S., Kanoun, O., & Derbel, N. (2022). Representativeness consideration in the selection of classification algorithms for the ECG signal quality assessment. *Biomedical Signal Processing and Control, 76*, 103686.

16. Wang, P., Lin, Z., Yan, X., Chen, Z., Ding, M., Song, Y., & Meng, L. (2022). A wearable ECG monitor for deep learning based real-time cardiovascular disease detection. *arXiv preprint arXiv:2201.10083.*

17. Hossain, M. B., Bashar, S. K., Lazaro, J., Reljin, N., Noh, Y., & Chon, K. H. (2021). A robust ECG denoising technique using variable frequency complex demodulation. *Computer Methods and Programs in Biomedicine, 200*, 105856.

18. Khan, A. H., Hussain, M., & Malik, M. K. (2021). Arrhythmia classification techniques using deep neural network. *Complexity, 2021*, 1–10

19. Subasi, A., Dogan, S., & Tuncer, T. (2021). A novel automated tower graph based ECG signal classification method with hexadecimal local adaptive binary pattern and deep learning. *Journal of Ambient Intelligence and Humanized Computing, 14*(2), 1–15.

20. Abdullah, S. M. S. A., Ameen, S. Y. A., Sadeeq, M. A., & Zeebaree, S. (2021). Multimodal emotion recognition using deep learning. *Journal of Applied Science and Technology Trends, 2*(02), 52–58.

21. Alarsan, F. I., & Younes, M. (2019). Analysis and classification of heart diseases using heartbeat features and machine learning algorithms. *Journal of Big Data, 6*(1), 1–15.

22. Schlosser, F., & Brockmann, D. (2021). Finding disease outbreak locations from human mobility data. *EPJ Data Science, 10*(1), 52.

23. Carrasco, M., Araya-Letelier, G., Velázquez, R., & Visconti, P. (2021). Image-based automated width measurement of surface cracking. *Sensors, 21*(22), 7534.

24. Joseph Michael Jerard, V., Thilagaraj, M., Pandiaraj, K., Easwaran, M., Govindan, P., & Elamaran, V. (2021). Reconfigurable architectures with high-frequency noise suppression for wearable ECG devices. *Journal of Healthcare Engineering, 2021*, 1–12.

25. Xie, X., Liu, H., Shu, M., Zhu, Q., Huang, A., Kong, X., & Wang, Y. (2021). A multi-stage denoising framework for ambulatory ECG signal based on domain knowledge and motion artifact detection. *Future Generation Computer Systems, 116*, 103–116.

26. Algarni, A. D., Soliman, N. F., Abdallah, H. A., El-Samie, A., & Fathi, E. (2021). Encryption of ECG signals for telemedicine applications. *Multimedia Tools and Applications, 80*(7), 10679–10703.

27. Gao, J., Zhang, H., Lu, P., & Wang, Z. (2019). An effective LSTM recurrent network to detect arrhythmia on imbalanced ECG dataset. *Journal of Healthcare Engineering, 2019*, 1–10

28. Chowdhury, M. H., & Cheung, R. C. (2019). Reconfigurable architecture for multi-lead ecg signal compression with high-frequency noise reduction. *Scientific Reports, 9*(1), 1–12.

29. Abdulbaqi, A. S., & Al-din, S. (2020, November). Feature extraction and classification of ECG signal based on the standard extended wavelet transform technique: Cardiology based telemedicine. In *IOP Conference Series: Materials Science and Engineering* (Vol. 928, No. 3, p. 032029). IOP Publishing.

30. Lin, Y. J., Chuang, C. W., Yen, C. Y., Huang, S. H., Huang, P. W., Chen, J. Y., & Lee, S. Y. (2019, May). An intelligent stethoscope with ECG and heart sound synchronous display. In *2019 IEEE International Symposium on Circuits and Systems* (ISCAS) (pp. 1–4). IEEE.

31. *MIT-BIH Arrhythmia Database*. (n.d.). MIT-BIH Arrhythmia Database | Kaggle. https:/// datasets/taejoongyoon/mitbit-arrhythmia-database.

Part 2

Role of Artificial Intelligence
and IoT in Health Care

9 Human Disease Prediction System – Application of AI Techniques in Chronic Diseases

Asha Joseph and Shiju George
Amal Jyothi College of Engineering

CONTENTS

9.1 INTRODUCTION: OVERVIEW

This chapter aims to describe the techniques used for "Human Disease Prediction" for possible chronic diseases such as diabetes, skin cancer, and heart problems. There are many recommended systems which take the user's symptoms as input and use data mining techniques to perform provisional diagnosis, similar to what is done at telemedicine centers. Symptoms, physical tests, and physical signs of the patient's body are frequently used to diagnose disease. Normally, doctors use their expertise and experience to detect illness. In the medical field, detecting and predicting diseases is a difficult challenge. Predicting disease based on multiple characteristics is a multi-layered problem that can lead to false assumptions and unanticipated outcomes. As a result, the healthcare sector now generates vast amounts of sophisticated information relevant to patients, disease diagnosis, electronic patient records, hospital resources, and medical gadgets, among other things. This results in processing the massive volume of data and getting evaluated to extract knowledge that can be used to help cost-cutting and decision-making. Significant progress in biomedical research has led to large amounts of data being generated. With the help of artificial intelligence (AI), meaningful information can be extracted from large volumes of data with very less human interference in a shorter time frame. Nonetheless, the pathological lesions of images have been taught in convolutional neural networks (CNNs) (a deep learning [DL] method).

This chapter generally discusses how artificial neural networks with genetic algorithms can be combined to reduce computing time and improve performance. Secondly, the chapter depicts more about the application of better machine learning (ML) or precisely DL techniques. Further, the chapter introduces the new technology of microrobots and nanorobots which are already in use for on-site diagnosis, precise therapy, and other biomedical applications because of their extraordinary biocompatibility and biodegradability.

9.2 RELATED WORKS

Human health is a relative state in which one can function well, i.e. physically, mentally, and live socially well-being within the environment in which one is living. The human body is an incredible machine; it can adapt, repair itself, and manage challenges throughout life. With the advancement of the world over time, humans have learned to recognize the signs of those who are afflicted and to provide treatment for dangerous diseases. Human development, uplifting the marginalized communities and groups, and improving the living standards in rural areas, all rely on the health sector. Though a nationwide collection of primary healthcare clinics has been established, due to a lack of educated personnel, pharmaceuticals, and medicines, among other factors, it has not been functioning successfully in several rural areas. Inadequate funding for necessary recurrent expenditures, resource misallocation, and limited capacity for supervision and coordination of the activities of other agencies providing healthcare services have all impacted the sector's overall performance.

The output of the developed applications like mobile android applications, which is similar to the telemedicine centers, does not provide full diagnostic results. For further treatment, the user should visit a doctor. Prediction is vital to lower the risk of disease. Discovering disease from multiple causes is a multi-faceted problem, which may lead to unpredictable outcomes and false assumptions. When people first become ill, they are often hesitant to visit a doctor or medical facility, which can lead to more serious problems. To address this, many systems are proposed that will assist people by providing an environment in which they can identify their symptoms and note down potentially detected diseases, enabling them to minimize further harm. The suggested systems will also provide basic illness preventive measures and an overview of the disease. At some point in their life, everyone has been a patient, and we all want to be treated well. Doctors, we believe, are all medical professionals who make recommendations based on extensive research. That, however, is not always the case. Analyzing data and combining it with the patient's medical profile would take time and skill even if they had access to the huge collection of data needed to compare with the treatment results for all the diseases they have come across. However, a physician's profession does not include in-depth study and statistical analysis. The current technology is complex in design and is only utilized for a specific type of disease. Most of the systems that have been built lack a proper prototype and implementing the systems that have already been developed is difficult.

9.3 DATA MINING TECHNIQUES IN DISEASE PREDICTION

Many strategies and models have been developed to date to use data mining techniques to predict diseases. Some of them are as follows:

9.3.1 INTELLIGENT HEART DISEASE PREDICTION SYSTEM

This work depicts the data mining techniques such as Naive Bayes, Decision Trees, and Neural Networks, which were used to create a prototype. This prototype handles the answers to the complex "what-if" queries, which traditional decision support system may not be able to answer. It is web-based, user-friendly, scalable, reliable, and expandable [6].

9.3.2 MEDICAL DIAGNOSIS USING BACK PROPAGATION ALGORITHM

The feed-forward back propagation technique is used in medical diagnosis as a classifier to discriminate between infected and non-infected patients. The technique used a multi-layer neural network with a relatively low learning rate, which is especially important when using a large training set size [5].

9.3.3 DISEASE PREDICTION SYSTEM

A study is conducted on how different classification algorithms can be used to predict cardiac diseases. To evaluate many types of heart-related problems, classification algorithms such as C4.5 Algorithm and Decision Trees and data mining techniques such as clustering and Association Rule mining are used. The Maximal Frequent Item set Algorithm (MAFIA) and C4.5 Algorithm, as well as Clustering Algorithms like K-Means, are used to extract maximal frequent item sets from a transactional database to draw a decision tree. The accuracy of disease can be corroborated with the support of this approach [4].

9.3.4 SMART HEALTH PREDICTION SYSTEM

Medical and educational aspects of clinical predictions are analyzed using the data mining techniques with their applications and an overview is presented in this work. A large amount of data is becoming available because of rules and the availability of computers in the medical and healthcare fields [3]. Humans cannot comprehend such a big volume of data in a short period of time to generate diagnoses and treatment plans. One of the main goals is to delve into data mining techniques in medical and healthcare applications to make accurate conclusions. In this ML combined with database management to discover new patterns and the information that goes along with them from enormous data sets. Clustering, forecasting, path analysis, and predictive analysis are some of the factors used in this system [3].

9.3.5 CHRONIC KIDNEY DISEASE PREDICTION

This work outlines diverse training algorithms like Scaled Conjugate, Bayesian regularization, Levenberg, and the Resilient back propagation Algorithm. After being trained using back propagation methods, the neural net system is utilized to detect kidney diseases in humans. The back propagation techniques proposed here can distinguish between infected and non-infected individuals [2].

9.3.6 MACHINE LEARNING OVER BIG DATA FOR PREDICTION

This work discusses an ML approach that is used for accurate disease prediction. The latent factor model is used to achieve the partial data. Naïve Bayes algorithm is used for clarification of large volumes of data from hospitals. To provide the results of disease prediction, the CNN-Based Multimodal Disease Prediction (CNN-MDRP) algorithm is used in this research [1].

9.4 NEURAL NETWORK MODELS

9.4.1 REAL-TIME HEART DISEASE PREDICTION SYSTEM

The most frequent diseases pertaining to the heart with high mortality rates around the globe include stroke, heart failure, arrhythmia, and myocardial infarction. Due to the excessive cost of the existing diagnostics, heart abnormalities are not detected in their early stages. As a result, a system that reliably estimates the probability of a patient developing heart disease must be evolved significantly, in real time. Through experimental study [7], an overall accuracy of 85.71% for UCI heart disease dataset and an accuracy of 87.30% for the cardiovascular dataset is designed and developed using the neural network model employing a multi-layer perceptron (MLP).

The increase in accuracy was roughly 12%–13% compared with the previous study. Using the Python programming language, a simple web application tool is created to test the prediction algorithm. This study aims to build a user-friendly tool for medical professionals as well as the public [7].

9.4.2 Recommendation System Using Machine Learning and IoT

People nowadays have become affected by a variety of conditions because of their unhealthy lifestyles and the environment. As a result, more people are searching for information about disorders, diagnoses, and solutions online. If a recommendation system for doctors and healthcare users can be created using the clinical profile, it will save a lot of time. Accurately predicting the condition is the most demanding challenge involved in this process. In the traditional technique of diagnosis, the patient visits a doctor, who performs a series of diagnostic tests before reaching a conclusion. Both the doctor and the patient must dedicate themselves to this procedure. This study provides a disease prediction system based on a Graphical user interface that leverages seven classification ML approaches to detect and predict problems. Along with the prediction based on symptoms and specific details on the expected condition, it provides alternate therapy as well. It analyzes body temperature and pulse rate and such readings over online with NodeMCU and ThinkSpeak, and maintains the collection of data in a real-time database on which the healthcare professional or user can have access in the future [9].

9.4.3 Decision Tree Classification Model

The healthcare service deals with billions of individuals around the globe and generates massive amounts of data. Models based on ML are analyzing multi-dimensional medical datasets and providing better options. This model uses various state-of-the-art Supervised ML algorithms that are specifically developed for disease prediction to categorize a cardiovascular dataset. The findings show that the Decision Tree classification model outperformed Naive Bayes, Logistic Regression, Random Forest, SVM, and KNN-based techniques in predicting cardiovascular disorders. With a 73% accuracy, the Decision Tree provided the best outcome. This approach enables the doctors to identify the onset of heart problems and provide adequate solutions in advance [10].

9.4.4 Classifier System Using Machine Learning Algorithms

The evolution, expansion, and application of various well-known data mining approaches have led to the ML approaches to derive useful information from stipulated data in biomedical communities, healthcare, and other industries. Early disease prediction, patient treatment, and community services all benefit from precise medical database analysis. The objective of implementing a classifier system using ML techniques is to significantly assist clinicians in early detection and diagnosis of diseases, which will substantially aid in the treatment of health-related concerns. For study, a sample of 4920 patient records diagnosed with 41 disorders was considered.

There were 41 diseases in the dependent variable. Researchers chose 95 out of 132 independent variables (symptoms) that are strongly associated with diseases and managed to optimize them. In this work, ML algorithms such as the Naive Bayes classifier, Decision Tree classifier, and Random Forest classifier were used to construct the disease prediction system [11].

AI techniques such as ML to DL are widely used in healthcare for drug research, diagnosis, and assessment of risks. To accurately detect diseases using AI approaches, a variety of medical data sources are necessary, including ultrasound, magnetic resonance imaging, mammography, genomics, computed tomography scans, and so on. AI also improved the hospital experience and accelerated the process of getting patients ready to continue their recovery at home. This study investigates how AI can be used to diagnose diseases like chronic heart diseases, diabetes, cancer, tuberculosis, stroke and hypertension, and skin diseases. Various sources on diagnosis were considered and the findings were compared using quality metrics such as accuracy, sensitivity, specificity, prediction rate, recall, area under curve precision, and F1-score [16].

9.5   DEEP LEARNING METHODS IN HUMAN DISEASE PREDICTION

The conventional methods are less accurate and incapable to extract the required features for the decision-making process due to the computational complexity of the medical data. However, with the introduction of DL such problems have been resolved. Below are some of the applications which are described for the effective dissemination and prediction of medical information for diagnosis through DL. It is understood that DL can deal with big data due to its ability to extract multiple and granular features through the hidden layers. Table 9.1 depicts the applications of DL approaches in medicine.

9.5.1   Diabetic Retinopathy

An MLP is used to classify various stages of diabetic retinopathy by taking the input from the integrated output of a classifier and a regression model [15]. This DL technique uses DenseNET architecture which does multi-task to categorize the output. But the technique has a limitation of comprehensiveness of input data and execution time for a large number of images.

9.5.2   Disease Diagnosis Based on Tongue Color Image Analysis

For any system to defeat human experience and intelligence is difficult, but a most appropriate model can be generated, which could help doctors with the diagnosis. An automated DL system can provide information to reveal many diseases [14]. The tongue color images are taken with the help of IoT devices. These images are processed with the help of feature extraction-based Synergic DL method and further uses deep neural network and optimization method. The weighted kappa score is used additionally to assess the performance of the classification done by the proposed algorithm.

TABLE 9.1

Application of Deep Learning Approaches in Medicine

Architecture/Work	Reference	Accuracy/Performance	Challenges
Artificial intelligence and COVID-19 using DL, GANs, ELM, and LSTM	Jamshidi et al. [25]	Bioinformatics approach, diagnosis, and treatment of COVID-19 more accurate	Improvement required in clinical data and medical imaging
Deep learning in skin diseases based on image recognition	Li et al. [26]	Better than the other computer-aided treatment methods	Need of high-performance graphics processors, philosophical, ethical, and legal bottlenecks
Detecting diseases by human physiological parameter-based DL	Qu & Liu et al (2019) [27]	Expanding learning system for detection of diabetes complications achieved high accuracy (95.6) and robust performance	Prevention of overfitting is not researched
Deep Learning for biomedical tongue color image analysis	Mansour et al. [14]	ADSL-TCL model, deep neural network (DNN)–based classifier, with maximum precision, recall, and accuracy 0.98, 0.97, and 0.98	Advanced DL architecture may be used to enhance the diagnostic performance
Multi-tasking DL model for diabetic retinopathy	Majumder & Kehtarnavaz [15]	Dense DNN with high accuracy	Comprehensiveness of the dataset and training time for large set of images, real-time implementation future work

9.5.3 Skin Disease Image Recognition

The advent of fusion of multiple DL models replaced the computer aided and a dermatologist for decision-making. Diseases like nevus, basal cell carcinoma, melanoma, eczema, psoriasis, and seborrheic need quantitative and quality feature extraction of lesion tissues using images [26]. The multi-modal fusion with AlexNet, VGG, Inception, and ResNet is used to break through the bottleneck of single models. Various DL frameworks like keras, tensorflow, and pytorch are used to do the skin disease predictions.

9.5.4 COVID Care

DL was most popularly used for the diagnosis and treatment of COVID. Specifically, the integrated bioinformatics approach in which data from various structured and unstructured data sources are used by the GAN, long short-term memory (LSTM), RNN, and hybrid models to retrieve important clinical information for

TABLE 9.2
DL Approaches in Healthcare

Model	Applications Used in Chronic Disease	Advantages of Models	Challenges
DBN	Diabetes	Reduce the dimensionality of the features	Not cost effective
RNN	Heart diseases	Quick for short duration prediction	Encounters gradient-vanishing problem for long data sequences
LSTM/GRU	Diabetes	Keep the capacity to memorize and predict longer-term prediction	Inclusion of optimization will help better results
DNN	Heart diseases	Better accuracy rate	The learning process is slow
GAN	CT image analysis	Generate features to identify more robust output	Training and validating the generated features for huge image set during the learning process is tedious
CNN	Lung, heart diseases, cancer	Quick learning and better performance for the 2D data inputs	Grouping has limitations of data categorization

decision-making [25]. The top techniques used to address COVID-19 issues are medical image processing, drug discovery, bioinformatics, toxicology, and natural language processing [13].

Table 9.2 describes the DL algorithms used in various applications, advantages, and challenges yet to be solved [8]. The basic ANN can influence the performance of classification due to being sensitive to conversion and modifications, with the advancement of DL techniques like CNN helps to guarantee the transformations and modifies invariances with most appropriate feature extractions. The DL methods in healthcare are depicted in Figure 9.1.

In healthcare-supervised learning provides output for decision-making considering multiple related tasks simultaneously with the help of DBN consisting of undirected layers called RBM, unlike DNN, DBN is faster and provides more robust results for medical data. The historical medical data provides a sequence of data evidence to predict cause or disease using RNN method but fails to remember long sequences leading to gradient-vanishing problems [20]. Therefore, to overcome such problems LSTM/GRu methods are adapted to deal with long-term dependency and complexity of medical data. It is also important to capture and generate images to do analysis and study of critical diseases, for which GAN is found to be robust.

9.6   USAGE OF MICRO- OR NANOROBOTS IN HEALTHCARE

Nanomedicine is a method that applies AI and robotics to diagnose, treat, prevent disease and severe damage, relieve pain, maintain, and improve human health using

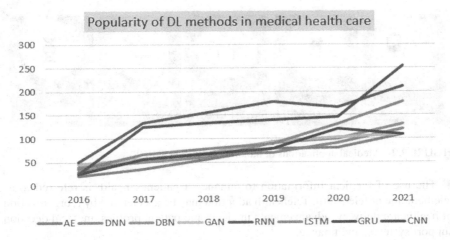

FIGURE 9.1   Popularity of DL methods in healthcare.

nanotechnology [18,24]. Nanomedical robots have a wide range of applications, including cancer diagnosis and early detection, medication administration, tissue engineering, gene delivery systems, cardiology, body vital analysis, diabetes monitoring, minimally invasive brain surgery, and imaging and detecting capabilities.

As mentioned by Giri et al. [19], challenges in the application of nanorobots are mainly for in vivo purposes, such as drug delivery, cargo transport, and for precision therapy. Micro/nanovehicles must be carefully designed to be used efficiently in a variety of biological applications. Biocompatibility and toxicity of nanorobots are also the factors to be considered. Researchers don't fully comprehend the interaction mechanisms between nanorobots and living systems, such as the complexities of the interaction of materials used to build nanorobots with biological matter, which could lead to changes in the surface characteristics of nanorobots depending on their environment [23]. As a result, the possible dangers and hazards are not completely understood. Figure 9.2 depicts the different medical applications of nanorobots.

Nanorobots have the potential to play a significant part in the elimination or treatment of common ailments, as well as advances in physical and mental skills, but their dynamic features are still being researched and tested. This is mostly owing to nanorobots' need to interact with their surroundings at a cellular level, which remains a substantial issue. Robots as small as the thickness of a human hair have recently been created. After being directed to a specific target area, the robot might administer medicine, eradicate malignant tumors, or remove plaque. A quest is on to explore and create a nanorobot that can be implanted into the eye and remain there for months, providing a treatment to prevent disease-causing blood vessel expansion. It is expected in the near future to consider nanorobotics a unique tool in medicine and humans may envisage their bodies being stuffed with tiny robots that do various diagnoses and therapeutic activities to keep them healthy on the inside.

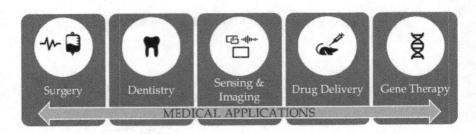

FIGURE 9.2   Medical applications of nanorobots (Giri et al. [19]).

The use of medical information to enhance a patient's health is referred to as telemedicine or telehealth. Telehealth adoption may be accelerated by reorganization of healthcare delivery, advancements in electronic patient profiles, medical decision support systems, and finance.

An AI and ML toolbox can greatly assist in identifying the essential attributes of nanomaterials pertinent to natural processes, that may be beneficial for nanotherapeutics implementations including toxicity reduction [22]. As an example, because the biophysiochemical interface of the NP corona dictates the biological identity of the NP, employing ML methods to uncover material qualities, size/shape, and surface features may give vital insights regarding NPs and their interactions with the environment. Electrostatic agglomeration and buildup, dissolution behavior, and competitive protein bonding above NPs may all be decoded using AI techniques. Traditional experimental procedures based on data association or identification of the most relevant factors are often complex and difficult to anticipate for these features. ML methods may be used to decode the nano-bio interface of nanotoxicology by establishing phase changes and a free energy release–based prediction relationship.

The extensive use of telemedicine allows tasks that were previously performed at the secondary level to be performed at the primary care level, as well as providing continuity and quality improvement in healthcare services. This technology can be cost effective too. By developing integrated systems that include the technological requirements of microsystems, nanorobotics, and telemedicine systems, new technologies will be able to offer unique capabilities in the prevention, diagnosis, treatment, and rehabilitation of isolated patients. Establish the benefits of these technologies, and respond quickly to any possible concerns by issuing alerts to physicians. And occasionally, in unextendible operations in distant regions such as Antarctic space stations or arctic areas and similar places, particularly remote ones may be effectively deployed as diagnostic procedures.

The miniaturization of robotic platforms could give researchers and doctors access to previously hard-to-reach regions of the human body and perform various microscopic medical procedures. However, the clinical usage of these miniature robots is still in the infant stage. In this direction, this review illustrates recent trends in micro/nanorobotics, focusing on their use in precision medicine for clinical usage as shown in Figure 9.3.

As defined by Soto et al. [21], a medical micro/nanorobot is an untethered micro/nanostructure whose goal is to perform any medical procedure and which has an

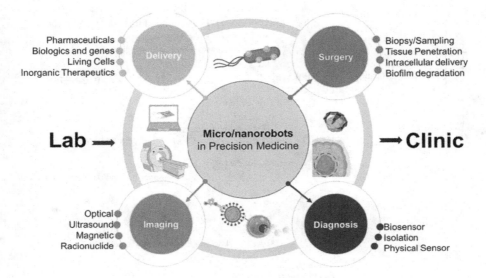

FIGURE 9.3 Use of micro/nanobots in precision therapy (Soto et al. [21]).

engine capable of changing different types of energy sources into mechanical force. In this review, the author depicts the most recent developments of micro/nanorobots from a precision medicine perspective, by introducing a comprehensive overview. He has tried to highlight the most anticipated opportunities for research on usage of nanorobots in healthcare, medical imaging, diagnosis, surgery, and precision therapy. The goals of each of these areas are to deal with diverse challenges in healthcare.

To perform precise diagnosis of disease and analyze the vital signals of the body, it is proved that micro/nanorobots are essential in healthcare. The use of these tiny robots could be in the field of measuring physical properties of tissue in real time or isolating pathogens. To obtain the accurate positioning of these inside the body the integration of micro/nanorobots with medical imaging modalities could be done. The existing challenges in the field of nanorobots are the potential risks associated with the translation of medical nanorobots from lab to clinic. Wearable devices for prevention medicine, daily health monitoring, and robotic control are the recent advances offered by flexible electronics. These sensors are providing the functions such as measuring and recording the physiological signals, vital signs, body kinetics, and dynamic biomolecular state. The implantable robots also play vital roles in detecting or monitoring the physiological or biomedical information and provide competent therapy for the degenerative diseases, once placed inside the body. Advanced functionalities which are not even heard of are emerging in this field as wearable robotic exoskeletons which assist or augment human mobility. BodyNET is one such new technology with new platforms merged, which is a network of implantable devices, wearable sensors, and exoskeletons for reinforced healthcare and health outcomes. In the article, He and Lee [20], sum up the progress of self-powered wearable sensors and convey a brief review of recent developments in flexible and wearable sensors, which are based on piezoelectric and triboelectric

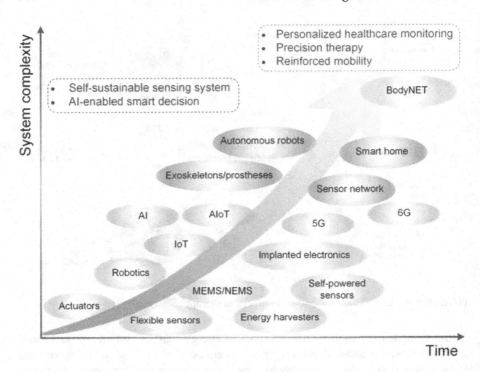

FIGURE 9.4 An overview of technology evolution (He & Lee [20]).

nanogenerators. Figure 9.4 shows an overview of technology revolution from discrete elements and platforms to a spatiotemporal and competent bodyNET for customized healthcare monitoring, reinforced mobility, and precision therapy.

The area of science dedicated to the research and development of machines whose size belongs to the micron scale is called microrobotics. These machines called micro- and nanorobots have a wide range of applications – especially in the biomedical domain where they can be used to perform tasks such as targeted drug delivery, minimally invasive surgeries, single-cell manipulation, and so on. Typically, a large number of micro- or nanorobots will be developed for this purpose. The development of these robots will be focused on their programmability for multiple tasks, reconfigurability for easy reuse for various medical tasks. Typically, the target application of these robots is in-place delivery of drugs to diseased cells, carrying out microsurgeries at the cellular level.

A special category of these robots is called biohybrid micro (and nano) robots. These robots are a combination of biological components such as DNA, enzymes, cells, and synthesized inorganic and polymer components. Biohybrid robots have special abilities such as sensing their surroundings and swarm actions that make them excellent tools for advanced drug delivery to the targeted cells. Another important aspect of biohybrid robots is their biodegradability that makes it relatively easy to get them out of the body once their targets are achieved (Table 9.3).

TABLE 9.3
Comparison of Studies on the Application of Micro/Nanobots in Healthcare

Architecture/Work	Reference	Applications	Challenges
Robotics hardware and bioinspired nanorobots	Giri et al. [19]	Surgery, dentistry, sensing and imaging, drug delivery, and gene therapy	Biocompatibility and toxicity of nanorobots
Robotics in telemedicine during COVID-19, used microbial dynamic analysis algorithm using Lagrange methods	Shahri & Sonia Sayyedalhosseini [22]	Nanorobots in pandemic diseases Diagnosis and drug delivery, surgery Cost-effective	Prediction of nanotoxicology needs improvement; binding of protein is complex and difficult to predict using conventional methods
Micro/nanorobots in precision medicine	Soto et al. [21]	Diagnosis, treatment, drug delivery, medical imaging, surgery and gene therapy	Clinical translation, improving the scalability of diagnostic tools, enabling the high-throughput detection, market challenges
Wearable devices	He & Lee [20]	Healthcare monitoring, precision therapy, AI-enabled smart decision	Feasibility of wearable devices vary person to person Social acceptance and privacy are problems
Intelligent drug delivery	Jinhua et al. [18]	Drug delivery, single-cell manipulation, and cell microsurgery	Clinical translation and application of biohybrid micro- and nanorobots

9.7 SUMMARY

This chapter presents recently released research findings that used AI-based learning approaches to diagnose diseases and AI strategies for disease prediction. AI is the ability of machines (computer systems) to do simulation of human tasks with learning, reasoning, and self-correction as part of the simulation. We need AI because the amount of work we must do is increasing every day. As a result, automating basic tasks is an excellent idea. It saves time and effort for any organization and its employees while increasing efficiency of the production [13].

By resolving some of the industry's most important priorities, AI has the potential to improve healthcare. Improved patient outcomes, as well as enhanced production and efficiency, are all possible results of AI. AI is a multi-dimensional realm of data, algorithms, analytics, DL, neural networks, and insights that are constantly evolving and adapting to the demands of the healthcare business and patients. AI techniques in the healthcare sector, particularly for disease diagnosis, are critical. This chapter is divided into many sections that include the diagnosis of chronic diseases such as heart disease, skin diseases, and diabetes with the purpose of providing insight into how machine and DL techniques perform over a variety of disease detection domains. An analysis of the quality of the works conducted and a discussion of AI techniques were included in the introduction. Later, numerous AI paradigms for disease detection models using data mining and neural networks were explored, as well as other AI applications in healthcare. The outcomes of applied ML algorithms in terms of several variables such as accuracy, sensitivity, and precision have also been portrayed. To summarize, medical experts now have a better understanding of how AI can be utilized for disease detection, which will lead to more acceptable ideas for future AI research. Even medical specialists realize the challenges that must be addressed before diseases may be recognized using AI. Doctors are hesitant to fully rely on AI-based treatments currently since they are uncertain of their ability to predict illnesses and symptoms. As a result, significant work must be done to train AI-based systems so that the accuracy of approaches for identifying diseases can be improved. As a result, AI-based research should be undertaken with the aforementioned factors in mind to ensure that AI and doctors have a mutually beneficial partnership.

The future of AI could be in privacy-preserving digital devices with AI as mentioned in Joseph [12], which may aid in the confidentiality and security of the patient records. In the healthcare industry, AI refers to the design, development, and deployment of micro- and nanorobots to detect, learn, comprehend, and perform administrative and clinical tasks. Micro- and nanobots have shown significant potential to conduct tasks which human beings find very difficult, such as drug delivery, cell manipulation, biosensing. Microrobots could be employed in minimally invasive surgery as well. Opening clogged veins or other channels, hyperthermia treatment, injection, electrical stimulation, biopsies, cauterization, cutting, drilling, or biomaterial removal are among surgical procedures that a microrobot could do [17]. The next work that should be undertaken by the researchers is the application of AI in forensic medicine which may require legal approval. With time, it is anticipated that more advanced technologies will help run models using huge datasets and explore underlying patterns of disease impact. This opens new opportunities for medical devices and diagnostic companies, with AI application, which will further lead to more accuracy enhancement in treatments, in turn adding opportunities for innovation.

REFERENCES

1. Shirsath, S.S. & Patil, S., (2018). Disease Prediction Using Machine Learning over Big Data. *International Journal of Innovative Research in Science, Engineering and Technology*, 7(6), 6752–6757.
2. Borisagar, N., Barad, D., & Raval, P. (2017). Chronic Kidney Disease Prediction Using Back Propagation Neural Network Algorithm. *Proceedings of International Conference on Communication and Networks*, India, pp. 295–303.

3. Kamble, N., Harmalkar, M., Bhoir, M., & Chaudhary, S. (2017). Smart Health Prediction System Using Data Mining. *International Journal of Scientific Research in Computer Science, Engineering, and Information Technology*, 2(2), 1020–1025.

4. Banu, M.A.N. & Gomathy, B. (2013). Disease Predicting System Using Data Mining Techniques. *International Journal of Technical Research and Applications*, 1(5), 41–45.

5. Shreevastava, M. & Gupta, A., (2011). Medical Diagnosis Using Back Propagation Algorithm. *International Journal of Emerging Technology and advanced Engineering*, 1(1), 55–58.

6. Palaniappan, S. & Awang, R. (2008). Intelligent Heart Disease Prediction System Using Data Mining Technique. *2008 IEEE/ACS International Conference on Computer Systems and Applications*, IEEE, France.

7. Bhoyar, S., Wagholikar, N., Bakshi, K., & Chaudhari, S. (2021). Real-Time Heart Disease Prediction System Using Multilayer Perceptron. *Proceedings of 2nd International Conference for Emerging Technology (INCET)*, Belgaum, pp. 1–4.

8. Al-Milli, N. (2013). Backpropagation Neural Network for Prediction of Heart Disease. *Journal of Theoretical and Applied Information Technology*, 56(1), 131–135.

9. Sanjay. J P, Naga, T., Deepak & Manimozhi, M. (2021). Prediction of Health Problems and Recommendation System Using Machine Learning and IoT. *Proceedings of Innovations in Power and Advanced Computing Technologies (i-PACT)*, Kuala Lumpur, pp. 1–8.

10. Princy, R.J.P., Parthasarathy, S., Hency Jose, P.S., Raj Lakshminarayanan, A., Jeganathan, S. (2020). Prediction of Cardiac Disease using Supervised Machine Learning Algorithms. *Proceedings of 4th International Conference on Intelligent Computing and Control Systems (ICICCS)*, Secunderabad, pp. 570–575.

11. Grampurohit, S. & Sagarnal, C. (2020). Disease Prediction Using Machine Learning Algorithms. *Proceedings of International Conference for Emerging Technology (INCET)*, Belgaum, pp. 1–7.

12. Joseph, A. (2020). Digital Evidence Acquisition Techniques for Crime Profiling based on Process Execution Context Analysis (*PhD Thesis*). VIT Vellore, India.

13. Vasal, S., Jain, S., & Verma, A. (2020). COVID-AI: An Artificial Intelligence System to Diagnose COVID 19 Disease. *Journal of Engineering Research and Technology*, 9(1), 1–6.

14. Mansour, R. F., Althobaiti, M. M., & Ashour, A. A. (2021). Internet of Things and Synergic Deep Learning Based Biomedical Tongue Color Image Analysis for Disease Diagnosis and Classification, *IEEE Access*, 9, 94769–94779.

15. Majumder, S. & Kehtarnavaz, N. (2021). Multitasking Deep Learning Model for Detection of Five Stages of Diabetic Retinopathy, *IEEE Access*, 9, 123220–123230.

16. Kumar, Y., Koul, A., Singla, R., & Ijaz, M.F. (2022). Artificial Intelligence in Disease Diagnosis: A Systematic Literature Review, Synthesizing Framework and Future Research Agenda. *Journal of Ambient Intelligence and Humanized Computing*, 13, 1–28.

17. Lamkin-Kennard, K.A. & Popovic, M.B. (2019). Molecular and cellular level—Applications in biotechnology and medicine addressing molecular and cellular level. Chapter 8, *Biomechatronics*, 201–233.

18. Li, J., Dekanovsky, L., Khezri, B., Wu, B., Zhou, H., & Sofer, Z. (2022). Biohybrid Micro- and Nanorobots for Intelligent Drug Delivery, *AAAS Journal of Cyborg and Bionic Systems*, 2022(1), 1–13.

19. Giri, G., Maddahi, Y., & Zareinia, K. (2021). A Brief Review on Challenges in Design and Development of Nanorobots for Medical Applications. *Applied Sciences*, 11(21), 10385.

20. He, T. & Lee, C. (2021). Evolving Flexible Sensors, Wearable and Implantable Technologies Towards BodyNET for Advanced Healthcare and Reinforced Life Quality, *IEEE Open Journal of Circuits and Systems*, 2(1), 702–720.

21. Soto, F., Wang, J., Ahmed, R., & Demirci, U. (2020). Medical Micro/Nanorobots in Precision Medicine. *International Journal of Advanced Science*, 7(21), 1–34.
22. Shahri, S.S.Z. & Sonia Sayyedalhosseini, S. (2021). Use of Medical Micro and Nano Robots in Telemedicine in COVID-19 Pandemic. *International Journal of Nanomedicine and Nanosurgery*, 5(1), 1–10.
23. Arvidsson, R. & Hansen, S.F. (2020). Environmental and Health Risks of Nanorobots: An Early Review. *Environmental Science Nano*, 7(10), 2875–2886.
24. Thangavel, K., Balamurugan, A., Elango, M., Subiramaniyam, P., & Senrayan, M. (2018). A Survey on Nanorobotics in Nanomedicine. *Journal of Nanoscience and Nanotechnology*, 2(5), 525–528.
25. Jamshidi, M., et al. (2020). Artificial Intelligence and COVID-19: Deep Learning Approaches for Diagnosis and Treatment. *IEEE Access*, 8(1), 109581–109595.
26. Li, L.F., Wang, X., Hu, J., Xiong, N.N., Du, X., & Li, B.S. (2020). Deep Learning in Skin Disease Image Recognition: A Review. *IEEE Access*, 8(1), 208264–208280.
27. Liu, Y., Zhang, Q., Zhao, G., Qu, Z., Liu, G., Liu, Z., An, Y. (2019). Detecting Diseases by Human-Physiological-Parameter-Based Deep Learning. *IEEE Access*, 7(1), 22002–22010.

10 Internet of Things in Mental Healthcare Worldwide – A Study

S. G. Hymlin Rose
R.M.D Engineering College

S. Janani
Periyar Maniammai Institute of Science & Technology

Anchana P. Belmon
Rajadhani Institute of Engineering and Technology

CONTENTS

DOI: 10.1201/9781003307778-12

10.1 INTRODUCTION

The Internet of Things (IoT) is slowly building its way into the healthcare and wellness industries. Based on recent research by Vodafone, 77% of healthcare respondents claimed an increase in disbursing more IoT compared to the previous year, and the scope of their initiatives has also grown simultaneously. Around 60% of those polled said they used sensors to keep track of people's blood pressure, sugar levels, and other vital signs in order to provide proper healthcare [1].

The Internet of Medical Things (IoMT) is a group of medical software and hardware that communicates with internet computer networks to link with healthcare IT systems. Wi-Fi-enabled medical devices provide the machine-to-machine connectivity that forms the core of IoMT [2]. IoMT examples include tracking patient medication orders and the whereabouts of patients admitted to hospitals, monitoring patients with chronic or long-term diseases remotely, and patients' wearable mHealth devices, which can relay information to caregivers. Medical devices that can be converted to or used with IoMT technology include hospital beds equipped with sensors that monitor patients' vital signs and infusion pumps that connect to analytics dashboards [3].

The emphasis is shifting toward health and prevention. People are living longer as a result of the adoption of IoT, which has also permitted self-reliance for longer periods of time, and the focus has shifted to chronic care [1]. The key component of the IoT is to swap the healthcare of a person into a modern healthcare system. The requirements for smart healthcare are as follows: (i) The accurate treatment should be given to the right person at appropriate time; (ii) It enables medical practitioners to accurately ascertain illness and heal patients' ailments; (iii) It enables all parties to communicate and exchange information effectively; (iv) Data availability in a conveniently accessible location; (v) Appropriate notification of patients for the perfect treatment without any delay; (vi) As a result of its cost-effective models, healthcare can be brought to remote areas; and (vii) It increases effectiveness by eliminating excess and increasing operational cost [4].

The healthcare market is divided into five sections: (i) hospitals, (ii) pharmaceuticals, (iii) medical devices, (iv) diagnostics and medical kits, and (v) telemedicine (Sethi & Sarangi [5]). In metropolitan regions, about half of the money spent on in-patient beds is for lifestyle-related complaints [4]. Obesity, alcohol consumption, poor diet, high cholesterol, and high blood pressure are the leading causes of lifestyle-related disorders. Due to internet advancements and telecommunication-associated technologies, the IoT in telemedicine is a rapidly increasing area.

Telemedicine has the potential to overcome the gap in healthcare between rural and metropolitan areas. It offers inexpensive consultation fees, remote diagnostic capabilities, and the ability to reach even the most remote locations [6]. Home healthcare is another IoT application. IT advancements and the incorporation of medical devices have made us achieve the best quality, low-cost healthcare for the needy people at home ourselves. Customers can save almost 20%–50% on their prices. The IoT incorporates a variety of technologies, one of which is mobile computing. Customers can now access healthcare services at lower costs because of advancements in mobile technologies such as 4G and 5G [7]. According to a PwC poll from 2017, 64% of Indian healthcare businesses claimed that they were investing in IoT [6].

10.2 HEALTHCARE SYSTEM ARCHITECTURE

An IoMT application connects a set of devices to a cloud server via gateways as shown in Figure 10.1 (e.g., smart medical devices for remote patient monitoring, RFID tags, and readers for IoT-based tracking).

10.3 CAN THE IOT HELP WITH YOUR MENTAL HEALTH?

Mental health awareness is growing, as are the skills to help everyone live happier, healthier lives. In a similar vein, the IoT is rapidly evolving. Combining the two,

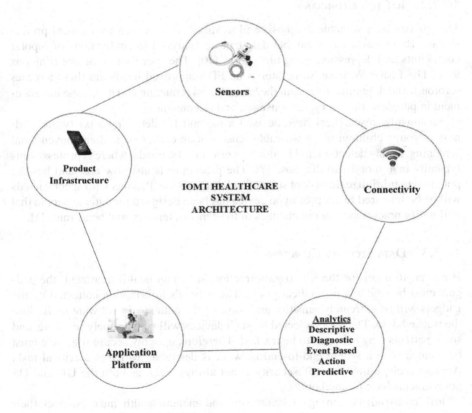

FIGURE 10.1 Architecture of IoMT.

through using IoT devices to promote mental health, has far-reaching implications for our thoughts, mental health, and research [8].

10.3.1 IoT for Self-Care

Mental health apps in IoT are aimed at reducing sadness and anxiety. To monitor symptoms of a panic attack, sensors that can be incorporated with a wristband are one idea. The "Breathe Watch" informs the user and their caregivers when an attack is impending and enables calming solutions for the user. Similarly, Alexa and Google Assistant skills can help users discover and address potential mental health issues. Early alleviation comes from taking breathing-related exercises and walking. The best way of basic diagnosis is to ask themselves how well they slept last night, eat, work, and so on. The device may give precise information (to enhance sleeping styles, for example) or inform users to consult the doctor based on their responses [9]. Of course, neither of these technologies is envisioned to completely replace doctors and psychiatrists. However, it can make facilities more handy and deliver support when alternative options aren't available. Any assistance is preferable to none at all.

10.3.2 IoT for Clinicians

The IoT can be a valuable diagnosis and treatment contrivance for medical professionals. Brain scans and wearable data can be analyzed for indications of bipolar complaints and depression using algorithms [10]. The success rate of one trial was 92%. The Fisher Wallace Stimulator is an FDA-approved headband that increases serotonin and dopamine release in the brain. Stress reduction and happiness enhancement in people with misery, nervousness, and sleeplessness.

Meanwhile, researchers have devised a method for detecting anxiety and sadness in young children using wearable sensors at an earlier stage than conventional screening. It may detect mental health concerns in 20 seconds, whereas professionals typically take months to diagnose [7]. The procedure is also low cost and has the potential to minimize the risk of suicide and drug misuse. Patients with special needs will be better cared for. A prototype device has been designed for autistic people that will notify practitioners about changes in their mood, tension, and heart rate [11].

10.3.3 Data Security Concerns

However, in order for the IoT to gain traction in mental health treatment, the gadgets must be safe and of medical grade. The patient's information collected by the gadgets will be extremely sensitive and some of the patients do not want to disclose the tracked data. The data collected by such devices will be extremely sensitive, and some patients may not want to be tracked. Therefore, a highly secure life cycle must be created with a secure end-to-end network is desirable, which is a critical task. Appropriately, up-to-date IoT security is not always ideal, as both the UK and US governments have pointed out.

IoT industrialists aiming at healthcare and mental health must connect their strict security measures to allay fears of data leaks. Using federated data to notice demographic patterns could be a viable approach that avoids the complexity of patient personal data. Still, it restricts the level of understanding required for optimal mental wellness [12,13].

10.3.4 PROGRESSIVE STEPS

Though the early experiments with the IoT for mental health are a stage in the accurate direction, opening up a conversation about the technology's options for our mental health and contributing to important societal discussions. Each mind matters, and the IoT will help us care for them all [14].

10.4 ROLE OF SMART DEVICES AND AI TO MONITOR MENTAL HEALTH

Smart phones and smart watches may be able to identify tiny changes in behavior and provide assistance to users. A new program aims to use smart phones and smart watches to detect minor changes in behavior and assist people in better monitoring and managing their behavioral health conditions [15].

Because mental illnesses like depression and bipolar disorder don't have obvious signs and are difficult to identify, doctors may be able to use smart devices and artificial intelligence (AI) to better monitor and treat their patients' behavioral health, according to a news release [16].

10.4.1 A NEW, AI-DRIVEN ERA

Tanzeem Choudhury of Cornell University founded the Precision Behavioral Health Initiative to help mobile health enter a new, AI-driven era. Bridges between the current gaps in reliable assessment, personalized intervention, and therapeutic impact could be constructed in this manner. The program seeks "precision technology" such as smart phones, smart watches, and other sensing IoT gadgets to continually and accurately monitor the signals of mental changes manifested in actions [17].

10.4.2 ROLE OF AI AND IoT TECHNOLOGY IN THE TREATMENT OF MENTAL HEALTH ISSUES

AI and IoT devices are lessening the problems that persons with mental health issues encounter when used together. Below are four ways that technology is leading the way into the future [18].

There is still a stigma connected with mental health issues, despite the fact that it is less prevalent than in the past. Some people are afraid of being judged if they acknowledge they need help from friends or if they schedule an appointment with an expert [19]. AI chatbots solve the above-said problem by letting people converse about their problems at any time. Some chatbots have been taught using mock transcripts from counselors, allowing them to answer queries about difficult issues like suicide. Other chatbots are free or have low monthly subscription rates, making them appealing to low-income patients. Mental health services may be particularly difficult to come by in small towns. Individuals may experience such low moods that leaving the house seems difficult. Distance or fear can create a hole, which chatbots fill. However, it is critical that users don't turn into so dependent on chatbots that they isolate themselves even more than before when they need human interaction the most [20].

When it comes to receiving mental health assistance, the internet may be a fantastic resource. However, what people view when accessing online information via devices with screens, thanks to things like social media channels, may make them feel worse. A skill exists that allows consumers to use an Amazon or Google smart speaker to address some of their mental health issues. It's called Mindscape, and it's aimed at the UK market. The skill begins by instructing individuals on breathing exercises before probing them further about the situations that are causing them emotional distress. People choose from a list of ten main categories, including sleep, money, and job. They are then given specific suggestions on how to deal with whatever is bugging them. It's simple to add other topics if the necessity arises, thanks to the skill's design.

The skill's inventors don't want the technology to take the role of mental health specialist, but they feel it might help people deal with everyday stress and those who wish to minimize their anxiety. They believe it could help someone who is having an early-morning panic attack and doesn't know who to call.

Smart speakers are becoming more popular as IoT devices as they become more ubiquitous in homes around the world. People with this skill can use their voices to request assistance. It should be clear that the data collected should not be compromised and the other smart speaker choices for the environment should develop applications based on the criteria. Some of the current ones want to address information which makes individuals uncomfortable [21].

According to research, 70% of people with mental health issues should also have other health issues. The telehealth platforms can provide a single nursing care for all of those patients' needs. They may, for example, talk about their growing depression and get their high blood pressure medication adjusted in one telemedicine appointment or at the very least a single service. Additionally, a growing number of high-quality software choices that integrate electronic health records (EHRs) and telemedicine to benefit doctors and patients are becoming available. A patient might access the portal at any time and safely view the treatment information on any connected device with a screen. Similarly, before or after an appointment, doctors might utilize EHR and analyze the patient's history [22].

Another telehealth alternative is SimpleC Companion, which operates on devices like laptops or PCs and provides patients with personalized movies, medicine aid memoir, and more. The system assists with chronic care supervision and sends alerts to household members or other guardians when a patient deviates from their treatment strategy. SimpleC Companion isn't just for those with mental illnesses; it also seeks to prevent admissions to the hospital and allow people to stay healthy at home or wherever they feel most at ease. A feature also provides mental stimulation, which helps the patients to take treatment and relax without any depression.

Even the most skilled doctors have trouble diagnosing individuals who are suffering from mental illnesses. Recent advancements suggest that AI could improve efficiency, allowing clinicians to provide therapies without protracted periods of uncertainty. Three months before people were formally diagnosed by doctors, an AI program that analyzed Facebook posts for symptoms of depression was able to detect the disease. Clinicians may eventually incorporate the AI system into other approaches for arriving at diagnosis. Another AI program examines brain scans and detects possible cases of disorders such as bipolar I disorder and severe depressive disorder. Researchers gathered people who had been diagnosed with mood disorders as well as those who had never been diagnosed with a mental illness to test the algorithm. More than 92% of the time, the AI properly identified patients with mental disorder [23].

Regrettably, that submission is static in its early stages and is not yet ready for extensive clinical use. Doctors, on the other hand, feel it could help distinguish between distinct mental illnesses that can present in similar ways. It may also provide a clearer portrait of how a patient with mental illness reacts to new drugs.

10.5 MODERNIZING MENTAL HEALTHCARE

The majority of the technology developments described here support professionals who are working to improve their patients' well-being. Even a chatbot may be the first thing that prompts a user to seek extra assistance. These four instances demonstrate how technology can be used to improve access to care, improve treatment quality, and provide other benefits. As a result, they may be able to provide extra mental health solutions to people who require them in order to live more fulfilling lives [24].

10.6 IOT WILL CHALLENGE THE IMPROVED PLEA ON
MENTAL HEALTH FACILITIES POST-PANDEMIC

During the Covid-19 pandemic, many mental health-focused IoT platforms saw a spike in demand. The Covid-19 pandemic has had a severe influence on people all around the world in a variety of ways, but one of the most significant has been on mental health. The problem has not only caused delays in the delivery of routine mental healthcare, but it has also put a huge pressure on the mental health of the general populace. Accessing mental health assistance has also been difficult, given that so many people have been forced to stay at home due to the storm, and healthcare facilities are already overburdened with emergency situations.

One of the most crucial factors to consider, especially in the aftermath of a pandemic, is an individual's mental health. The public's mental health has been worsening and the number of instances has been increasing as a result of recent recessions, global geopolitical turmoil, and increased rates of addiction. The American Psychological Association published research in 2019 that revealed a particularly noticeable trend in mental health issues among teenagers and young adults, with a 50% increase in symptom reporting for serious depression from 2005 to 2017.

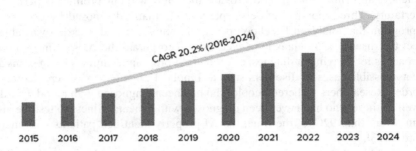

Global trend of IOT in mental Health care

FIGURE 10.2   Increase in demand of IoMT.

According to Global Data's epidemiological estimates, major depressive disorder (MDD) [25] affects over 40% more people than previously thought in the United States, France, Germany, Italy, Spain, the United Kingdom, and Japan. After the pandemic, global MDD prevalence is anticipated to rise even more, from 53.4 million persons in 2019 to 55.4 million in 2029 as in Figure 10.2. There is also a shortage of mental health and addiction treatment providers, making it difficult for many people to get help.

As the number of individuals suffering from mental illnesses rises, innovation in the mental health field will accelerate, resulting in greater use of new technologically assisted care and diagnosis approaches. Consumers will be able to choose from a variety of customized, digital solutions in the mental health arena in the future, according to global data.

Internet of Things (IoT) solutions that gather patient data, such as mobile health (mHealth), are fast developing, with publicly available mobile apps becoming widespread, and a major section of population in the United States and Europe are now possessing smart phones. Mobile apps are especially well suited to treat mental diseases like depression and anxiety, where stigma and a lack of self-confidence are hurdles to therapy and involvement. For example, the non-specific terms 'mental health' or 'depression' bring up over 8,000 medical, lifestyle, or health and fitness apps in the Apple and Google app stores [26].

Many mental health telemedicine platforms, such as Teladoc Health's Betterhelp and TheraPlatform, have reported increased demand since the outbreak began. Between October 2019 and March 2019, the average monthly traffic to Teladoc Health's Betterhelp site was more than three million visits. Last April, this figure jumped to about 4.4 million visits. TheraPlatform is a video conferencing-enabled practice management tool for teletherapy. From September to February, the website received an average of roughly 32,000 monthly hits, increasing to around 617,000 monthly visits from March to June [27].

Virtual health interventions will play an increasingly crucial role in addressing demand as health spending rises and people become more interested and involved. This will necessitate a major redesign to ensure that everyone has access to integrated community and home-based medical care, as well as a future healthcare model that emphasizes prevention, wellness, and early intervention.

10.7 IOT AND THE FUTURE OF MENTAL HEALTH

Around 79% of British own a smart phone and use it an average of 30 times per day and over 10,000 times each year. The advent of stylish and smart phones substituted and incorporated practically the day-to-day aspects of people's life and transforms the physical life into a digital life. The use of smart phones and the integrated technology of IoT develop, modify, and enhance the life we live as easy, efficient, and connected than ever before.

The IoT allows physical devices, houses, and sensors to share data in real time, allowing for a closer link between the actual world and computer-based systems. The potential of IoT is endless, from smart wearables, smart homes, and smart cars to every digital technology, which enriches our lives. We can see how IoT and smart technology can help us regulate and treat our mental health as they become more prevalent in our daily lives. From correctly monitoring and tracking the EHR to boosting message and offering admission to relevant online resources, IoT provides one of the keys to enriched mental health.

Everyday stress and demands, such as job and income, as well as personal connections and experiences, can have an impact on our mental health and well-being. When you add in the current Covid-19 virus and the necessity for communal distance, it is no surprise that many of us are feeling overwhelmed and alone. The trend of increase is expected to increase in the future also as indicated in Figure 10.2. The way we deal with these difficulties differs from person to person. As we turn to digital gadgets to treat people's need to be a car, IoT can assist to link the gap. Some of the ways in which the IoT assists humans with mental health are listed as follows [28].

10.7.1 SMART WEARABLE

Smart sensors are used in wearable technology to observe, detect, and convey the information what our brain is thinking and body is experiencing. The smart watch is the most ubiquitous smart wearable, and the new Apple Watch Series 6 claims to be the future of health on your wrist. One can track sleep, check oxygen levels, and can even conduct an ECG with the Series 6. Building on this, Takeda Pharmaceuticals' Cognition Kit app examines and observes the mental health via a series of quick understanding and attitude investigations, and the outcomes stand fairly hopeful, allowing those who are most afflicted to live a more independent lifestyle.

10.7.2 MOBILE APPLICATIONS AND ALGORITHMS

AI technology is used in mental healthcare and therapy through apps and algorithms. They can provide persons suffering from mental health issues with healthcare and support that they might not otherwise receive, due to distance or economics, for example. AI can talk and listen to people via apps and algorithms, assisting in the detection, prediction, diagnosis, management, and treatment of mental health issues.

10.7.3 Artificial Intelligence

Recently, researchers used a Facebook AI algorithm to analyze user postings and were able to predict indicators of clinical depression three months before the individuals' medical workers spotted them. Persons who use terms like "alone", "ugh", or "tears" in their posts about the emotional state of isolation or segregation could be early cautionary emblems. Investigators believe that if depression is detected and preserved early enough, the negative effects on a person's learning, career, and associations can be minimized.

10.7.4 Chatbots

Woebot and Wysa, for example, are mental health chatbots that give first-line care for those coping with mental health issues. Chatbots are not intended to replace established therapeutic methods, but they can provide additional support and real-time assistance while maintaining clients' privacy and anonymity.

10.7.5 E-Therapy

Anyone with a mental health problem can use an internet connection to get virtual and real-time counseling and advice through online therapy. Individuals can get support and treatment from a real therapist by enrolling in an online program or using video chat capabilities from the comfort of their own homes.

10.7.6 Smart Security and GPS Trackers

It may be said that mental tranquility is everything. People all around the world experience a great sign of relief with the unveiling and the emerging reputation of the smart security. Smart security systems can provide us with a sense of security and peace. We can use our smart phones and smart devices to inspect, act, control, and interconnect with physical devices such as security cameras, alarm systems, thermostats, and doorbells [22,28].

A smart tracking device within the house of the person to be treated and linked to your apps and devices is doing a remarkable thing in the world. It makes advantage of our worldwide network to keep you connected to your favorite things. Curve can be followed in present through the application and areas and personalized warnings can be created.

We are living in an era when the IoT is transforming everything. It allows us to connect our lives in a variety of ways, delivering ease and confidence whether we are keeping track of our health or monitoring our houses and personal possessions. And that is comforting. Some might wonder if we truly need specified applications and AI techniques to manage our mental health, but given how far technology has progressed in our lives, the following is the real question: Can we afford to ignore the potential and beneficial impact it could have on our mental health? [29]. Definitely, the answer should be yes.

10.8 BENEFITS OF IOT IN HEALTHCARE

In the healthcare industry, there are various advantages to implementing IoT. The most important benefit is that, thanks to the very accurate data generated by IoT healthcare devices, treatment outcomes can be substantially improved or maximized, allowing for informed choices. Because all the health records of the patient can be measured at instant and delivered to the team of doctors to which the patient is monitored through healthcare cloud platform, there is a possibility of less error. On these IoT devices, AI-powered algorithms could also support in reaching comprehensible inferences or making endorsements based on the information provided.

Another substantial benefit of IoT in healthcare is cost reduction. Patients who are not in critical condition can stay at home while IoT-based connected devices record and deliver all vital data to the healthcare facility, which avoids the hospital stay and frequent doctor visits. The healthcare facilities come to the conclusion by combining data from a variety of IoT devices. The patient's data will be collected more in real time than the previous records. Despite this, there is a figure of challenges to astound [30].

10.9 CHALLENGES OF IOT IN HEALTHCARE

10.9.1 DATA SECURITY AND PRIVACY

Data security and privacy are two of the most persistent concerns for IoT. The information of the patient is collected using the IoT-enabled devices in real time. However, most of the collected information does not adhere to data protocols and standards.

There is a lot of ambiguity when it comes to data proprietorship and legislation. As a result, data stored in IoT-enabled devices are vulnerable to data theft, making it easier for criminals to get access to the system and compromise vital health information. False health claims and the establishment of phone IDs for buying and vending pharmaceuticals are two examples of IoT device data abuse.

10.9.2 INTEGRATION: MULTIPLE DEVICES AND PROTOCOLS

The integration of different types of equipment makes IoT applications in the healthcare sector difficult. Device manufacturers have yet to agree on communication protocols and standards, which is why this stumbling block exists. As a result, each manufacturer creates their own IoT ecosystem, which is incompatible with other manufacturers' devices and apps. In this instance, there is no way to use a synchronous data aggregation technique. This inconsistency slows the procedure and hinders the use of IoT in healthcare [31].

10.9.3 DATA OVERLOAD AND ACCURACY

Aggregating data for key insights and analysis is tough due to the non-uniformity of data and communication routes. In order to undertake good data analysis, IoT captures data in bulk, which must be separated into chunks without being overwhelmed by absolute accuracy. Furthermore, an abundance of data could have a long-term effect on the hotel industry's decision-making process.

10.9.4 Cost

The design cost of the IoT apps for the mental healthcare solutions is one of the most essential ones to consider. It is desirable, if the IoT solutions to healthcare are genuine and if the application is worthy. While putting an IoT application in place takes time and money, the advantages will surpass the expenses if the firm avoids time and money but improves business processes, creates novel income streams, and increases business trends [32].

10.10 CONCLUSION

IoT is slowly but steadily being integrated into a variety of healthcare applications and services. Despite the fact that IoT has numerous uses in the healthcare sector, many healthcare organizations are still hesitant to completely integrate it into their operations because it is still in its infancy and is not yet standardized. In this chapter, an overview of the IoT technology in mental healthcare is provided. The future of IoT with AI technology will become a high trend within the year 2025 as per the studies undertaken by many corporates. The ways how the IoT can tackle the mental healthcare with AI are also explained in detail. Finally, some of the important challenges of IoT in healthcare and the benefits of using IoMT technology are also summarized.

REFERENCES

1. A. Sawand, S., Djahel, Z. Zhang, F. Nait-Abdesselam (2015). Toward energy-efficient and trustworthy eHealth monitoring system (vol. 12, no. 1, pp. 46–65), *China Communications*.
2. B. Pradhan, S. Bhattacharyya, K. Pal (2021). IoMT-based applications in healthcare devices (vol. 2021, Article ID 6632599), *Journal of Healthcare Engineering*.
3. M. Umair, M. A. Cheema, O. Cheema, H. Li, H. Lu (2021). Impact of COVID-19 on IoMT adoption in healthcare, smart homes, smart buildings, smart cities, transportation and industrial IoMT (vol. 21, no. 11, p. 3838), *Sensors*.
4. S. B. Baker., W. Xiang, I. Atkinson (2017). Internet of things for smart healthcare: Technologies, challenges, and opportunities (vol. 5, pp. 26521–26544), *IEEE Access*.
5. P. Sethi., S. R. Sarangi (2017). Internet of things: Architectures, protocols, and applications (vol. 2017, Article ID 9324035), *Journal of Electrical and Computational. Engineering*.
6. S. Movassaghi, M. Abolhasan, J. Lipman, D. Smith, A. Jamalipour (2014). Wireless body area networks: A survey (vol. 16, no. 3, pp. 1658–1686), *IEEE Communications Survey Tutorials*.
7. H. A. E. Zouka, H. A. El Zouka, M. M. Hosni (2019). Secure IoT communications for smart healthcare monitoring system (vol. 13, p. 100036), *Internet of Things*.
8. F. Shanin., H. A. Aiswarya Das, G. Arya Krishnan, L. S. Neha, N. Thaha., R. P. Aneesh, S. Embran (2018). Portable and centralized e-health record system for patient monitoring using Internet of Things (IoT) (pp. 165–170), *International CET Conference on Control, Communication, and Computing*.

9. K. N. Swaroop, K. Narendra Swaroop, K. Chandu, R., Gorrepotu, S. Deb (2019). A health monitoring system for vital signs using IoT (vol. 5, pp. 116–129), *Internet of Things*.

10. M. M. Rathore, A. Ahmad, A. Paul, J. Wan, D. Zhang (2016). Real-time medical emergency response system: Exploiting IoT and big data for public health (vol. 40, no. 12, p.283), *Journal of Medical Systems*.

11. V. M. Rohokale, N. R. Prasad, R. Prasad (2011). A cooperative Internet of Things (IoT) for rural healthcare monitoring and control, *2nd International Conference on Wireless Communication, Vehicular Technology, Information Theory and Aerospace & Electronic Systems Technology (Wireless VITAE)*, Chennai.

12. J. Mohammed, C.-H. Lung, A. Ocneanu, A. Thakral, C. Jones, A. Adler (2014). Internet of things: Remote patient monitoring using web services and cloud computing, *Physical and Social Computing (CPSCom)*, Taipei.

13. K. B. S. Kumar, K. B. Sundhara Kumar, K. Bairavi (2016). IoT based health monitoring system for autistic patients (pp. 371–376), *Proceedings of the 3rd International Symposium on Big Data and Cloud Computing Challenges (ISBCC 16')*, Chennai.

14. A. Onasanya, M. Elshakankiri (2019). Smart integrated IoT health-care system for cancer care (vol. 27, pp. 4297–4312), *Wireless Networks*.

15. S. K. Sood, I. Mahajan (2017). Wearable IoT sensor based healthcare system for identifying and controlling chikungunya virus (pp. 33–44), *Computers in Industry*.

16. A. Abdelgawad, K. Yelamarthi, A. Khattab (2017). IoT-based health monitoring system for active and assisted living (vol. 195, pp. 11–20), *Smart Objects and Technologies for Social Good*.

17. L. Yang, Y. Ge, W. Li, W. Rao, W. Shen (2014). A home mobile healthcare system for wheelchair users, *Proceedings of the IEEE 18th International Conference on Computer Supported Cooperative Work in Design (CSCWD)*.

18. Z. Yang, Q. Zhou, L. Lei, K. Zheng, W. Xiang (2016). An IoT-cloud based wearable ECG monitoring system for smart healthcare (vol. 40, p. 286), *Journal of Medical Systems*.

19. L. Cerina, S. Notargiacomo, M. G. Paccanit, D. Santambrogio (2017). A fog-computing architecture for preventive healthcare and assisted living in smart ambients, *IEEE 3rd International Forum on Research and Technologies for Society and Industry (RTSI)*, Italy.

20. C. S. Nandyala, H.-K. Kim (2016). From cloud to Fog and IoT based real-time U-healthcare monitoring for smart homes and hospitals (vol. 10, no. 02, pp. 187–196), *International Journal of Smart Home*.

21. P. Verma, S. K. Sood (2018). Fog assisted-IoT enabled patient health monitoring in smart homes (vol. 5, no. 3, pp. 1789–1796), *IEEE Internet of Things Journal*.

22. I. Zimi, A. Arman, A. M. Rahmani, T. Pahikkala (2017). HiCH: Hierarchical Fog-assisted computing architecture for healthcare IoT (vol. 16, no. 5s, pp. 1–120), *ACM Transactions on Embedded Computer Systems*.

23. N. Kumar (2017). IoT architecture and system design for healthcare systems, *International Conference on Smart Technologies for Smart Nation (SmartTechCon)*, Bengaluru.

24. A. P. Plageras, K. E. Psannis, Y. Ishibashi, B. G. Kim (2016). IoT-based surveillance system for ubiquitous healthcare (vol. 82, pp. 349–357), *IECON -IEEE Industrial Electronics Society*.

25. M. T. Villalba, M. Teresa Villalba, M. de Buenaga, D. Gachet, F. Aparicio (2016). Security analysis of an IoT architecture for healthcare (vol. 1, pp. 454–460), *Internet of Things. IoT Infrastructures*.

26. R. Mahmud, F. L. Koch, R. Buyya (2018). Cloud-Fog interoperability in IoT-enabled healthcare solutions, *Proceedings of the 19th International Conference on Distributed Computing and Networking - ICDCN '18*, United States.

27. S. M. R. Islam., S. M. Riazul Islam, D. Kwak, M. H. Kabir, M. Hossain, K. S. Kwak (2015). The internet of things for health care: A comprehensive survey (vol. 03, pp. 678–708), *IEEE Access*.

28. T. N. Gia, A. M. Rahmani, T. Westerlund, P. Liljeberg, H. Tenhunen (2015). Fault tolerant and scalable IoT-based architecture for health monitoring, *2015 IEEE Sensors Applications Symposium (SAS)*, Zadar.

29. T. Muhammed, R. Mehmood, A. Albeshri, I. Katib (2018). UbeHealth: A personalized ubiquitous cloud and edge-enabled networked healthcare system for smart cities (vol. 6, pp. 32258–32285), *IEEE Access*.

30. B. Farahani, F. Firouzi, V. Chang, M. Badaroglu, N. Constant, K. Mankodiya (2018). Towards fog-driven IoT eHealth: Promises and challenges of IoT in medicine and healthcare (vol. 78 part 2, pp. 659–676), *Future Generation Computer Systems*.

31. T. Wu, F. Wu, J. M. Redoute, M. R. Yuce (2017). An autonomous wireless body area network implementation towards IoT connected healthcare applications (vol. 5, pp. 11413–11422), *IEEE Access*.

32. F. Touati, R. Tabish, A. Ben Mnaouern (2013). Towards u-health: An indoor 6LoWPAN based platform for real-time healthcare monitoring, *6th Joint IFIP Wireless and Mobile Networking Conference (WMNC)*, Dubai.

11 Internet of Things
A Promise to Smart Healthcare

Arifa Begum S. K.
Bharat Institute of Technology

Shaheen Begum
Sri Padmavati Mahila Visvavidyalayam (SPMVV)

C. Sadak Vali
Browns college of Pharmacy

P. Haritha
Bharat School of Pharmacy

K. V. L. D. Spandana
Avanthi Institute of Pharmaceutical Sciences

S. Swathi Goud
Vishnu Institute of Pharmaceutical
Education & Research (VIPER)

CONTENTS

DOI: 10.1201/9781003307778-13

11.1 INTRODUCTION

Smart healthcare system broadly includes the M-health (Mobile-health) systems and e-health (electronic-health) systems which are purely based on IoT technology. M-health system devices include sensors, which are connected to a mobile or any other smart device inclusive of a facility for storage and personalization of data based on which feedback are given to the patient which makes the patient understand his health condition [1,2]. The e-health system comprises two components mainly, the department of mental health and the robot, which work in collaboration with others to manage the health of the patient. Internet of Things (IoT), the most emerging innovative trend in the modern era, plays a significant role in personalized care. Artificial intelligence (AI) which mimics human intelligence is a science and a set of computational technologies that can be created as software or tools [3,4]. These tools in combination with the data storage tools like cloud databases drive smart healthcare toward providing a promising approach for patients suffering from depression (depression and mood monitoring), asthma (smart inhalers), cardiovascular disorders (heart rate monitoring), neuronal disorders (Parkinson's disease monitoring) and diabetes (glucose monitoring). Smart devices like mobile phones, tablets, smartphones and smart watches are being utilized in the evaluation of brain functioning in tremors, dementia, and movement disorders [5–7].

IoT-based healthcare systems can improve a patient's health by collecting a variety of patient data and inputs from medical professionals to improve hospital workflows [7,8]. The protocol involves the transformation of the data from the sensors and the medical devices to the healthcare network which involves a systematic approach starting with a record of patient's vital information (blood pressure, heart rate, electrocardiogram [ECG], oxygen saturation, etc.), storage of the patient data in cloud and continuous monitoring through the utilization of smartphones, computers, etc. as shown in Figure 11.1 [9].

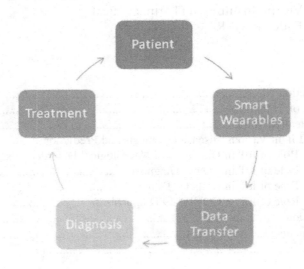

FIGURE 11.1   Internet of Things.

11.2 INTERNET OF THINGS

There are three basic components: (i) Identification Technology –Universally Unique Identifier (UUID) and Globally Unique Identifier (GUID), (ii) communication technology (majority of the healthcare systems make use of the short-range communication systems viz.body area network (BAN), radiofrequency identification (RFID), near-field communication etc.,) and (iii) location technology, viz.real-time location systems, Global Positioning System etc. [10–12].

The significance of the IoT ranges from smart hospital space (where the cloud-connected sensors and the ambient sensors provide a comfortable hospital stay to the patient) to its application in the detection and management of the most dreadful diseases like cancer, diabetes, neurological disorders as well as the COVID-19 as shown in Figure 11.2 [13,14]. Machine learning (ML) paved tremendous change in healthcare departments with the best examples being the physical robots, which perform the tasks like delivering supplies in the hospitals. The super robots are the biggest revolution in the field of IoT-based technological developments, which minimize invasive incisions during common surgical procedures like gynec, prostate, head and neck surgeries [15]. AI and ML techniques are been extensively used in the computer-aided diagnosis of patients by procuring the patient's data from the cloud server. These techniques are also utilized to gain insights into the disorders such as Parkinson's, Alzheimer's, ischemic diseases as well as sclerosis, epilepsy, etc. [16].

AI-based techniques are gaining importance in neurology, and other neurological disorders making use of imaging and medical data. The brain-related disorders could be well explored using the Preferred Reporting Items for the Systematic Reviews and Meta-Analyses guidelines (PRISMA). The risk of bias can be calculated using the PRISMA search models to study Parkinson's disease–related tremors and imbalanced coordination, which are characterized progressively with time [17]. The significance of IoT in healthcare management is depicted in Figure 11.2.

The highly cost-effective treatment and challenging diagnosis of cancer are encouraging medical professionals to suggest the patients in preventive care strategies by creating a decision-making predictive model tool [18,19]. These predictive models assist in the determination of a person's chances of developing various types of cancer. Extensive research is being carried out at the University of Colorado Cancer Centre by making tools for women who received breast cancer diagnosis [20]. Figure 11.3 depicts IoT layout in the healthcare sector.

The recent treatment of disorders is more focused on the use of the IoT due to the several advantages associated with it. IoT in medicine is based on the components like communication, collection, analysing and storing of the data of patients with the help of the internet. The ease of communication between the physician and patient with the help of smart devices, avoiding the hospital atmosphere with the help of home treatment and rehabilitation, reduction in the cost of treatment etc. makes it more reliable for use by patients as shown in Figure 11.3. The use of sensors, storing of patient data in the database and other automated techniques for the treatment also help the physician to identify the patient easily and treat the patient much more easily. The different types of sensors are shown in Figure 11.4.

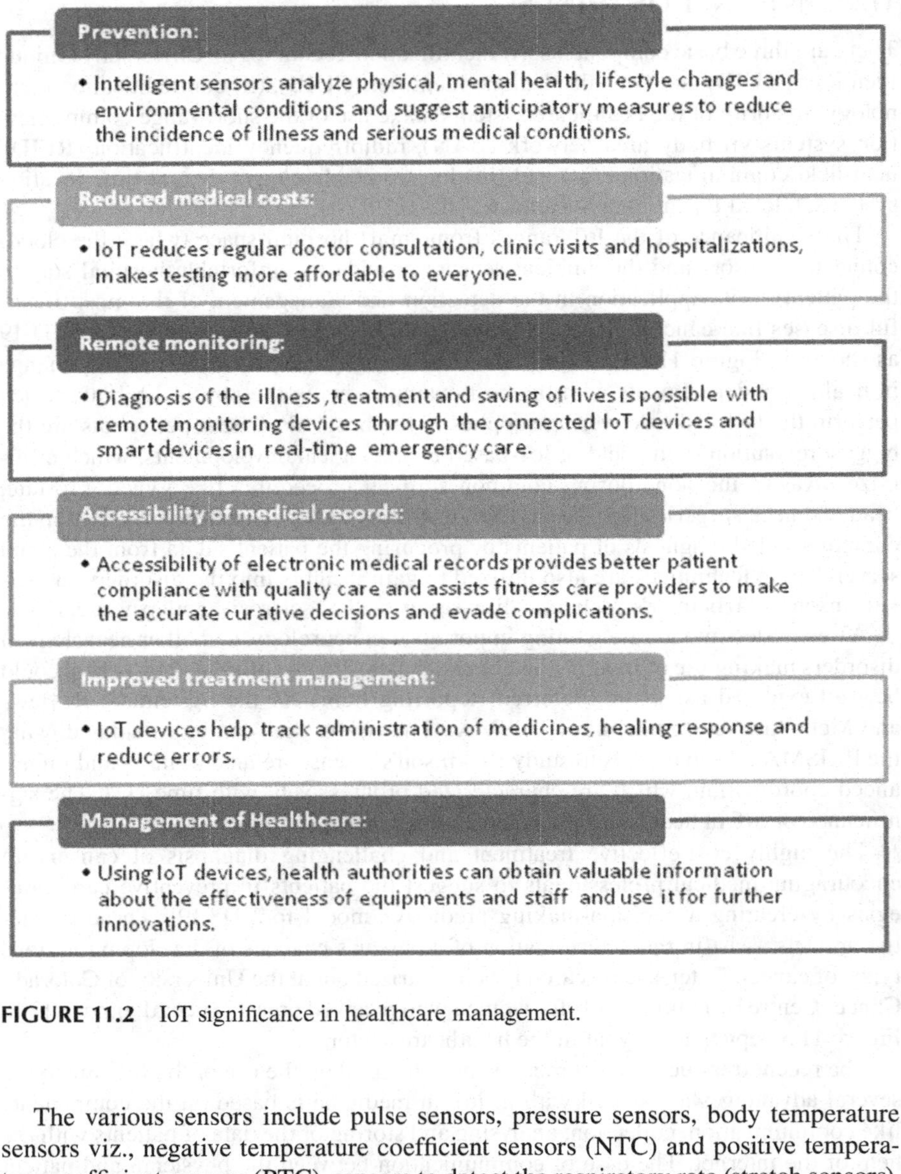

Prevention:

- Intelligent sensors analyze physical, mental health, lifestyle changes and environmental conditions and suggest anticipatory measures to reduce the incidence of illness and serious medical conditions.

Reduced medical costs:

- IoT reduces regular doctor consultation, clinic visits and hospitalizations, makes testing more affordable to everyone.

Remote monitoring:

- Diagnosis of the illness, treatment and saving of lives is possible with remote monitoring devices through the connected IoT devices and smart devices in real-time emergency care.

Accessibility of medical records:

- Accessibility of electronic medical records provides better patient compliance with quality care and assists fitness care providers to make the accurate curative decisions and evade complications.

Improved treatment management:

- IoT devices help track administration of medicines, healing response and reduce errors.

Management of Healthcare:

- Using IoT devices, health authorities can obtain valuable information about the effectiveness of equipments and staff and use it for further innovations.

FIGURE 11.2   IoT significance in healthcare management.

The various sensors include pulse sensors, pressure sensors, body temperature sensors viz., negative temperature coefficient sensors (NTC) and positive temperature coefficient sensors (PTC), sensors to detect the respiratory rate (stretch sensors), pulse oximeter sensors, ECG sensors in helmets and chest straps, electroencephalogram (EEG) sensors, blood glucose monitoring sensors and various other wireless sensor networks (WSNs), wireless body area network (WBAN) and wireless personal area network (WPAN). The critical care required for COVID-19 patients can be provided by the IoT-based healthcare monitoring systems. The most promising ones include the devices meant for the measurement of body temperature, pulse rate and oxygen saturation of the patients [21]. IoT-based tools could be the most valuable

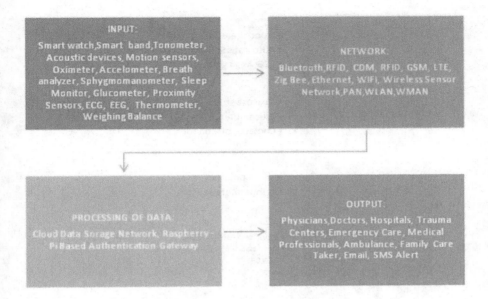

FIGURE 11.3 IoT layout in Healthcare.

for the diagnosis, treatment and management of various health disorders. This chapter also focuses on the significance of IoT in neurological disorders, cancer, diabetes, and COVID-19.

11.3 IOT IN HEALTHCARE

The benefits of IoT in the healthcare sector are as follows:

Real-time diagnosis and treatment: IoT helps in monitoring the condition of patients using electronic devices and gadgets to diagnose and treat diseases in an emergency. IoT improves patient compliance and quick recovery.

Prevention of diseases and medical errors: Healthcare devices and sensors detect the changes in physiological functions of the body and transfer the same to healthcare professionals. IoT prevents further worsening of the patient's condition and reoccurrence of the disease. IoT helps in the prevention of medical errors.

Lowering of treatment costs: IoT reduces the physician consultation charges. The quality of treatment is improved with the use of IoT in the healthcare sector. It makes the physicians and nursing staff suggest the right dose at right time without any complications.

Maintenance of medical records: Maintenance of a patient's previous medical history database is easier with the application of IoT wearable and gadgets in the healthcare sector.

The limitations of IoT are as follows:

Deficient of standardizations: There is no specific organization or council to standardize the data gathered from devices manufactured by various companies. Lack of harmony is the backdrop for use of IoT devices in healthcare units.

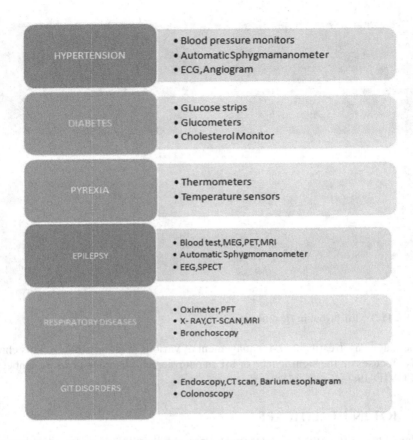

FIGURE 11.4   Types of sensors used in different diseases.

Security problems: IoT networks may cause security problems due to network security deficiencies, bugs, software updates, hardware failure, hacking.

Data leakage and corruption: The personal information of a patient is at risk as IoT healthcare systems collect the personal health information of patients, which may lead to data corruption.

Difficulty in operation: The crafting, usage, and handling of IoT devices are difficult for unprofessional and unskilled operators.

11.4   ROLE OF IOT IN VARIOUS DISEASE DIAGNOSIS AND PREDICTION

11.4.1   ROLE OF IOT IN DIAGNOSIS OF NEUROLOGICAL DISORDERS

Neurological disorders like Parkinson's disease, Alzheimer's disease, stroke, multiple sclerosis involve either the central or peripheral nervous system and are characterized by symptoms that include partial or complete paralysis, muscle weakness, partial or complete loss of sensation, seizures, difficulty reading and writing, poor cognitive abilities, unexplained pain, decreased alertness depending upon the disorder with which the patient is suffering.

The inability of the drugs to cross the blood brain barrier has been a great challenging task for physicians in the treatment of neurological disorders. The progression in the treatment strategy gave rise to the use of stem cells along with the utilization of brain stimulation techniques. It was suggested that some disorders are due to the destruction or loss of neurons and glial cells, and hence to restore these neurons researchers have proposed the use of stem cells derived from the adult brain. The stem cells thus obtained will be stimulated and can be implanted in the place of lost cells [22]. Deep brain stimulation (DBS) with electric high-frequency impulses can be an alternative for the treatment of some neurological disorders. This involves the stimulation of impaired motor and non-motor regions by providing continuous impulses to the electrodes placed in those specific regions. This therapy was helpful in the treatment of Parkinson's disease compared with epilepsy treatment [23]. As the systemic data differ from individual to individual; the mapping study will be particular to each individual rather than following pooled treatment techniques for all similar individuals. With the help of the data collected from each patient, after the analysis, individualization of treatment confined to those particular symptoms can also be carried out using these techniques. ML, considered a part of AI, is now regarded as an important tool in the treatment of various disorders and diseases. In the current scenario, there is a great need for novel techniques and methods for the treatment of neurodegenerative disorders, which is due to the difficulty in understanding the degeneration of neurons and diversified patients as shown in Figure 11.5 [24,25].The best examples are the utilization of wearable accelerometer sensors for the monitoring of the position and the angle of the joints, as well as the behavioural parameters associated with arthritic and neurological disorders. The role of IoT in the diagnosis of neurological disorders is depicted in Figure11.5.

11.4.2 ROLE OF IoT IN CANCER DIAGNOSIS

Cancer, the leading global challenge, has become the most important risk-identified disease due to the global pandemic caused by SARS-COVID. This has necessitated the development of the round-the-clock observation system. Current developments in the technology using IoT shows its significance to timely detect symptoms associated with early stages of cancer and also to monitor both the patients diagnosed and cured from cancer. This can assist physicians in the detection and management of different types of cancers. Among the various types of cancer, breast cancer is the most common and dreadful with the highest death rate. The main aim is to prevent the spreading after immediate detection of the lumps by biopsy. The proverb "Prevention is better than cure" holds apt to deal with cancer. Wearables assist in the detection of breast cancer. These wearable consist of thermistors that are located around the breast for monitoring the variation of temperature through time, thereby helping to detect abnormal changes in temperature produced by cancer cells. These wearable are also being utilized in the monitoring of testicular cancers [26,27]. Wearable medical devices are the future of smart healthcare which will provide the data via IoT to the cloud, big

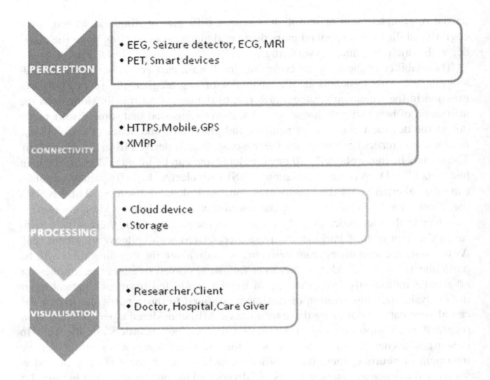

FIGURE 11.5   Role of IoT in the diagnosis of neurological disorders.

data analysis, and algorithms which can easily diagnose the disease. Other methods to detect breast cancer include the auger electron-emitting therapeutic agents, which assist in the detection of the variation of density in the tissue of the breast by the use of ultra-sounds. Thermistor-based wearable are promising as they show less percentage of false positives than mammography screening methods [28]. AI and IoT can improve cancer treatment as shown in Figure 11.6. AI assists to recognize images and, thus, transforms image interpretation from subjective to reproducible quantifiable tasks with the utilization of multiple data streams, integrated diagnostic systems, radiographic images, electronic health records and social networks [29]. ML techniques for Computer-Aided Detection (CADe) and Computer-Aided Diagnosis (CADx) play a significant contribution in the distinction between malignant and benign breast lesions. These AI methods for CADx involve the automatic characterization of a tumour, from which the computer characterizes the suspicious lesion thereby helping the physician in patient management by estimating the probability of disease [30]. The role of IoT in cancer diagnosis and treatment is depicted in Figure 11.6.

11.4.3   ROLE OF IOT IN DIABETES DIAGNOSIS

Diabetes characterized by long-term high blood glucose levels should be diagnosed before reaching a dangerous level, which is possible through the self-management

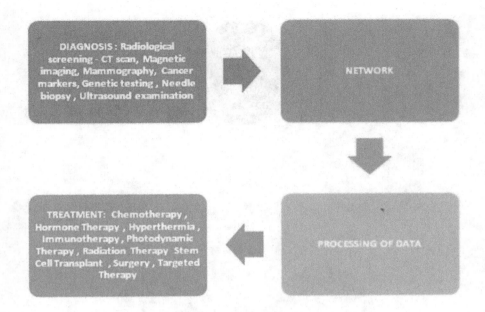

FIGURE 11.6 Role of IoT in cancer diagnosis and treatment.

of the disease utilizing the sensor support system. The software-based continuous monitoring technologies include the utilization of the wireless ad hoc and sensor devices based on IoT as shown in Figure 11.7. Robot-assisted management of diabetes is gaining significance in the management of this disease. Web-centric disease management hubs assist in the monitoring and management of the disease. Al-Odat et al. proposed an IoT system for monitoring diabetic patients using a cloud computing system, employing a hardware system consisting of an Alaris 8100 infusion pump, Keil LPC-1768 board, and IoT cloud to monitor the diabetic patients [31]. Rastogi et al. proposed an IoT method for examining diabetes concerning other disorders/diseases such as coronary heart disease, hypertension and ocular disorders, which in some cases are the serious effects caused due to diabetes [32]. IoT-based embedded healthcare system, which makes use of the secure hash algorithm (SHA) proposed by Al-Odat et al. [31], ensures the maintenance of the security and authenticity of the diabetic patient's records. Catarinucci et al. proposed a three-hardware component – RFID, WSN and smart mobile–based smart hospital system implemented with a graphical user interface (GUI) for making the data easily available to the specialist [33]. The role of IoT in diabetes care is depicted in Figure 11.7

11.4.4 ROLE OF IoT IN COVID-19 DIAGNOSIS

The major challenges in the healthcare sector due to the COVID-19 pandemic have made a breakthrough in the field of IoT-based health monitoring systems. The pandemic necessitated the continuous monitoring of the patient's body temperature,

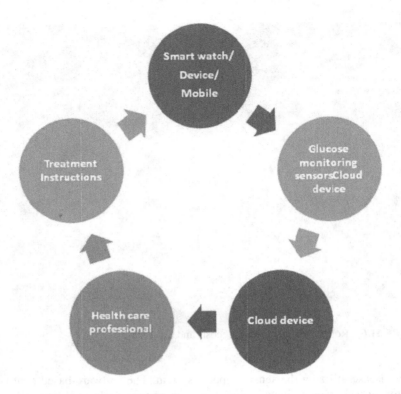

FIGURE 11.7   IoT in diabetes care.

oxygen saturation levels (SpO_2 levels) and pulse rate. IoT plays a significant role in the tackling of COVID-19 patients by providing effective control and diagnosis, reducing expenditure and providing superior treatment. The setup of the significance of the IoT in COVID-19 is depicted in Figure 11.8. The civilians of different countries were given awareness regarding the pandemic through smart mobile apps like Arogya Setu in India, Close Contact detector in China and Taiwan Social Distancing app [34]. The communication system was spread by using different applications like tele health consultations (video chats between patients and physicians), digital diagnostics (tracking the health data after digital diagnosis) and robot assistance (using robots to assist in delivering medicines, cleaning and disinfection of hospitals). IoT-based system (nCapp) was developed by Bai et al. to diagnose COVID-19 [35]. A smart helmet with a provision to identify the COVID-19-infected persons in the crowd was developed and reported by Mohammed et al., which makes use of thermal imaging systems [36–38]. The role of IoT in COVID-19 diagnosis is depicted in Figure 11.8.

11.5   CONCLUSION

The era of smart devices is going to change the perspective in the prevention, treatment and maintenance of the healthcare system paving the promise to manage highly

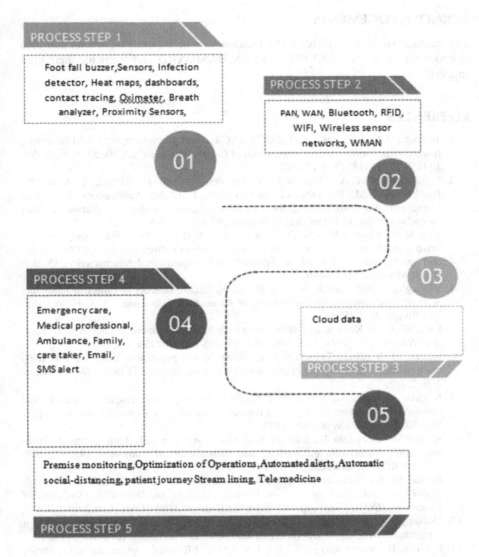

FIGURE 11.8 IoT in COVID-19 diagnosis.

dreadful diseases. So our future is the "SMART DEVICES". IoT warrants health maintenance experts to be more observant and connect with the patients practically. Data processed from IoT devices can aid healthcare professionals to recognize the finest healing procedure for patients and achieve the anticipated result. We conclude that IoT technology perks up the safety of patients by dropping medication errors, reducing adverse drug events, and fulfilling practice guidelines. There should be no doubt that IoT is a vital means for improving healthcare value and well-being.

ACKNOWLEDGEMENTS

The authors would like to thank the management of Bharat Institutions and also extend their thanks to HOD CSE, JAMIA HAMDARD and team for their kind support.

REFERENCES

1. Tessmer, M. S., & Flaherty, K. T. (2017). AACR cancer progress report 2017: Harnessing research discoveries to save lives. *Clinical Cancer Research*, 23(18), 5324–5325. doi: 10.1158/1078–0432.CCR-17-2302.

2. Myszczynska, M. A., Ojamies, P. N., Lacoste, A., Neil, D., Saffari, A., Mead, R., Hautbergue, G.M., Holbrook, J.D. & Ferraiuolo, L. (2020). Applications of machine learning to diagnosis and treatment of neurodegenerative diseases. *Nature Reviews Neurology*, 16(8), 440–456. doi: 10.1038/s41582-020-0377-8.

3. Kim, N. H., Yang, D. W., Choi, S. H., & Kang, S. W. (2021). Machine learning to predict brain amyloid pathology in Pre-dementia Alzheimer's disease using QEEG features and genetic algorithm heuristic. *Frontiers in Computational Neuroscience*, 15. doi: 10.3389/fncom.2021.755499.

4. Sadoughi, F., Behmanesh, A., & Sayfouri, N. (2020). Internet of things in medicine: A systematic mapping study. *Journal of Biomedical Informatics*, 103, 103383. doi: 10.1016/j.jbi.2020.103383.

5. Lindvall, O., & Kokaia, Z. (2006). Stem cells for the treatment of neurological disorders. *Nature*, 441(7097), 1094–1096. doi: 10.1038/nature04960.

6. Sharifi, M. S. (2013). Treatment of neurological and psychiatric disorders with deep brain stimulation; raising hopes and future challenges. *Basic and Clinical Neuroscience*, 4(3), 266.

7. Nakhla, Z., Nouira, K., & Ferchichi, A. (2019). Prescription adverse drug events system (PrescADE) based on ontology and internet of things. *The Computer Journal*, 62(6), 801–805.doi: 10.1093/comjnl/bxy076.

8. Kumar, M. A., Vimala, R., & Britto, K. A. (2019). A cognitive technology based healthcare monitoring system and medical data transmission. *Measurement*, 146, 322–332. doi: 10.1016/j.measurement.2019.03.017.

9. Bansal, M., & Gandhi, B. (2019). IoT & big data in smart healthcare (ECG monitoring). In *2019 International Conference on Machine Learning, Big Data, Cloud and Parallel Computing (COMITCon)* (pp. 390–396). IEEE. doi:10.1109/COMITCon.2019.8862197.

10. Onasanya, A., & Elshakankiri, M. (2021). Smart integrated IoT healthcare system for cancer care. *Wireless Networks*, 27(6), 4297–4312.doi: 10.1007/s11276-018-01932-1.

11. Pradhan, B., Bhattacharyya, S., & Pal, K. (2021). IoT-based applications in healthcare devices. *Journal of Healthcare Engineering*, 2021.doi: 10.1155/2021/6632599.

12. Khan, M. M., Mehnaz, S., Shaha, A., Nayem, M., & Bourouis, S. (2021). IoT-based smart health monitoring system for COVID-19 patients. *Computational and Mathematical Methods in Medicine*, 2021.doi: 10.1155/2021/8591036.

13. Efat, M., Alam, I., Rahman, S., & Rahman, T. (2020). IoT based smart health monitoring system for diabetes patients using neural network. In *International Conference on Cyber Security and Computer Science* (pp. 593–606). Springer, Cham. doi: 10.1007/978-3-030-52856-47.

14. Karthick, G. S., & Pankajavalli, P. B. (2020). A review on human healthcare Internet of things: A technical perspective. *SN Computer Science*, 1(4), 1–19. doi: 10.1007/s42979-020-00205-z.

15. Kelly, J. T., Campbell, K. L., Gong, E., & Scuffham, P. (2020). The Internet of Things: Impact and implications for health care delivery. *Journal of medical Internet research*, 22(11), e20135. doi: 10.2196/20135.

16. Panchatcharam, P., & Vivekanandan, S. (2019). Internet of things (IoT) in health-care–Smart health and surveillance, architectures, security analysis and data transfer: A review. *International Journal of Software Innovation (IJSI)*, 7(2), 21–40. doi: 10.4018/IJSI.2019040103.

17. Baker, S. B., Xiang, W., & Atkinson, I. (2017). Internet of things for smart health-care: Technologies, challenges, and opportunities. *IEEE Access*, 5, 26521–26544. doi:10.1109/access.2017.2775180.

18. Javaid, M., &Khan, I. H. (2021). Internet of Things (IoT) enabled healthcare helps to take the challenges of COVID-19 pandemic. *Journal of Oral Biology and Craniofacial Research*, 11(2), 209–214.doi:10.1016/j.jobcr.2021.01.015.

19. Alansari, Z., Soomro, S., Belgaum, M. R., & Shamshirband, S. (2018). The rise of Internet of Things (IoT) in big healthcare data: Review and open research issues. *Progress in Advanced Computing and Intelligent Engineering*, 675–685. doi:10.1007/978-981-10-6875-166.

20. Issa, B. A., & Thabit, Q. Q. (2021). Review in IoT for healthcare in our life. *IJEEE*, 18(1), 9–20. doi: 10.37917/ijeee.18.1.2.

21. Kumar, S., Tiwari, P., & Zymbler, M. (2019). Internet of Things is a revolutionary approach for future technology enhancement: A review. *Journal of Big Data*, 6, 111. doi: 10.1186/s40537-019-0268-2.

22. Qadri, Y.A., Nauman, A., Zikria, Y.B., Vasilakos, A.V., & Kim, S.W. (2020). The future of healthcare internet of things: A survey of emerging technologies. *IEEE Communications Surveys & Tutorials*, 22, 1121–1167. doi:10.1109/COMST.2020.2973314.

23. Coenen, V. A., Amtage, F., Volkmann, J., & Schläpfer, T. E. (2015). Deep brain stimulation in neurological and psychiatric disorders. *Deutsches Arzteblatt International*, 112(31–32), 519–526. doi: 10.3238/arztebl.2015.0519.

24. Barrachina-Fernández, M., Maitín, A. M., Sánchez-Ávila, C., & Romero, J. P. (2021). Wearable technology to detect motor fluctuations in Parkinson's disease patients: Current state and challenges. *Sensors*, 21(12), 4188. doi: 10.3390/s21124188.

25. Tzallas, A. T., Tsipouras, M. G., Rigas, G., Tsalikakis, D. G., Karvounis, E. C., Chondrogiorgi, M., & Fotiadis, D. I. (2014). PERFORM: A system for monitoring, assessment and management of patients with Parkinson's disease. *Sensors*, 14(11), 21329–21357. doi: 10.3390/s141121329.

26. Warner, E., Messersmith, H., Causer, P., Eisen, A., Shumak, R., & Plewes, D. (2008). Systematic review: Using magnetic resonance imaging to screen women at high risk for breast cancer. *Annals of Internal Medicine*, 148(9), 671–679. doi:10.7326/0003-4819-148-9-200805060-00007.

27. Villegas, D., Martínez, A., Quesada-López, C., & Jenkins, M. (2020, June). IoT for cancer treatment: A mapping study. In *2020 15th Iberian Conference on Information Systems and Technologies (CISTI)* (pp. 1–6). IEEE. doi: 10.23919/CISTI49556.2020.9141031.

28. Humm, J. L., & Charlton, D. E. (1989). A new calculational method to assess the therapeutic potential of Auger electron emission. *International Journal of Radiation Oncology* Biology* Physics*, 17(2), 351–360. doi: 10.1016/0360-3016(89)90450-1.

29. Drukker, K., Sennett, C. A., & Giger, M. L. (2014). Computerized detection of breast cancer on automated breast ultrasound imaging of women with dense breasts. *Medical Physics*, 41(1), 012901. doi: 10.1118/1.4837196.

30. Gao, B., Zhang, H., Zhang, S. D., Cheng, X. Y., Zheng, S. M., Sun, Y. H., ...& Tian, J. (2014). Mammographic and clinicopathological features of triple-negative breast cancer. *The British Journal of Radiology*, 87(1039), 20130496. doi:10.1259/bjr.20130496.

31. Al-Odat, Z. A., Srinivasan, S. K., Al-Qtiemat, E. M., & Shuja, S. (2019). A reliable IoT-based embedded health care system for diabetic patients. *ArXiv/abs preprint*. doi: 10.48550/arXiv.1908.06086.

32. Rastogi, R., Singhal, P., Chaturvedi, D. K., & Gupta, M. (2021). Investigating correlation of tension-type headache and diabetes: IoT perspective in health care. In *Internet of Things for Healthcare Technologies* (pp. 71–91). Springer, Singapore. doi: 10.1007/978-981-15-4112-44.

33. Catarinucci, L., De Donno, D., Mainetti, L., Palano, L., Patrono, L., Stefanizzi, M. L., & Tarricone, L. (2015). An IoT-aware architecture for smart healthcare systems. *IEEE Internet of Things Journal*, 2(6), 515–526.

34. Jahmunah, V., Sudarshan, V. K., Oh, S. L., Gururajan, R., Gururajan, R., Zhou, X., Tao, X., Faust, O., Ciaccio, E. J., Ng, K. H., & Acharya, U. R. (2021). Future IoT tools for COVID-19 contact tracing and prediction: A review of the state-of-the-science. *International Journal of Imaging Systems and Technology*, 31(2), 455–471. doi: 10.1002/ima.22552.

35. Bai, L., Yang, D., Wang, X., Tong, L., Zhu, X., Zhong, N., Bai, C., Powell, C. A., Chen, R., Zhou, J., Song, Y., Zhou, X., Zhu, H., Han, B., Li, Q., Shi, G., Li, S., Wang, C., Qiu, Z., Zhang, Y., ... & Tan, F. (2020). Chinese experts' consensus on the Internet of Things-aided diagnosis and treatment of coronavirus disease 2019 (COVID-19). *Clinical eHealth*, 3, 7–15. doi: 10.1016/j.ceh.2020.03.001.

36. Singh, R. P., Javaid, M., Haleem, A., & Suman, R. (2020). Internet of things (IoT) applications to fight against COVID-19 pandemic. *Diabetes & Metabolic Syndrome: Clinical Research & Reviews*, 14(4), 521–524.doi: 10.1016/j.dsx.2020.04.041.

37. Kumar, K., Kumar, N., & Shah, R. (2020). Role of IoT to avoid spreading of COVID-19. *International Journal of Intelligent Networks*, 1, 32–35. doi: 10.1016/j.ijin.2020.05.002.

38. Mohammed, M. N., Syamsudin, H., Al-Zubaidi, S., AKS, R. R., & Yusuf, E. (2020). Novel COVID-19 detection and diagnosis system using IoT based smart helmet. *International Journal of Psychosocial Rehabilitation*, 24(7), 2296–2303.

12 A Brief Review on Wireless Capsule Endoscopy Image Compression

P. Linu Babu
IES College of Engineering

S. Sridevi
Veltech Rangarajan Dr. Sagunthala R & D
Institute of Science and Technology

CONTENTS

12.1   INTRODUCTION

Endoscopy is a medical procedure used to detect numerous digestive problems by examining various digestive system organs such as the esophagus, colon, and small intestine (Abdelkrim, 2018), (Ahn, 2018). Fiber optic endoscopy is the most dependable and least intrusive way of screening the gastrointestinal (GI) tract (Al-Shebani, 2019) Invention of transistor significantly developed the microelectronic devices, which introduced a novel endoscopy in the form of a capsule (Babu, C.,2020). Wireless capsule endoscopy (WCE) is a novel alternative solution for reducing the discomfort and some of the risks associated with flexible endoscopy during GI tract screening. PillCam SB, the first capsule endoscope gadget, was created to treat cryptic GI bleeding. WCE has advantages such as being less intrusive and allowing for a thorough examination of the small intestine (Bouyaya, 2021). WCE procedure involves swallowing a small electronic pill in the size of 26 mm × 11 mm which contains a tiny wireless camera and electronic devices. The capsule freely moves to GI tract, it continuously captures the image and transmits it to the recording device through wireless technology. Images are downloaded in the workstation and analyzed by the experts for medical diagnosis. The capsule mechanism runs on a small battery which supplies power for 8–10 hours. It is vital to have a clinical specialist present to examine each video series for diagnostic purposes. Despite its many advantages, it has a short life span; finding the disease within that time frame is necessary. WCE transmits numerous images in a single inception, which increases RF transmitter power and occupies memory storage. Analyzing each WCE video could take up to an hour; even for an expert viewer. Image compression is the main approach to deal the power consumption and buffer memory reduction. It minimizes the quantity of image data while maintaining image quality. Medical endoscopy employs lossless image compression, which focuses on reducing redundant data from an image. Image compression blocks consist of color space conversion, compression filter, quantization, and encoder.

Many researchers have created many compression algorithms with the goal of improving compression ratios (CRs), reducing power consumption, and lowering hardware costs. Practical implementation of existing algorithms remains difficult due to their complexity. This study presents a review of the most important existing compression algorithm on image compression. The survey focuses on various modifications in traditional compression techniques. The schematic diagram of the WCE model is shown in Figure 12.1.

The main purpose of the review is to examine all the up-to-date compression techniques based on WCE images. All the recent lossy, lossless, and near-lossless compression approaches are reviewed with a detailed vision of existing techniques along with their drawbacks. The key focus of the review is précised as follows:

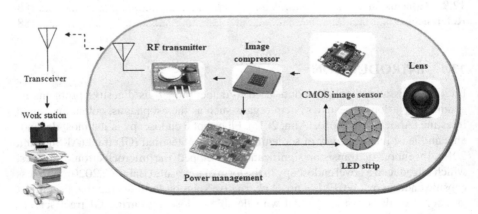

FIGURE 12.1   Wireless capsule endoscopy block diagram.

    i. To study all advanced WCE image compression algorithms in various parts of the GI tract images.
    ii. To present a detailed view of the basic requirement of the WCE algorithm.
    iii. To discuss the challenges faced by the recent compression algorithm.
    iv. To provide a future guideline to overcome the existing limitations and design an efficient system to compress the GI images.

The rest of the chapter is laid out as follows: Section 12.2 explains the clinical perspective of the WCE compression; Section 12.3 narrates a review of the existing compression algorithms; Section 12.4 describes the near-lossless image compression algorithms; Section 12.5 explains low power and low complexity image compression algorithms; Section 12.6 describes the WCE compression using intelligent learning models; Section 12.7 highlights the results and discussion; Section 12.8 describes the research findings and limitations; and conclusion is stated in Section 12.9.

12.2 IMAGE COMPRESSION CLINICAL PERSPECTIVE

From the clinical perspective, image compression method is utilized for the operation of WCE with limited bandwidth. Also, it must be lossless and reduce the data size without affecting the image quality. As illustrated in Figure 12.2, a typical WCE

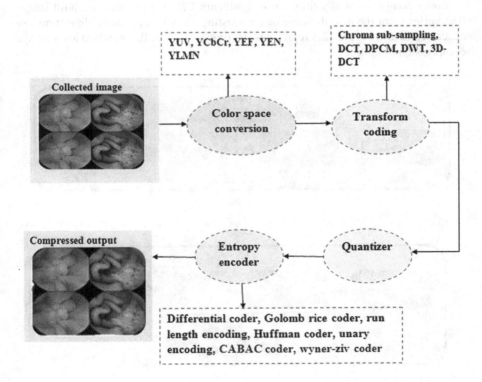

FIGURE 12.2   Image compression system for diagnosing GI tract disease.

compression system comprises a color space converter, transform coding, quantizer, and entropy encoder. Most of the existing algorithms convert the color space of the image to reduce the interpolation of the image (Chen et al., 2009). However, certain systems, in order to decrease computing strain or achieve a lossless system, do not employ any color space converters or quantizers. Lossy compression utilizes the DCT and DWT (Li & Deng, 2009). The near-lossless and lossless algorithms are primarily based on JPEG-LS and DPCM (Xie et al., 2006) predictive coding. To eliminate uninformative parts, several approaches use corner clipping. This review shows the methodology of the best existing compression techniques.

12.3   REVIEW OF COMPRESSION ALGORITHMS FOR WIRELESS CAPSULE ENDOSCOPY IMAGES

Lossy, lossless, and near-lossless compression strategies are the image compression strategies in WCE. Data duplication cannot be removed through lossless compression, which is reversible and does not sacrifice data. Some deformations are introduced into near-lossless compression without any valuable information being lost. Meanwhile, lossy compression techniques are used to obtain a significant CR of 50:1, keeping the overall image quality of the obtained image. In power-constrained scenarios, lossy compression is preferable.

Lossy compression algorithms use significant CRs yet produce a rebuilt image that varies from the actual. Some of the existing lossy compression algorithms are described below. Figure 12.3 represents the process flow of the standard lossy image compression module.

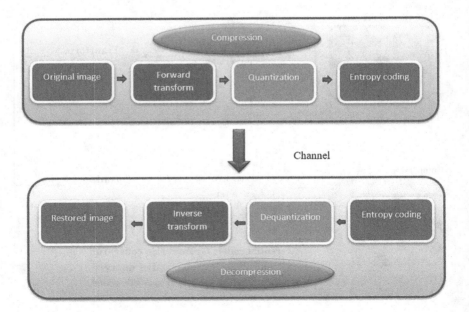

FIGURE 12.3   Block diagram of a common lossy compression operation.

(Xue et al. 2021) suggested a unique 3D DCT technique for compressing WCE images. This method divides the entire operation into two sections: in vivo and in vitro processes, respectively. In in vivo process, the 2D Bayer image pattern was restored into a 3D data pattern to overcome the color components correlation. The 4-point DCT butterfly structure was adapted to eliminate the complexity of the 3D DCT without multiplication. The 3D data pattern was quantized for further optimization by using the hybrid meta-heuristic algorithm. 3D zig-zag scan was employed before encoding to align the 3D block spectrum parameters. The blocking artifacts in the decompressed images were adaptively removed by using a frequency-domain filter. This method exceeds state-of-the-art methods with a CR of 22.94:1 and a PSNR of 40.72 dB. Although this technology improves compression rates and overall image quality, it had the major drawback of high-power consumption.

(Sushma 2021) developed a novel chroma compression method on WCE by using wyner-ziv coder. Existing techniques use a lot of electricity by compressing the luminance and chrominance of the endoscopic picture. As a result, this approach compresses just the luminance of the picture and reconstructs the chroma components on the decoder side using a GAN network. To improve the chroma prediction, wynerziv encoding was used. This method obtained a CR of 94.72% at a PSNR of 43.58 dB when compared to earlier WCE video compression methods.

(Khan and Wahid 2014) developed a WCE image compressing technique for white band images (WBIs) and narrow band images (NBIs). This technique removed the requirement for a huge temporary buffer storage system. The dual-band photograph comprises WBIs and NBIs. The suggested technique employs a basic predictive coding and a new color area for improved and efficient performance. Endoscopic images are taken by the sensor, according to the features of the narrow band and white band. The WBI CR was 80.4% and the NBI ratio was 79.2%. Firstly, the RGB image was transformed to YUV and then sub-sampled and compressed using the JPEG prediction. Lastly it was encoded and transmitted to workstation. In comparison with the transform-based algorithms for endoscopic applications, this dual-band approach considerably reduces the complexity of the calculation, eliminates memory needs, lowers hardware costs, and reduces low latency and power consumption.

(Sushma and Aparna 2019) implemented a WCE image compression based on texture classification. JPEG-based DCT classifier was utilized for image compression. This technique combines the block classification approach with DCT to distinguish blocks based on texture. Using 2D DCT, each block was converted to a frequency domain. Zig-zag scan was used to obtain the compressed bit stream and Golomb–Rice encoder (GRE) was used for entropy coding. When compared to JPEG-based compression algorithms, the proposed technique enhances compression rate by 9% without losing quality. (Fante et al. 2020) presented an image quality assessment model to evaluate the lossy algorithms.

Lossless compression algorithms provide a high CR while maintaining the image's information. Figure 12.4 shows the block diagram of the lossless algorithm.

(Mohammed et al. 2017) developed a compression method for Color filter array (CFA) capsule endoscopy images. In this chapter, a new color space transformation termed YLMN is presented, which completely exploits the inter-color correlation in a CFA image. A memory-effective adaptable GRE was used to encode the

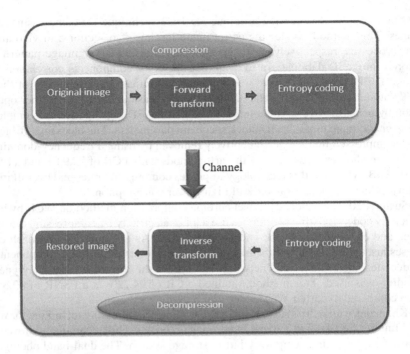

FIGURE 12.4   Block diagrams of lossless compression operation.

leftover signal using raster-order prediction. Finally, by removing the image's non-informative corner portions, the corner clipper technique reduces the lossless bit rate even more. Compared with earlier techniques, the algorithm uses a 65-nm TSMC CMOS process with a gate count reduction of 38.9% and a reduction in memory requirement of 71.2%.

(Lee et al. 2018) designed image compression hardware for WCE. The output of a CMOS image sensor is translated to the YUV color space and fed to the DPCM. Then, to obtain a high CR, zero-skipping coding, and mode-switcher architecture were used. Forward Error Correction block was introduced to reduce the bit error rate. With a throughput of 2 frames per second on a VGA resolution image, it utilizes just 0.78 mW of power at 40 MHz.

(Khan and Wahid 2011) developed a low-power WCE image compressor. For this procedure, the YUV color space was used. The algorithm was a static prediction system that combined Golomb–Rice with unary encoding. Low-power commercial image sensor was used, it was compatible with all raster-scan image sensors. The lossless compression for endoscopic images provides a CR of approximately 73%.

12.4   NEAR-LOSSLESS IMAGE COMPRESSION ALGORITHMS

(Turcza and Duplaga 2017) have established a near-lossless algorithm for reducing the power consumption during image WCE image compression. In this method, the newly implemented compressor utilizes predictive coding with DCT. Bayer CFA images from the CMOS sensor were directly applied for compression. By exploiting inter-pixel coherence to condense pixel energy into a minimal number of conversion factors, DCT provides excellent efficiency. DCT is implemented row-wise to the arriving pixels of the compressed image to minimize the memory demands of the suggested compressor. Image corners were ignored for the purpose of reducing data size using simple circuitry integrated into the compressor. The intended image compressor was developed with a 1 KB FIFO data serializer and a stream buffer, which makes the interface to an RF transmitter a low-cost option. In comparison to much more complex JPEG-LS-based coding techniques, this compressor attains superior average quality (46.68 DB) and a lower bit rate. It consumes ultra-low power (44 µJ) for a single image frame, yet this was not enough for better WCE diagnosis.

(Chen et al. 2016) developed a cost-effective VLSI for near-lossless WCE image compression. Here, a novel JPEG-LS-based near-lossless CFA image compression approach was designed for VLSI implementation. In a typical JPEG-LS method, the context module selects a pixel for the run mode, which was used more than 81% of the hardware cost. Because eliminating the context model reduces compression efficiency, a unique prediction, run mode, and MGR coding approach were employed to boost compression efficiency. To begin, RGB line buffers of a specific length were used to recover the pixels of the CFA image. The novel prediction method was applied in JPEG-LS for better compression. A run length database and an encoder make up the run mode module. A run length coder plus a modified Golomb–Rice coder comprise the entropy coding circuit. This method increases the average PSNR values for the identical test images by 0.96 and 0.43 dB, respectively.

12.5 LOW-POWER AND LOW-COMPLEXITY IMAGE COMPRESSION

(Abdelkrim et al. 2018) designed a WCE architecture to minimize the power consumption and hardware complexity. For WCE image compression, this approach investigates the benefits of coupled DCT and DWT transformations. To begin, 2D-DWT decomposed the sub-blocks of the original frame. After that, 2D-DWT was used to process the selected low-frequency components. Aside from that, the coefficients were quantified using an 8-point DCT and scaled down using a numerical scale factor. An MCLA method was used to accomplish the calculation in both the 2D-DCT and 2D-DWT sections. A CABAC coder performs the coding phase, which was divided into three stages: binarization, context modeling, and arithmetic coding. The AMBA bus was used to control the endoscopy system and ensure communication with external devices. Temporary storage buffer is used for hybrid compression technology, thereby increasing the power consumption.

(Turcza and Duplaga 2013) introduced a unique picture compression approach that was effective and practical to accomplish low power in wireless endoscopy. An adaptive Golomb–Rice (AGR) algorithm and a scalar version of the discrete cosine transform were included in the proposed method. FEC encoder was applied to prevent random and explosive mistakes from wirelessly transmitted data. In the color alteration step, RGB portions were down-sampled and transformed to CFA color space. The parameters were compressed by 2D block-wise integer discrete cosine transform. AGR encoder was adapted for encoding the quantized parameters. The picture was rebuilt back to the raw image in the workstation via reverse operations. However, in order to store the DCT coefficients, the buffer memory was necessary, which necessitates more space and, as a result, greater power.

(Malathkar and Soni 2019) developed hybrid DPCM-based image compression on WCE images. This technique provides efficient bandwidth utilization and high image quality. Firstly, a new YEN color space for WCE was developed. The RGB color image was converted to the YEN color space, which resulted in improved compression performance. Following conversion, a hybrid DPCM compression approach was used, which resulted in a mix of adaptive threshold (AT-DPCM) and DPCM codes. Basic predictive coding resulted in better results for both soft and crisp endoscopic images. The result obtained after Golomb family codes were used to transform hybrid DPCM into binary form. In terms of CR, the hybrid DPCM surpasses the regular DPCM and AT-DPCM. This approach has a high CR (64%) without requiring any additional buffer capacity and has low computational complexity. This, however, is insufficient for accurate diagnosis.

(Turcza and Duplaga 2019) designed an energy-efficient algorithm to achieve a high frame rate in multi-view capsule endoscopy. The method achieves both great overall energy efficiency and cheap implementation cost by acting directly on Bayer CFA images. To de-correlate image values in each 4×4 block, it employs a two-dimensional discrete cosine transform. The resultant coefficients were encoded with low complexity. On the decoder side, an adaptive deblocking filter eliminates blocking effects and tiling artifacts from very flat images, improving the final picture quality.

(Intzes et al. 2020) developed a high-performance low-complexity image compressor. Using sample RGB endoscopic photos, Huffman coding books were proposed in this work. It was a simple arithmetic-based method that was with minimal energy complexity. The blue and green planes' DPCM encoders used a single reduction operation. The output of the DPCM encoders was a signed number that we consider as an unmarked value because of the statistics provided by the Huffman encoder. The efficiency and energy conservation of the recommended system was improved by employing a Huffman representation relying on basic logic gates and avoiding the use of memory tables.

(Babu et al. 2020) designed a low-complexity and low-power compression module. Here, compression approach was based on some endoscopic image characteristics, as well as suitable for hardware implementation. The chroma sub-sampling module was a key component of the preprocessing stage, as it can significantly reduce the amount of data that must be transferred. Encoder block consists of two stages respectively differential coder and Golomb–Rice coder. Finally, the decompression module performed the compression module's contrast operation to obtain the original image. The 22:1:2 compression patterns produce better results, with an average PSNR of 37 dB and a 70% compression rate.

12.6 WIRELESS CAPSULE COMPRESSION USING INTELLIGENT LEARNING MODELS

In recent years, intelligent systems like machine learning and deep learning algorithm play a significant role in image compression. In WCE, the capsule that compresses every redundant image exhausts the battery life of the module.

(Bouyaya et al. 2021) proposed an intelligent compression module to compress the endoscopy images. The goal is to use a deep learning-based categorization feedback loop to examine the relevance of the images. This classification is supplemented with a rudimentary prediction-based compression mechanism to wisely manage the capsule's minimum energy. The capsule achieves this by transmitting a low-rate subsampled rendition of each image. To find any potential lesions, the pictures will be digitally encoded and categorized. Following classification, the photographs that are regarded as crucial for the diagnosis will be enhanced with extra content, while the images that are judged less essential will be taken in low resolution. This allows large amounts of data to be saved without affecting the diagnosis.

(Ahn et al. 2018) built a WCE compression module using an intelligent approach to focus on damaged spots even more. The paper suggested using deep-learning algorithms to automatically evaluate and detect lesions in collected images in real-time, allowing the capsule to take further images of a given spot, modify its focus level, or increase image resolution. Through the intelligent model, analyzing the affected region gets easier by collecting even more images. But the need for power to access the intelligent model is a significant roadblock of this model.

12.7 RESULT AND DISCUSSION

This section compares the existing WCE compression techniques and analyzes their performance in detail. In WCE, low power consumption devices existed compression module is mandatory to escalate the life span of the WCE (Wang & Chen, 2016). Through the compression algorithm and power consumption factor, we can assess how far WCE can travel for excavation (Malathkar & Soni, 2020). Different approaches came with a high CR but failed to minimize the power utilization (Usman et al., 2017). Some of the existing model's power consumption metrics are shown in Figure 12.5.

Achieving a better CR without affecting its quality is a satisfactory factor of a good compression algorithm (Xie et al., 2006). Existing lossy algorithms had provided a highly compressed image, though it will help to minimize the power usage, less quality of the received images creates the reliability issue between pathology analysts (Chen et al., 2009). Lossless compression achieved a good diagnostic quality image without missing any informative portion of the captured image but was unable to beat the CR performance of the lossy algorithms (Al-Shebani et al., 2019). Near-lossless algorithms came to a solution between the controversial limitations of the abovementioned compression techniques. This algorithm gains a good CR without losing rich image attributes. Figure 12.6 shows the CR metric comparison of the existing frameworks (Liu et al., 2016).

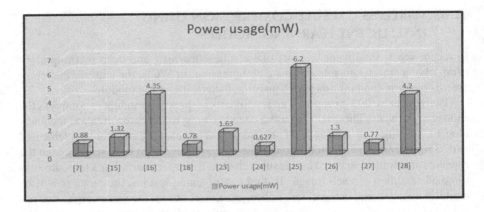

FIGURE 12.5   Comparison chart of existing algorithms' power usage.

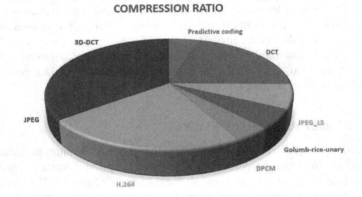

FIGURE 12.6   Comparison of various baseline techniques based on compression ratio.

Figure 12.7 shows the test images of the different locations of the GI tract. Figure 12.8 depicts relevant images of compression performance (Wang & Chen, 2016).

Table 12.1 shows the algorithm's complexity and noise-sensitive levels (Shabani & Timarchi, 2017).

The algorithm with high PSNR indicates the proficiency of the algorithm. Algorithms' high memory requirement may increase the size aspect of the capsule, which will lead to swallowing discomfort in patients (Al-Shebani et al., 2019).

12.8   RESEARCH FINDINGS AND LIMITATIONS

Image compression in capsule endoscopy in the medical image processing area is still a hot subject in research (Li & Deng, 2009). This study offered an extensive

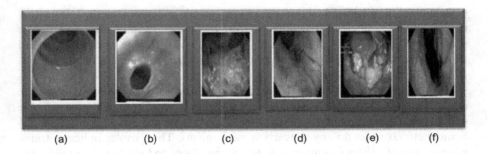

FIGURE 12.7 Test images (a) Lumen (b) contents (c) mucosa (d) flat lesion (e) protruding lesions (f) excavated lesions.

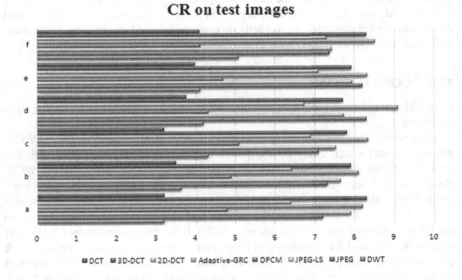

FIGURE 12.8 Various existing methods CR of test images.

TABLE 12.1

Performance Comparison of Different WCE Compression Models

Method	PSNR	Complexity	Clock Rate	Memory
JPEG	51.32	$O(n^3)$	150 MHz	Yes
JPEG-LS	∞	$O(n\log n)$	42 MHz	Yes
MPEG	49.23	$O(n\log n)$	144 MHz	Yes
3D-DCT	40.74	$O(n)$	98 MHz	No
DPCM	43.23	$O(n)$	76 MHz	No
DCT	39.23	$O(n)$	89 MHz	Yes
ODA	43.96	$O(n)$	65 MHz	No

evaluation of the advanced GI tract diagnostic capsule endoscopy method. Detecting Crohn's disease, intestine bleeding, cancer, esophagus examination, and polyps screening is achieved by endoscopy images (Gu et al., 2016). The workstation record capsule screenings and pathologists examine the images to locate the abnormalities (Varma Malathkara & Soni, 2018).

Most of the reviewed compression mechanism focuses on improving the image quality and increasing the CR with less complex hardware (Goyal et al., 2017). Color space conversion is mainly performed by YUV, YEN, YEF, YCbCr, and YLMN. Some methods never do any conversion mechanisms. This chapter indicates transform coding of existing techniques in two forms: lossy and lossless (Mostafa et al., 2011). DCT and DWT are lossless, and they consume more memory and power. The newly developed mechanism utilized DPCT, AT-DPCM, and sub-sampling, which are lossless and near-lossless methods (Fante et al., 2015). Some techniques used quantization to further reduce the data. Entropy coding is mostly performed by using conventional, modified, and AGR coder, CABAC coder, Huffman coder, differential coder, and run length coder. Some methods used the hybrid form to achieve the limitations of the separate ones (Jarray et al., 2018).

12.9   CONCLUSION

In this chapter, a brief review of existing WCE image compression technologies is presented.

Image compression was used to reduce the amount of data transferred from WCE; it is significant for increasing the life span to fully screen the GI tract. Several different compressing modules have to be taken into account, when designing the WCE. WCE is a new approach for GI disorders, focusing on small intestine pathology. Despite the varied quality of the pictures, capsule endoscopy offers a very decent sensitivity for evaluating the small intestine and identifying abnormalities due to the large number of images. Compression in WCE images is significant for efficient diagnosis. The need for a perfect real-time smart capsule to give accurate and quick detection of various GI illnesses, including cancer, as well as particular features of endoscopic pictures, still leaves space for specialized compression research. Issues such as power consumption, memory usage, and hardware complexity still needed to enhance for better performance.

REFERENCES

Abdelkrim, Z., et al, (2018). Low power design of wireless endoscopy compression/communication architecture. *Journal of Electrical Systems and Information Technology*, 5(1), 35–47.

Ahn, J., et al, (2018). Finding small-bowel lesions: Challenges in endoscopy-image-based learning systems. *Computer*, 51(5), 68–76.

Al-Shebani, Q., et al, (2019). The development of a clinically tested visually lossless Image compression system for capsule endoscopy. *Signal Processing: Image Communication*, 76, 135–150.

Babu, C., et al, (2020). Novel chroma subsampling patterns for wireless capsule endoscopy compression. *Neural Computing and Applications*, 32(10), 6353–6362.

Bouyaya, D., et al, (2021). An intelligent compression system for wireless capsule endoscopy images. *Biomedical Signal Processing and Control*, *70*, 102929.

Chen, S. L., et al, (2016). VLSI implementation of a cost-efficient near-lossless CFA image compressor for wireless capsule endoscopy. *IEEE Access*, *4*, 10235–10245.

Chen, X., et al, (2009). A wireless capsule endoscope system with low-power controlling and processing ASIC. *IEEE Transactions on Biomedical Circuits and Systems*, *3*(1), 11–22.

Fante, K. A., et al, (2015, January). A low-power color mosaic image compressor based on optimal combination of 1-D discrete wavelet packet transform and DPCM for wireless capsule endoscopy. In *Proceedings of the International Conference on Biomedical Electronics and Devices - BIODEVICES, (BIOSTEC 2015)* (pp. 190–197). Portugal.

Fante, K. A., et al, (2020). An ingenious application-specific quality assessment methods for compressed wireless capsule endoscopy images. *Transactions on Environment and Electrical Engineering*, *4*(1), 18–24.

Goyal, K., et al, (2017, February). DWT based low power image compressor for wireless capsule endoscopy. Proceedings of the 10th International Joint Conference on Biomedical Engineering Systems and Technologies - BIODEVICES, (BIOSTEC 2017), Porto, Portugal, (pp. 17–24).

Gu, Y., et al, (2016, October). An image compression algorithm for wireless endoscopy and its ASIC implementation. In *2016 IEEE Biomedical Circuits and Systems Conference (BioCAS)* (pp. 103–106). IEEE, Shanghai.

Intzes, I., et al, (2020). An ingenious design of a high performance-low complexity image compressor for wireless capsule endoscopy. *Sensors*, *20*(6), 1617.

Jarray, N., et al, (2018, March). Efficient hybrid DWT-DCT architecture for wireless capsule endoscopy. In *2018 15th International Multi-Conference on Systems, Signals & Devices (SSD)* (pp. 263–268). IEEE, Yasmine Hammamet.

Khan, T. H., & Wahid, K. A. (2011). Lossless and low-power image compressor for wireless capsule endoscopy. *VLSI Design*, *2011*, 1–12.

Khan, T. H., & Wahid, K. A. (2014). White and narrow band image compressor based on a new color space for capsule endoscopy. *Signal Processing: Image Communication*, *29*(3), 345–360.

Lee, J., et al, (2018, May). A 0.78 mW low-power 4.02 high-compression ratio less than 10− 6 BER error-tolerant lossless image compression hardware for wireless capsule endoscopy system. In *2018 IEEE International Symposium on Circuits and Systems (ISCAS)* (pp. 1–4). IEEE, Florence.

Li, J., & Deng, Y. (2009, October). Fast compression algorithms for capsule endoscope images. In *2009 2nd International Congress on Image and Signal Processing* (pp. 1–4). IEEE, Tianjin, China.

Liu, G., et al, (2016). Design of a video capsule endoscopy system with low-power ASIC for monitoring gastrointestinal tract. *Medical & Biological Engineering & Computing*, *54* (11), 1779–1791.

Malathkar, N. V., & Soni, S. K. (2019). Low complexity image compression algorithm based on hybrid DPCM for wireless capsule endoscopy. *Biomedical Signal Processing and Control*, *48*, 197–204.

Malathkar, N. V., & Soni, S. K. (2020). Low cost image compression algorithm with colour reproduction algorithm for transmitting video frame of capsule endoscopy using low power. *Biomedical Signal Processing and Control*, *60*, 101995.

Mohammed, S. K., et al, (2017). Lossless compression in Bayer color filter array for capsule endoscopy. *IEEE Access*, *5*, 13823–13834.

Mostafa, A., et al, (2011, December). An efficient YCgCo-based image compression algorithm for capsule endoscopy. In *14th International Conference on Computer and Information Technology (ICCIT 2011)* (pp. 219–222). IEEE, Dhaka, Bangladesh.

Shabani, A., & Timarchi, S. (2017). Low-power DCT-based compressor for wireless capsule endoscopy. *Signal Processing: Image Communication*, *59*, 83–95.

Sushma, B. (2021). Endoscopic wireless capsule compressor: A review of the existing image and video compression algorithms. In *Sustainable Communication Networks and Application: Proceedings of ICSCN 2020* (pp. 275–293), India.

Sushma, B., & Aparna, P. (2019, April). Texture classification based efficient image compression algorithm for wireless capsule endoscopy. In *2019 5th International Conference on Computing Engineering and Design (ICCED)* (pp. 1–6). IEEE, Singapore.

Turcza, P., & Duplaga, M. (2013). Hardware-efficient low-power image processing system for wireless capsule endoscopy. *IEEE Journal of Biomedical and Health Informatics*, *17*(6), 1046–1056.

Turcza, P., & Duplaga, M. (2017). Near-lossless energy-efficient image compression algorithm for wireless capsule endoscopy. *Biomedical Signal Processing and Control*, *38*, 1–8.

Turcza, P., & Duplaga, M. (2019). Energy-efficient image compression algorithm for high-frame rate multi-view wireless capsule endoscopy. *Journal of Real-Time Image Processing*, *16*(5), 1425–1437.

Usman, M. A., et al, (2017). Quality assessment for wireless capsule endoscopy videos compressed via HEVC: From diagnostic quality to visual perception. *Computers in biology and Medicine*, *91*, 112–134.

Varma Malathkara, N., & Soni, S. K. (2018, April). Low-complexity and lossless image compression algorithm for capsule endoscopy. In *Proceedings of 3rd International Conference on Internet of Things and Connected Technologies (ICIoTCT)* (pp. 26–27), Jaipur.

Wang, Q., & Chen, S. (2016, October). A low power prediction SAR ADC integrated with DPCM data compression feature for WCE application. In *2016 IEEE Biomedical Circuits and Systems Conference (BioCAS)* (pp. 107–110). IEEE, Singapore.

Xie, X., et al, (2006). A low-power digital IC design inside the wireless endoscopic capsule. *IEEE Journal of Solid-State Circuits*, *41*(11), 2390–2400.

Xue, J., et al, (2021). 3D DCT based image compression method for the medical endoscopic application. *Sensors*, *21*(5), 1817.

13 A Comprehensive Review on Leukemia Diseases Based on Microscopic Blood Cell Images

Della Reasa Valiaveetil
Christ College of Engineering

Kanimozhi T
VelTech Ranagarajan Dr. Sagunthala R and D
Institute of Science and Technology

CONTENTS

13.1 INTRODUCTION

Abnormal cell mutation can affect any organ in the body and result in dysfunction, which results in the cause of cancer [1]. Leukemia is a cancer of the blood and bone marrow that affects people of all ages, especially children. In leukemia, the bone marrow undergoes an aggressive, out-of-control proliferation of abnormal cells [2]. According to WHO, about 60,530 new leukemia cases have been reported in 2020, of which about 23,100 have attained death. Most leukemia cases are reported in individuals above 45 years of age, but the syndrome is found widely among the younger population below 15 years of age [3]. Acute myelogenous leukemia (AML), chronic lymphocytic leukemia (CLL), acute lymphocytic leukemia (ALL), and chronic

DOI: 10.1201/9781003307778-15

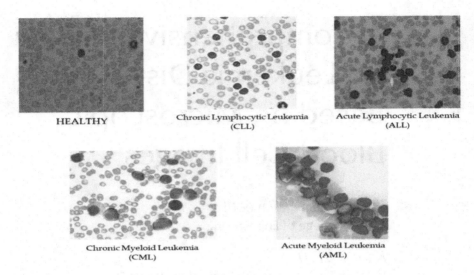

HEALTHY   Chronic Lymphocytic Leukemia   Acute Lymphocytic Leukemia
                          (CLL)   (ALL)

Chronic Myeloid Leukemia   Acute Myeloid Leukemia
         (CML)   (AML)

FIGURE 13.1   Different variants of leukemia.

myeloid leukemia are the four stages of leukemia that are based on the acute and chronic stages [4,5]. Figure 13.1 shows the blood cell appearance for normal and different types of leukemia. The variants of leukemia differ based on the type of white blood cells (WBCs) get affected. Unlike normal cancers, leukemia is highly perilous due to its frequent occurrence [6]. Leukemia develops in the spongy layer of bone marrows beneath the bone, which makes the diagnosis process highly difficult [7,8]. In most cases, leukemia was identified in its second and third stages making the treatment highly challenging.

To cope with this problem, researchers put forward some diagnostic technologies such as bone marrow biopsy [9] and blood smear tests [10]. Physical signs of leukemia such as pale skin are examined by a physician. The conditions of lymph nodes and spleen were also examined to diagnose any sort of leukemia. The blood smear test is an examination of both blood cells and plasma in the blood. It analyses the morphological characteristics of blood cells and detects mutant cells. Blood cells are classified into three types. They are WBCs, which include monocytes, lymphocytes, neutrophils, eosinophils, basophils, and macrophages; red blood cells which are erythrocytes, and platelets which are red blood cells. The atypical mutation of the blood cells converges the property of healthy cells to a malignant cell, which does not limit itself to a particular cell but spreads rapidly to nearby cells, resulting in the blockage of function [11]. Manual examination of the blood cells is considerably ineffective with tremendous loss of time and energy. Here evolves the integration of artificial intelligence (AI) technology that matches up the work of physicians with high accuracy and less time and power. The survey explores the imaging and classification process of microscopic leukemia cells (MLCs) using machine learning

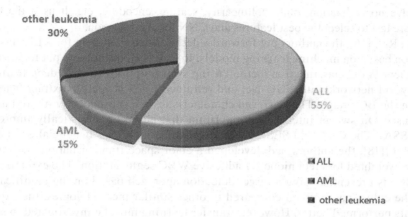

FIGURE 13.2   Different types of leukemia in MLC images.

(ML) and deep learning (DL) technology. Figure 13.2 illustrates the different types of leukemia using MLC images.

The structure of the proposed work has the following sectional parts: the first section specifies some of the significant preliminary studies on leukemia. The systematic review describes the exploration areas of the current leukemia survey and problem statement, the result section provides the comparative study on existing ML and DL techniques and finally the conclusion part summarizes the contribution of the survey.

13.2   PRELIMINARIES STUDY ON LEUKEMIA

The entire architecture of a computer vision system for leukemic cancer diagnoses involves data acquisition, pre-processing, fragmentation, feature extraction, and classification. The preliminary section analyses all recent studies on leukemic cancer and provides a detailed structure of the existing technique, its outcome, and its limitations. In Ref. [12], the authors have developed an image segmentation technique to detect acute lymphoblastic leukemia from microscopic images. This work surveyed different ML techniques to detect leukemia from blood cells. Initially, all shapes of the nucleus in blood cells are segmented using k-medoids. It segments the nuclei and WBC cytoplasm with different stains. Then the processed data are classified using KNN, Random Forest, Decision tree, and Naive Bayes classifiers. The deep learning based algorithms for the analysis of microscopic images are highlighted in [13][14].

To eradicate the occurrence of errors in manual processes, the authors of Ref. [15] developed a deep convolutional neural network (CNN) architecture. The key objective of this method is to reduce the error rate, inconsistencies in labor work of manual classification, and the requirement for trained professionals. The datasets ALL-IDB and multiple myeloma were used for the training process. The noise data are removed from the input samples to reduce the overfitting problem. The pre-processing steps involve normalization, multi-collinearity, scaling, encoding, etc. It used the Chi-square test to select the best features and CNN for classification.

In Ref. [16], the authors put forward a decision-based system for ALL classification based on machine learning models. In Ref. [17], the authors put forward an efficient WBC classification method using swarm optimization of deep features. A hybrid network with VGG-Net and retrained CNN is used to extract features from the BC image. The retrieved characteristics are subsequently filtered using a Based-On swarm intelligence algorithm that has been statistically improved (SESSA). The CNN and SESSA feature combination yields beneficial outcomes. In Ref. [18], the authors had developed a color space transformation and multi-class weighted loss technique for adhesive WBC segmentation. The extraction of WBCs is presented using a target detection approach based on the modification of the color space. When compared to other similar methodologies, the experiments performed better. However, transfer learning must be investigated to solve the problem of tiny medical sample data and make the approach applicable to other similar types of data. A local pixel segmentation technique for ALL classification was proposed in Ref. [19]. The dataset collected contains 108 MBC images. The statistical features were measured for local pixel extraction and classified using an ANN classifier. Finally, the characteristics of blast cells were recognized accurately. Furthermore, blast cells were correctly identified (with 97% accuracy) in MBCs. Furthermore, this approach outperformed watershed and MBS procedures in terms of outcomes.

13.3 MACHINE LEARNING AND DEEP LEARNING APPROACHES IN LEUKEMIA DETECTION

Researchers have used ML and computer-aided diagnostic approaches to help in the detection and classification of leukemia. The images of blood smears were examined for diagnosing, distinguishing, and counting the cells in distinct forms of leukemia in these investigations, Google Net architecture was employed for classification [20]. The advanced and innovative concept of DL architecture insisted on a way to design a neural network architecture for leukemic cancer [21]. ML and DL, two AI methods, are essential for the segmentation and classification of many kinds of medical data and images [22]. This technique integrates mathematical and scientific concepts and develops architecture for leukemic cancer. Recent research has resulted in a series of studies on microscopic blood cell (MBC) images [23]. The output produced through the ML techniques is fast and efficient with a minimum error rate. But these techniques face a lot of challenges in training large data, complex architectural design, and high computation costs [24]. To overcome all these points there is a need to develop an advanced network that practically overcomes all the drawbacks of all existing techniques with minimum computation cost and less processing time. The survey describes the existing ML concepts of leukemia as well as the flaws in the current system. It also leads to some futuristic prospection of DL techniques to minimize the current loopholes in the imaging system. Figure 13.3 shows the overall work process of MBC classification in an ML system.

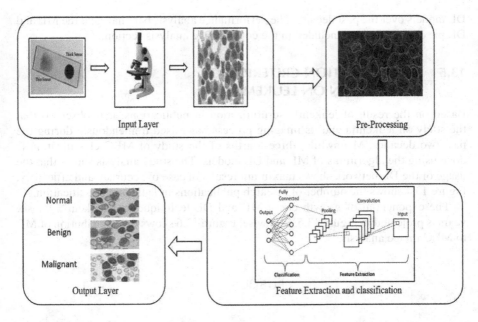

FIGURE 13.3 Overall work process of microscopic blood cell classification in machine learning system.

13.4 SYSTEMATIC REVIEW

A systematic review of all recent studies on leukemia is done in the present work. The work mainly analyses the study of microscopic blood smear images and ML techniques for leukemia. The study analyzes the existing technique and states the drawbacks of existing techniques and also provides a theoretical Statement to overcome the existing target.

This review mainly focuses to respond the following questions:

1. What is the available ML algorithm for leukemia detection?
2. Which technique is more efficient for microscopic smear images?
3. What are the major challenges in training the leukemia blood smear images?
4. How effective is the performance of ML networks in the detection of leukemia?

The researcher came to the conclusion that PubMed, Elsevier, Springer, Scopus, Web of Science, and Science Direct have the most papers relevant to the subject and objectives of this study after reviewing electronic databases that offer scholarly publications in the two fields of medicine and computer sciences. From 2016 to November 10, 2022, suitable papers were retrieved from the databases using the keywords leukemia, microscopic leukemia cells, classification of leukemia diagnosis and detection, and ML.

The survey analyses the efficiency of ML and DL models on the microscopic leukemia blood cells. The comparative section portrays the growth and evolution of

DL models over the past decade. The performance analysis bar chart and the ML and DL pie chart were also included in the comparative analysis section.

13.5 SCRUTINIZATION CRITERION OF PUBLICATION ON LEUKEMIA

Based on the result of leukemia scrutinization in publications, it is observed that the study on leukemia and its imaging process has raised tremendously during the past two decades. Meanwhile, three-fourths of the study of MBC classification is done using the algorithms of ML and DL models. The study analysis shows that the usage of the DL network shows maximum results in case of accuracy and efficiency. Figure 13.4 shows the number of research publications in leukemia classification.

The exponential of growth curve ML and DL techniques for leukemia for six years is projected in Figure 13.5. Likewise, Figure 13.6 shows the contribution of ML to MLC image analysis.

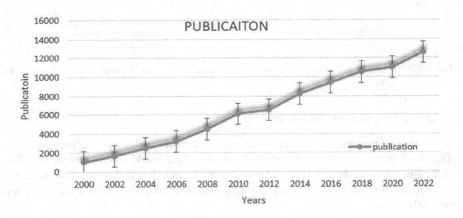

FIGURE 13.4   Number of research publications in leukemia classification.

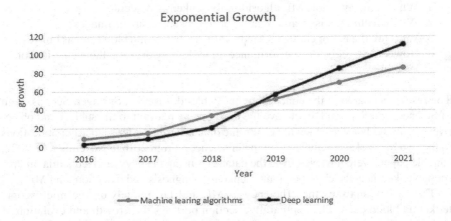

FIGURE 13.5   Exponential growth prediction of ML and DL technique in leukemia classification.

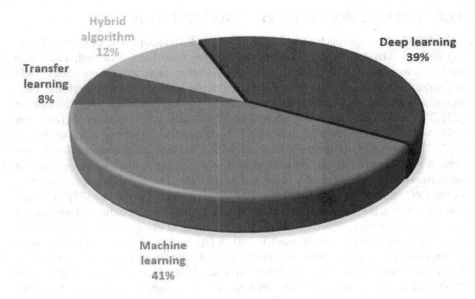

FIGURE 13.6   Machine learning contribution on MLC image analysis.

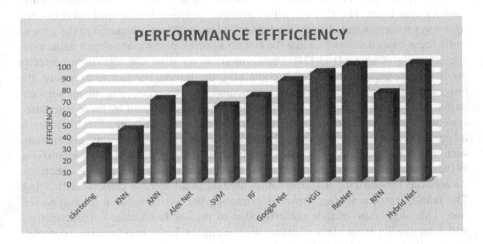

FIGURE 13.7   Performance efficiency of ML and DL model on leukemia cell classification.

13.6   PERFORMANCE ANALYSIS

The performance of the ML and DL models in the existing model is calculated with parameters such as accuracy, Jaccard index, sensitivity, recall, Dice index, and F1 score. These parameters measure the true-positive, true-negative, false-positive, and false-negative values from the output image and compare those results with the ground truth values to predict maximum efficiency of the trained model. Figure 13.7 portrays the performance efficiency of some DL and ML models compared with the ground truth images.

13.7 OVERALL REVIEW OF RESEARCH FINDINGS

The classification approach of leukemia in DL and ML adopts the three-step learning process. The data are pre-processed once they have been collected. The entire dataset is verified for missing values in the preparation stage, as missing values might skew the classification result. The complete dataset is split into two subgroups once the missing value is checked. DNN classifier or algorithm is used for classification [25]. The leukemia dataset was created using publicly available datasets [26]. The collection includes microarray data with 72 bone marrow expression samples including 7128 genes, ALL-IDB image database, MPCTRC dataset, and several local datasets. A multi-layered neural network model in which input data are represented at numerous levels of abstraction is known as a DNN. The hierarchical architecture of the DNN makes it much simpler to explain complicated problems [27]. A seven-layer DNN is used to categorize the leukemia lesion to extract the vast amount of gene expression data. When compared to other types of classifiers, the classification accuracy is much greater in DL models [28]. A DL-based classifier has the advantage of improving accuracy while requiring the least amount of processing work [29]. The classification accuracy of the DNN, AlexNet, VGG, GoogleNet, MobileNet, and ResNet classifiers is about 98.34%–99.57%, which is higher than that of the SVM, KNN, and Naive Bayes classifiers [30].

To produce full blood cell counts on blood smear images, a convolution neural network was used. The CNN can be modified, combined, and optimized in multiple ways to detect and classify the leukemia lesion. When compared to the ground truth, these trials demonstrate that the system's overall performance has a mean average accuracy of above 0.95 [31]. Furthermore, every time, the algorithm correctly predicts the contaminated images containing the tumor. For fast prototyping, the program is also ported to a low-cost microcomputer. Pre-processing, image segmentation, feature extraction, and classification techniques are used by these automated systems. Noise reduction, color correction, and picture enhancement techniques are all part of the pre-processing step. The segmentation stage separates cell components such as the nucleus and cytoplasm, which is particularly important for identifying WBCs, and various kinds of blood cells, but has different forms and architectures. As a result, generalizing a segmentation method to all sorts of cells is challenging. The feature extraction stage involves extracting the attributes used for categorization. This stage may include the extraction of present handcrafted characteristics, which may suffer from a lack of generality once again. Leukemia detection, complete blood cell count, and WBC distribution are all done in the same system. To enhance detection accuracy, partly visible WBCs are dealt with individually. The system's performance is also evaluated on a small off-the-shelf embedded device such as the Raspberry Pi 3. The system as a whole is cost-effective, and its performance is comparable to that of a human pathologist. As a result, its application may enable patients to receive therapy at a lower cost and more quickly.

In addition, a color feature termed cell energy was included, and findings suggest that this feature effectively distinguishes cancer cells from non-cancer cells. The survey firmly suggests that the DL model with a pre-trained or hybrid network has the maximum efficiency for the classification of MLC. The efficiency of the model considerably increases if the system is subjected to some optimization model.

13.8   DEFECTS WITH THE CURRENT SYSTEM

The classification of leukemia has reached its zenith in image processing. However, this does not place a priority on collecting more samples to improve performance and cancer categorization and faces several shortcomings due to its complex nature and processing method. Some of them are listed below:

- The complex structure of the neural network results in time complexity.
- The classification of blood smear images has limitations in feature selection and has limited the number of labeled smear images.
- It has insufficient training data and small datasets.
- It has limited public dataset and samples.
- Existing techniques have a high error rate and false positives.
- The complex network structure causes an overfitting problem.
- A vast study of DL networks is not done to train leukemic images.

13.9   CONCLUSION

This chapter shows a systematic review of the existing DL and ML techniques for the classification of leukemia cells. Several classification modules have to be taken into account while developing an architecture for classifying MBCs. The ML and DL technique shows remarkable results in predicting and classifying the MLC images. The output produced through the DL techniques is fast and efficient with a minimum error rate. Additionally, it lists the research problems that have been satisfactorily resolved and the open problems that are still present in the field. The survey analysis points out that the DL models work better on the classification process than other techniques. Moreover, the classification accuracy of the DL technique ranges around 98.36%–99.57% in the hybrid network while the ML stays around 86%–92%. But these techniques face a lot of challenges in training the large data, complex architectural design, and computation cost. To tackle these factors, the system can be developed with pre-trained and hybrid networks. The optimization model can also be applied to improve the robustness of the network.

REFERENCES

1. Samra, B., et al, (2020). Evolving therapy of adult acute lymphoblastic leukemia: state-of-the-art treatment and future directions. *Journal of Hematology & Oncology, 13*(1), 1–17.
2. Philip, A. T., et al, (2021, June). Detection of acute lymphoblastic leukemia in microscopic images using image processing techniques. In *Journal of Physics: Conference Series* (Vol. 1937, No. 1, p. 012022). IOP Publishing.
3. Yang, X., et al, (2021). Secular trends in the incidence and survival of all leukemia types in the United States from 1975 to 2017. *Journal of Cancer, 12*(8), 2326.
4. Kassani, S. H., et al, (2019, October). A hybrid deep learning architecture for leukemic B-lymphoblast classification. In *2019 International Conference on Information and Communication Technology Convergence* (ICTC) (pp. 271–276). IEEE, Lucknow Campus.
5. Kumar, D., et al, (2020). Automatic detection of white blood cancer from bone marrow microscopic images using convolutional neural networks. *IEEE Access, 8*, 142521–142531.

6. Negm, A. S., et al. (2018). A decision support system for Acute Leukaemia classification based on digital microscopic images. *Alexandria Engineering Journal, 57*(4), 2319–2332.

7. Sahlol, A. T., et al, (2020). Efficient classification of white blood cell leukemia with improved swarm optimization of deep features. *Scientific Reports, 10*(1), 1–11.

8. Li, H., et al, (2020). Color space transformation and multi-class weighted loss for adhesive white blood cell segmentation. *IEEE Access, 8*, 24808–24818.

9. Al-jaboriy, S. S., et al, (2019). Acute lymphoblastic leukemia segmentation using local pixel information. *Pattern Recognition Letters, 125*, 85–9

10. Acharya, V., & Kumar, P. (2019). Detection of acute lymphoblastic leukemia using image segmentation and data mining algorithms. *Medical & Biological Engineering & Computing, 57*(8), 1783–1811.

11. Genovese, A., et al, (2021, June). Acute Lymphoblastic Leukemia detection based on adaptive unsharpening and Deep Learning. In *ICASSP 2021-2021 IEEE International Conference on Acoustics, Speech and Signal Processing (ICASSP)* (pp. 1205–1209). IEEE, Toronto, ON..

12. Bodzas, A., et al, (2020). Automated detection of acute lymphoblastic leukemia from microscopic images based on human visual perception. *Frontiers in Bioengineering and Biotechnology, 8*, 1005.

13. Rehman, A., et al, (2018). Classification of acute lymphoblastic leukemia using deep learning. *Microscopy Research and Technique, 81*(11), 1310–1317.

14. Rajpurohit, S., et al, (2018, September). Identification of acute lymphoblastic leukemia in microscopic blood image using image processing and machine learning algorithms. In *2018 International Conference on Advances in Computing, Communications and Informatics (ICACCI)* (pp. 2359–2363). IEEE, MIT, Pune.

15. Vogado, L. H., et al, (2018). Leukemia diagnosis in blood slides using transfer learning in CNNs and SVM for classification. *Engineering Applications of Artificial Intelligence, 72*, 415–422.

16. Kashef, A., et al, (2020). Treatment outcome classification of pediatric Acute Lymphoblastic Leukemia patients with clinical and medical data using machine learning: a case study at MAHAK hospital. *Informatics in Medicine Unlocked, 20*, 100399.

17. Sneha, D., et al. *A Novel Segmentation Approach for Acute Lymphocytic Leukemia Detection Using Deep Learning.*

18. Li, H., Zhao, X., Su, A., Zhang, H., Liu, J., & Gu, G. (2020). Color space transformation and multi-class weighted loss for adhesive white blood cell segmentation. *IEEE Access, 8*, 24808–24818.

19. Dese, K., et al, (2021). Accurate machine-learning-based classification of leukemia from blood smear images. *Clinical Lymphoma Myeloma and Leukemia, 21*(11), e903–e914.

20. Aftab, M. O., et al, (2021, April). Executing spark BigDL for leukemia detection from microscopic images using transfer learning. In *2021 1st International Conference on Artificial Intelligence and Data Analytics (CAIDA)* (pp. 216–220). IEEE, Pakistan.

21. Ghaderzadeh, M., et al, (2021). Machine learning in detection and classification of leukemia using smear blood images: a systematic review. *Scientific Programming, 2021*, 1–14.

22. Dasariraju, S., et al, (2020). Detection and classification of immature leukocytes for diagnosis of acute myeloid leukemia using random forest algorithm. *Bioengineering, 7*(4), 120.

23. Fan, H., et al, (2019). LeukocyteMask: an automated localization and segmentation method for leukocyte in blood smear images using deep neural networks. *Journal of Biophotonics, 12*(7), e201800488.

24. Khilji, I. Q., et al, (2020). Application of homomorphic encryption on neural network in prediction of acute lymphoid leukemia. *International Journal of Advanced Computer Science and Applications, 11*(6), 350–360.
25. Shafique, S., & Tehsin, S. (2018). Acute lymphoblastic leukemia detection and classification of its subtypes using pretrained deep convolutional neural networks. *Technology in cancer research & treatment, 17*, 1533033818802789.
26. Zolfaghari, M., & Sajedi, H. (2022). A survey on automated detection and classification of acute leukemia and WBCs in microscopic blood cells. *Multimedia Tools and Applications, 81*(5), 6723–6753.
27. Jha, K. K., & Dutta, H. S. (2020). Nucleus and cytoplasm–based segmentation and actor-critic neural network for acute lymphocytic leukaemia detection in single cell blood smear images. *Medical & Biological Engineering & Computing, 58*(1), 171–186.
28. Shaheen, M., et al, (2021). Acute myeloid leukemia (AML) detection using AlexNetmodel. *Complexity, 2021*, 1–8.
29. Bukhari, M., et al, (2022). A deep learning framework for leukemia cancer detection in microscopic blood samples using squeeze and excitation learning. *Mathematical Problems in Engineering, 2022*, 1–18.
30. Lavitt, F., et al, (2021). Deep learning and transfer learning for automatic cell counting in microscope images of human cancer cell lines. *Applied Sciences, 11*(11), 4912.
31. Elhassan, T. A. M., et al, (2022). Feature extraction of white blood cells using CMYK-moment localization and deep learning in acute myeloid leukemia blood smear microscopic images. *IEEE Access, 10*, 16577–16591.

14 Effects of Numerical Mapping Techniques on Performance in Genomic Signal Processing

Seda Nur Gulocak and Bihter Das
University of Firat

CONTENTS

14.1   INTRODUCTION

Deoxyribonucleic acid (DNA) is a nucleic acid that performs the vital functions of all organisms and carries genetic characteristics. Consisting of two long polymers, DNA includes a phosphate group, a sugar group, and a base linked by ester bonds. There are four bases: adenine, thymine, guanine, and cytosine. DNA strands are held together by hydrogen bonds. The base corresponding to adenine base is thymine while the base corresponding to guanine is cytosine [1]. The sequence formed by these bases encodes the genetic information. The nucleotide sequence that contains genetic information and forms a certain part of DNA is called a gene. A gene is a region in the genome sequence that has identifiable regulatory or functional regions that are transcribed. Three-nucleotide sequences in DNA are called "codons", and codons code for different amino acids that make up proteins. There are 64 possible codons. UGA, UAG, and UAA are stop codons. These codons do not code for an amino acid-like the other 61 codons. Since there are 20 amino acids (aa) in total, there may be more than one codon coding for the same aa [2]. Messenger RNA (mRNA) carries the information in DNA to the ribosomes, the protein synthesis site.

DOI: 10.1201/9781003307778-16

Carrier RNA is responsible for the transport of aa to be used in protein synthesis. RNA is synthesized by the enzyme RNA polymerase reading DNA. This process is called transcription. In other words, mRNA (messenger RNA) is created from DNA. The genetic code is extracted from the cell nucleus and taken to the cytoplasm. Protein synthesis takes place here. The translation is the process of translating the code carried by mRNA into proteins. The transfer of genetic information from DNA to RNA is called transcription, and the translation of the code carried by mRNA into proteins is called translation [3]. DNA bases are divided into two classes according to their derivatives. The guanine and adenine bases are called purines, while the thymine and cytosine bases are called pyrimidines. The two strands of DNA are complementary due to base pairings. Purines and pyrimidines form hydrogen bonds. There are two hydrogen bonds between adenine and thymine, while a triple hydrogen bond exists between guanine and cytosine. Genes contain small protein-coding sequences called exons. Exons are the regions where the polymerase enzyme synthesizes mRNA and genetic information is transferred from meaningful DNA to mRNA [2]. Figure 14.1 shows the representation of genetic and intergenetic regions in eukaryotic DNA. Between the exon sequences are long, non-protein-coding regions called introns. The first exons of the genes start with the start codon "ATG" and the last exon of the gene ends with one of the stop codons. The start codon is the codon of formylated (AUG) methionine that signals initiation for transcription on mRNA [4].

In this section, studies that examine the techniques used for digitization of DNA data in various genomic fields are presented. In this study, all numerical mapping

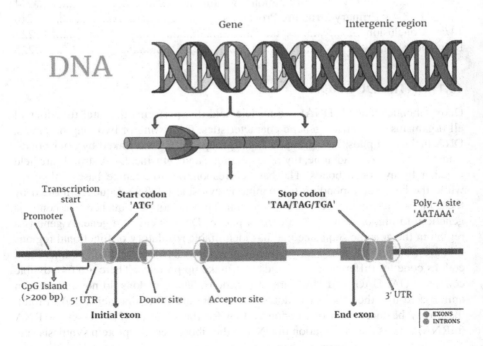

FIGURE 14.1 Genetic and intergenetic regions in eukaryotic DNA.

techniques developed in the last 10 years in the literature and used to digitize DNA sequences were examined and the benefits and shortcomings of these numerical techniques in genomic study areas. Digitization of DNA sequences is extremely important in order to achieve targeted high-performance accuracy in genomic studies such as detection of exon regions, exon-intron classification, disease-causing gene detection, phylogenetic analysis, and promoter recognition. Therefore, in this study, all the digital mapping techniques of the last 10 years were introduced in detail, and a review study presenting all the techniques was actualized. Das et al. introduced two group mapping techniques such as nucleotide and amino acid for the prediction of exon regions [5]. Wisesty et al. used binary and information encoding (BIE) techniques to diagnose breast cancer [6]. Raman Kumar et al. used position based, 2-bit neural networks based, hamming distance based, integer, and trigonometric encoding techniques to detect protein-coding regions [7]. Yu et al. separate numerical encoding techniques into five groups. These are biochemical properties, primary structure properties, Cartesian coordinate properties (CCPs), BIE, and graphical representation (GR). They performed genomic signal processing implementations using these techniques [8]. Kumari used three groups of numerical techniques for genomic signal processing in another study [9]. Das et al. compared the performance of techniques in CCP group for the prediction of exon regions [10]. Ahmad et al. used GR encoding techniques for genomic signal processing applications [11]. Jin et al. compared the performance of the techniques based on GR for the detection of similarity between species [12]. Mendizabal et al. used techniques in the Cartesian coordinate group for the identification of similarity of DNA sequences [13]. Saini et al. compared the performance of the techniques in the BIE group for genomic signal processing applications [14]. Mabrouk used genetic code context (GCC), frequency of nucleotide occurrence, atomic number, 2-bit binary, Electron-Ion Interaction Pseudopotential (EIIP) encoding techniques for the prediction of exon regions [15]. Das compared the performance of three numerical mapping techniques to detect type 2 diabetes from nucleotide sequences [16]. Das and Turkoglu introduced entropy-based encoding technique for the identification of protein-coding regions in another study [17].

14.2   EXAMINATION OF DNA NUMERICAL MAPPING TECHNIQUES AND THEIR NUMERICAL REPRESENTATIONS

In this section, the coding techniques developed for the digitization of DNA sequences are comprehensively examined under five main headings. In the literature, coding techniques are also called different names as digital mapping techniques, numerical methods, and coding schemes. However, all the nomenclatures mean the same. Fifty digital mapping techniques developed in the last 10 years are classified into five groups according to their general characteristics. These groups are Cartesian coordinate coding techniques, biochemical and physicochemical coding techniques, binary and information coding, primary structure coding techniques, and graphically represented coding techniques. Figure 14.2 shows the hierarchical scheme of all DNA mapping techniques.

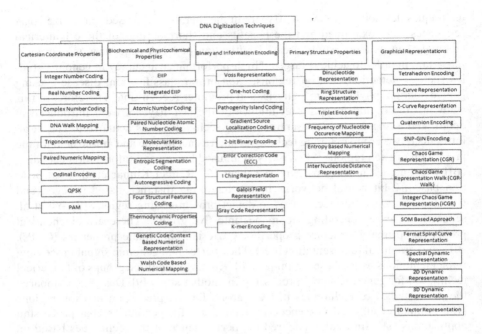

FIGURE 14.2 Hierarchical scheme of all DNA mapping techniques.

14.2.1 CARTESIAN COORDINATE PROPERTIES

The first group of DNA numerical mapping techniques is CCP digitization techniques. In DNA numerical mapping techniques, which have Cartesian coordinates, the nucleotides that make up DNA are given the formalized values of the points on the Cartesian coordinate system according to certain properties. Within this group, there are nine numerical coding techniques, namely integer number coding, real number coding, complex number coding, DNA walk mapping, trigonometric coding, paired numeric coding, ordinal encoding, quadrature phase shift keying (QPSK), pulse amplitude modulation (PAM) are examined.

The integer encoding technique is one-dimensional that uses arbitrary integer values such as 0, 1, 2, and 3, which is realized by encoding DNA nucleotides with integers. In the DNA sequence, if purine (A, G)>pyrimidine (C, T), four bases are given the values $T=0$, $C=1$, $A=2$, $G=3$. If $T>A$ and $G>C$, bases are given the values $A=0$, $C=1$, $T=2$, $G=3$ [18]. The advantage of this technique is that the computational complexity is low since a one-dimensional numerical array is obtained. The disadvantage is that coding with arbitrary assignment does not provide real DNA signals [8]. In real number coding, the bases in the DNA sequence are encoded with real numbers $A=-1.5$, $C=0.5$, $T=1.5$, $G=-0.5$ [19]. The advantage of this technique is that since the mean of the signal values is zero and the deviations are symmetrical, it is useful in neural network applications, data training, and feature learning [8].

It also provides less noisy output. However, since it represents the DNA signal with arbitrary real numbers, it is a disadvantage of this technique that it cannot reflect the DNA structure very well.

Complex number coding is a two-dimensional (2D) numerical mapping technique performed with complex numbers according to the complementary structure of A-T and C-G pairs. Coding is done with A=1+j, G=−1−j, C=−1+j, T=1−j values. Nucleotides are placed at different corners in the 2D Cartesian coordinate plane, giving different coding values for A, T, G, and C. The advantage of this technique is that it reduces three-dimensional (3D) digitization to two dimensions. Two different digitization representations can be created by changing the planes. In the first, C-G and A-T nucleotide pairs have mathematically complex conjugate values, purine and pyrimidine have equal complex values and opposite sign real number values (A=1+j, G=−1+j, C=−1−j, T=1 −j). In the latter, the two complementary strands of DNA have equal complex values and opposite signs (A=−1+j, G=1+j, C=−1−j, T=1−j). Thus, their algebraic sum becomes zero and is complementary, which is advantageous in signal processing. The coding scheme created by rotating the Cartesian coordinate plane by 45 degrees takes the values (A=−1, C=−j, G=j, T=1) [8].

Complex number coding is the only signal sequence that reduces the computational load of the four binary Voss coding schemes by 75% [11].

DNA Walk coding performs the digitization according to the purine pair (A-T) and pyrimidine pair (C-T). In the DNA sequence, the A and T bases are given the value −1, and the C and T bases are given the value +1. This coding technique is preferred for evolutionarily visualizing base pairs in DNA [8]. The disadvantage of this technique is that it is not useful for DNA sequences longer than 1000 bases.

$$\hat{X}(i) = \begin{cases} X(i-1)+1 & \text{if } X(i) = C \vee T \\ X(i-1)+(-1) & \text{otherwise} \end{cases} \tag{14.1}$$

Trigonometric coding is the technique of assigning trigonometric values to DNA nucleotides. The advantage of this technique is that it is designed to be well suited to the Gauss–Newton-tuned adaptive Kaiser window used to define exon positions, and it performs well for long DNA sequences [20]. However, the disadvantage of this technique is that it needs some improvements when applied to spectral analysis. Equation 14.2 shows the formula for the numerical representation of trigonometric coding [21].

$$\begin{aligned} A &= \cos(\theta) + j \times \sin(\theta) & C &= -\cos(\theta) - j \times \sin(\theta) \\ G &= -\cos(\theta) + j \times \sin(\theta) & T &= \cos(\theta) - j \times \sin(\theta) \end{aligned} \tag{14.2}$$

Figure 14.3 shows the graphic representation of trigonometric coding.

In the paired numerical coding technique, the G-C and A-T base pairs in the two strands of DNA are encoded with the values (+1) and (−1). The advantage of this

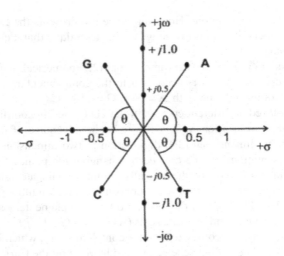

FIGURE 14.3 The graphic representation of trigonometric coding [21].

technique is that it reduces the complexity of DNA. There are seven rules for digitizing nucleotide pairs with this technique. Among these rules, the most used one in studies is the RY rule. The most commonly used purine is the pyrimidine rule. This digitization technique is most commonly used for exon and gene prediction. It takes advantage of the frequency of bases in exons and introns. Introns have more A and T bases, and exons have more G and C bases. Thus, this distinction can be used with the values given by matching [22]. Sequential coding technique, A=0.25, G=0.75, C=0.50, T=1.00 values are given to nucleotides and coding is done. A value of 0.00 is given for the unknown nucleotide. The advantage of this technique is to reduce the size of the input array in systems using neural networks. For example, in one-hot encoding, the number of input values for each input string of length l is 4×1. The disadvantage of this technique is that it causes a long training time and can be applied mostly for short sequences [23].

QPSK coding is performed by assigning complex values A=1+j, C=−1−j, G=−1+j, T=1−j to bases based on the complementary property of the gene sequence. It is accepted as one of the constellation diagrams commonly used in signal processing. It represents DNA on the 2D plane and provides the symmetry of genetic codes [8]. The advantage of this technique is that a symbol mapping helps visualize the DNA sequence in digital communication followed by information transfer. In addition, this technique can reveal some aspects of DNA, such as the analysis of DNA sequences, and the error correction ability of DNA [24]. PAM coding represents the real-numbered representation of nucleotides. It is the coding of the pulse levels of bits in a data string [25]. PAM, like QPSK, is a constellation diagram. Coding is done by giving the bases A=−1.5, G=−0.5, C=0.5, T=0.5 values. The advantage of this technique is that it provides symmetry of genetic codes with real numbers in a one-dimensional plane [8]. Figure 14.4 shows constellation notation for real and complex numbers.

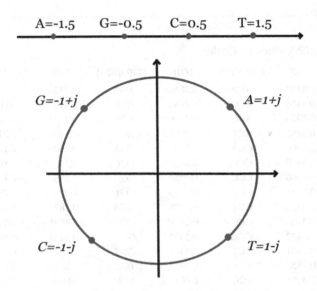

FIGURE 14.4 Constellation notation for real and complex number representations [8].

14.2.2 BIOCHEMICAL AND PHYSICOCHEMICAL PROPERTIES

The second group of DNA numerical mapping techniques is the biochemical and physicochemical (BPP) numerical techniques. Techniques with biochemical and physicochemical properties include the techniques in which digitization is performed using the chemical and physical values of DNA obtained in the laboratory environment. Within this group, 11 coding schemes such as EIIP, integrated EIIP, atomic number coding, paired nucleotide atomic number coding, molecular mass representation, entropic segmentation coding, autoregressive coding, four structural features coding, thermodynamic properties coding, GCC-based numerical coding, Walsh code–based numerical mapping are examined.

Electromagnetic resonance resulting from the electromagnetic oscillation between biomolecules is called EIIP [20]. For the four nucleotides of EIIP coding, values of A=0.1260, T=0.1335, C=0.1340, G=0.0806 are given. The DNA sequence encoded by the EIIP values constitutes the numerical sequence showing the distribution of the pseudopotential energies of the free electrons along the DNA sequence. The advantage of this technique is that it performs well in areas such as neural networks, wavelet transform, and genomic signal processing [8]. EIIP coding reduces the computational burden of coding by 75%, of the four binary signal strings offered by Voss [11]. However, the disadvantage of this technique is that it cannot fully detect protein-coding regions in some genomes.

In the integrated EIIP coding technique, bases are realized by assigning electron-ion pseudopotential energy values to codons in the form of triple nucleotides. EIIP mapping used the electron potential of a single nucleotide to encode biological information. In the integrated EIIP, the EIIP values of all three nucleotides are summed, and the total numerical value is assigned to the codon, then shifted and moved one by one, and the same digitization is continued for each codon [26] in Table 14.1.

TABLE 14.1

Integrated EIIP Values of Codons

A (0.1260)	IEIIP	C (0.1340)	IEIIP	G (0.0806)	IEIIP	T (0.1335)	IEIIP
AAA	0.3780	ACA	0.3860	AGA	0.3326	ATA	0.3885
AAC	0.3860	ACC	0.3940	AGC	0.3406	ATC	0.3935
AAG	0.3326	ACG	0.3406	AGG	0.2872	ATG	0.3401
AAT	0.3885	ACT	0.3935	AGT	0.3401	ATT	0.3930
CAA	0.3860	CCA	0.3940	CGA	0.3406	CTA	0.3935
CAC	0.3940	CCC	0.4020	CGC	0.3486	CTC	0.4015
CAG	0.3406	CCG	0.3486	CGG	0.2952	CTG	0.3481
CAT	0.3935	CCT	0.4015	CGT	0.3935	CTT	0.4010
GAA	0.3326	GCA	0.3406	GGA	0.2872	GTA	0.3401
GAC	0.3406	GCC	0.3486	GCG	0.3935	GTC	0.3481
GAG	0.2872	GCG	0.2952	GGG	0.2418	GTG	0.2947
GAT	0.3401	GCT	0.3481	GGT	0.2947	GTT	0.3476
TAA	0.3855	TCA	0.3935	TGA	0.3401	TTA	0.3930
TAC	0.3935	TCC	0.4015	TGC	03481	TTC	0.4010
TAG	0.3401	TCG	0.3481	TGG	0.2947	TTG	0.3476
TAT	0.3930	TCT	0.4010	TGT	0.3476	TTT	0.4005

The advantage of this technique is that it can better complement the deficiencies of the EIIP technique in determining exon regions. The disadvantage is that this technique cannot achieve 100% success in protein-coding regions.

The atomic number coding technique is performed by assigning atomic numbers to each nucleotide in the DNA sequence. It is coded by giving atomic numbers $A = 70$, $G = 78$, $C = 58$, $T = 66$. The advantage of this technique is that it is widely used in exon separation, signal processing techniques, and measuring fractal size differences between genomic sequences of species [8]. The disadvantage is that it cannot fully reflect the structure of DNA, as it assigns a numerical value to the bases.

The coding technique with the representation of paired atomic numbers is performed not by assigning atomic numbers to each base, but by assigning atomic numbers to purines and pyrimidines. $G-A = 62$ is encoded with $C-T = 42$ values. The advantage of this technique is that it is preferred in studies on the detection of ATCG nucleotide fluctuation [11]. However, this technique cannot fully reveal the properties of DNA such as atomic number coding.

The molecular mass coding technique is performed by assigning molecular masses to four nucleotides. DNA sequence mapping is performed by assigning masses $A = 134$, $T = 125$, $C = 110$, and $G = 150$ [11,17]. The advantage of this technique is that it is an easy and convenient method and does not require additional research.

The entropic segmentation coding technique is performed by representing the 12-letter nucleotide formation to identify large DNA segments. Thus, it defines the differential base pairs with each codon position in the DNA sequences and performs the boundary search by the entropic segmentation method [27,28]. The 12-symbol alphabet is based on nucleotide statistics within the codons. The symbols numbered with the 12-letter alphabet are assigned according to the first, second, and third order of the codon. The entropy calculation is then performed for the sequence coded according to the alphabet. The advantage of this technique is its good performance in exon and intron classification [11].

The autoregressive coding technique is based on the structural features of DNA sequences. While coding, DNA bending stiffness (DBS) values and propeller twist (PT) are used [11]. The twist angle, measured in degrees, is called dinucleotide PT. The higher the PT value, the stronger the DNA helix in that region. A lower propeller bend value means the helix is relatively flexible. Numerical values are assigned by reading the DNA sequence as binary nucleotides by shifting them by one, and coding is performed [29]. The advantage of this technique is great convenience in finding the three periodic properties of short exons in a DNA sequence. Table 14.2 shows PT values.

Twisting stiffness is considered as the sequence correlation of DNA with anisotropic flexibility. High values indicate more rigid regions in the DNA regions, lower values indicate less rigid regions [29]. Table 14.3 shows bending stiffness values.

In four structural features coding technique, coding is done using the four physical properties of the DNA molecule. Structural property values of DNA have been obtained by physical models or biological experiments [30]. Dinucleotides (DN) is obtained by shifting the DNA sequence by one and $\tilde{x}_\alpha(n) \to$ DBS, $\tilde{x}_\beta(n) \to$ duplex disrupt energy, $\tilde{x}_\gamma(n) \to$ duplex free energy, $\tilde{x}_\delta(n) \to$ PT sequences are obtained according to numerical values. The advantage of this technique is that it preserves the physical properties of DNA. It also performs well in the application of gene

TABLE 14.2
Propeller Twist Values

Dinucleotide	Coding	Dinucleotide	Coding	Dinucleotide	Coding	Dinucleotide	Coding
AA	−18.66	GA	−13.48	CA	−9.45	TA	−11.85
AC	−13.10	GC	−11.08	CC	−8.10	TC	−13.48
AG	−14.00	GG	−8.10	CG	−10.03	TG	−9.45
AT	−15.01	GT	−13.10	CT	−14.00	TT	−18.66

TABLE 14.3
Bending Stiffness Values

Dinucleotide	Coding	Dinucleotide	Coding	Dinucleotide	Coding	Dinucleotide	Coding
AA	35	GA	60	CA	60	TA	20
AC	60	GC	85	CC	130	TC	60
AG	60	GG	130	CG	85	TG	60
AT	20	GT	60	CT	60	TT	35

TABLE 14.4

The Conversion Table of Four Structural Features

DN	DBS	DDE	DFE	PT	DN	DBS	DDE	DFE	PT
AA	35	19	−12	−1866	GA	60	16	−15	−1348
AC	60	13	−15	−1310	GC	85	31	−23	−1108
AG	60	16	−15	−1400	GG	130	31	−23	−810
AT	20	9	−9	−1501	GT	60	13	−25	−1310
CA	60	19	−17	−945	TA	20	15	−9	−1185
CC	130	31	−23	−810	TC	60	16	−15	−1348
CG	85	36	−28	−1003	TG	60	19	−17	−945
CT	60	16	−15	−1400	TT	35	19	−12	−1866

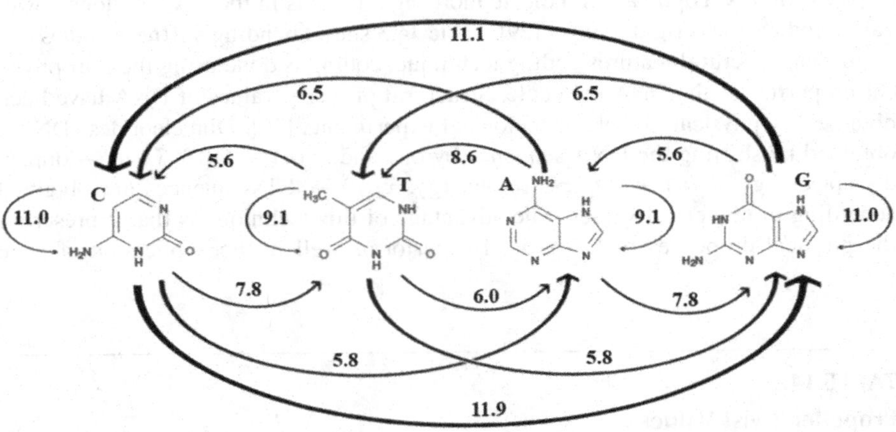

FIGURE 14.5 Enthalpy values for intermolecular thermodynamic interactions [8].

prediction to identify protein-coding regions. Table 14.4 shows the conversion table of four structural features.

Coding according to thermodynamic properties is carried out by enthalpy values of thermodynamic interactions of adjacent nucleotides [8]. The thermodynamic interactions' enthalpy values between DNA molecules are shown in Figure 14.5.

For the biological and chemical enthalpy values of close nucleotide combinations, when the nucleotides are placed in A, C, G, and T order, the enthalpy values reflecting the biochemical properties show asymmetrical features. The advantage of this technique is that in ascending order according to the physical size and weight of the molecules, the best ordering corresponding to the symmetrical codes as C, T/U, A, G [31]. The disadvantage is that it does not give satisfactory results in determining the exon regions. Table 14.5 gives the enthalpy values of the dinucleotides.

In digitization with the GCC, the DNA sequence is read with the reading frame in the form of triplet codons. The reading frame rereads the sequence by shifting one

TABLE 14.5
Enthalpy Values of Dinucleotide

Dinucleotide	Coding	Dinucleotide	Coding	Dinucleotide	Coding	Dinucleotide	Coding
AA	9.1	GA	5.6	CA	5.8	TA	6.0
AC	6.5	GC	11.1	CC	11.0	TC	5.6
AG	7.8	GG	11.0	CG	11.1	TG	5.8
AT	8.6	GT	6.5	CT	7.8	TT	9.1

TABLE 14.6
GCC-Based Values of Twenty Amino Acids

Bases	Amino Acid	Numerical Representation	Bases	Amino Acid	Numerical Representation
GCU, GCC, GCA, GCG	A – alanine (Ala)	$0.61 + 88.3i$	AUG	M – methionine (Met)	$1.18 + 162.2i$
UGU, UGC	C – cysteine (Cys)	$1.07 + 112.4i$	UAU, UAC	Y – tyrosine (Tyr)	$1.88 + 193i$
GAU, GAC	D – aspartic acid (Asp)	$0.46 + 110.8i$	UGG	W – ryptophan (Trp)	$2.65 + 227i$
GAA, GAG	E – glutamic acid (Glu)	$0.47 + 140.5i$	GUU, GUC, GUA, GUG	V – valine (Val)	$1.32 + 141.4i$
UUU, UUC	F – phenylalanine (Phe)	$2.02 + 189i$	CCU, CCC, CCA, CCG	P – proline (Pro)	$1.95 + 122.2i$
GGU, GGC, GGA, GGG	G – glycine (Gly)	$0.07 + 60i$	AAU, AAC	N – asparagine (Asn)	$0.06 + 125.1i$
CAU, CAC	H – histidine (His)	$0.61 + 152.6i$	CAA, CAG	Q – glutamine (Gln)	$148.7i$
AUU, AUC, AUA	I – isoleucine (Ile)	$2.22 + 168.5i$	CGU, CGC, CGA, CGG, AGA, AGG	R – arginine (Arg)	$0.60 + 181.2i$
AAA, AAG	K – lysine (Lys)	$1.15 + 175.6i$	AGU, AGC, UCU, UCC, UCA, UCG	S – serine (Ser)	$0.05 + 88.7i$
UUA, UUG, CUU, CUC, CUA, CUG	L – lucine (Leu)	$1.53 + 168.5i$	ACU, ACC, ACA, ACG	T – threonine (Thr)	$0.05 + 118.2i$

base per turn and obtains the amino acids made up of codons. Each aa is encoded with a unique complex number given in Ref. [15]. Table 14.6 gives the GCC-based numerical values of 20 amino acids. For example, the codons obtained by the reading frame for an X = AGCTACCGTGT sequence are as follows:

First reading frame AGC TAC CGT → amino acids [S, Y, R], second reading frame GCT ACC GTG → amino acids [A, T, V], third reading frame CTA CCG TGT → [L. P, C] amino acids

The numerical sequence was obtained by coding the amino acids with their complex number values:

[0.05 + 88.7i, 0.6 + 88.3i, 1.88 + 193i, 0.06 + 125.1i, 0.60 + 181.2i, 1.32 + 141.4i].

In the Walsh coding technique, the basic definition of the k-degree Walsh code is given in Equation 14.3.

$$w_k = \begin{pmatrix} W_i & W_i \\ W_i & \overline{W_i} \end{pmatrix}$$
(14.3)

Here, $k = 2^i$, $i = \{1, 2, 3, \ldots\}$, $\overline{W_i}$, W_i, W_1 *is* the complement $\{1 \text{ or } 0\}$. $i = 1$ is a matrix. If $W_1 = 0$, WCs of order-2 are in the form of Equation 14.4.

$$W_2 = \begin{pmatrix} 0 & 0 \\ 0 & 1 \end{pmatrix}$$
(14.4)

The core matrix W_2 is iterated to get the order-4 WC. The order-4 WC codes for $i = 2$ and $k = 4$ are Equation 14.5. 64 different permutations of binary codes are produced.

$$w_k = \begin{pmatrix} W_2 & W_2 \\ W_2 & \overline{W_2} \end{pmatrix}$$
(14.5)

The advantage of this technique is that it is widely used in code division multiple access communication and exon region determination, and it performs well compared to digitization methods such as WCBNE trigonometric, complex number, binary, and hamming distance-based encoding [25]. In addition, Walsh codes provide good correlation and orthogonal properties. As in Equations 9.3 and 9.4, fourth-degree WCs are determined. Four arbitrary WCs are selected from 64 possible combinations and assigned to nucleotides as in Equation 14.6.

$$\left(\begin{matrix} 00:00 \\ 01:01 \\ \hline 00:11 \\ 01:10 \end{matrix} \right) \Rightarrow \left\{ \begin{matrix} A \\ G \\ T \\ C \end{matrix} \right\} \Rightarrow \left\{ \begin{matrix} W_A \\ W_G \\ W_T \\ W_C \end{matrix} \right\}$$
(14.6)

14.2.3 BINARY AND INFORMATION ENCODING

The third group of DNA numerical mapping techniques is BIE digitization techniques. In binary and information coding techniques, DNA data are mostly encoded by giving binary numerical values. Within this group, ten coding techniques as Voss representation, one-hot coding, pathogenicity island coding, gradient source localization coding, 2-bit binary encoding, error correction code, I Ching representation, Galois field representation, gray code representation, k-mer encoding are examined.

In the Voss representation, four separate binary sequences are created to represent the genome sequences. In the sequences created for each base, the sequence position with "1" is given to the relevant base, and "0" is given for other positions. The advantage of this technique is its high performance in the Fourier transform method in detecting short exon regions [8]. Although simple and easy to use, the disadvantage of this technique is the computational complexity as four sequences are obtained. One-hot encoding is also called 4-bit binary encoding. It is realized by assigning A =1000, C=0010, T=0100, and G=0001 values in 4-bit binary base to A, T, C, and G nucleotides. The advantage of this technique is that it is very easy to use in the detection of specific regions in genomes, such as the classification of 4mC positions in the mouse genome, detection of coding regions, and various areas where digitization is needed [1].

In the pathogenicity island coding technique, "1" is assigned to the C and G bases, and "0" is assigned for the A and T bases. The advantage of this technique is that it significantly detects G+C patterns in genome signals [11]. It gives good results in the detection of coding regions in exon regions.

The gradient source localization coding technique was created by considering the biologically inspired gradient source localization when designing the indicator array. The nucleotides in the DNA sequence are given the values of A = 0, T = 2 C = 1, and G = 3 [11]. In 2-bit binary encoding, coding is performed by assigning 2-bit binary values such as A = 00, T = 01, G = 10, and C= 11 to the nucleotides of the sequence. The advantage of this technique is that it is very easy for using [15]. Error correction coding technique has been developed in many different forms. Encoding is performed by assigning X- and Y-coordinate values to codons according to purine-pyrimidine, strong-weak H bond, and amino-keto groups. The advantage of this technique well reflects the nature of genome coding, genome redundancy, and detection of gene mutations [8,32]. The I Ching coding technique is a genetic code based on symmetry and periodicity patterns. Nucleic acids are organized according to biochemical properties such as h-bonds, purine-pyrimidine, and keto-enol. Mapping is carried out according to the I Ching table. Some codons represent the same aa [8,33]. Bases take values in three different axes.

1. Axis x: A, T=0=2-H bond, T; C, G=3-H bond=1; y axis: Pyrimidine=1=T, C, Purine=0=A, G
2. Axis x: Keto/Amino (A=C=1, G=T=0); y axis: Pur/Pyr (C=T=1, A=G=0)
3. Axis x: H-bonds (C=G=1, A=T=0); y axis: Keto/Amino (A=C=1, G=T=0)

The Galois field-based coding technique performs the digitization of the sequence of nucleotides of DNA as a linear sequence. The array (n, k) is converted to orthogonal code words. With the Galois domain, the bases are labeled with four finite GF domains. Numerical assignments of bases A, T, G, and C with this technique corresponding to polynomial representations are shown in Equation 14.7 [7]. The advantage of this technique is the easy digitization of DNA sequences.

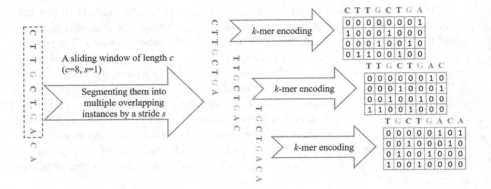

FIGURE 14.6   The k-mer encoding representation [35].

$$0 = 0 \Leftrightarrow 0 \Leftrightarrow A$$

$$x^0 = 1 \Leftrightarrow 1 \Leftrightarrow C \qquad (14.7)$$

$$x^1 = x \Leftrightarrow 2 \Leftrightarrow T$$

$$x^2 = x + 1 \Leftrightarrow 3 \Leftrightarrow G$$

In the gray coding technique, integer values are assigned to each base and expressed with binary symbols. Some rules must be observed when assigning values. These rules are that the codes should not be the same or repeat in a set, and any two adjacent codes should not be separated by a bit. So, the hamming distance should be 1. For this reason, these codes are called single-distance codes [7]. The advantage of this technique is that it increases the accuracy of prediction in the detection of protein-coding regions.

The k-mer coding technique is used to split a sequence into multiple k-based subsequences. If the entire DNA sequence is considered a sentence, the k-mer segments are the words that make up the sentence. With a step size of 1, a base 1 array $(1 - k + 1)$ is split into k-mers. For example, the AGCCT sequence splits into three 3-mers: (AGC, GCC, CCT) [34,35]. Figure 14.6 shows the working logic of the k-mer coding technique.

14.2.4   PRIMARY STRUCTURE PROPERTIES

The fourth group of DNA numerical mapping techniques is primary structure feature digitization technique. In primary structure coding techniques, DNA data is usually read as dinucleotides or triplet codons and digitized with values given according to certain properties or distance values between nucleotides. In this group, six coding techniques are examined, namely dinucleotide representation, ring structure representation, triplet encoding, frequency of nucleotide occurrence mapping, entropy-based numerical mapping, and internucleotide distance representation.

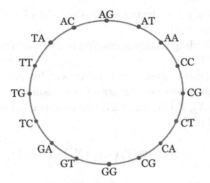

FIGURE 14.7 Arrangement of dinucleotides in the unit circle [8].

TABLE 14.7
Angle Values of Dinucleotides in the Unit Circle

Dinucleotide	Coding	Dinucleotide	Coding	Dinucleotide	Coding	Dinucleotide	Coding
AA	$\pi/4$	GA	$5\pi/4$	CA	$7\pi/4$	TA	$3\pi/4$
AC	$5\pi/8$	GC	$13\pi/4$	CC	$\pi/8$	TC	$9\pi/8$
AG	$\pi/2$	GG	$3\pi/2$	CG	2π	TG	π
AT	$3\pi/8$	GT	$11\pi/8$	CT	$15\pi/8$	TT	$7\pi/8$

In dinucleotide representation, dinucleotide sets consisting of the combination of two adjacent bases are coded with the angle values of the dinucleotides placed around a unit circle. A, T, G, and C bases of DNA come together to form 16 binary dinucleotide sets: {AA, AG, AT, AC, TA, TG, TT, TC, GA, GG, GC, GG, CA, CG, CC, CT}. The "magic circle" approach has been established to evenly distribute binary nucleotides around the unit circle [36,37]. Dinucleotides that are evenly distributed around the unit circle are assigned a numerical value with the corresponding polar angle at the position of the circle [36]. Figure 14.7 gives the arrangement of dinucleotides in the unit circle. Table 14.7 shows angle values of dinucleotides placed properly around the unit circle. The advantage of this technique is that it provides advantages in all genomic fields where the binary dinucleotide structure is used. The disadvantage is that it does not reflect the structure of DNA very well in digitization.

The ring structure encodes the bases in the DNA sequence according to the ring structure of these bases and their matching molecular masses. At the corners of Figure 14.8 are the purine-pyrimidine, amino-keto, and strong hydrogen bond-weak hydrogen bond classes, resulting in six different combinations for mapping. In Figure 14.8, each drawing corresponds to a different coding system [8]. Sixteen dinucleotides are placed on the surface of the hexagon to preserve the chemical properties and position information of the nucleotide. The advantage of this technique is that it gives high accuracy in comparing DNA sequences for similarity. It also gives good results in phylogenetic analysis for the detection of evolutionary relationships between different species [38].

Table 14.8 contains coding values according to the placement of the groups in the first hexagon in Figure 14.8.

Triplet encoding performs digitization using weights based on the properties of their codons. The distance between the arrays is measured. If the first codon (X_1, Y_1) and the second codon (X_2, Y_2) are encoded, the distance between them is calculated as shown in Equation 14.8.

$$|\psi(X_1) - \psi(Y_1)| < |\psi(X_2) - \psi(Y_2)| \tag{14.8}$$

Here ψ is the weight mapping of the codons. Weight values consist of two parts as integer and fractional number parts. The integer part represents the amino acid; the fractional part represents the codon. For example, the corresponding number for the

TABLE 14.8

Ring Structure Coding Values

Dinucleotide	Coding	Dinucleotide	Coding	Dinucleotide	Coding	Dinucleotide	Coding
AA	(0, 1)	GA	(1, 0)	CA	(1,1)	TA	(−1, 1)
AC	(−0.5, 1.25)	GC	(−0.5, −1.25)	CC	(−0.5, 0)	TC	(−1, 0)
AG	(0, 1.5)	GG	(0, −1)	CG	(1, −1)	TG	(−1, −1)
AT	(0.5, 1.25)	GT	(0.5, −1.25)	CT	(0, −1.5)	TT	(0.5, 0)

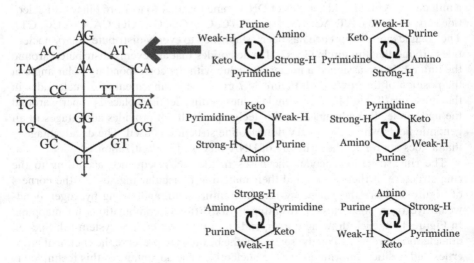

FIGURE 14.8 The coding system [8].

amino acid Alanine is 1. The GCT first codon has a weight of 1.1 while the GCC second codon has a weight of 1.2. In this way, the codons are digitized with their weight values [8,39]. The advantage of this technique is that it performs quite well in calculating intersequence similarity.

The coding technique according to the frequency of nucleotide formation, the idea that the DNA nucleotide has different frequencies in regions such as exons and introns is used. Coding is performed by assigning nucleotide formation frequencies to statistically computable fractional values. Nuclear values can be assigned according to the frequency of single nucleotides, as well as the frequency values of dinucleotides or triplets can be calculated and used for digitization [8,15]. The advantage of this technique is that it gives good results in the detection of specific areas such as the detection of the protein-coding region.

The entropy-based numerical mapping technique is based on the use of a new entropy-based digitization, which is a fractional derivative of Shannon entropy, in the analysis of nucleotide sequences, in the analysis of the distribution of exons, introns and amino acids, and in many genomic fields. In the fractional entropy equation (Equation 14.9) the α and $p(x_i)$ values were changed. It is based on the principle of performing entropy calculations for DNA codon distributions. The entropy value for each codon reflects the balance between 64 possible codons.

$$Sf = -\sum \left[\left(-p(x_i) \right)^{\alpha} p(x_i) \log \left(p(x_i) \right) \right] \tag{14.9}$$

Here, $p(x_i)$ is the repetition frequency of each codon in the DNA sequence and the formula in Equation 14.10 is used for α.

$$\alpha = \frac{1}{\log \left(p(x_i) \right)} \tag{14.10}$$

The value of α is the logarithm of the repetition frequency of the codon divided by 1. The advantage of this technique is its high accuracy in applications, detection of exon regions, diagnosis of disease-causing genes, and phylogenetic analysis [17].

In the internucleotide distance coding technique, each base in the DNA sequence is coded with the value of the base distance between it and the same base that follows it. For example, if the distance between the first adenine base in the sequence and the next adenine base is n, the value n is given instead of the first adenine base, and the coding continues for each similar expression. If there is no similar expression in the continuation of the sequence, the length of the remaining sequence is assigned instead of that base [14]. The advantage of this technique is that if used to represent the peptide chain, the measured distance values have a direct effect on the protein folding points [40]. The downside is that this technique is not digitization that preserves the information of DNA. The encoding output of some of the digitization techniques examined in this group cannot be expressed as an aggregate graphic because it contains different representations or the value ranges are very small numbers.

The fifth group of DNA numerical mapping techniques is GR digitization techniques. In graphical coding techniques, when DNA data are digitized with the rules of each technique, various graphics are obtained as numerical data. Within this

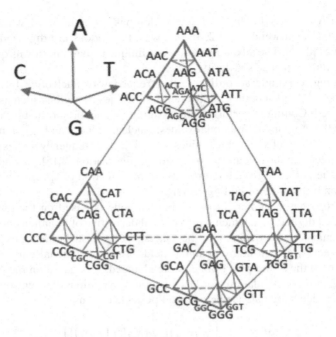

FIGURE 14.9   Tetrahedron representation [8].

group, there are fourteen coding techniques, namely tetrahedron encoding, H-curve representation, Z-curve representation, quaternion encoding, single-nucleotide polymorphism (SNP)–genetic identity number (GIN) encoding, chaos game representation, (CGR), chaos game representation walk (CGR-Walk), integer chaos game representation (iCGR), self-organizing map (SOM)-based approach, Fermat spiral curve representation, spectral dynamic representation, 2D dynamic representation, 3D dynamic representation, and 8D dynamic representation are examined.

In the tetrahedron coding technique, each nucleotide is placed in one of the four corners of a regular tetrahedron. The numerical representation of A, G, C, and T bases is represented as a 3D coordinate system in Figure 14.9 [8]. For numerical representations of nucleotides $A = k$, $G = -\dfrac{2\sqrt{2}}{3}i - \dfrac{\sqrt{6}}{3}j - \dfrac{1}{3}k$, $C = -\dfrac{2\sqrt{2}}{3}i + \dfrac{\sqrt{6}}{3}j - \dfrac{1}{3}k$, $T = \dfrac{2\sqrt{2}}{3}i - \dfrac{1}{3}k$.

The advantage of this technique is in the applications of obtaining the DNA spectrum of biomolecular sequences. Obtained spectra give local frequency information for bases [17]. The disadvantage of this technique is that it is not suitable for DNA sequences longer than 5000 bases.

The H-curve coding technique provides a 3D representation of the functions formed by the i, j, and k unit vectors on the x, y, and z axes of each nucleotide in the DNA sequence. The H-curve is defined in Equation 14.11.

$$h(z) = \sum_{w=1}^{n} g_w(z) \qquad (14.11)$$

Here, $z \in \{C, T, A, G\}$ and n are length of the sequence. The basic functions are, respectively, $g_w(A) = i + j - k$, $g_w(G) = -i + j - k$, $g_w(C) = -i - j - k$, $g_w(T) = i - j - k$. The endpoints of the H-curve define the nucleotide combination of the sequence. The advantage of this technique is that it makes imaging, comparison, and sequencing of gene structures simpler. The disadvantage is that calculating coordinates in this technique are complicated. A loop or circuit is likely to occur. Information loss can occur because arrays are not uniquely identified. To avoid this loss, the coding functions are reduced to the 2D Cartesian coordinate plane. Functions assigned to nucleotides for regulated coding, respectively, $g_w(A) = \dfrac{1}{2}i - \dfrac{\sqrt{3}}{2}j$, $g_w(T) = \dfrac{1}{2}i + \dfrac{\sqrt{3}}{2}j$, $g_w(C) = \dfrac{\sqrt{3}}{2}i + \dfrac{1}{2}j$, $g_w(G) = \dfrac{\sqrt{3}}{2}i - \dfrac{1}{2}j$. Here, w represents the position of a nucleotide in the sequence, while i and j represent vectors in the Cartesian plane [8,41].

The Z-curve representation enables 3D visualization and analysis of DNA sequences with unique vector sets. $\{x_n, y_n, z_n\}$ components represent the coordinates of DNA sequence nucleotides in the Z-curve. A_n, C_n, G_n, and T_n nucleotides are converted to x_n, y_n, z_n coordinate vectors. Vectors toward each surface in Figure 14.10 represent nucleotides. The sum of the vectors moving in these four directions (n) is equal to the number of nucleotides [8]. Equation 14.12 shows the conversion between (x_n, y_n, z_n) and (A_n, C_n, G_n, T_n). Figure14.10 depicts tetrahedron-based coordinate system of the Z-curve.

$$\begin{vmatrix} A_n \\ C_n \\ G_n \\ T_n \end{vmatrix} = \frac{n}{4} \begin{vmatrix} +1 \\ +1 \\ +1 \\ +1 \end{vmatrix} + \frac{1}{4} \begin{vmatrix} +1 & +1 & +1 \\ -1 & +1 & -1 \\ +1 & -1 & -1 \\ -1 & -1 & +1 \end{vmatrix} \begin{vmatrix} x_n \\ y_n \\ z_n \end{vmatrix} \qquad (14.12)$$

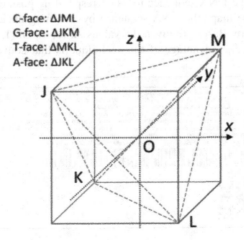

C-face: ΔJML
G-face: ΔJKM
T-face: ΔMKL
A-face: ΔJKL

FIGURE 14.10 Tetrahedron-based coordinate system of the Z-curve [8].

The advantage of this technique is that it can be applied to any sequence length and provides high-accuracy identification by converting DNA data into a curve-based sequence signal for quantification of protein-coding regions [42]. It provides success in identifying long-range correlation intron regions [43].

Quaternion encoding is N-dimensional complex number coding. It is equivalent to the tetrahedron. $h = a_0 i_0 + \dots + a_j i_j + \dots + a_N i, N \in Z^+$. When $j = 3$ in the equation, it is a 4D quaternion [8]. Four types of quaternions have been developed for the detection of protein-coding regions. The bases take, respectively, $A = i + j + k$, $G = -i - j + k$, $C = -i + j - k$, $T = i - j - k$. The advantage of this technique is that it performs better for the classification of quaternion-coding protein-coding regions than sequential and complex number coding [44].

The SNP-GIN coding technique was developed to assign a unique GIN to individuals based on their biological characteristics. SNPs are used as individual DNA markers. The advantage of this technique is that the genotype frequencies are easy to calculate. A computer can easily interpret the SNP-typing results. SNPs have advantages such as low sensitivity to re-genetic rearrangements when encountered with repetitive elements, applicability to highly degraded DNA, and rapid genotyping. Digitizing polymorphic nucleotides provides a great advantage. Each specific SNP is taken as a 4-bit bin ACGT (SNP value). Values of 1 or 0 are assigned based on the presence or absence of nucleotides. The hyphen (-) symbolizes the situation where the second nucleotide cannot be identified. If the SNP is not found in both paired chromosomes, the value "0000" is assigned for digitization. Homozygous SNPs are coded with one 1 and three 0s, while heterozygous SNPs are coded with two 1s and two 0s. Data in binary format obtained by analyzing all SNPs can be easily encoded into a hexadecimal format or represented graphically and used in any identification document. It is called the GIN [45]. Example digitization of 72 SNPs for SNP data processing and generation of GINs in digital and graphic formats is shown in Figure 14.11.

Chaos game coding (CGR) is a technique that provides image mapping that assigns each nucleotide in the DNA sequence to its corresponding position in the plane. The CGR coding scheme maps the DNA sequence by assigning nucleotides to each corner of the unit square. Bases are given the values A: (0, 0), G: (1, 1), T: (1, 0), and C: (0, 1), respectively. The advantage of this technique is that conversion to numerical

<table>
<tr><th>Form</th><th>SNP data</th></tr>
<tr><td>Genotypes</td><td>A|G C|C G|G A|G C|G A|A A|G A|C T|T A|A G|G A|C G|G C|T A|A C|C C|C A|G G|G C|C A|G G|G G|T A|A C|C T|T C|G A|G T|T A|G G|G G|T A|A C|C A|C A|
G C|C G|G A|T C|T C|C G|G T|T A|G A|A G|T A|G A|A C|G G|G T|T A|T T|T A|G G|G G|G A|A A|C C|C G|G C|T C|G T|T A|C C|C A|G A|A T|T A|A C|G G|T T|T</td></tr>
<tr><td>Nucleotides</td><td>AGCCGGAGCGAAAGACTTAAGGACGGCTAACCCAGGGCCAGGGGTAA
CCTTCGAGTTAGGGGTAACCACAGCCGGATCTCCGGTTAGAAGTAGAACGGGTTATTTAGGGGGAAACCCGGCTCGTTACCCAGAATTAACGGTTT</td></tr>
<tr><td>Binary encoding</td><td>1010010000101010011010001010110000011000000101100001001011000010001001010001001001010001000111 0000
1000001011010100001101000100011100001001100101001000010100101010100001000011010100000111010100001
1000100001100100011010001000101000110001000010010101100001110001001010100000001100001100011 0001</td></tr>
<tr><td>Hexadecimal</td><td>A42A68AC182C25844A24A238416A1A2384CA4295421A83A862191A228C42561C4A818631</td></tr>
<tr><td>Linear</td><td></td></tr>
<tr><td>Two-dimensional</td><td></td></tr>
</table>

FIGURE 14.11 Sample digitization consisting of SNP [45].

sequence can be performed while preserving the main features of the original biological sequence, and it performs well in the analysis of evolutionary relationships. The CGR coding scheme maps the DNA sequence by assigning nucleotides to each corner of the unit square [8]. Subsequent nucleotides are mapped between the position of the preceding nucleotide and its corresponding peak. The mathematical coding scheme is given in Equation 14.13 [8].

$$\left\{ \begin{array}{l} X_i = 0.5\left(X_{i-1} + g_{ix}\right), \\ Y_i = 0.5\left(Y_{i-1} + g_{iy}\right) \end{array} \right. \tag{14.13}$$

Here (g_{ix}, y_i) indicates the peak corresponding to this nucleotide. (X_i, Y_i) indicates the current points drawn on the coordinate, while (X_{i-1}, Y_{i-1}) indicates the previous points.

The CGR-Walk technique is a mapping technique that considers thermodynamic properties. Three 2D CGR planes were created. The peaks in these three planes are assigned to nucleotides according to their thermodynamic properties of amino-keto, purine-pyrimidine, and strong-weak H bonds. The basic coding structure is the same as CGR [8]. The advantage of this technique is that it performs better in measuring similarity and difference between exons of species [46,47].

The iCGR technique provides a lossless coding method. With iCGR, the DNA sequence is represented by the repeating function of nucleotides and their position in the sequence and can be encoded and decoded again. Considering that as seen in the definition of CGR coding, the coordinates of the current nucleotide are determined by the coordinate of the previous nucleotide and its vertex coordinate, it is argued that the last coordinate of a DNA sequence includes the information of the complete DNA sequence, according to this recursive relationship. The bases are represented by the coordinates A = (1,1), C = (−1, −1), T = (−1, 1), G = (1, −1), respectively, forming the vertices of a square, these are the CGR vertices. The advantage of this technique is that it performs well in interspecies similarity detection. The disadvantage is that long DNA sequences cannot be fully recovered due to floating points in the calculations [48]. The CGR coordinate of the four nucleotides is calculated as in Equation 14.14.

$$p_{i,x} = p_{i-1,x} + 2^{i-1}\alpha_{i,x}$$

$$p_{i,y} = p_{i-1,y} + 2^{i-1}\alpha_{i,y}$$

$$\alpha_i = S(i), \alpha_i \in \{A,T,C,G\} \quad i = 1,2,3,\ldots n \tag{14.14}$$

Here, i is the number of nucleotides, p_i is the coordinate of the current nucleotide, p_{i-1} is the coordinate of the previous nucleotide, and α_i is the value of the corner point of the current nucleotide [48].

In SOM-based coding, genomic sequences are encoded with fixed-size and metric-based vectors. The C, T, A, and G nucleotides map to the four corners of an irregular tetrahedron. The distance between the AG and CT vertices is set as 1, and the distance between the other pairs as 2 [8]. Bases are given the values A: (0, 0, 0), T: (0.289, 0.5, 0.816), C: (0.866, 0.5, 0), G: (0, 1, 0) [49]. The advantage of this technique is that it performs well in unsupervised learning in artificial neural networks. In addition, new digitization has been achieved in the phylogenetic analysis of distant species with SOM [49].

The Fermat spiral curve representation provides a graphical numerical representation that combines the global and local position information of the DNA sequence. Each base in the subsequences corresponds to a point in the cluster. A GR of the DNA sequence is realized by coding nucleotides into the Fermat spiral curve. The advantage of this technique is that it is a monotonically increasing function that can hold the position information of the original sequence in the polar coordinate system. It performs well in detecting different species and comparing first exons [50].

Spectral dynamic representation is a GR in which the distributions of bases A, G, C, and T in the DNA sequence are expressed by a series of discrete lines. The base positions in the array correspond to the base positions of the original array, and the lengths of the lines are equal to 1. The GR of this representation is similar to a molecular, atomic, or stellar spectrum consisting of a series of sharp spectral lines. That is why it is called the spectral representation of the DNA sequence. Thus, a dynamic representation is obtained [51]. The advantage of this technique is that it performs well in the spectroscopy and dynamics fields of physics.

Two-dimensional dynamic representation, which is one of the Dynamic Representation of Biological Sequences (DRBS) methods, is the representation of biological sequences with point masses in Euclidean space. This sequence can be DNA, RNA, or protein. In DRBS methods, each base is represented by a vector. The GR is performed by the execution (shift) of nucleotides representing the bases in the Cartesian coordinate system. In the 2D dynamic representation of DNA/RNA sequences, the bases take the values $A = (-1, 0)$, $C = (0, 1)$, $G = (1, 0)$, $T/U = (0, -1)$, respectively [52]. The advantage of this technique is that it is effective in characterizing the biological sequence.

Another DBRS method is 3D dynamic representation. What is explained in the 2D dynamic representation of DBRS methods is also valid here. Conflicts caused by degeneration of 2D representation have been resolved in 3D representation. DNA/RNA bases $A = (-1, 0, 1)$, $G = (1, 0, 1)$, $C = (0, 1, 1)$, $T/U = (0, -1, 1)$ in 3D representation represented as Refs. [52,53]. The advantage of this technique is that it is still highly effective in characterizing the biological sequence.

The eight-dimensional vector representation was developed based on the 2D GR of DNA sequences with the concepts of mean and variance probability. The DNA sequence is mapped in eight-dimensional Euclidean space. With this mapping, exons of different species were compared and their similarities/differences were examined [35]. The vectors as $(1, 0.2) \rightarrow A$, $(1, -0.2) \rightarrow T$, $(1, 0.3) \rightarrow C$, $(1, -0.3) \rightarrow G$ are assigned to the bases sequentially. By obtaining an 8D vector in the space of DNA sequences, a new map is created in eight-dimensional Euclidean space. After the vectors of the sequences are determined, the distance between them is calculated as $d = E_1 - E_2$, and a measure of similarity/difference between species is obtained. The smaller the value, the more similar the species. The advantage of this technique is that it performs well in detecting interspecies similarity and analyzing protein sequence [35].

14.3 CONCLUSION

This study is an attempt to review the DNA numerical mapping techniques used in the analysis of DNA sequences and to present the advantages and disadvantages of each technique to researchers. With a rich literature review, how every coding technique in the last 10 years digitizes DNA sequences is explained in detail. This section will guide researchers in developing new coding techniques and make it easier for previous researchers to improve their work. It will also guide researchers in exploring new techniques using innovative ideas.

REFERENCES

1. Abbas, Z., Tayara, H., & Chong, K. T. (2021). 4mCPred-CNN—prediction of DNA N4-methylcytosine in the mouse genome using a convolutional neural network. *Genes*, *12*(2), 296.
2. Nei, M., & Kumar, S. (2000). *Molecular Evolution and Phylogenetics*. Oxford University, England.
3. Clancy, S. & Brown, W. (2008). Translation: DNA to mRNA to protein. *Nature Education*, *1*(1), 101.
4. Akhtar, M., Epps, J., & Ambikairajah, E. (2008). Signal processing in sequence analysis: Advances in eukaryotic gene prediction. *IEEE Journal of Selected Topics in Signal Processing*, *2*(3), 310–321.
5. Das, J. K., Sengupta, A., Choudhury, P. P., & Roy, S. (2021). Mapping sequence to feature vector using numerical representation of codons targeted to amino acids for alignment-free sequence analysis. *Gene*, *766*, 145096.
6. Wisesty, U. N., Mengko, T. R., & Purwarianti, A. (2020). Gene mutation detection for breast cancer disease: A review. *IOP Conference Series: Materials Science and Engineering*, *830*(3), 032051.
7. Raman Kumar, M., & Naveen Kumar, V. (2020). A numerical representation method for a DNA sequence using gray code method. In K. N. Das, J. C. Bansal, K. Deep, A. K. Nagar, P. Pathipooranam, & R. C. Naidu (Eds.), *Soft Computing for Problem Solving, Advances in Intelligent Systems and Computing, vol 1057*. Springer, Singapore, (pp. 645–654).
8. Yu, N., Li, Z., & Yu, Z. (2018). Survey on encoding schemes for genomic data representation and feature learning—From signal processing to machine learning. *Big Data Mining and Analytics*, *1*(3), 191–210.
9. Kumari, P. K. (2018). A survey on numerical representation of DNA sequences. *Asian Journal for Convergence in Technology (AJCT)*, *4*, 1–5, ISSN 2350-1146.
10. Das, L., Das, J. K., Nanda, S., & Mohapatra, S. (2018). DNA coding sequence prediction: A review. *2018 International Conference on Applied Electromagnetics, Signal Processing and Communication (AESPC)*, Bhubaneswar, India, vol. 1, pp. 1–6.
11. Ahmad, M., Jung, L. T., & Bhuiyan, A.-A. (2017). From DNA to protein: Why genetic code context of nucleotides for DNA signal processing? A review. *Biomedical Signal Processing and Control*, *34*, 44–63.
12. Jin, X., Jiang, Q., Chen, Y., Lee, S.-J., Nie, R., Yao, S., Zhou, D., & He, K. (2017). Similarity/dissimilarity calculation methods of DNA sequences: A survey. *Journal of Molecular Graphics and Modelling*, *76*, 342–355.
13. Mendizabal-Ruiz, G., Román-Godínez, I., Torres-Ramos, S., Salido-Ruiz, R. A., & Morales, J. A. (2017). On DNA numerical representations for genomic similarity computation. *PloS One*, *12*(3), e0173288.

14. Saini, S., & Dewan, L. (2017). Comparison of numerical representations of genomic sequences: Choosing the best mapping for wavelet analysis. *International Journal of Applied and Computational Mathematics*, *3*(4), 2943–2958.
15. Mabrouk, M. (2017). Advanced genomic signal processing methods in DNA mapping schemes for gene prediction using digital filters. *American Journal of Signal Processing*, *7*(1), 12–24.
16. Das, B. (2022). A deep learning model for identification of diabetes type 2 based on nucleotide signals. *Neural Computing & Applications*, *34*, 12587–12599.
17. Das, B., & Turkoglu, I. (2018). A novel numerical mapping method based on entropy for digitizing DNA sequences. *Neural Computing & Applications*, *29*, 207–215. doi: 10.1007/s00521-017-2871-5.
18. Das, B., & Toraman, S. (2022). Deep transfer learning for automated liver cancer gene recognition using spectrogram images of digitized DNA sequences. *Biomedical Signal Processing and Control*, *72*, 103317.
19. Kwan, H. & Arniker, S. (2009). Numerical representation of DNA sequences. 307–310. doi: 10.1109/EIT.2009.5189632.
20. Das, L., Das, J. K., Mohapatra, S., & Nanda, S. (2021). DNA numerical encoding schemes for exon prediction: A recent history. *Nucleosides, Nucleotides & Nucleic Acids*, *40*(10), 985–1017.
21. Das, L., Nanda, S., & Das, J. K. (2019). An integrated approach for identification of exon locations using recursive Gauss Newton tuned adaptive Kaiser window. *Genomics*, *111*(3), 284–296.
22. Zhang, X., Shen, Z., Zhang, G., Shen, Y., Chen, M., Zhao, J., & Wu, R. (2016). Short exon detection via wavelet transform modulus maxima. *PloS One*, *11*, e0163088. doi: 10.1371/journal.pone.0163088.
23. Choong, A. C. H., & Lee, N. K. (2017). Evaluation of convolutionary neural networks modeling of DNA sequences using ordinal versus one-hot encoding method. *2017 International Conference on Computer and Drone Applications (IConDA)*, Sarawak Branch, Malaysia, pp. 60–65.
24. Chakravarthy, N., Spanias, A., Iasemidis, L. D., & Tsakalis, K. (2004). Autoregressive modeling and feature analysis of DNA sequences. *EURASIP Journal on Advances in Signal Processing*, *2004*(1), 952689.
25. Kumar, M. R.., & Vaegae, N. K. (2020). Walsh code based numerical mapping method for the identification of protein coding regions in eukaryotes. *Biomedical Signal Processing and Control*, *58*, 101859.
26. Varadwaj, P. K., Purohit, N., Lahiri, T., & Antisiperov, V. (2021). Digital signal processing-based approach to identify splicing mutations for detecting genetic diseases. *Zhurnal Radioelektroniki* [Journal of Radio Electronics], *1*, 1–8.
27. Bernaola-Galván, P., Grosse, I., Carpena, P., Oliver, J. L., Román-Roldán, R., & Stanley, H. E. (2000). Finding borders between coding and noncoding DNA regions by an entropic segmentation method. *Physical Review Letters*, *85*(6), 1342–1345.
28. Nicorici, D., & Astola, J. (2004). Segmentation of DNA into coding and noncoding regions based on recursive entropic segmentation and stop-codon statistics. *EURASIP Journal on Advances in Signal Processing*, *2004*(1), 832471.
29. Song, N. Y., & Yan, H. (2010). Autoregressive modeling of DNA features for short exon recognition. *2010 IEEE International Conference on Bioinformatics and Biomedicine (BIBM)*, Hong Kong, pp. 450–455.
30. Zheng, Q., Chen, T., Zhou, W., Xie, L., & Su, H. (2021). Gene prediction by the noise-assisted MEMD and wavelet transform for identifying the protein coding regions. *Biocybernetics and Biomedical Engineering*, *41*(1), 196–210.

31. Liu, B., Liu, C.-M., Li, D., Li, Y., Ting, H.-F., Yiu, S.-M., Luo, R., & Lam, T.-W. (2016). BASE: A practical de novo assembler for large genomes using long NGS reads. *BMC Genomics*, *17*(5), 499.

32. Zhang, L., Tian, F., Wang, S., & Liu, X. (2012). A novel coding method for gene mutation correction during protein translation process. *Journal of Theoretical Biology*, *296*, 33–40.

33. Castro-Chavez, F. (2012). Defragged binary I Ching genetic code chromosomes compared to Nirenberg's and transformed into rotating 2D circles and squares and into a 3D 100% symmetrical tetrahedron coupled to a functional one to discern start from non-start Methionines through a Stella Octangula. *Journal of Proteome Science and Computational Biology*, *2012*(1), 3.

34. Deng, L., Wu, H., Liu, X., & Liu, H. (2021). DeepD2V: A novel deep learning-based framework for predicting transcription factor binding sites from combined DNA sequence. *International Journal of Molecular Sciences*, *22*(11), 5521.

35. Zhang, D. (2019). A new numerical method for DNA sequence analysis based on 8-dimensional vector representation. *Journal of Applied Mathematics and Physics*, *7*(12), 2941–2949.

36. Liu, Z., Liao, B., Zhu, W., & Huang, G. (2009). A 2D graphical representation of DNA sequence based on dual nucleotides and its application. *International Journal of Quantum Chemistry*, *109*(5), 948–958.

37. Randić, M., Butina, D., & Zupan, J. (2006). Novel 2-D graphical representation of proteins. *Chemical Physics Letters*, *419*(4), 528–532.

38. Bari, A. T. M., Reaz, M., Islam, A. T., Choi, H.-J., & Jeong, B.-S. (2013). Effective encoding for DNA sequence visualization based on nucleotide's ring structure. *Evolutionary Bioinformatics Online*, *9*, 251–261.

39. Zou, S., Wang, L., & Wang, J. (2014). A 2D graphical representation of the sequences of DNA based on triplets and its application. *EURASIP Journal on Bioinformatics and Systems Biology*, *2014*(1), 1.

40. Sankar, A., Nair, A., & Thiru, M. (2005). Visualization of genomic data using internucleotide distance signals. *Proceedings of IEEE Genomic Signal Processing*, Thiruvananthapuram, India.

41. Yau, S. S. -T., Wang, J., Niknejad, A., Lu, C., Jin, N., & Ho, Y. (2003). DNA sequence representation without degeneracy. *Nucleic Acids Research*, *31*(12), 3078–3080.

42. Zhang, C.-T., & Wang, J. (2000). Recognition of protein coding genes in the yeast genome at better than 95% accuracy based on the Z curve. *Nucleic Acids Research*, *28*(14), 2804–2814.

43. Yu, C., Deng, M., Zheng, L., He, R. L., Yang, J., & Yau, S. S.-T. (2014). DFA7, a new method to distinguish between intron-containing and intronless genes. *PloS One*, *9*(7), e101363.

44. Kwan, H. K., Kwan, B. Y. M., & Kwan, J. Y. Y. (2012). Novel methodologies for spectral classification of exon and intron sequences. *EURASIP Journal on Advances in Signal Processing*, *2012*(1), 50.

45. Garafutdinov, R. R., Sakhabutdinova, A. R., Slominsky, P. A., Aminev, F. G., & Chemeris, A. V. (2020). A new digital approach to SNP encoding for DNA identification. *Forensic Science International*, *317*, 110520.

46. Deng, W., & Luan, Y. (2013). Analysis of similarity/dissimilarity of DNA sequences based on chaos game representation. *Abstract and Applied Analysis*, *2013*, e926519.

47. Yu, Z. -G., & Anh, V. (2001). Time series model based on global structure of complete genome. *Chaos, Solitons & Fractals*, *12*(10), 1827–1834.

48. Yin, C. (2019). Encoding and decoding DNA sequences by integer chaos game representation. *Journal of Computational Biology*, *26*(2), 143–151.

49. Boyle, A. P., Araya, C. L., Brdlik, C., Cayting, P., Cheng, C., Cheng, Y., Gardner, K., Hillier, L. W., Janette, J., Jiang, L., Kasper, D., Kawli, T., Kheradpour, P., Kundaje, A., Li, J. J., Ma, L., Niu, W., Rehm, E. J., Rozowsky, J., … Snyder, M. (2014). Comparative analysis of regulatory information and circuits across distant species. *Nature*, *512*(7515), 453–456.

50. Mo, Z., Zhu, W., Sun, Y., Xiang, Q., Zheng, M., Chen, M., & Li, Z. (2018). One novel representation of DNA sequence based on the global and local position information. *Scientific Reports*, *8*(1), 7592.

51. Bielińska-Wąż, D., & Wąż, P. (2017). Spectral-dynamic representation of DNA sequences. *Journal of Biomedical Informatics*, *72*, 1–7.

52. Bielińska-Wąż, D., Panas, D., Waz, P. (2019). Dynamic representations of biological sequences. *MATCH Communications in Mathematical and in Computer Chemistry*, 82, 205–218.

53. Czerniecka, A., Bielińska-Wąż, D., Wąż, P., & Clark, T. (2016). 20D-dynamic representation of protein sequences. *Genomics*, *107*(1), 16–23.

15 Importance of 5G/6G in Telemedicine System during the Pandemic Situation

Jayanta Kumar Ray
Sikkim Manipal University

Ramsundar Ghorai
Sikkim Manipal University

Rogina Sultana
Aliah University

Arpita Sarkar
Assam Science and Technology University

Rabindranath Bera
Sikkim Manipal University

Sanjib Sil
Calcutta Institute of Engineering and Management

Quazi Mohmmad Alfred
Aliah University

CONTENTS

DOI: 10.1201/9781003307778-17

15.1   INTRODUCTION

The first occurrence of COVID-19, "Coronavirus disease 2019" [1] took place at the end of 2019. The spreading of this virus originated in a city in Central China, namely Wuhan. Within few days, this spread took place globally and infected a large number of persons [2]. Risk of life was created among human beings. Administrations throughout the world were thinking about the ways regarding human safety and rescue. Various scientists were dedicated to combat the spread of this virus. In order to reduce the spreading of the virus, the lockdown [3] or curfew was imposed by the government in many countries. To protect people from infection, various rules were imposed on individual persons such as wearing masks, usage of sanitizers and avoiding crowd, offices and corporates. During lockdown [4] or curfew, few persons were allowed to go outside their residence. Hence, in these situations, telemedicine played a vital role in providing medical help remotely. The chapter organization is as follows: 4G, 5G and 6G technologies, importance of telemedicine and realization of telemedicine.

The third generation was updated to fourth generation and started in 2010. It denotes the existence of a new technology called mobile broadband (MBB) internet access, which provides utilities to millions of users around the world. The minimum data rate is 200 Mbps, and the maximum data rate is 1 Gbps. The fourth generation specifies the introduction of Long-Term Evolution (LTE). The internet was accessed from anywhere and any place. It gave good support during pandemic situation. Due to the facility of internet provided by 4G, there was an availability of online mode in various applications such as office work, education, marketing, finance, ticketing and health. The applications in real mode had been transferred to virtual mode. As the facilities were available from home, there is no requirement for any person to go outside their residence. Hence, the requirement for COVID-19 protocols is properly maintained, and the spreading of the virus had been controlled. The transition from 3G to 4G provides huge facilities like access methodology, data transfer rate, transmission terminology and security [5]. As a result, the user can access the multimedia data at any time and any place. The frequencies are ranging from 2 to 8 GHz. The usage of high-speed data access (HSPA) provides the user to access the internet in an easy mode. Orthogonal Frequency Division Multiple Access (OFDMA) achieves the high spectral efficiency. This high spectral efficiency reduces the interference and increases the reliability of the signal. The smartness in mobile phones had been started with the 4G technology, which provides facilities in online mode such as finance, marketing, health, meeting and education during a pandemic situation. As a result, these applications were availed by sitting at residence.

Figure 15.1 shows the smart health system in which the patient interacts with the doctor through an online system. The doctor issues a prescription for the patient and uploads it in the online system, and then from the online system, the patient downloads the soft copy of the prescription from the internet. Then the patient purchases the set of medicines in online mode. Hence, the procedure of proper treatment was totally fulfilled in online mode, and the patient had a remedy for the health problem.

The update of 5G technology from 4G technology denotes the increase in smartness. In 4G technology, smartness is available only in smartphones, but in 5G, the extension of smartness is toward factories, vehicles, robots etc. [7]. The smart functioning

FIGURE 15.1   Smart health. (Courtesy [6].)

specifies the execution of smart data. The operation of devices is executed through online mode. On the other hand, 5G is far more advanced than 4G. In 4G, only one service is available, which is called MBB but in 5G, there are three services, i.e. eMBB (enhanced Mobile Broadband), mMTC (massive Machine Type Communication), URLLC (Ultra Reliable Low Latency Communication) given in Figure 15.2.

In 5G, high reliability, low latency and massive bandwidth are available. The target of 5G is to transform the real world into smart world. The smart world involves smart transport, smart institution, smart home, smart health, smart farming, smart irrigation, smart industry, smart machine etc. When the online mode is utilized in industry and transport, the problematic situation due to pandemic will be solved to a broad extent [8]. The smart industry includes the combination of mMTC and eMBB. On the other hand, smart transport involves the combination of eMBB and URLLC. The aim of 5G is to execute the operation on machines utilizing the internet. In 5G, the presence of large bandwidth, low latency and high reliability fulfills the requirements for manufacture, production and critical situations. The smart factory [9] includes various features like manufacturing, production, maintenance, logistics and management by following the process of automation. Smart irrigation includes the process of automation in irrigation through the monitoring of sensors. For developing smartness in the environment, many scientists are dedicated upon the utilization of internet.

Smart health involves efficient hospital facilities having robotic systems, health checkup devices etc. The 4G specifies the communication between users, but in 5G, the communication is from user to user and user to device. The features of 5G technologies include ultra-speed, reduction of delays, massive connectivity, improvement of data management, reduction of battery consumption, wider coverage, increase in data rates, smartness of the antenna system etc. Figure 15.3 depicts the applications of 5G. The launching of 5G technology was already started in 2020. When

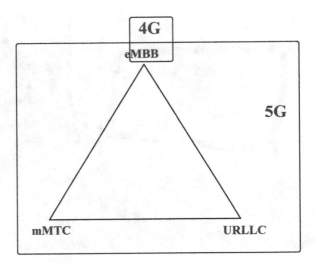

FIGURE 15.2   4G and 5G technology.

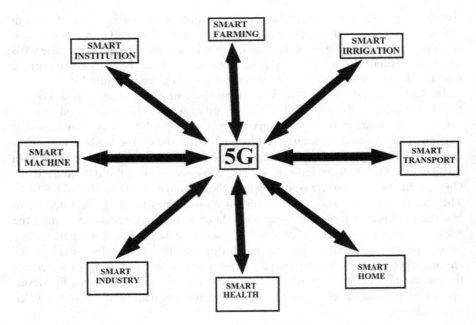

FIGURE 15.3   5G and its applications.

5G wireless communication was implemented; a new term called New Radio (NR) has emerged. The 5G new interface according to the Third-Generation Partnership Project (3GPP) can facilitate according to the requirements of the user in future. Due to the presence of NR [10], new features such as high data rates, reduction of latency, improvement of reliability and increase in coverage and capacity are available. There is an improvement in performance of the network energy and utility of spectrum for high-frequency bands. The deployment of radio access technology was done through the expansion of the range of spectrum.

From 3GPP, it should be realized that the operation of NR is ranging from 1 to 52.6 GHz, utilized for both licensed and unlicensed spectrum. The Orthogonal Frequency Division Multiplexing (OFDM) along with discrete Fourier transform (DFT) is used for transmission in 5G NR. It was utilized for increasing amplification in the uplink direction. In place of OFDM, another multiplexing is utilized which is called filter bank multiple carrier (FBMC). In 4G LTE, the subcarrier spacing is only 15 kHz but in 5G NR, there is flexibility in which the range of subcarrier spacing varies from 15 to 240 kHz. NR is the new air interface standardized by the 5G technology released on December 2017 [11]. In 5G technology, the NR will be utilized along with the existing 4G LTE. While transmitting from 4G to 5G; it has been observed that there is a large difference in parameters such as data rate, latency, connectivity, mobilization and traffic capacity. The peak data rate for 4G is 1 Gbps, while it is 20 Gbps for 5G. The speed for mobilization in 4G is 350 kilometers per hour, but for 5G, it is 500 kilometers per hour. The connectivity for 4G is 10^5 devices per square kilometer, but for 5G, the connectivity will convert into massive connectivity, i.e. 10^8 devices per square kilometer. The range of bandwidth for 4G varies from 1.4 to 20 MHz, but for 5G, maximum bandwidth is 60 GHz. The usage of coding in 4G is turbo coding due to presence of moderate code rate while in 5G, high code rates are present; hence, low-density parity check (LDPC)[12] coding will be used in place of turbo coding. They realized that LDPC performs better than turbo coding [13].

For 4G, the techniques utilized are OFDMA and CDMA (Code Division Multiple access) and for 5G, it will be BDMA (Beam Division Multiple Access) and CDMA. The term smart originated in 4G technology and it was applicable only in mobile phones. During COVID-19, many organizations utilized 4G technology for their data transmission. From the comparison between 4G and 5G, it is clear that 5G technology is far more advanced than 4G. In 4G, microwave horn antennas are used, but in 5G, millimeter wave dish antennas are used. The operating frequency for microwave antenna is sub-6 GHz, while the operating frequency for millimeter wave antenna is 28 GHz. The microwave horn antenna is shown in Figure 15.4a, whereas the millimeter wave dish antenna is shown in Figure 15.4b. By comparing the efficiencies of microwave horn antenna with millimeter wave dish antenna, it was observed that millimeter wave antennas are more efficient than microwave antennas. The experimental results were obtained by executing the experimental procedure in hardware mode. The vector signal generator utilized is connected with the transmitting antenna and on the other hand the spectrum analyzer is connected to the receiving antenna. The experimental results have been obtained by utilizing the spectrum analyzer. The SystemVue software is used for the analysis of signals being transferred to the vector signal generator. From the vector signal generator, the signals are transferred to the transmitting antenna and then to the wireless environment. From the wireless environment, the signals are received by the receiving antenna. These signals are passed to the spectrum analyzer. From the spectrum analyzer, the signals are uploaded into the computer, i.e. from the hardware to the software platform. The experimental procedure as described in Ref. [14] for microwave and millimeter wave antennas is

(a)

(b)

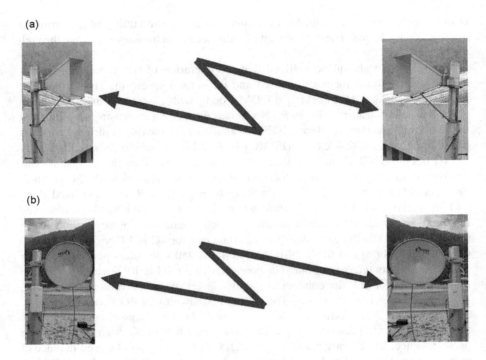

FIGURE 15.4   (a) Microwave horn antennas. (b) Millimeter wave dish antennas.

mostly similar, but there are a few differences. Before starting the experiments, it must be observed that the distance between the transmitter and the receiver for both microwave and millimeter wave antennas are the same.

The parameters for experimental results include the received signal strength indicator (RSSI) and signal-to-noise ratio (SNR). From the experimental results, it has been realized that the value of RSSI and SNR for millimeter wave antenna is very large in comparison with microwave antenna. Due to the large difference in RSSI and SNR, while comparing the millimeter wave with the microwave, it has been confirmed that millimeter wave is far more superior to microwave. The parameters for millimeter wave and microwave are specified in Table 15.1.

From Table 15.1, it is confirmed that the millimeter wave is much more reliable than microwave signal, possible only during clear sky conditions. During rainy conditions, the performance of both millimeter wave and microwave is deteriorated. The experimental results given in Refs. [14] and [15] prove that the performance of millimeter wave becomes much more deteriorated in comparison with microwave. It is necessary to shift from millimeter wave to microwave utilizing cognitive radio as mentioned in Ref. [16].

Around 2030, the 5G technology will update to 6G [17]. It specifies the increase in smartness with the development of artificial intelligence. Every operation on machines or devices can be executed in online mode. Hence, the Internet of Things (IoT) will convert into the Internet of Everything (IoE). As the 6G technology is

TABLE 15.1

Comparison of Millimeter Wave and Microwave

References	Distance between Transmitter and Receiver	Types of Antenna	Frequency (GHz)	Received Signal Strength Indicator (dBm)	Signal-to-Noise Ratio	Feedback
[14]	99.6 ft	Microwave horn antenna	3	−97.2	>31 dB	The performance of millimeter wave is far better than microwave
[14]	99.6 ft	Millimeter wave dish antenna	28	−43.8	>49 dB	
[15]	100 ft	Microwave horn antenna	3	−97.6	>30 dB	
[15]	100 ft	Millimeter wave dish antenna	28	−44	>50 dB	

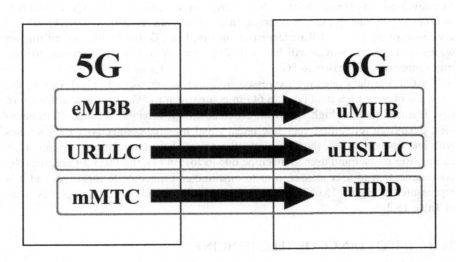

FIGURE 15.5 Conversion from 5G to 6G.

based on artificial intelligence, it provides high capacity, increase in data rate, reduction of latency and Quality of Service (QoS) in comparison to 5G. There is a large transition due to the upgradation from 5G to 6G [18]. While converting from 5G to 6G as given in Figure 15.5, URLLC will be converted to uHSLLC (ultra High Speed and Low Latency Communications), eMBB will convert to uMUB (ubiquitous Mobile Ultra Broadband), mMTC will convert to uHDD (Ultra High Data Density) [19]. There is a conversion from connectivity of things to connectivity of intelligence.

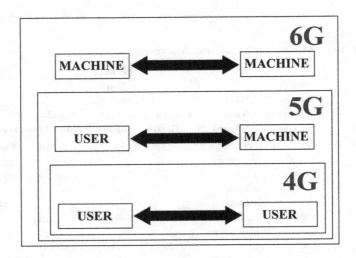

FIGURE 15.6   4G, 5G and 6G communication.

The development of 6G includes various things such as artificial intelligence increase in efficiency of energy, tactile internet, increase in data security, low backhaul and accession of network. Millimeter waves are used in 5G, but in 6G, submillimeter waves or Terahertz waves will be used. The capacity of 6G will increase 10–100 times more in comparison to 5G.

For 6G, the data rates are expressed in Terabyte per second (Tb/s). Due to the presence of very high data rates in 6G in comparison to 5G, there is availability of new features such as high spectrum efficiency, high broadband range of frequencies, ultra-high reliability, very low latency and massive connectivity of machines with intelligence. In 4G, the communication takes place among users only; in 5G, it can be user to user and user to machine due to IoT; in 6G, the IoE [20] specifies the communication of user to user, user to machine and machine to machine, and it is represented in Figure 15.6. The comparison of 4G, 5G and 6G technologies is given in Table 15.2.

15.2   IMPORTANCE OF TELEMEDICINE

Telemedicine [23] relies on IoT and artificial intelligence. Electronic gadgets like android mobiles, laptops, desktop computers and minicomputers are used in telemedicine with the help of which the patient can be able to communicate with the doctor. Telemedicine is a new platform in which the contents and documents for medical services are transferred from one place to another by using internet. Telemedicine was already initiated in 1920 [23] during the previous pandemic situation. At that time, the telemedicine system was not expanded due to the presence of various problems. One reason was the lack of development of a technical system both in hardware and software platforms. Another one was that the system was not suitable for the health environment. Earlier, telemedicine had been applied in few developed

TABLE 15.2

Comparison of 4G, 5G and 6G Technologies

Parameters	4G	5G	6G
Peak data rate for each device [21]	1 Gbps	10 Gbps	1 Tbps
Vehicular speed [21]	350 km per hour	500 km per hour	1000 km per hour
Integration of satellite [21]	NA	NA	Fully applicable
Artificial intelligence [21]	NA	Partially	Fully
Process of automation in vehicles [21]	NA	Partially	Fully
Extended reality [21]	NA	Partially	Fully
Holographic communication [21]	NA	Partially	Fully
Service type [21]	Video	Virtual reality, augmented reality	Tactile
Highest frequency [21]	6 GHz	90 GHz	10 THz
Spectral efficiency(maximum) [21]	15 bps per hertz	30 bps per hertz	100 bps per hertz
Latency (E2E) [21]	100 ms	10 ms	1 ms
Core network [22]	Internet	Internet of Things (IoT)	Internet of Everything (IoE)
Periodicity [22]	2010–2020	2020–2030	2030–2040
Architecture [22]	MIMO	Massive MIMO	Intelligent surface
Focus [22]	Real-time applications	Extreme data rates	Privacy, secrecy and security
Data rate (maximum) [22]	1 Gbps	35.46 Gbps	100 Gbps

countries such as the United States. Telemedicine is expanding the medical sector in a rapid process.

Earlier, the American Telemedicine Association had published a telemedicine journal, which included various features [23] such as the following:

- Development of communication between doctors and hospitals regarding the delivery of patient information having diagnostic reports, schedules, consultations and exchanging of diagnostic information, i.e. electrocardiograms, X-rays having teleradiology.
- Internetworking among healthcare groups, hospitals, research centers, rural health clinics etc.
- Establishment of the video communication between patients and doctors for proper consultation, interview, interaction, etc.
- Proper guidance to healthcare professionals for applying remote clinic system by the usage of video and satellite relays.
- Proper access to information using databases or electronic library in an easy procedure.

The benefits of telemedicine include improvement of access and quality of care, minimizing cost and isolation [24]. In future, the development of telemedicine will provide the availability of various opportunities. It is applicable to remote places such as rural hospitals and health centers. This new platform assists and facilitates patients in critical conditions residing in rural areas [25]. The doctors collect the data from the medical instrument displayed on the screen of the computer and then execute the treatment of the patient residing in rural areas.

15.3 REALIZATION OF TELEMEDICINE

The experiment shown in Figure 15.7 was carried out at Sikkim and Midnapore district in West Bengal. The place where the doctor's chamber is present is at SMIT, Sikkim. The clinic is present in the village namely Kolaghat, Midnapore district in West Bengal. The 5G NR is installed in the patient chamber so that the doctor was able to monitor the patient and able to undergo the proper treatment. The antenna used in the doctor's chamber was the microwave antenna, which is the horn antenna, and the antenna used in the patient's clinic is millimeter wave antenna, which is the dish antenna. The frequency of the microwave horn antenna is sub-6 GHz specifically 3 GHz, which is the microwave frequency. The frequency for the millimeter wave dish antenna is 28 GHz which is the millimeter wave frequency. Cameras are used at both 4G LTE and 5G NR so that the interaction between doctor and the patient was done by video conference. The video conference includes both audio and video signals. With the help of the audio signal, the doctor was able to communicate with the patient. To develop the communication between 4G LTE and 5G NR, there is a need for gateway.

The experiment was conducted using simulation software, i.e. SystemVue 2020. Using a computer, the signals are downloaded into the 4G transmitter viz. Vector Signal Analyzer (VSA) using signal downloader option present in the SystemVue 2020. The VSA is connected to the microwave horn antenna. The microwave antenna is connected to 4G-5G gateway in wireless mode. The 4G-5G gateway acts as a relay and converter of 4G signal to 5G signal and vice versa. It created entry to the 5G

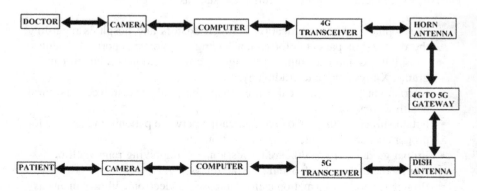

FIGURE 15.7   Realization of telemedicine.

(a)

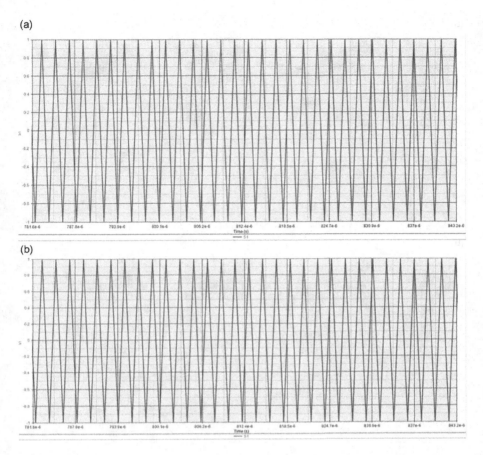

(b)

FIGURE 15.8 (a) Output of the audio signal at the 4G data sink. (b) Output of the audio signals at the 5G baseband receiver.

environment. There will be a transition from 4G LTE signal to 5G NR signal. The baseband signals are generated by the LTE receiver, and data available in the audio or video data sink are stored in a text file. The dish antenna is connected to a 5G receiver viz. Spectrum Analyzer. Data from the spectrum analyzer are uploaded into the computer via SystemVue 2020. Figure 15.8a and b shows the output of the audio signals at 4G data sink and 5G baseband receivers. Figure 15.9a and b shows the output of the video signals at 4G data sink and 5G baseband receivers.

15.4 CONCLUSION

The improvement of telemedicine system gives good support to a large number of patients in rural areas. The development of telemedicine reduces the need for a physical visit to the hospital. Therefore, a patient can communicate with a doctor or hospital via any electronic device, including a mobile phone, laptop etc. It is possible

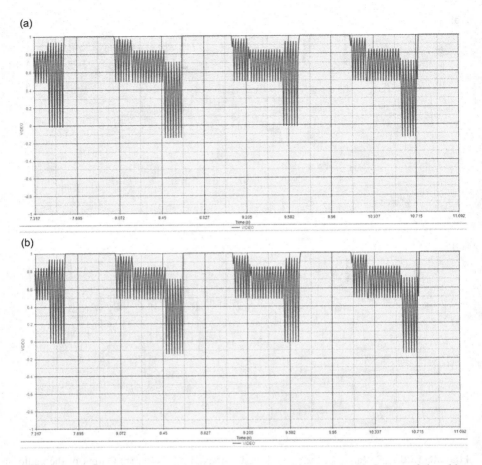

FIGURE 15.9 (a) Output of the video signal at the 4G data sink. (b) Output of the video signal at the 5G NR receiver.

to do this from the comfort of their home or at a nearby health clinic. This helps in reducing the spread of infectious diseases, and it will be convenient for the patient. During the pandemic situation in 2019, many patients were able to interact with doctors in online mode due to the facility provided by 4G LTE. When 4G is updated to 5G, the facilities regarding telemedicine will increase. The facilities are telesurgery, telediagnostics, telemedical devices etc. In future, if any pandemic situation arises, then telemedicine system will be the best alternative for the treatment of patients.

REFERENCES

1. V. Chamola, V. Hassija, V. Gupta and M. Guizani, (2020), A Comprehensive Review of the COVID-19 Pandemic and the Role of IoT, Drones, AI, Blockchain, and 5G in Managing its Impact, *IEEE Access*, vol. 8, pp. 90225–90265, doi: 10.1109/ACCESS.2020. 2992341.

2. Q. -V. Pham, D. C. Nguyen, T. Huynh-The, W. -J. Hwang and P. N. Pathirana, (2020), Artificial Intelligence (AI) and Big Data for Coronavirus (COVID-19) Pandemic: A Survey on the State-of-the-Arts, *IEEE Access*, vol. 8, pp. 130820–130839, doi: 10.1109/ ACCESS.2020.3009328.

3. O. Nadeem, M. S. Saeed, M. A. Tahir and R. Mumtaz, (2020), A Survey of Artificial Intelligence and Internet of Things (IoT) Based Approaches Against Covid-19, *IEEE 17th International Conference on Smart Communities: Improving Quality of Life Using ICT, IoT and AI (HONET)*, pp. 214–218, doi: 10.1109/HONET50430.2020.9322829.

4. N. Afroz, M. Boral, V. Sharma and M. Gupta, (2021), Sentiment Analysis of COVID-19 Nationwide Lockdown Effect in India, *International Conference on Artificial Intelligence and Smart Systems (ICAIS)*, 2021, pp. 561–567, doi: 10.1109/ICAIS50930.2021.9396038.

5. E. Ezhilarasan and M. Dinakaran, (2017), A Review on Mobile Technologies: 3G, 4G and 5G, *Second International Conference on Recent Trends and Challenges in Computational Models (ICRTCCM)*, Tindivanam, 2017, pp. 369–373, doi: 10.1109/ICRTCCM. 2017.90.

6. http://medicalbinders.com/quarantine-time-binder-update-time-part-1/.

7. G. Barb and M. Otesteanu, (2020), 4G/5G: A Comparative Study and Overview on What to Expect from 5G, *43rd International Conference on Telecommunications and Signal Processing (TSP)*, Milan, Italy, 2020, pp. 37–40, doi: 10.1109/TSP49548.2020.9163402.

8. C. Bockelmann, et al., (2018), Towards Massive Connectivity Support for Scalable mMTC Communications in 5G Networks, *IEEE Access*, vol. 6, pp. 28969–28992, doi: 10.1109/ACCESS.2018.2837382.

9. J. Cheng, W. Chen, F. Tao and C. -L. Lin, (2018), Industrial IoT in 5G Environment Towards Smart Manufacturing, *Journal of Industrial Information Integration*, vol. 10, pp. 10–19, ISSN 2452-414X, doi: 10.1016/j.jii.2018.04.001, (www.sciencedirect. com/science/article/pii/S2452414X18300049).

10. P. Popovski, K. F. Trillingsgaard, O. Simeone and G. Durisi, (2018), 5G Wireless Network Slicing for eMBB, URLLC, and mMTC: A Communication-Theoretic View, *IEEE Access*, vol. 6, pp. 55765–55779, doi: 10.1109/ACCESS.2018.2872781.

11. Noohani, M., (2020), A Review Of 5G Technology: Architecture, Security and wide Applications, *International Research Journal of Engineering and Technology (IRJET)*, vol. 07, no. 05, e-ISSN: 2395-0056, https://www.researchgate.net/publication/341541673.

12. G. Prasad, H. A. Latchman, Y. Lee and W. A. Finamore, (2014), A Comparative Performance Study of LDPC and Turbo Codes for Realistic PLC Channels, *18th IEEE International Symposium on Power Line Communications and Its Applications*, Glasgow, UK, pp. 202–207, doi: 10.1109/ISPLC.2014.6812365.

13. M. H. Alwan, M. Singh and H. F. Mahdi, (2015), Performance Comparison of Turbo Codes with LDPC Codes and with BCH Codes for Forward Error Correcting Codes, *IEEE Student Conference on Research and Development (SCOReD)*, Kuala Lumpur, Malaysia, 2015, pp. 556–560, doi: 10.1109/SCORED.2015.7449398.

14. J.K. Ray, S. Sil, R. Bera, P. Biswas, A.S. Biswas and Q.M. Alfred, (2022), Millimeter Wave Based Reliable V2X Communication. In: Mandal J.K., De D. (eds.) *Advanced Techniques for IoT Applications*. EAIT 2021. Lecture Notes in Networks and Systems, vol 292. Springer, Singapore. doi: 10.1007/978-981-16-4435-1_59.

15. J. K. Ray, P. Biswas, R. Bera, S. Sil and Q. M. Alfred, (2020), TSN Enabled 5G Non Public Network for Smart Systems, *5th International Conference on Computing, Communication and Security (ICCCS)*, 2020, pp. 1–6, doi: 10.1109/ICCCS49678.2020.9277016.

16. J. K. Ray, A. Singh, Q. M. Alfred, S. Shome and R. Bera, (2019), 5G URLLC Communication System with Cognitive Radio and Frequency Diversity Reception for Improving Reliability in Smart Factory E-cranes Operation, *IEEE MTT-S International Microwave and RF Conference (IMARC)*, 2019, pp. 1–5, doi: 10.1109/IMaRC45935. 2019.9118760.

17. E. C. Strinati, S. Barbarossa, J. L. Gonzalez-Jimenez, D. Ktenas, N. Cassiau, L. Maret, C and Dehos, (2019), 6G: The Next Frontier, From holographic messaging to artificial intelligence using subterahertz and visible light communication, *IEEE Vehicular Technology Magazine*, vol. 14, no. 3, pp. 42–50.

18. W. Saad, M. Bennis and M. Chen, (2020), A Vision of 6G Wireless Systems: Applications, Trends, Technologies, and Open Research Problems, *IEEE Network*, vol. 34, no. 3, pp. 134–142, doi: 10.1109/MNET.001.1900287.

19. P. Yang, Y. Xiao, M. Xiao and S. Li, (2019), 6G Wireless Communications: Vision and Potential Techniques, *IEEE Network*, vol. 33, no. 4, pp. 70–75, doi: 10.1109/MNET. 2019.1800418.

20. T. Ho, K. Nguyen, H. Le and L. Hanzo, (2019), Next-generation Wireless Solutions for the Smart Factory, Smart Vehicles, the Smart Grid and Smart Cities, *arXiv:1907.10102*.

21. M. Z. Chowdhury, M. Shahjalal, S. Ahmed and Y. M. Jang, (2020), 6G Wireless Communication Systems: Applications, Requirements, Technologies, Challenges, and Research Directions, *IEEE Open Journal of the Communications Society*, vol. 1, pp. 957–975, doi: 10.1109/OJCOMS.2020.3010270.

22. S. A. H. Mohsan, A. Mazinani, W. Malik, I. Younas, N. Q. H. Othman, H. Amjad and A. Mahmood, (2020), 6G: Envisioning the Key Technologies, Applications and Challenges, *International Journal of Advanced Computer Science and Applications (IJACSA)*, 11(9), doi: 10.14569/IJACSA.2020.0110903.

23. M. Krol, (1997), Telemedicine, *IEEE Potentials*, vol. 16, no. 4, pp. 29–31, doi: 10.1109/ 45.624339.

24. M. Touil, L. Bahatti and A. E. Magri, (2020), Telemedicine Application to Reduce the Spread of Covid-19, *IEEE 2nd International Conference on Electronics, Control, Optimization and Computer Science (ICECOCS)*, pp. 1–4, doi: 10.1109/ICECOCS5012 4.2020.9314459.

25. K. Kolisnyk, D. Deineko, T. Sokol, S. Kutsevlyak and O. Avrunin, (2019), Application of Modern Internet Technologies in Telemedicine Screening of Patient Conditions, *IEEE International Scientific-Practical Conference Problems of Infocommunications, Science and Technology (PIC S&T)*, pp. 459–464, doi: 10.1109/PICST47496.2019.9061252.

16 Applications of Artificial Intelligence Techniques in Healthcare Industry

P. T. Vasanth Raj, K. Pradeep,
R. Dhanagopal, and R. Suresh Kumar
Chennai Institute of Technology

CONTENTS

16.1 INTRODUCTION

In the field of healthcare and disease diagnosis, there have been several instances demonstrating the potential benefit of artificial intelligence (AI) approaches that are based on deep learning (DL). While doing fundamental research into these methods is likely to lead to significant advances, we strongly recommend that parallel efforts be directed into building rigorous testing and validation processes for AI algorithms in clinical settings. This is necessary in order to build trust in the healthcare field and offer input to the basic research community on areas where further development is

DOI: 10.1201/9781003307778-18

most required. We bring attention to an important aspect of the challenge of balancing expectations, namely that it is not reasonable to anticipate that AI systems, including DL, would perform better than the training sets. On the other hand, in clinical settings, where robust training sets represent the highest levels of medical expertise, DL algorithms have the potential to consistently produce high-quality results. As a consequence of this, one of the goals that such applications should strive to achieve is to broaden people's access to services that are of a high standard of quality.

16.2 AI IN CHRONIC DISEASES

Chronic health problems may be either physical or mental diseases. Patients who suffer from a number of chronic conditions have an increased risk of being hospitalized, early death, requiring the services of several specialists, and having high rates of access to the hospital. Patients over the age of 65 are at an increased risk of a variety of chronic health disorders, which affect approximately one-third of the world's population. It is predicted that the rates of patients having more than four chronic diseases in the same period will triple between the years 2015 and 2035. In addition to high rates of morbidity and mortality, the management of the repercussions of chronic disease results in significant financial losses for communities as well as significant reductions in productivity. The World Health Organization (WHO) estimates that there will be a global shortage of 12.9 million healthcare workers by the year 2035. Patients sometimes get therapy that is not as effective as it may be owing to the complexity of chronic illness management, as well as time restrictions faced by primary care physicians and a worldwide scarcity of healthcare providers (approximately 46.3% of patients with these diseases do not agree to take care according to guidelines). In addition, the management systems that are now in place for chronic illnesses are not well equipped to cope with the complexities of individual individuals. Machine learning (ML) is a subset of AI that uses computer algorithms to evaluate data and determine correlations between risk factors and health problems. Models that are based on ML give scalable solutions, which can assist to reduce some of the load that is being caused by the increasing incidence of chronic illnesses throughout the world. In addition to this, they may be used to do analyses of unstructured data and develop sickness predictions in order to provide individualized and patient-specific medical guidance. In contrast to traditional statistical modeling, ML approaches do not rely on any assumptions about the variables used in the analysis, which might result in improved classifications and predictions. Personalized medicine's primary objective is the use of patient insights and features in order to determine patient risk factors, followed by the formulation of treatment options that are based on the individual patient's unique risk profile [1]. ML models may play a significant role in the development of personalized medicine by contributing to the consolidation of several healthcare datasets, including electronic health records (EHRs), imaging data, genetic data, data from mobile sensors, and biomarker analyses [2]. It is possible that the use of ML algorithms will assist in the promotion of individualized treatment, the anticipation of illness or complication risk, the prescribing of actionable measures, and the prevention of acute occurrences. As a consequence of the fast use of digital health, mobile apps, patient activity, and habit datasets may be combined with EHR data. Using a wide variety of data sources, ML models are able to do real-time patient demand analysis, which may assist medical practitioners in their efforts to improve the treatment of chronic diseases such as diabetes, cardiovascular disease (CVD), and dementia.

16.2.1 ML IN DIABETES

Hyperglycemia is the defining feature of diabetes, which is a disease caused by glucoregulatory failure. It may be broken down into two distinct classes (type 1 and type 2 diabetes). Diabetes mellitus type 1 is defined by a complete absence of insulin production, while diabetes mellitus type 2 is characterized by insulin resistance as well as a relative shortage of insulin [3]. The incidence of type 2 diabetes is predicted to soar in the next years since it is now the most common form of diabetes, accounting for 90% (425 million) of all cases of diabetes worldwide [4]. The four different kinds of ML research on diabetes that may be categorized are as follows:

• The diagnosis as well as the forecasting of type 2 diabetes.
• Blood glucose regulation.
• Diabetes phenotyping as a diagnostic tool.
• Problems related to diabetes are identified at an early stage.

16.2.2 ML IN CARDIOVASCULAR DISEASE

A stroke, high blood pressure, coronary heart disease, heart failure, and atrial fibrillation are all examples of CVDs, which are conditions that affect the heart or blood arteries. To this day, CVD remains one of the leading causes of mortality and illness worldwide, accounting for one-third of all deaths [5,6]. There are about 102 million individuals in the United States who are affected by at least one cardiovascular condition (41.5%), and it is anticipated that 131 million people, or 45%, will have CVD by the year 2035. It was estimated that the expense of CVD in the United States would be 555 billion dollars in 2014–2015, and it is anticipated that this number would quadruple to 1.1 trillion dollars by the year 2035. The death rate from CVD has dropped significantly when adjusted for age during the last half-century. Despite a significant reduction in prevalence, CVD is still the leading cause of death in the United States [7]. The present stability of death rates due to CVD may be linked to a variety of different factors.

• Patients do not make any modifications to the elements that contribute to their risk.
• Patients do not follow the prescribed course of treatment.
• An inability to correctly identify the issue.
• Failure to adhere to treatment regimens that are supported by evidence.

In addition, there are significant disparities in the rates of cardiovascular mortality across different groups of people depending on factors such as race, gender, and ethnicity. These may be the result of a patient's resistance to the treatment designed to modify CVD risk factors, or they may be the result of socioeconomic conditions or behavioral disorders [7]. AI may be able to assist solve some of the challenges associated with the treatment of CVD by customizing medicine, giving high-risk patients priority, and maybe eliminating inequities in cardiovascular results. The following is a list of the four categories of studies that are now being conducted in cardiology ML:

- Estimation of the risk of CVD.
- Research into phenotypic characteristics and prognostic variables.
- Advances made in the reliability of the ECG and the diagnostic.
- Improvements in the accuracy of diagnostic and imaging procedures.

16.2.3 CARDIOVASCULAR RISK PREDICTION

The inability to recognize and prevent CVDs is still a problem today. Even though a vast percentage of individuals seem to be healthy and have no symptoms leading up to their death, a significant proportion of people continue to pass away unexpectedly [8]. Traditional algorithms for predicting the risk of CVDs, such as the Framingham risk score, are only able to assess at the population level, which results in low discriminating accuracy at the individual level (75%). As a direct result of this, individual patients run the risk of receiving inappropriate treatment, which may lead to morbidity as well as increased costs [9], [10]. Traditional models for predicting the risk of CVD have low predictive performance because they utilize constrained modeling methodologies and a limited set of variables. The identification of asymptomatic persons who are at high risk of CVD and the beginning of intense preventive treatment is still a challenging task, particularly when employing traditional CVD risk models [11]. Comprehensive tools that have a better level of precision are necessary in order to solve these challenges. ML models may afford answers to questions regarding the prediction of CVD risk by identifying both known and undiscovered risk factors for CVD, conducting exhaustive analyses of patient characteristics and possibly locating novel approaches to the treatment of CVD.

16.2.4 CREDENTIALS OF NOVEL CARDIOVASCULAR DISEASE PHENOTYPES

ML has been helpful in the classification of new genotypes and phenotypes related to heart disease. Within a variety of illnesses, such as heart failure with preserved ejection fraction (HFpEF), coronary artery disease, and pulmonary hypertension, these models have been successful in identifying therapeutically homogeneous patient subgroups [12]. As a result, these models may help patients and medical professionals choose between prognostic and treatment options, as well as choose invasive treatments and how much resources to use.

16.2.5 SUMMARY

In the field of medicine, AI has made great strides in improving the diagnosis and prognosis of chronic health problems. They may potentially progress patient care by supporting physicians in rapidly digesting massive amounts of data in order to make decisions that are time-sensitive. AI models will not be able to replace doctors, but they may be able to improve physician performance for patients. This could be accomplished by improving the accuracy of diagnosis; lowering the risk of medical errors; reducing costs and economizing on both time and money; and generally enhancing patient-physician interaction. There are still uncertainties about the accuracy and repeatability of ML systems, despite the rapid pace of innovation and hype around the benefits of AI. Despite this, there is a lot of optimism surrounding AI. It is vital to have strong regulations in place before the implementation of ML's industry-wide healthcare system in order to address concerns over accuracy, bias, and safety. When it comes to the risk-to-benefit ratios that are involved with the installation of ML systems, healthcare administrations, insurance firms, and government agencies should all have a realistic assessment of the situation. If the government were to provide financial incentives to encourage the research, development, and deployment of AI systems in healthcare industry, the benefits could be enormous in terms of enhancing patient outcomes, broadening patient access, and reducing the overall cost of ongoing medical care.

16.3 AI IN ALGORITHMIC MEDICINE

The healthcare industry has been struggling with a variety of challenges for quite some time, the most major of which are rising prices and workforce shortages, but there are currently no strong solutions in sight [13]. At the same time, a quantity of medical data that has never been seen before has been produced. These data come from places like EHRs, medical imaging, and laboratory facilities [14]. Since it is difficult for humans to examine such complex and large datasets, clinicians have long depended on computers to do this task. Computers can process far more data in a much shorter amount of time. In this context, the advent of AI, which has the potential to substantially enhance the process of data analysis, has presented healthcare administrators and clinicians with the opportunity to get better insights [15]. It is an opportunity to enhance the delivery of care, reduce the expenses of healthcare, and provide assistance to an overworked workforce. The most effective AI method for doing data analysis is known as ML. This method draws from the fields of mathematics, statistics, and computer science [14]. The use of AI is driving significant advancements in the medical field, with ML serving as the driving force behind these improvements. Unlike non-AI methodology and software, ML software relies on pattern recognition and probabilistic methods to estimate medical outcomes, as opposed to the more traditional statistical methods that are used by other software [15]. The application of ML algorithms and other forms of AI technology in the practice of medicine is referred to as "algorithmic medicine." It's possible that AI systems that can accurately predict important medical outcomes could make healthcare more efficient and precise. AI may assist with healthcare administration, population health screening, drug development, and social aid in addition to medical treatment [15]. This broadens the scope of algorithmic medicine beyond clinical care, which refers to care that is provided directly from a clinician to a patient. Because of its potential and promise, AI has gained the attention of governments as well as other stakeholders in the healthcare industry. Because of this, they have begun investigating how it may be used in the management and provision of medical care.

16.3.1 COMPUTER VISION

Computer vision (CV) is the term used to describe the process in which computers assist with the identification and interpretation of images and videos [16]. DL has come to play an increasingly important role in the operation of CV. This is due to the fact that DL is comprised of numerous layers, each of which is useful in recognizing and modeling the different properties of a picture. Convolutional neural networks (CNNs), one kind of DL, in particular, include a sequence of convolutions and max-pooling layers. This is due to the fact that the fundamental architecture of CNNs has been found to be particularly beneficial in picture categorization (see Figure 16.1) [17]. CNNs are largely responsible for the recent increase in interest that has been shown in neural networks. In order for CNNs to function properly, they begin their analysis with low-level image characteristics and work their way up to higher-level features that represent the more complex aspects of the picture. In order to determine the target class, for example, the earlier levels may be able to distinguish lines, points, and edges, while the last layers may combine the information. CNN was developed after its predecessor, AlexNet, which was an image classification model [17]. The most recent variants of CNNs include those that include specialized layers, such as ResNet, ResNeXt, and region-based CNN [17].

CNNs are being used in the interpretation of medical pictures at an increasing rate [17]. One application of this technology is to classify chest X-rays according to whether or not they contain cancerous nodules. In this particular investigation, a number of chest X-rays that have been categorized or otherwise marked up are cast-off to learn neural networks and how to compute attributes that are reliable indicators of the presence or absence of cancer. Additionally, CNNs may be used for segmentation, which involves dividing a group of interest from the remainder of an area that is not interesting. As a result of the fact that CNNs have also been used for the interpretation of CT and MRI scans, fundoscopies, and histopathological images, their usage is not restricted to the study of chest X-rays.

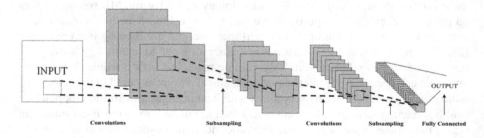

FIGURE 16.1   CNN architecture.

16.4   AI IN THYROIDOLOGY

Hypothyroidism is one of the most common conditions that affect the endocrine system. According to Ref. [18], thyroid nodules can affect up to 67% of the general population. There has been a correlation established between the rise in the occurrence of thyroid nodules and the increased use of imaging modalities as well as the developments in imaging technology [19]. The diagnostic accuracy of ultrasound has been improved because of technological developments such as elastography, quantitative ultrasound, and 3D ultrasound [20,21]. Along these same lines, AI-based algorithms have been utilized to identify and treat thyroid diseases. They used a learning vector quantization network and a multilayer perceptron that were trained by back-propagation in order to examine the robustness of these models when subjected to noisy diagnostic data. The diagnosis and treatment of thyroid nodules has been the primary focus of the vast bulk of recent AI research in the field of thyroidology. Texture analysis was one of the first techniques used in the classification of thyroid ultrasound images.

16.4.1   ULTRASOUND IMAGE CLASSIFICATION

At present, in the event that an ultrasound reveals the presence of a thyroid nodule, either an endocrinologist or a radiologist will examine the images in order to assess the risk that the lesion is malignant by using one of the several classification systems now in use. The ACR-TIRADS classification and the classification used by the American Thyroid Association (ATA) are the two classification methods that are used the majority of the time [22,23]. For instance, according to the ATA classification, a thyroid nodule has a high likelihood of developing into cancer if its edges appear to be uneven, if it includes microcalcifications, and if there is increased blood flow. This is because all three of these characteristics are associated with the development of cancer. These classification systems are rather open to interpretation [23]. A direct result of this subjectivity is the existence of variations both between and among observers. Numerous radiology and endocrinology groups adopted similar methods in their own clinics, and the results were quite varied. In addition, these approaches find the majority of cancerous nodules, but they also find a significant number of non-cancerous nodules that are classed as possibly malignant. As a direct consequence of this, thyroid biopsies are carried out on millions of patients every year all over the world. Researchers have used a wide array of approaches, such as logistic regression and CNNs, in order to classify the many types of thyroid nodules. Using a multivariate binary logistic regression model, thyroid nodules less than one centimeter in size were identified in 2014 [24]. The positive predictive value of their model was found to be 66.4%, while the negative predictive value was found to be 85.6%. In a separate piece of research, [25] evaluated the accuracy of radiologists in classifying thyroid nodules in comparison to the performance of a computer-aided diagnostic system. They used support vector machines for the development of a binary classification system, and they improved the parameters of the support vector machines using a grid search [25]. The accuracy of their model was higher when measured against that of radiologists. Radiologists gathered data from ultrasound images and categorized nodules with the help of Wu and colleagues' radial basis function neural network [26]. Their system achieved a sensitivity of 92.31%. Nevertheless, each of these models made use of a variety of subjective input parameters. So, the techniques that were talked about did not solve the problem of subjectivity.

CNNs were ultimately used to directly classify thyroid nodules from ultrasound images in later versions. [27] categorized thyroid nodules using the Google Net methodology, and they did it using an open-access database. The level of accuracy achieved by AI models increased along with their level of complexity. Their DL model was able to perform at the same level as radiologists, as stated in a study that was presented at the 2019 meeting of the Radiological Society of North America [28]. Molecular markers and ultrasound imaging were used in another study that was conducted in 2019, and the results let researchers classify thyroid nodules according to their level of genetic risk [29].

16.5   AI AND DRUG DISCOVERY

The process of creating new medicines extends back untold numbers of years [30]. Since the beginning of civilization, people have had the knowledge to heal ailments with natural resources such as plants, animals, and inorganic materials. In traditional Persian medicine, rose oil is used for aromatherapeutic treatments of heart conditions. In old Chinese medicine, *Artemisia annua* was used to treat fever. In ancient Greek medicine, opium was used to relieve pain. These are just a few of the well-known examples of understanding the miraculous power of natural-based resources [31,32]. Extraction of morphine from poppies, artemisinin from wormwood plants, penicillin from penicillium fungus, and quinine from cinchona trees are some examples of no-table discoveries of small molecules for use in medicine. Other examples include the discovery of antibiotics [31,33]. The research based on trial and error that led to the identification of these chemicals has not been sufficient to meet the enormous demand for potential medicinal possibilities.

16.5.1   HIGH-THROUGHPUT SCREENING

As a consequence of recent discoveries in biotechnology and pharmaceutical sciences, as well as developments in automation technology, the process of developing new drugs has entered a new era. Robots are able to screen hundreds of compounds per day for use in the development of functional scaffolds [34]. First, synthetic compounds are now being investigated as a potential replacement for natural product-based compounds for a variety of reasons, including the fact that natural product-based compounds are particularly incompatible with high-throughput screening (HTS). Second, both the quantity of samples and the concentration of those samples are lower than the minimum required for the automated screening process. Third, they raise the possibility of extinction for all living things, including plants and animals. In addition, the synthesis of their structures is a difficult task because of the enormous structural complexity possessed by these organisms. And last, the cost of providing them for early drug research is lower than it would be otherwise. As a direct consequence of this, companies and research centers are shifting their focus to the screening of millions of synthetic compounds [35,36]. Converting to synthetic HTS, on the other hand, comes with a number of problems, one of which is that it has driven the research of small-molecule pharmaceuticals into an industry that is not economically feasible. The low hit rates that have previously been associated with synthetic libraries may be attributed to their lack of complexity and variation (hit is a candidate active compound). Second, the procedure as a whole consumes a great deal of time, necessitates a great deal of effort, and is expensive [34]. Costly and time-consuming, the early stages of drug development might take up to 5 years [37]. Additionally, there has been a rise in the need for creative approaches to either predict or develop novel active molecules [38]. Computer-aided drug discovery, also known as CADD and which has recently gained a lot of popularity, makes use of algorithm-based models. These models have the potential to provide successful hits without the necessity for actual cell or enzyme-based assays. When using this method, locating effective hits requires spending less time and money than normal. The fact that most chemists and biologists have little to no familiarity with computational sciences is the primary obstacle facing progress in this area. Due to the sheer amount of data that are produced each day in the field of biological sciences, there will be a great deal of unrealized potential.

16.5.2 Deep Learning–Based Virtual Screening

In spite of the fact that it is highly interpretable, fingerprint-based VS keeps feature extraction and classification completely distinct. The knowledge of human professionals is replicated by ECFP when it comes to the method by which they examine and describe molecules, including the determination of whether or not sub-graphs are present. On the one hand, this approach, to the extraction of features, is analogous to what was done in the imaging field before DL became common practice. On the other hand, the use of DL has made it possible to automatically extract features from the molecules that are fed into the system as shown in Figure 16.2.

In recent years, new designs and methods have emerged that encourage training while learning molecular representations. These new designs and methods are

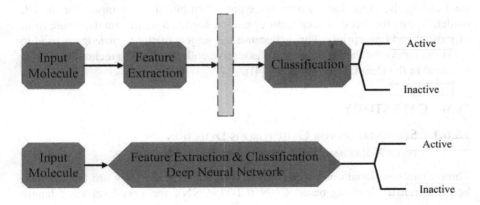

FIGURE 16.2 Feature extraction of DL.

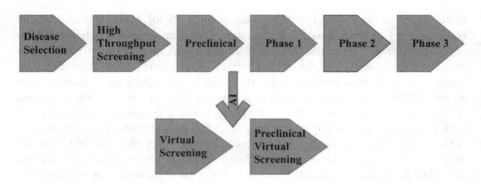

FIGURE 16.3   Discovery of drug.

described as training while learning. These techniques make use of a variety of DL models, as seen in Figure 16.3, in order to automatically extract features from the molecules that are fed into the system. The ability to produce "deep features" often known as extremely non-linear properties is one of the benefits offered by DL algorithms. These characteristics encode molecules in a manner that is distinct from the conventional fingerprinting methods, which often provide results that cannot be deciphered. On the other hand, research has shown that taking into account these traits might result in more precise categorization and generalization. Because molecules have an inherent structure that is comparable to that of graphs, the technique known as graph convolutional neural networks (GCNNs), has been the one that has seen the most amount of use in this area. In a graph that depicts a molecule, the atoms are represented by the nodes, and the bonds are represented by the edges.

In the study that was conducted by Ref. [39], the authors trained a GCNN to learn fingerprints that were similar to the ECFP concept [40] were successful in expanding the possibilities of graph convolutions. They accomplished this by improving the input feature stage. In the input featurization step, the molecules are converted into graphs, and two arrays, one for storing the atoms and the other for storing the bonds, are used for this purpose. Nevertheless, the subject matter knowledge is still used during the input featurization stage and when building the inputs for the DL model, despite the fact that deep features may be seen as a significant departure from expert-defined fingerprints. This is because the subject matter knowledge is used to build the inputs for the DL model. An extensive collection of DL technologies may be found in the DeepChem repository [41].

16.6   CASE STUDY

16.6.1   Segmentation for Osteoporosis Detection from X-Ray and CT Images

Three main functional components make up CBTCNNOD. They are the channel-boosted transfer learning-based CNN (CBTL-CNN), the gray-level zone length

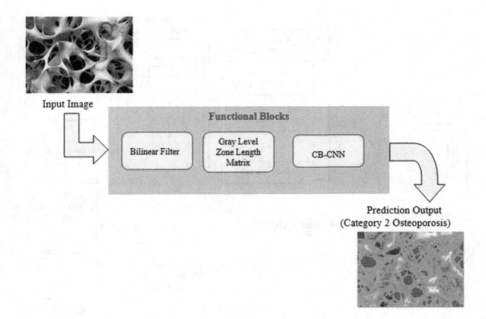

FIGURE 16.4 Flow diagram of CBTCNNOD.

matrix (GLZLM), and the bilinear filter. The suggested approach to CBTCNNOD's flow diagram is shown in Figure 16.4.

A bilateral filter is used in the preprocessing step of the proposed CBTCNNOD to preserve the edges of pictures by smoothing them down. It combines neighboring pixels based on their geometric proximity and photometric similarity. A pixel value at a position is replaced by the average values of nearby and comparable pixels after being computed. When computed in a smooth zone, the values of the next pixels in the immediate area are roughly the same. The result of normalizing this pixel value is unity. The suggested method's subsequent step for feature extraction is GLZLM.

GLZLM is used to extract picture features. It is a sophisticated statistical matrix that is used to characterize texture. Its other name is "gray-level size zone matrix" (GLSZM). The specifics of the estimate of the probability density function of the image distribution are provided by the GLZLM for an image f, denoted by GSF, where N numbers of gray levels are taken into consideration. Zone-length matrices adhere to the same principles as run-length matrices. The number of zones with a size of s_n and the number of gray levels g_m are both represented by the matrix value GSF (s_n, g_m).

The number of rows in the resulting matrix will be N, as determined by the gray levels, and the number of columns will be determined by the greatest zone size. Because of this, the matrix has a fixed number of rows and a variable number of columns. The matrix will be larger and flatter when the texture is more homogenous. Unlike RLM and co-occurrence matrix, ZLM does not call for estimates in many

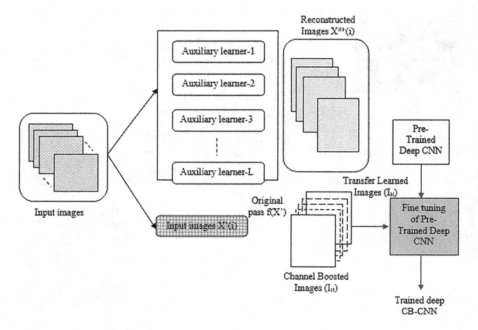

FIGURE 16.5 CBTL-CNN architecture.

dimensions (COM). To choose the best gray-level quantization test, several must be run during the training phase of picture categorization.

To transfer information from a trained model of a big dataset to an untrained model of a small dataset, one uses the transfer learning (TL) technique. In a CNN, the first few layers are frozen while the latter few layers are trained independently on a dataset to provide accurate predictions. This study introduces an improved method of implementing CNN using "channel boosting." By using channel boosting, the number of input channels is increased for improved NN representation. Figure 16.5 depicts the general model of the CBTL-CNN. This model uses L numbers of auxiliary learners to extract local and global invariance in the input picture distribution.

These support learners may adopt any model of the generators and choose various characteristics from the applied input photos. These auxiliary learners' primary goal is to extract intricate details from pictures in order to enhance the input representation of the image dataset in CB-CNN. These characteristics are sometimes combined to provide a concise description of the picture collection, and other times they take the place of the actual features of the input photographs. CNN is taught via TL in the next phase. This TL-based CB-CNN speeds up generalization and cuts down on training time. Once further trained, channel boosting is used to fine-tune this TL-based CNN. This enhances the network's capacity for learning and allows for additional fine-tuning. As a result, the TL-based CB-CNN helps to boost the classifier representation capacity.

As a platform for osteoporosis diagnostic support, ARBKSOD is created. This system's suggested inputs may be divided into three categories. X-ray, DEXA, and

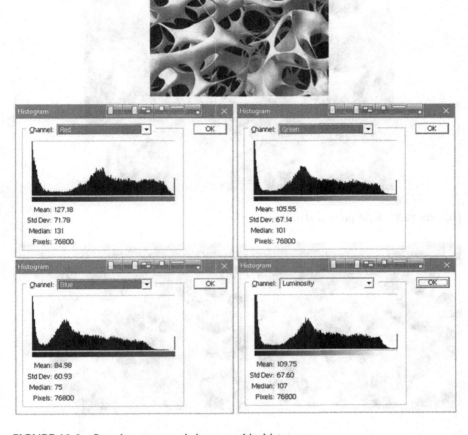

FIGURE 16.6 Sample osteoporosis image and its histograms.

CT scan image types may be used as input images. The goal of FHMIC is to figure out what kind of picture to send for more specialized analysis. While CT accuracy is measured in micrometers, X-ray and DEXA pictures are processed in millimeters (mm). Classifying the input photos is a process that must be done in order to get acceptable accuracy since these procedures are created in a manner to leverage various knowledge base parts. Figure 16.6 shows sample osteoporosis image and its histograms.

KOA module produces a diagnostic report regarding the presence of osteoporosis and the level of impairment based on the processed picture and the separation distance in bone trabecular microarchitecture. Figure 16.7 shows the processed image.

While comparing the proposed method's classification performance to that of the current approaches, 200 users' worth of image datasets is taken into account.

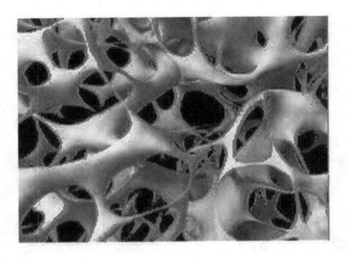

FIGURE 16.7   KOA processed image.

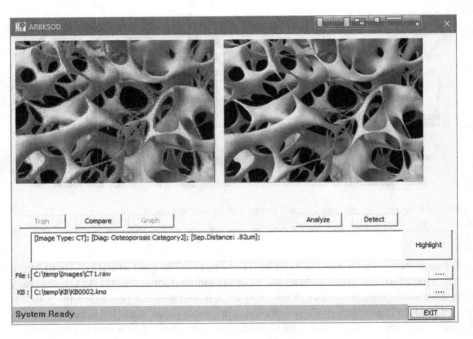

FIGURE 16.8   CBTCNNOD user interface.

The 200 users' CT scans, dual X-ray images, and X-ray images are divided into batches of 20 each. You may obtain the osteoporosis training dataset from the NCBI website. The user interface constructed using Visual Studio IDE is shown in Figure 16.8. This user interface is used to send information about TL from the server to a personal computer.

The harm that osteoporosis poses to human civilization, particularly to older people, is widely known. By giving adequate medications and nutrients at an early stage, osteoporosis may be greatly slowed in its progression. Different phases of osteoporosis are identified and diagnosed using X-ray, DEXA, and CT scan imaging technologies. This study introduces an integrated system to aid and automate the diagnosis of osteoporosis using all of the imaging methods mentioned above. The suggested ARBKSOD approach worked well in terms of all the crucial assessment criteria, according to the observed data. With this level of accuracy and precision in diagnosing osteoporosis, the suggested method could be very helpful in the orthopedic field and help people in general.

16.6.2 DEEP LEARNING FRAMEWORK FOR RETINAL SEGMENTATION

According to Figure 16.9, the encoding process for the BiDCU-contracting Net is broken down into four stages. Each phase employs a ReLU, a 2×2 maximum pooling method, and two 3×3 convolutional filters. With each level, the number of feature maps doubles. Layer after layer, the contracting technique recovers images more quickly while also lengthening the layer size of those representations. The final layer of a multidimensional picture definition, which contains significant semantic information, is traversed by the encoding path to complete the process. After the encoding process was complete, the primary U-Net had a number of convolutional layers. In order to identify distinctive features, the method works by feeding a network a number of convolutional layers. As convolutions proceed, the network might, however, acquire duplicate properties. It often includes merging the feature maps of all previous convolutional layers with the feature map obtained from the current layer and used as input data for the next convolution.

Compared to conventional convolutions, the idea of entirely linked convolutions has a number of benefits. Instead of using duplicate feature maps, the network is able to employ a variety of feature maps. This idea enhances the network's representational capability by enabling information to circulate within

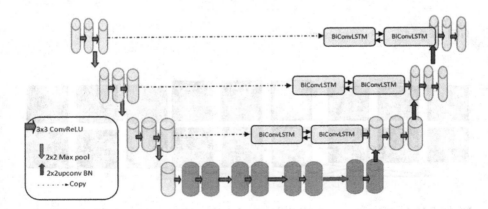

FIGURE 16.9 Framework for disease prediction.

it and reusing functionality. Fully connected convolutions should use all capabilities before usage in order to avoid the network from exploding or deleting gradients. The gradients will also be restored to the network's original places at a quicker pace. The theory of completely connected convolutions is used in the suggested network. As a consequence, a single block has two convolutions that follow one another. As seen in Figure 16.10, the last convolutional layer of the encoding pathway shows a series of N blocks. Blocks link in a dense manner.

BConvLS layer is receiving the output of the BN phase via a BConvLS layer. The LSTM model has a key flaw in that; there is no spatial connection between these networks since these models use complete linkages between state-to-state and state transitions. ConvLSTM was proposed as a solution to this issue and ought to be put into practice since it transforms operations into input-to-state and state-to-state transformations. The circuit has a memory cell C, an input gate, an output gate, a forgotten gate, and an input gate. It is separated into four parts. Input, output, and forget gates are used to track access to, update, and clear memory cells.

The segmentation of retinal blood vessels was examined using three significant datasets: DRIVE, STARE, and CHASH DB1. This dataset consists of 40 color retinal pictures, 20 of which were used for testing and the remaining 20 for training. The DRIVE dataset is structured as follows: The original states that the picture is 565×584 pixels in size. The images are only cropped to include information from columns 9 to 574 in order to generate a square data collection, yielding a frame size of 565×565 pixels (in this case).

From a total of 190,000 patches found from 20 images in the DRIVE dataset, we selected 171,000 patches at random for training. Each of the three datasets shown in Figure 16.11 has a patch size of 48×48 pixels on each side.

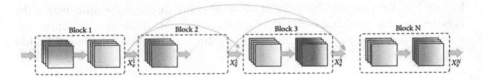

FIGURE 16.10   Block representation.

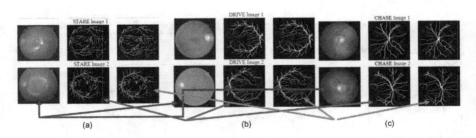

FIGURE 16.11   Output of EDLFDPRS method. (a) Input image, (b) ground truth masks, (c) predicted masks.

Each of the 20 color images in STARE measures 700×605 pixels in both width and height. Due to the short sample size, two frequently used approaches must be used for both training and testing on this dataset. First of all, from each set of 20 photographs, certain training examples were randomly selected. The "leave-one-out" process is used to examine a sample, after which the remaining 19 specimens are trained using the findings. This implementation, which is described in more depth below, employs the 'leave-one-out' technique for STARE datasets. There are 28 photos in the CHASH DB1 data collection, each of which has a resolution of 999×960 pixels. The dataset would be split into two groups, and samples within each group would be picked at random. The last eight samples are used for testing, so there are 20 samples left for training.

In this study, a combination of a bi-directional LSTM network, U-Net, and a fully connected layer is employed to build an efficient framework. In order to increase the amount of biased data accessible and provide more accurate segmentation results, the network additionally incorporates a densely coupled convolutional layer block. By adding BN after the up-convolutional layer, this effort was also able to increase the network's speed by around six times. The suggested technique has an accuracy of 97.32%, 97.33%, and 97.44%, respectively, for the datasets: DRIVE, STARE, and CHASE. When compared to the current approach, the suggested method's accuracy is 2.24% higher. Additionally, the segmentation activities for all three datasets using the same amount of network parameters are compared between the proposed work and other designs such as U-Net, RU-Net, and Dense U-Net models.

Automated segmentation of brain tumors using MR data is crucial for disease development analysis and surveillance. Because gliomas are aggressive and varied, tumors are divided into intra-tumoral groups using accurate and efficient segmentation procedures. The gray-level co-occurrence matrix feature extraction method is employed in the study to extract attributes from the picture. CNNs, which are often used in biomedical image segmentation, have significantly improved the state-of-the-art accuracy in the segmentation of brain tumors. In this study, a significant yet straightforward method that combines a U-Net with a 3D CNN segmentation network is presented to provide better and more accurate estimates. In order to produce division maps that differed fundamentally in terms of divided growth sub-districts, the two models were created entirely using the dataset and assessed. They were then ensemble in various ways to appear in the final prediction.

As shown in Figure 16.12, the 3D CNN is a multifiber unit-based array that uses dilated weighted convolutions to find feature properties at different scales for volumetric segmentation.

Pre-processing: The training data are upgraded using a number of techniques before being put into the network (mirroring, rotation, and cropping). Training: A redesigned loss function that incorporated the focused loss with the generalized loss was utilized to train the model with a patch size of 128×128. Inference: The 240×240×155 voxels in the original MRI data were altered to 240×240×160 voxels so that the network could split them into smaller units. When the trained network is prepared for inference, pass the data through it to create probability maps. The ensemble then makes the final forecast.

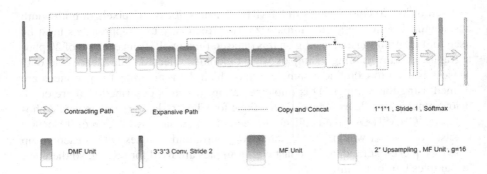

FIGURE 16.12   3D CNN architecture—multifiber unit-based array.

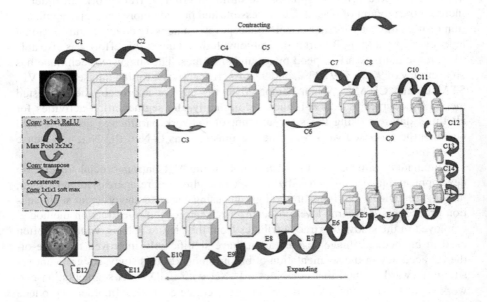

FIGURE 16.13   Proposed 3D CNN architecture.

The second model in our ensemble is a 3D U-Net variant, which varies from the traditional U-Net design in that leaky ReLUs are utilized in place of the ReLU activation function and instance normalization is used in place of batch normalization. The model is made from scratch with our dataset and has a similar layout as shown in Figure 16.13.

Collect the information necessary to reduce the size of the MRI slice during pre-processing. Then, normalize the z-scores after resampling the images and the median voxel spaces of the otherwise diverse data. In order to train the network, use a $128 \times 128 \times 128$ voxel input patch size and a batch size of 2. To prevent overfitting and raise the segmentation accuracy of the model, numerous data augmentation techniques (gamma correction, mirroring, and rotation) are applied to the data during runtime. It uses a patch-based approach for the inference step, where each patch overlaps by half its size and the voxels closest to the center are given more weight. The patch axes and mirroring give further augmentation throughout the test time.

Feature extraction was the first step in the classification of images. The feature extraction technique used was the gray-level co-occurrence matrix texture feature extraction. The GLCM characteristics used were correlation, dissimilarity, homogeneity, contrast, and energy with angles (0, 45, 90, and 135). Using VPTs, the test features vectors' closest neighbors' indices are looked up, and their labels are retrieved. The chance of each label at each grid place is determined using these data. The label probabilities are then linearly interpolated over the whole image. Both anecdotal and quantitative findings from the enhancing tumor experiment imply that CNN is more adept at segmenting. On the other hand, the tumor core segmentation accuracy of the U-Net is higher. However, both networks fare equally well when detecting the whole tumor segmentation on their own after accounting for expectations. Because of this, we only employed U-output Nets to generate the final ensemble predictions for three regions: (1) tumor core (TC), (2) enhancing tumor (ET), and (3) overall tumor (WT) as shown in Figure 16.14.

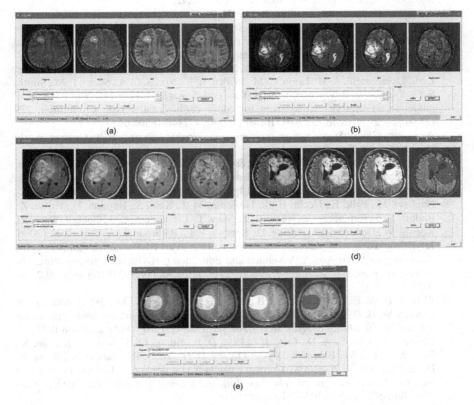

(a)

(b)

(c)

(d)

(e)

FIGURE 16.14 Feature selection of GLCM and VTP along with segmentation for the brain tumor. (a) TC = 1.04, ET = 2.49, WT = 5.85, (b) TC = 4.15, ET = 2.08, WT = 7.76, (c) TC = 5.95, ET = 6.02, WT = 14.23, (d) TC = 9.31, ET = 4.43, WT = 18.60, (e) TC = 18.80, ET = 3.92, WT = 23.80.

The ensemble of the two networks and the feature extraction of the GLCM and VPT are discussed. The difficulty of segmentation in biomedical images is typically overcome by using both these networks. The brain cancer ensemble outperforms predictions from multiple other state-of-the-art algorithms in effectively and accurately identifying brain tumors from MRI data. We aggregate the model's outputs using the variable ensemble method to get the best outcomes. The suggested ensemble provides an automated way of creating brain tumor segmentation for disease planning and patient care that is therapeutically beneficial.

REFERENCES

1. Redekop, W. K., & Mladsi, D. (2013, September). The faces of personalized medicine: A framework for understanding its meaning and scope. *Value in Health*, *16*(6), S4–S9. https://doi.org/10.1016/j.jval.2013.06.005.
2. Rumsfeld, J. S., Joynt, K. E., & Maddox, T. M. (2016, March 24). Big data analytics to improve cardiovascular care: Promise and challenges. *Nature Reviews Cardiology*, *13* (6), 350–359. https://doi.org/10.1038/nrcardio.2016.42.
3. American Diabetes Association (2009). Diagnosis and classification of diabetes mellitus. *Diabetes Care*, *32*(Suppl 1), S62–S67. https://doi.org/10.2337/dc09-S062.
4. IDF diabetes atlas–2017 atlas. (n.d.), Retrieved September 28, 2019, Available at https://diabetesatlas.org/resources/2017-atlas.html.
5. Eckel, R. H., Jakicic, J. M., Ard, J. D., de Jesus, J. M., Miller, N. H., Hubbard, V. S., Lee, I. M., Lichtenstein, A. H., Loria, C. M., Millen, B. E., Nonas, C. A., Sacks, F. M., Smith, S. C., Svetkey, L. P., Wadden, T. A., & Yanovski, S. Z. (2014, June 24). 2013 AHA/ACC guideline on lifestyle management to reduce cardiovascular risk. *Circulation*, *129* (25_suppl_2). https://doi.org/10.1161/01.cir.0000437740.48606.d1.
6. A. Alwan, *Global Status Report on Noncommunicable Diseases 2010*, Geneva: World Health Organization, 2011.
7. McClellan, M., Brown, N., Califf, R. M., & Warner, J. J. (2019, February 26). Call to action: Urgent challenges in cardiovascular disease: A presidential advisory from the American Heart Association. *Circulation*, *139*(9). https://doi.org/10.1161/cir.0000000000000652.
8. Naghavi, M., Falk, E., Hecht, H. S., Jamieson, M. J., Kaul, S., Berman, D., Fayad, Z., Budoff, M. J., Rumberger, J., Naqvi, T. Z., Shaw, L. J., Faergeman, O., Cohn, J., Bahr, R., Koenig, W., Demirovic, J., Arking, D., Herrera, V. L., Badimon, J., … Shah, P. K. (2006, July). From vulnerable plaque to vulnerable patient—Part III: Executive summary of the Screening for Heart Attack Prevention and Education (SHAPE) task force report. *The American Journal of Cardiology*, 98(2), 2–15. https://doi.org/10.1016/j.amjcard.2006.03.002.
9. Wilson, P. W. F., D'Agostino, R. B., Levy, D., Belanger, A. M., Silbershatz, H., & Kannel, W. B. (1998, May 12). Prediction of coronary heart disease using risk factor categories. *Circulation*, *97*(18), 1837–1847. https://doi.org/10.1161/01.cir.97.18.1837.
10. Detrano, R., Guerci, A. D., Carr, J. J., Bild, D. E., Burke, G., Folsom, A. R., Liu, K., Shea, S., Szklo, M., Bluemke, D. A., O'Leary, D. H., Tracy, R., Watson, K., Wong, N. D., & Kronmal, R. A. (2008). Coronary calcium as a predictor of coronary events in four racial or ethnic groups. *The New England journal of medicine*, *358*(13), 1336–1345. https://doi.org/10.1056/NEJMoa072100.
11. Franco, M., Cooper, R. S., Bilal, U., & Fuster, V. (2011). Challenges and opportunities for cardiovascular disease prevention. *The American Journal of Medicine*, *124*(2), 95–102. https://doi.org/10.1016/j.amjmed.2010.08.015.
12. Krittanawong, C., Zhang, H., Wang, Z., Aydar, M., & Kitai, T. (2017). Artificial intelligence in precision cardiovascular medicine. *Journal of the American College of Cardiology*, *69*(21), 2657–2664. https://doi.org/10.1016/j.jacc.2017.03.571.

13. Topol, E. J. (2019). High-performance medicine: The convergence of human and artificial intelligence. *Nature Medicine, 25*, 44–56. https://doi.org/10.1038/s41591-018-0300-7

14. Harrison, C. J., & Sidey-Gibbons, C. J. (2021, July 31). Machine learning in medicine: A practical introduction to natural language processing. *BMC Medical Research Methodology, 21*(1). https://doi.org/10.1186/s12874-021-01347-1.

15. Reddy, S. (2018). Use of artificial intelligence in healthcare delivery. In *eHealth - Making Health Care Smarter.* IntechOpen. https://doi.org/10.5772/intechopen.74714.

16. Howarth, D., & Jaokar, A. (2019). Deep learning and computer vision with CNNs. *Data Science Central.* https://doi.org/10.1017/CBO9781107415324.004.

17. AAIH, (2019). Artificial intelligence in healthcare: A technical introduction, *Alliance for Artificial Intelligence in Healthcare (AAIH) White Paper,* (September), pp. 1–45.

18. Ezzat, S. (1994, August 22). Thyroid incidentalomas. Prevalence by palpation and ultrasonography. *Archives of Internal Medicine, 154*(16), 1838–1840. https://doi.org/10.1001/archinte.154.16.1838.

19. Singh, S., Singh, A., & Khanna, A. K. (2011, November 23). Thyroid incidentaloma. *Indian Journal of Surgical Oncology, 3*(3), 173–181. https://doi.org/10.1007/s13193-011-0098-y.

20. Liang, X. W., Cai, Y. Y., Yu, J. S., Liao, J. Y., & Chen, Z. Y. (2019). Update on thyroid ultrasound: A narrative review from diagnostic criteria to artificial intelligence techniques. *Chinese Medical Journal, 132*(16), 1974–1982. https://doi.org/10.1097/CM9.0000000000000346.

21. Goundan, P., Korpaisarn, S., Smith, J., Rohrbach, D., Mamou, J., Patel, H., Wallace, K., Feleppa, E., & Lee, S. (2019). MON-571 the performance of an advanced ultrasound technique, quantitative ultrasound, compared to conventional ultrasound in the evaluation of thyroid nodules. *Journal of the Endocrine Society, 3*(Suppl 1), MON-571. https://doi.org/10.1210/js.2019-MON-571.

22. Tessler, F. N., Middleton, W. D., Grant, E. G., Hoang, J. K., Berland, L. L., Teefey, S. A., Cronan, J. J., Beland, M. D., Desser, T. S., Frates, M. C., Hammers, L. W., Hamper, U. M., Langer, J. E., Reading, C. C., Scoutt, L. M., & Stavros, A. T. (2017). ACR Thyroid Imaging, Reporting and Data System (TI-RADS): White paper of the ACR TI-RADS committee. *Journal of the American College of Radiology: JACR, 14*(5), 587–595. https://doi.org/10.1016/j.jacr.2017.01.046.

23. Choi, S. H., Kim, E. K., Kwak, J. Y., Kim, M. J., & Son, E. J. (2010). Interobserver and intraobserver variations in ultrasound assessment of thyroid nodules. *Thyroid: Official Journal of the American Thyroid Association, 20*(2), 167–172. https://doi.org/10.1089/thy.2008.0354.

24. Zhang, M., Zhang, Y., Fu, S., Lv, F., & Tang, J. (2014). Development of a logistic regression formula for evaluation of subcentimeter thyroid nodules. *Journal of Ultrasound in Medicine: Official Journal of the American Institute of Ultrasound in Medicine, 33*(6), 1023–1030. https://doi.org/10.7863/ultra.33.6.1023.

25. Chang, Y., Paul, A. K., Kim, N., Baek, J. H., Choi, Y. J., Ha, E. J., Lee, K. D., Lee, H. S., Shin, D., & Kim, N. (2016). Computer-aided diagnosis for classifying benign versus malignant thyroid nodules based on ultrasound images: A comparison with radiologist-based assessments. *Medical Physics, 43*(1), 554. https://doi.org/10.1118/1.4939060.

26. Wu, H., Deng, Z., Zhang, B., Liu, Q., & Chen, J. (2016). Classifier model based on machine learning algorithms: Application to differential diagnosis of suspicious thyroid nodules via sonography. *American Journal of Roentgenology.* https://doi.org/10.2214/AJR.15.15813.

27. Chi, J., Walia, E., Babyn, P., Wang, J., Groot, G., & Eramian, M. (2017). Thyroid nodule classification in ultrasound images by fine-tuning deep convolutional neural network. *Journal of Digital Imaging.* https://doi.org/10.1007/s10278-017-9997-y.

28. Buda, M., Wildman-Tobriner, B., Hoang, J. K., Thayer, D., Tessler, F. N., Middleton, W. D., & Mazurowski, M. A. (2019). Management of thyroid nodules seen on US images: Deep learning may match performance of radiologists. *Radiology, 292.* https://doi.org/10.1148/radiol.2019181343.

29. Daniels, K., Gummadi, S., Zhu, Z., Wang, S., Patel, J., Swendseid, B., … Eisenbrey, J. (2019). Machine learning by ultrasonography for genetic risk stratification of thyroid nodules. *JAMA Otolaryngology–Head & Neck Surgery*, 1–6. https://doi.org/10.1001/jamaoto.2019.3073.

30. Ji, H. -F., Li, X. -J., & Zhang, H. -Y. (2009). Natural products and drug discovery. Can thousands of years of ancient medical knowledge lead us to new and powerful drug combinations in the fight against cancer and dementia? *EMBO Reports 10*(3), 194–200. https://doi.org/10.1038/embor.2009.12.

31. Willcox, M. L., & Bodeker, G. (2004). Clinical review traditional herbal medicines for malaria. https://doi.org/10.1136/bmj.329.7475.1156.

32. Mohebitabar, S., Shirazi, M., Bioos, S., Rahimi, R., Malekshahi, F., & Nejatbakhsh, F. (2017). Therapeutic efficacy of rose oil: A comprehensive review of clinical evidence. *Avicenna Journal of Phytomedicine*, *7*(3), 206–213. http://www.ncbi.nlm.nih.gov/pubmed/28748167.

33. Gaynes, R. (2017). The discovery of penicillin—New insights after more than 75 years of clinical use. *Emerging Infectious Diseases*, *23*(5), 849–853. https://doi.org/10.3201/eid2305.161556.

34. Li, J. W.-H., & Vederas, J. C. (2009). Drug discovery and natural products: End of an era or an endless frontier? *Science*, *325*(5937), 161–165. https://doi.org/10.1126/science.1168243.

35. Amirkia, V., and Heinrich, M. (2015). Natural products and drug discovery: A survey of stakeholders in industry and academia. *Frontiers in Pharmacology*, *6*(October), 1–8. https://doi.org/10.3389/fphar.2015.00237.

36. Koehn, F. E., & Carter, G. T. (2005). The evolving role of natural products in drug discovery. *Nature Reviews Drug Discovery*, *4*(3), 206–220. https://doi.org/10.1038/nrd1657.

37. Strovel, J., Sittampalam, S., Coussens, N. P., Hughes, M., Inglese, J., Kurtz, A., Andalibi, A., et al. (2004). *Early Drug Discovery and Development Guidelines: For Academic Researchers, Collaborators, and Start-Up Companies. Assay Guidance Manual.* Eli Lilly & Company and the National Center for Advancing Translational Sciences. http://www.ncbi.nlm.nih.gov/pubmed/22553881.

38. Kennedy, J. P., Williams, L., Bridges, T. M., Daniels, R. N., Weaver, D., & Lindsley, C. W. (2008). Application of combinatorial chemistry science on modern drug discovery. *Journal of Combinatorial Chemistry*, *10*(3), 345–54. https://doi.org/10.1021/cc700187t.

39. Duvenaud, D., Maclaurin, D., Aguilera-Iparraguirre, J., Gómez-Bombarelli, R., Hirzel, T., Aspuru-Guzik, A., & Adams, R. P. (2015). Convolutional networks on graphs for learning molecular fingerprints. In *NIPS'15 Proceedings of the 28th International Conference on Neural Information Processing Systems* - Volume 2, pp. 2224–2232, Montreal.

40. Kearnes, S., McCloskey, K., Berndl, M., Pande, V., & Riley, P. (2016). Molecular graph convolutions: Moving beyond fingerprints. *Journal of Computer-Aided Molecular Design*, *30*(8), 595–608. https://doi.org/10.1007/s10822-016-9938-8.

41. Ramsundar, B., Eastman, P., Walters, P., & Pande, V. (n.d.) *Deep Learning for the Life Sciences: Applying Deep Learning to Genomics, Microscopy, Drug Discovery, and More.* O'Reilly Media, Inc., Sebastopol, CA.

Index

265

Printed in the United States
by Baker & Taylor Publisher Services

Printed in the United States
by Baker & Taylor Publisher Services